An Introduction to General Linguistics

An Introduction to

General Linguistics

FRANCIS P. DINNEEN, S.J.

Georgetown University

Institute of Languages and Linguistics

HOLT, RINEHART AND WINSTON, INC.

New York, Chicago, San Francisco, Toronto, London

Preface

This *Introduction to General Linguistics* is intended to acquaint the student with a linguist's approach to language. Since the student is presumed to know nothing whatever about linguistics, the initial chapters, dealing with some elementary concepts of linguistic science, the description of language as sound, and some of the problems encountered in the formal description of grammar, are deliberately simplistic. The succeeding chapters introduce more complete and probing investigations of the same topics. All of the chapters deal with the basic problems of how to organize, describe, and interrelate the data we call "linguistic."

Although the organization of the book is historical, it is clearly not a history of linguistics. This would require more information and space than are presently available. Instead, the movements and individuals that show some of the most important developments in linguistics have been selected for study and comparison. Like the proverbial iceberg, the history of linguistics has a largely invisible foundation consisting of many ideas and authors who are left unmentioned, but whose influence and importance are undeniable; those studied here are only the more visible peaks of this foundation.

The "historical" approach is employed for several reasons:

First, there are several excellent texts available that deal with one or another of the techniques of linguistic description according to modern methods, but they do not describe how these techniques were developed and why they are to be preferred to alternative approaches. In a dynamic field such as linguistics, all positions are also counter-positions, and a historical treatment makes this evident.

Second, linguistics is just one of many kinds of language study, and there is more than one kind of "linguistics." As the structural method of language analysis, linguistics defines the object of study most clearly when it indicates both what the object is and what it is not in explicit terms. Although this approach contrasts with traditional presentations of linguistic data, it is worth showing how structural linguistics is coming to share some of the goals and presuppositions of traditional studies, while avoiding some of their inherent defects.

Third, a historical approach can show the radical compatibility of the modern scientific approach to language with the traditional humanistic point of view, since it details the growth in our knowledge about language, and the conditions under which progress has been made.

Fourth, this book is based on the lectures on general linguistics given to the undergraduate majors in both linguistics and languages in the Institute of Languages and Linguistics of Georgetown University. For both, this is a required course, but linguistics majors receive thorough training in various kinds of descriptive methods, while language majors are unlikely to require such extensive practical training. This *Introduction* is intended to give both a familiarity with various conceptions of linguistic form and to enable them to evaluate them. Consequently, it is designedly a cultural introduction to the study of linguistic science. It should equip language majors with an appreciation of the methods and viewpoints in the field and give linguistics majors a perspective they would not ordinarily receive in their specialized courses.

The *Introduction* has been planned for a one-year, two-semester course, and I have found that the material can be covered adequately in that time, with approximately half of the first semester spent on Chapters 1, 2, and 3 and the other half on Chapters 4, 5, and 6. The basic terminology, with illustrations in English, is introduced in the first three chapters; these chapters provide a glossary of the linguistic terms and viewpoints used to criticize and evaluate the other presentations, as well as the actual experience of discussing a language the students know in linguistic terms. In the second semester, the modern contributions from de Saussure on are examined. If a one-semester course is scheduled, the instructor can select several authors for concentrated study and assign the rest as supplementary reading.

The organization of this work is a consequence of its purposes. First, the concept of linguistic science and some basic techniques and problems in the phonological and grammatical study of language are considered. These enable us to criticize the foundations of language study as initiated by the Greeks, adapted by the Romans, and handed on as the basis of grammatical study in the West. The medieval period contributed a more sophisticated semantic theory, which is implicit in our traditional grammatical orientation. For English speakers, traditional grammar includes the use of etymology, at first, intuitively, then on a more scientific basis, and the composition of dictionaries and prescriptive grammars.

Modern descriptive linguistics started with the rejection of the nineteenth-century historical study as the sole scientific approach to language. De Saussure initiated this work on a sociological model, advocating a dualistic treatment of meaning; Sapir continued the developing interest in linguistic patterning, showing similarities among linguistic, psychological, and anthropological factors and stressing relations between language and culture; Bloomfield started a tradition of empirical linguistic description in an effort to make linguistics an autonomous science; Firth rejected the phonemically based studies of Bloomfield, and although agreeing with his monistic approach, he suggested a new situational approach to the statement of meanings; Hjelmslev formulated the immediate constituent description of language in logico-deductive terms; Chomsky returns to the acceptance of many traditional grammatical goals and presuppositions with the rigorous formal methods that have been developed in linguistics and other sciences.

The questions of general linguistic interest with which all of these authors deal include the problem of defining "language" in such a way that the various kinds of language uses and studies can be distinguished according to their purposes, materials, and methods, while providing for a view of language that is basic to all particular studies. The specification and usefulness of such concepts as "sentence," "word," "grammar," and "meaning" are discussed, and the reasons for labeling certain language uses as correct or incorrect are treated. The problems of how to represent language as sound in a faithful and systematic way and the most accurate and suggestive methods of describing the grammar of a language are investigated. Especially, an attempt is made to define the word "meaning" as it appears in various studies, to describe the different proposals for dealing with meaning, and to compare their relative merits.

It will be found in this work that there is more attention paid to the synchronic (ahistorical) than to the diachronic (historical) study of language itself. This is a deliberate restriction in view of the amount of information that would be required for a useful historical study of languages and because the methods of synchronic linguistics, when fully understood, readily show the methods and merits of historical work. For similar reasons, not all schools of linguistics, nor fundamental individual views, have been dealt with.

A consequence of the study of general linguistics should be an informed and critical awareness of the difference between a speaking knowledge of languages and the discussion of language. The ability to speak several languages superbly is no guarantee that the speaker can offer any opinion about language that would be even minimally interesting. The study of linguistics brings to light the bases of informed and uninformed opinions about language, offers new insights into the relations between the dialects of a single language and between different languages, and shows how cultural differences can be correlated with language differences. It provides the understanding basic to a scientific approach to language learning and language teaching and the foundations for a critical evaluation of certain philosophic or pseudo-philosophic problems connected with language. Much more than the information accumulated in a course in general linguistics, the structural attitude toward social phenomena should be the most valuable acquisition. The ability to see familiar facts in a new light is equivalent to acquiring a new sense.

FRANCIS P. DINNEEN, S.J.

Washington, D.C.
September 1966

Contents

1

Linguistics as a Scientific Study of Language

There are as many studies that deserve the adjective "linguistic" as there are uses of language. "Linguistics," however, has been defined as "the scientific study of language," because the empirical methods of the sciences are employed as much as possible in order to bring the precision and control of scientific investigation to the study of language. Many people have doubted that the methods of the sciences can be fruitfully applied in such a field. It is part of the purpose of this book to show the accomplishments and advantages of scientific linguistics.

Within the discipline of linguistics there are several areas of study, all of which are obviously interdependent, but which can be distinguished because of their concentration on specific aspects of language. We could list general, or theoretical, linguistics, descriptive, comparative, and historical linguistics, and applied linguistics. Any one of these areas can be involved in the study of a particular language, so that we can speak, for example, of comparative Germanic linguistics, or applied French linguistics.

While the boundaries that separate the studies of clearly different languages can be sharply drawn, it is not easy to distinguish the topics and methods peculiar to general and descriptive linguistics. The tentative distinctions proposed here, therefore, could be formulated in several other ways.

One of the principal tasks of the linguist is to describe languages in a scientific fashion. This activity, and the development of the techniques required for its practice, can be called **descriptive linguistics.** A course in descriptive linguistics usually includes training in phonetics as well as in phonological and grammatical analysis. But one might ask where the units, categories, and descriptive techniques discussed in such a course come from, what their value is, and how they are justified. Their justification must evidently come from a general theory of language. Such a theory would very likely be useless unless it were founded on a good deal of experience in describing languages scientifically. Thus there is an interdependence between descriptive and **general,** or **theoretical, linguistics,** and each must be constantly revised in the light of the other.

Since this book is an introduction to general linguistics, it is not intended to provide practical training in the techniques that linguists use in describing languages. Their methods will be examined, but it will be clear to the reader that formal training in phonetics, and methods of analysis are required in order to make practical use of the insights of scientific linguistics.

General linguistics is concerned with such questions as how the linguist defines his object of study; the properties he assumes all languages must have; how these are best described and compared; and, especially, how such a description differs from the traditional approach to language taken in most of our school grammars. The development of traditional grammar will be examined, and this survey will show the advances that linguistic science makes possible, as well as the degree of continuity that exists between the older and more modern traditions.

"Linguistics" was almost always understood to mean "descriptive linguistics" until recently, when a demand developed for linguistic explanation as well as description. This shift has called for some refinements in linguistic theory, which are still in progress, because factors were introduced that many linguists had not thought of as part of their field of study, although they have long been part of the traditional approach to language study. This volume is intended to give a more informed appreciation of the strengths and weaknesses of both the traditional and the scientific study of language. Above all, it is hoped that these two approaches will be seen as complementary, rather than antagonistic.

Some of the problems that should be the province of general linguistics, then, can be considered by discussing this field as (1) an activity, (2) a doctrine, and (3) a theory. As an activity, general linguistics includes a search for the most universal features of human languages, in order to describe language simply, exactly, and objectively. Our reliance on descriptive work for information and testing is obvious here.

General linguistics as a doctrine or body of information should focus on theories and descriptions of language advanced by various scholars. We could restrict ourselves to an examination of the modern linguists, if we would be content with largely descriptive work. But if we require that language be explained as well, we would do well to consider the traditional work in language study. This work was not scientific, but it is unlikely that we would not find points of value, if only by contrast, by following such a developed and sustained study. The reason for reconsidering many outmoded views about language is, therefore, for critical, rather than purely historical, purposes. This account focuses on the goals others had in mind in studying language, and it pays careful attention to the number of elements required to explain and describe language and to the number of systematic relations that were seen to link such elements. We can inquire whether the elements distinguished were apt for the purpose of the study undertaken, whether the features examined were peculiar to an individual language or to a single language use, and whether the study brought out any insights into language that we might have overlooked. Such a consideration will also help us to avoid the mistakes of the past.

Just as descriptive linguistics can be viewed as deriving its categories and criteria of relevance from general linguistic theory, so too we can view **historical** and **comparative linguistics** as deriving their methods from descriptive linguistics. In order to pursue the historical development of a language we require a precise description of an earlier and later stage of a language. For comparative work we must have two equally precise accounts of the languages to be compared. General linguistics, viewed as a theory, will therefore be seen to depend on historical and comparative work as well as on descriptive linguistics. This interplay of general descriptive, historical, and comparative linguistics should result in a general linguistic theory on which we can draw in **applied linguistics.** Without a background in linguistic theory the descriptive linguist would not be in a position to select the units of his description intelligently. Except in the light of some theory, facts about language cannot be related to language description. The general linguistic theory at which we aim will, therefore, be the result of much experience in descriptive, historical, comparative, and applied linguistics. It will contain those basic presuppositions about language to which we are driven, both by our failures and successes, in describing language simply and intelligibly.

This book will consider how far linguists have advanced in their work toward the goal of establishing a general linguistic theory. No final answer, and no final theory, will be given, since linguistics is still in a stage of dynamic development. No linguist has yet produced a program that convinces all other linguists that the final answers are in sight. But so much has been done in the field that we will be in a position to estimate the promise of linguistic science and to anticipate how far linguistics, by itself or with the aid of other disciplines, can go.

SOME CHARACTERISTICS OF THE LINGUISTIC STUDY OF LANGUAGE

This section will point up some of the views in linguistics that were developed from the late 1930s to the 1950s. While they are still characteristic of the structural, descriptive approach, not all of the qualities discussed here and in the following section now delimit all work in linguistics. The reasons for this will appear in the accounts of more recent work in later chapters.

Linguistics Is a Scientific Study

The most important claim linguists make is that their study of language is scientific. Although both scientists and linguists disagree to some extent concerning the nature of their respective activities, there does seem to be general agreement about some requirements for a scientific method. These include the use of controlled experiment, in which the variable factors involved have been precisely identified in an objective way, as well as the requirement that the methods used be made public, so that the results of an experiment can be verified. Thus a scientific study should be **empirical, exact,** and, therefore, **objective.**

Some simple illustrations of how these requirements are applied in the physical sciences will indicate how the linguist approaches language in his scientific study. First, an objective study is to be understood as contrasting with one that is subjective. Instead of saying that something is hot, the scientist would measure the degree of heat by means of a standard thermometer. Instead of making the subjective observation that something is heavy, the scientific approach would be to count the number of standard weights required to balance an object on a scale. A nonscientific approach can be called subjective because it requires two observers to take the same mental attitude toward a subject, while the objective approach of science merely requires them to see the conformity of the subject in question to some sort of standard measure.

Requiring an observer to see the conformity between objects is another way of saying that the scientific method is empirical. As much as possible, it restricts evidence to what can be seen or felt or heard. This requirement facilitates objective communication about the subject under study, because it is easier to make two people see the same thing than to make them think or feel the same way about it.

From the emphasis placed on the empirical method in some commentaries on scientific investigation one gets the impression that empiricism obviates the need for thinking, and in particular, the need for a unifying hypothesis to explain what has been observed. While this is a naïve view indeed, it is still worth keeping in mind that hypotheses cannot substitute for observation, any more than can observation be informed without some theory. Another way of formulating the requirement of empiricism is that the evidence offered must be made public. Hypotheses are not immediately public, in the same sense as the objects they concern, but discussion and explanation can make the hypothesis mediately public.

Because it uses this approach, scientific method is exact, and the findings of the physical sciences can often be stated in mathematical terms, the most precise way we have found of describing things in relation to each other. Measurements, as described above, reduce to counting, since we number the quantity of standard measures required to equate, for instance, a body and its weight or length.

When scientific investigation is described as being exact and objective because it employs an empirical approach this is not to imply that other studies must be inexact if they are subjective, nor that they must be empirical in order to be exact. Traditional logic, whose object of study is a concept or idea in relation to other concepts or ideas, is neither empirical nor objective in the sense used above. But it is certainly exact, even though it is not "scientific," as this term is used here. It is desirable, therefore, to distinguish **scientific, unscientific,** and **nonscientific** studies. An unscientific study is one that employs no consistent method, so that its results are unpredictable and cannot be verified. A nonscientific study could be one in which empirical evidence is not required, but which employs a method that is publicly available and so allows properly trained workers to check the consistency of its results. One way to understand the difference is to contrast the scientific study of language with the **humanistic** approach, since the goals and methods of these two kinds of study are so different. Much of the traditional approach to language has been humanistic in the sense that establishing human values has been its goal. This approach is subjective in the best sense of the word, since it requires the thinking subject to assume the same value system as the one proposing such norms. For example, the statements "That is a vulgar expression" or "The noun stands for something *conceived* as a thing" require subjective agreement. From this point of view it should be clear that the term "objective" in the scientific sense and "true" in the nonscientific sense are not synonymous. Further, it should be clear that the traditional approach to language, is not rejected by the linguist merely because it is predominantly humanistic. Rather, the linguist has been dissatisfied by the traditional approach because deficiencies in its method have led to a lack of precision.

Linguistics Is Descriptive

One way of pointing out differences between the traditional and the linguistic approaches to language is to say that the scientific view of language is primarily descriptive while a large part of traditional grammatical work, especially as reflected in the usual school grammar, has been prescriptive. It is one of the tasks of school grammars to give rules to distinguish "correct" and "incorrect" speech. On the other hand the linguist, as an initial part of his investigation, merely records what the speakers of a language say, just as he hears it. Since many linguistic descriptions have not observed differences that are of importance to purists, the impression has been given that successful communication is the sole criterion by which the linguist judges language. This is not at all a necessary conclusion, but merely a division of labor and a recognition of the source of judgments about "correct" and "incorrect" language. Such judgments are always social, human decisions about the relative desirability of utterances. There is nothing in the utterances themselves, as sounds we hear, that brands them as right or wrong. The linguist first records all there is to hear, as accurately and objectively as he can. It is not his task to lay down rules for usage, although he would obviously be in a favorable position to do this objectively. The difference between the linguist's approach to language and that of the school grammarian is obviously the difference between a scientific and a humanistic goal. Both objectives are sensible in their own spheres.

SOME CHARACTERISTICS OF LANGUAGE

Linguists have found by experience that there are several characteristics of language that provide a basis for accurate description. The first is that all languages are **sound** and, as a consequence, can be represented as **linear.** Second, all languages are **systematic,** both in the permissible combinations of language sounds and in the combination of meaningful elements of the language. Third, language is **meaningful,** since the sounds speakers make are connected with factors other than language itself. When the relation between the sounds the speakers make and their meanings is investigated we find that the relation is both **arbitrary** and **conventional.**

Language Is Sound

The statement that language is sound may appear obvious, since the most common experience all men have of language is in speaking and listening to it. But this statement is meant to point out that the sounds of language have primacy over their representation in writing. While the writing systems of languages have their systematic aspects, the linguist considers writing and other methods of representing language secondary to the basic phenomenon of speech. All traditional orthographies symbolize only part of the important signals given in speech, and the letters used in common alphabets, such as the familiar Roman alphabet, represent different sounds in different languages.

By regarding language primarily as sound the linguist can take advantage of the fact that all human beings produce speech sounds with essentially the same equipment. While the sounds of foreign languages may sound strange or difficult to us, all of them can be described with reasonable accuracy by accounting for the movements of the articulatory organs that produce them.

Language Is Linear

Since the sounds of language are produced by successive movements of the speech organs (which, of course, have other functions independent of the production of speech), we can say that a fundamental feature of spoken language is that it is **linear**. That is, we can accurately represent language by using separate symbols for each distinct sound and arrangeing the symbols in a linear succession that parallels the order in which the sounds are produced. The order of the symbols is immaterial: we are accustomed to a left-to-right order in our writing system, but any other consistent sequence would do as well.

Language Is Systematic

When language is said to be linear, it is meant only that it can be represented by a string of symbols. An examination of many languages will show that the number of symbols required will not be indefinite. As few as a dozen may suffice, while perhaps fifty or more may be required. But whatever the number of symbols, not all possible combinations of sounds (and, therefore, of symbols) will occur. This is an illustration of part of what is meant by saying that language is **systematic:** It is describable in terms of a finite number of units that can combine only in a limited number of ways.

This combination of linearity and systematic restriction of combinations provides us with a convenient frame of reference, in terms of which we can describe and compare languages accurately, whether we are describing the sound system or the grammatical system. A simple illustration can be seen in a few English words: *table* is a common word with a sequence of sounds recognizable as an English word, and so is *stable*. To each of these words we can suffix another single sound, to give *stables* and *tables,* both of which are acceptable English words. But there is not a single sound in English that we could prefix to *stable* that would give us a recognizable sequence in English, nor is there a single sound or sound sequence that we could suffix to *tables* or *stables* to result in an acceptable English word.

Language Is a System of Systems

Speakers of English would probably discuss the examples involving *table* and *stable* and their permissible forms in terms of two kinds of reasoning. For example, they might say that there is no such word as *gstable* and that it is not grammatical to put another suffix after the *-s* of *stables*. Another way of putting this is to say that languages have both a phonological (or sound) system and a grammatical system, each with its proper units and rules of permissible combination and order. Units are not permitted to combine for several reasons, phonological, grammatical, stylistic, or semantic. Language is a system of systems, all of which operate simultaneously, but we can distinguish, for the sake of analysis, the units and combinatory rules proper to each.

Language Is Meaningful

The reason the linguist, or anyone else, is interested in studying language is that the sounds produced in speech are connected with almost every fact of human life and communication. There is a stable relation between the kinds of sounds speakers of various languages make and their cultural environment. It is principally through the acquisition of language that the child becomes an effective member of the community, and the leaders in a society preserve and advance their leadership largely through their ability to communicate with people through language.

Language Is Arbitrary

Communication through speech alone between speakers of different languages is impossible because there is no necessary connection between the sounds that each language uses and the message that is expressed, even if the message in both languages is identical. When we say that language is **arbitrary** we are simply pointing out the condition required for the existence of more than one language: that there be no direct, necessary connection between the nature of the things or ideas language deals with and the linguistic units or combinations by which these things or ideas are expressed. This statement is clear enough when we consider that there are alternative expressions for *baby* or *infant* in English, and that other languages employ quite different-sounding words to express the same thing—for example, German *Kind,* Spanish *criatura,* Turkish *cojuk.* If there had to be a direct connection between the nature of the things languages talk about and the expressions used to represent them, there could only be one language, or there would have to be a one-to-one set of conversion rules to account for the different sounds used in different languages. Onomatopoeia, the use of words that imitate the sounds of their referents, for example, *buzz, hum, bang,* may seem to invalidate this statement, but such words are comparatively few in languages, and the accuracy of the imitation depends on the sounds available in the language.

Language Is Conventional

If it is true that there is no predictable connection between the things that language deals with and the expressions we use to represent these things, it would appear that there is nothing predictable about language at all. This is obviously not true, since people use language according to fixed analogical rules. It is only when we consider an item of language as isolated that its arbitrariness is clear; but no linguistic unit is really isolated. It is part of a system of systems, with regular and clearly specifiable relations to the other units of the language. In fact, the use and formation of linguistic units is so regular that these units almost seem to be employed according to an agreement among the speakers.

Language, therefore, can be said to be **conventional** as a consequence of this apparent agreement. This agreement is not, nor could it be, explicit; rather, it is an agreement of fact, of action. Speakers in a given community, for example, use the same sort of expressions to name the same things, and the same sorts of constructions to deal with similar situations. It is this implicit convention that constitutes and stabilizes linguistic systems. An important consequence of the conventional nature of language is that we can be confident that an accurate description of the speech of a single representative speaker will be applicable to the speech habits of others in the same community.

Language Is a System of Contrasts

One reason a description of a single speaker's habits will be valid for the speech of a community is that language is a system of differences to be observed. How these differences are made is relatively unimportant. For example, parakeets cannot produce sounds exactly like human speakers because they do not have the vocal cords or nasal cavities that men have. Yet the sounds that they produce differ from each other in a manner analogous to speech sounds and are understood to represent human speech. Individuals do not and cannot speak in direct imitation of each other; they speak alike, and in the same language, when they make the same number of phonetic and grammatical distinctions as other speakers.

Language Is Creative

Viewed as a system of contrasts, language can be understood as a pattern common to an indefinite number of utterances that differ completely in reference. This patterning provides the analogical basis for our ability to produce novel sentences or to understand sentences we hear for the first time. By imaginative manipulation of the standard interlocking of the phonological, grammatical, and lexical systems poets and creative writers or speakers can extend our awareness of possible relations among things. In this way they may be said to create a new world for us through language.

Languages Are Unique

Since languages are arbitrary, systematic networks of contrasts, each language must deservedly be considered unique. For example, two languages may differ in the number of parts of speech, or may require quite different combinations of these parts, even though the number is the same. For such reasons we have new patterns to learn in the study of foreign languages.

Languages Are Similar

Apart from the more evident cases of historically related languages, such as the Romance group, it is not surprising that all languages have certain features in common. All speakers experience the material world about them with the same senses and in substantially the same way. The differences in the phonological, grammatical, and lexical systems alluded to above reflect the social organization of speech, a subject discussed earlier in this chapter. While this arbitrary selection of important features of experience makes learning languages that are unrelated to one's own difficult, there are still pervasive similarities to be found among different languages. That is why languages can be learned.

SOME CHARACTERISTICS OF LINGUISTIC ANALYSIS

The units and relations that the linguist discusses when describing a language are generally selected as a consequence of the nature of spoken language. Since language is sound, all the units will be stated basically in terms of sounds or sound differences. Since language is meaningful, all the units will be established according to the meanings or meaning differences that they signal. Since language is arbitrary, the connection between sounds and meanings will always be indirect. All sounds will, therefore, at least make a difference in meaning, and some sounds and sound sequences will have a constant, conventional connection with some feature of the nonlinguistic environment. Since the primary focus of the description is on the patterns of sounds and sound sequences of a language, the description is called formal; since another primary focus of the description is on the contrasts among units and patterns of units, the description is called structural. In brief, each linguistic unit will be definable in terms of its characteristic **composition, distribution,** and **function.**

The Composition of Linguistic Units

To define a thing in terms of its composition is to give a positive, additive list of its component parts, a process that will distinguish it from other things that have more or fewer parts. For example, the individual sounds used in a language can be defined in terms of their composition by listing the articulatory movements that are required to produce them. The simple words of a language can be defined according to the sounds that make them up, and larger constructions in terms of the words or parts of words that compose them.

The Distribution of Linguistic Units

As a consequence of the nature of spoken language we have seen that the individual sounds of a language can occur only in a restricted number of combinations. The same is true of parts of words, words, and larger constructions. It is possible, therefore, to define linguistic units in terms of their **distribution** in relation to each other. To do this more accurately, we can specify a particular **environment** in which items can occur. A linguistic environment is a selected point in the linear representation of language. For example, we can list all the sounds that can occur in syllable-initial, syllable-medial, or syllable-final position, or all the words that could substitute for a given form in a sentence.

The Function of Linguistic Units

The units of which a language is composed can also be defined in terms of their function—that is, in terms of what they do or in terms of the use made of them. It is the over-all function of language to communicate meanings, and this is done through sounds and sound differences. Every unit of language will, therefore, have at least a differential function. It will distinguish one message from another, even though it does not have a meaning itself. This is the usual function of the individual sounds. Other units of language, in addition to their **differential** function, will have a **referential** function. That is, there will be a conventional connection between the unit and some aspect of the nonlinguistic environment. An obvious example of this would be the name for anything, which can be said to have a referential function when it is used to point to some subject of discussion and a differential function, because it makes clear that we are discussing what it names and not something else.

Meaning in Linguistic Analysis

Because of the primarily formal approach of linguistic analysis, which defines linguistic units in terms of their composition or distribution, many traditional scholars have objected that the study of meaning in language has been neglected or ignored. If we consider the nature of language, however, we can see that this objection is not justified. There are two readily distinguishable aspects of language. First, language is made up of sounds and sound sequences whose systematic patterns can be accurately described. Second, language is used to communicate messages about the nonlinguistic environment. We can call the first aspect the expression side of language, and the second, the content. The following diagram suggests some of the ways in which these two aspects of language are related:

$$\text{CONTENT} \longleftrightarrow \text{CONTENT}$$
$$\overline{\phantom{\text{CONTENT}}} \qquad \overline{\phantom{\text{CONTENT}}}$$
$$\text{EXPRESSION} \longleftrightarrow \text{EXPRESSION}$$

The arrows represent the systematic relations between the units and suggest (1) that we could establish units of content or meaning without reference to any particular linguistic expression and discuss their systematic combinations; (2) that we could study units of expression according to their possible combinations without reference to content; or (3) that we could study the parallel systems of expression and content in terms of the units and combinations that are possible.

If we were to study the systematic relations that exist among elements of meaning without reference to expression in language, we could hardly be said to be studying a particular language, whatever else might be said in criticism of such an undertaking. If we were to study systems of expression elements without relating them to meanings, we might be said to be studying a code without attempting to break it. Here too we would not be studying a particular language. It would seem that the most promising study of language is one that considers both the system of formal expression and the system of meanings that language represents. While most linguists focus primarily on the expression, they do not and cannot ignore meaning.

One reason linguists have been presumed to be studying language without reference to meaning is that they do not presuppose that there is a single content system which all languages must manifest. When we consider that all languages are presumed to be arbitrary, conventional, and systematic, this view does not seem to be unreasonable. It has been part of the method of a good deal of traditional grammar, however, to discuss languages that are very different from Latin and Greek in terms of the content system of those languages. Their content system, like any other, had first to be discovered through the formal distinctions of the two languages. The linguist believes that discussing the formal system of one language in terms of the content system of another imposes a structure upon the language. Structure, according to the linguist, should, rather, be discovered through the obvious and necessary signals that are found in the expression side of language.

It is, therefore, nothing more than a reaffirmation of the linguist's basic insight into the nature and working of language, and of his plan to attack these problems in the most objective, simple, and exact manner, that he prefers to examine languages first according to the form of their expression and then according to their content system. The linguist cannot wholly ignore meaning, of course. For instance, he identifies meaningful units in the initial stages of his investigation of an unknown language by means of a "gloss"—that is, by some sort of translation of the meaning or meaning difference involved. But the linguist will not assume that the meaning has the same systematic relations in the language he is studying as it does in his own language. For example, he might learn from a Hawaiian informant who also speaks English that *kaua* can be glossed as "we," *'oukou* as "you" (pl.) and *laua* as "they." Later he finds that the pronominal systems of the two languages are quite different, since English pronouns contrast singular vs. plural in the first, second, and third persons, with a distinction of masculine, feminine, and neuter in the third person singular, but not in the plural. The Hawaiian pronouns do not distinguish gender in any number, but they contrast singulars with duals (pairs) and plurals (more than pairs) and then subdistinguish these latter forms into inclusive and exclusive: *kaua* = "I" and "you"; *maua* = "I" and "he"; *kakou* = "I" and "you" (pl.); and *makou* = "I" and "they" (pl.). None of these forms is as vague as English "we" although this is a legitimate gloss for identifying a form as meaningful in the initial investigation. In this limited sense the linguist is dealing with the language without reference to meaning. In the case of his own native language, or when dealing with another language he knows equally well, different procedures may be possible for the linguist.

Functional Relation of Expression and Content

The arrows in the sketch shown on p. 12 indicate that there are systematic relations between the sounds speakers produce and the messages they communicate. This relation can be called a functional relation, and the word "function" can be given two definitions: (1) "what something does" and (2) "covariation." "Covariation" simply means that there is a functional relation between two things when a change in one is paralleled by a change in the other. Applied to language this statement suggests that differences in meaning are signaled by differences of expression, so that in one sense the function of a linguistic unit is to indicate difference in meaning, or to signal a meaning. For example, the *s* of *tables* signals a difference in the meaning between *table* and *tables* and also has the positive meaning of "plural," whereas the *t* of *table,* meaningless in itself, signals the difference between *table* and *sable*. In another sense linguistic units can be said to be functionally related to each other when a change in one entails a change in the other without signaling a difference in meaning. For example, the final sounds in the plural forms of English *cat, dog,* and *rose* have the same function of signaling "plural," but they covary directly with the kind of sounds that precede them. The final sound of *cats* is like the initial sound of *sue;* the final sound of *dogs* is like the initial sound of *zoo,* while the sound that signals "plural" in *roses* is like the sounds in *is*. While the sounds [s], [z], and [iz] elsewhere make differences in meaning, the sound changes in these words are automatically conditioned by preceding sounds. This aspect of language will be covered more fully in Chapter 2.

There is, therefore, a basic and important functional relation between expression and content: (1) It is the function of the expression plane to communicate and differentiate meanings; (2) all other things being equal, it is impossible to communicate or differentiate meanings without employing differences in expression. Since expression is taken here to be basically sound, the differences that concern us must be differences we can hear and produce. The difference is indicated by the composition or the distribution of the linguistic unit.

Types of Meanings

The word "meaning" is applied in so many senses by so many disciplines that it is difficult to use it with clarity. In linguistics we are primarily concerned with (1) meanings attached to linguistic units and (2) meanings attached to patterns or arrangements of units. This division is often discussed as the difference between lexical and grammatical meaning, but the distinction requires further refinement. Lexical meanings are usually considered to be the meanings of words. The most familiar type of lexical meaning can be called referential or denotational, for example, the naming of things. Grammatical meanings are usually concerned with the relations between words and the things words denote. Different arrangements of the same words can convey different grammatical meanings, for example, "dogs hate cats" and "cats hate dogs." But there are many words that typically indicate relations between the things we name, such as the preposition in "he goes *to* school" or the selection of the inclusive or exclusive forms in Hawaiian pronouns. Referential meaning is often discussed as though it were an invariable function of words in isolation. In ordinary speech people do not use single words, but combine them into a complete utterance and then in successive sentences. The same word may be used but with a different effect. Sometimes the same word does not really refer to the same thing, as in "the dog bit him" and "he's a sly dog." Such uses are often termed **metaphoric,** which is another kind of meaning languages have. This use, along with many others (for example, metonymy, synechdoche), is often grouped under the heading "stylistic meanings."

The same sort of distinction is often made between **referential** and **connotational** meanings. The difference can be understood by comparing sentences like "There's a gentleman to see you" and "There's a guy to see you." In these two sentences the words *guy* and *gentleman* can be said to have the same referential or denotational meaning (that is, they refer to the same *person*), but the selection of the one instead of the other conveys more information than the basic reference. In this particular case the connotation could be explained as indicating either something about the speaker's impression of the person referred to or something about the speaker's relation to the one spoken to, without implying any judgment about the other person.

Since one must have considerable experience as a member of a culture in order to sort out these various kinds of meanings, and since such values vary considerably from one culture to another, the linguist, in the earlier stages of investigating an unknown language, tries to avoid them. He confines his attention principally to the differential function of linguistic units, even in the case of those that have a referential function as well. He is concerned first to establish that the items he deals with are functional in the language and tries to establish their characteristic composition and distribution before examining their function. This approach, too, has led to the misunderstanding that the linguist tries to examine language without reference to meaning. In a complete description of a language, of course, information about *all* the systems must be given, including the semantic system. What characterizes the linguist's approach to this problem has already been indicated: every system of a language is assumed to be a structure, in which the composition, distribution, and function of a linguistic unit must be given according to the unique organization of the language. Since all differences in all systems can be communicated only by some contrast in the forms of the language, the linguist takes it to be a sensible procedure to first describe the formal system of the language.

Distribution and Meaning

In a formal description of language the linguistic units are identified through their composition and distribution, without reference to their function, as explained above. Since languages are systematic and conventional, there will be clues to the meaning or function of the units of language that can be derived from their composition (for example, English compounds ending in -*hood*), but the more reliable clue to the meaning type of linguistic units is their distribution. However, because language is arbitrary, distribution is neither a direct nor an infallible indication of the meaning type; languages are essentially patterns of contrasting units, and these patterns are typically filled by units that have a similar function.

Linguists distinguish two basic kinds of distribution, **contrastive** and **noncontrastive**. The latter is often called **complementary distribution** and the former, **parallel distribution**. Linguistic units are said to be in, or to have in relation to each other, complementary distribution when they do not appear in the same linguistic environment. Units that can substitute for each other in the same environment are said to be in contrastive or parallel distribution, since the distribution, or "privileges of occurrence," of one unit is parallel to that of the others which can also appear there. For example, in the word *pan* we can consider the *-an* part of the word to be the linguistic environment in which the sound of *p* occurs. Almost all the consonants of English can substitute for the *p* of *pan* to form a normal word, but not the initial sound in *thigh, high, why, yes,* or *zoo,* for example, nor the final sounds in *rouge* or *sing.* Using these sounds in place of the *p* of *pan* would possibly produce a pronounceable sequence in English, but one that is meaningless. In the environment *-an* the initial sounds in *thigh, high, why, yes, zoo* and the final sounds in *rouge* and *sing* are in complementary distribution with all the other sounds that occur there. Another way of expressing this is to say that all the other sounds that can be substituted in this environment have a differential function in that position, while the others do not.

Nonsense verse is often used to illustrate the fact that items in contrastive or parallel distribution have similar meanings. In Lewis Carroll's "Jabberwocky," a frequently cited example, we can identify the "adjectives," "verbs," and "nouns" because of our familiarity with the distribution of these categories in normal language:

> 'Twas brillig, and the slithy toves
> Did gyre and gimble in the wabe . . .

A formal analysis of language soon reveals the typical constructions the language uses, the members that can and cannot form part of these constructions, and the characteristics of constructions that contrast with each other. Such an analysis assists us in determining the function of the units, patterns, and contrasts of the language, whether differential, referential, or both.

LINGUISTIC TERMINOLOGY

Students beginning the study of linguistics often find the terminology they encounter to be formidable and not justified in view of the grammatical terminology they have already learned. However, the new linguistic terminology is used for two main reasons. First, linguistics, like traditional grammar, is largely a way of talking about language, and, therefore, a precise vocabulary is required so that specialists in the field can communicate accurately with each other. Second, many of the insights of linguistics result from the fact that linguists assume a point of view different from that of the traditional grammarians. New terms are thus required to distinguish what the linguist and the traditionalist have to say about the same units.

Still, the language of linguistics is set by linguists, and not all linguists share the same background and interests. While it will be found that their terminology is sometimes divergent, it will also be found that they define terms accurately. Despite the individual differences or interests, as well as different national traditions, all linguists share a basic understanding and agreement as the result of the influential work of scholars like de Saussure, Troubetzkoy, Martinet, and others among the European scholars, and Boas, Sapir, Bloomfield, Harris, Pike, Hockett, and Chomsky among the Americans.

One aspect of learning linguistics, therefore, is learning to talk about language in the same way that linguists do. Our "native tongue" for talking about language involves the vocabulary of traditional grammar. Learning the terminology of linguistics is similar to the learning of a second language: at first we can only repeat the new expressions we learn, but gradually we are able to make original responses in the language as we learn how these expressions are used in the proper circumstances. Just as in learning a second language we must avoid using words according to the rules and references of our native language, so too we must not assume that similar terms in traditional grammar and linguistics are to be understood and defined in the same way. Since much of the criticism in this book of the work of earlier scholars is presented in the language of linguistics, it will be useful to sketch one structural linguistic approach to two of the most fundamental systems of language: the phonological and grammatical systems. This approach will be illustrated in English, since the student presumably knows this language best.

Review Questions

1. Define "linguistics."
2. How does the linguistic study of language differ from other studies?
3. Explain scientific, unscientific, and nonscientific studies.
4. Is "scientific" completely synonymous with "exact"? Explain.
5. Give an example of a study that is exact but not scientific.
6. What is the chief difference between linguistics and traditional school grammar?
7. Contrast the descriptive and prescriptive approaches to language.
8. Explain what is meant by the "objectivity" of linguistics and the "subjectivity" of humanistic language study.
9. What features does the linguist assume to be characteristic of all languages?
10. Explain what is meant by the statement that language is sound.
11. Explain what is meant by the statement that language is linear.
12. Explain what is meant by the statement that language is systematic.
13. Explain what is meant by the statement that language is meaningful.

14. Explain what is meant by the statement that language is a system of systems.
15. Explain what is meant by the statement that language is arbitrary and conventional.
16. Explain what is meant by the statement that language is a system of contrasts.
17. Explain what is meant by the statement that language is creative.
18. Explain how languages are both unique and similar.
19. Explain the difference between the differential and referential functions of linguistic units.
20. Explain what is meant by a formal, structural analysis.

Suggested Readings

Standard references for all chapters:

Bloomfield, L., *Language* (New York, 1933).
De Saussure, F., *Cours de linguistique générale* (Paris, 1915); English edition, *A Course in General Linguistics*, trans. Wade Baskin (New York, 1959).
Gleason, H. A., *An Introduction to Descriptive Linguistics*, 2d ed. (New York, 1961).
———, *Linguistics and English Grammar* (New York, 1965).
Hill, A. A., *Introduction to Linguistic Structures* (New York, 1958).
Hockett, C. F., *A Course in Modern Linguistics* (New York, 1958).
Hughes, J. P., *The Science of Language* (New York, 1962).
Jespersen, O., *Language, Its Nature, Development and Origin* (London, 1922).
Robins, R. H., *General Linguistics, An Introductory Survey* (London, 1964).
Sapir, E., *Language* (New York, 1921).

Readings for Chapter 1

Bloomfield, L., "A Set of Postulates for the Science of Language," *Language*, 2 (1926), 153–164; also in *Readings in Linguistics*, ed. Martin Joos (Washington, D.C., 1957).
Bolling, G. M., "Linguistics and Philology," *Language*, 5 (1929), 27–32.
Carroll, J. B., *The Study of Language* (Cambridge, Mass., 1953).
Collitz, H., "The Scope and Aims of Linguistic Science," *Language*, 1 (1925), 14–16.
Conant, J. B., *Science and Common Sense* (New Haven, Conn., 1951).
Hall, R. A., *Linguistics and Your Language* (New York, 1960).
Hamp, E. P., *A Glossary of American Technical Linguistic Usage 1925–1950* (Utrecht, 1958).
Schlauch, M., *The Gift of Language* (New York, 1956).
Trager, G. L., "The Field of Linguistics," *Studies in Linguistics*, Occasional Papers, 1 (Norman, Okla., 1949).

2

The Study of Language as Sound

One aspect of both traditional grammar and linguistics is talking about language, and any efficient system of communication requires shared experience as its basis. The most universal experience all of us have of language is speaking it and hearing it. We have already seen that most writing systems do not conform exactly to the sounds people make in speaking, so that it is easy to appreciate the need for some accurate method of transcribing the sounds of languages. Phonetics provides us with an accurate means of describing language sounds, and phonemics with an efficient system of writing the sounds. Since the linguist takes sound to be the basic manifestation of language, it will be useful to give a brief sketch of how the sounds of English can be described phonetically and phonemically. We will then be able to appreciate the shortcomings of earlier work and the progress that has been made in language study in recent years.

The sounds of a language can be described in three principal ways: according to (1) their composition, (2) their distribution, and (3) their function. Phonetics is primarily concerned with the composition of sounds, while phonemics treats the distribution and function of sounds.

THE COMPOSITION OF LANGUAGE SOUNDS

The sounds of a language can be studied in terms of the articulatory movements required to produce them or as disturbances in the air in the form of sound waves or according to the manner in which they strike our ears. **Articulatory phonetics** is concerned with the first sort of study while **acoustic phonetics** deals with the second. The third type of investigation is often called **impressionistic phonetics.**

Working with language as sound defined from any of these three points of view gives us information that differs widely in usefulness and reliability. Articulatory phonetics deals with an aspect of sound with which we are all familiar, since we all have the same vocal apparatus and we can see and feel how we produce sound. Acoustic phonetics, which employs electrical or mechanical equipment to register speech as sound waves, provides more objective information about sounds than articulatory descriptions. While it would be impossible to discount the importance of hearing, it is well known that individuals vary widely in their ability to hear and discriminate sounds. Such information as "it sounds like the American Midwest *r*" is impressionistic and subjective and is of little help to someone unfamiliar with such a sound.

Because of their objectivity, the findings of acoustic phonetics give promise of providing us with the most reliable and accurate information about language sounds, but the equipment involved is expensive, complex, and requires training to operate with confidence. In practice most linguists rely first on articulatory descriptions, which give information about the positions and movements of the articulatory organs during the production of language sounds.

PRESUPPOSITIONS AND METHODS OF ARTICULATORY PHONETICS

At the outset the phonetician assumes that any sound he can produce to the satisfaction of a native speaker of a particular language has been produced by the same articulatory movements the native speaker uses. In practice the phonetician finds that many articulatory refinements have to be made, but this assumption provides a useful beginning. The linear nature of language implies that there is a temporal sequence of articulatory movements that can be represented by a linear sequence of symbols. The phonetic units that the symbols represent should ideally be sounds composed only of **simultaneous,** and not **successive,** components. Actually, this is neither completely true nor possible in practical phonetic description.

As part of his training the phonetician studies general phonetics. In his work in this area he does not describe the sounds of an actual language but, rather, sounds that are typical and frequent in various languages. By analyzing the components of familiar sounds he is better able to describe other sounds he has not heard before, since the latter are usually different arrangements of the same components. By showing how we can analyze the sounds of English into their components, we can illustrate what sort of information articulatory phonetics gives us.

Although he need not be a physiologist, the phonetician needs to be familiar with the organs of speech. Sounds in languages are generally produced when air which has been taken into the lungs is expelled through the two exits open to it, the mouth, the nose, or both. In Figure 1 it can be seen that the air from the lungs passes through the

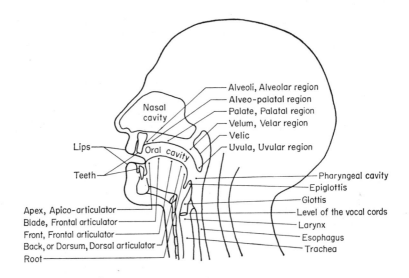

Fig. .1. The Organs of Speech.

trachea. The air in normal breathing takes the same route, but since breathing is a constant factor and is not generally used for conventional language functions, its audible sound and its wave form are usually ignored in phonetics.

The Production of Language Sounds

In the channel above the trachea is the **larynx,** a cartilaginous enclosure in which are contained the vocal cords. From the outside the larynx is called the **Adam's apple.** If we look down into the throat with a laryngoscope or a mirror properly placed, we can see that the vocal cords resemble two lips hinged together at the front. When they are completely closed air cannot pass through them from the lungs. The liplike closure is called the **glottis,** and the stoppage it effects is called a **glottal stop.** In normal breathing the lips are spread open, resembling the sides of a printed capital *A;* in whispering the cords close down to about the middle of the *A* opening. When engaged in the production of the vowels, the vocal cords open and close at very high rates of speed, often hundreds of times per second. The vibration causes the air stream coming from the lungs through the trachea and the vocal cords to pulsate in the typical fashion called **voice,** and a sound produced in such a manner is called **voiced sound.** The vibration in the larynx can be readily felt by putting a finger on or near the Adam's apple and humming; it is also noticeable when holding the hand on the top of the head.

The wave form of the air after passing through the vocal cords can be differentiated in many ways, depending on the shape of the cavities through which it passes (for example, the **pharyngeal, oral,** and **nasal** cavities) or on an overlay of friction imparted to it by narrowing the passages of exit. If the **velum** is lowered, there is no **velic closure** of the nasal cavity and the voiced sounds passing through the nasal cavity acquire a quality called **nasality.** Many other important modifications can be introduced, depending on the contacts made by the various movable and immovable parts of the mouth.

The Points of Articulation in English

To articulate something is to break it down into segments, links, or joints. Language sounds are said to be articulated with respect to each other through interruption or change of quality. While "change of quality" is not an articulatory description, it is possible to detect the correspondence between the organic adjustments that give rise to qualitative differences and the wave forms caused by such sounds by means of electronic analysis. Devices such as the sound spectrograph show that speech is generally a continuous passage from one type of articulation to another, but the ear appears to discriminate centers or peaks in this continuous flow. It is these centers that the phonetician principally attempts to describe and symbolize. Transitions from one such state of the articulatory organs to the next are often difficult to analyze and describe.

Figure 1 is labeled to show the places where speech sounds are commonly articulated as a result of the approach of one of the movable parts to an immovable one or of two movable parts to each other. The upper teeth and the hard section of the mouth behind the teeth are comparatively immovable, while the lips, lower jaw, velum, and, above all, the tongue, are more easily moved. The movable parts are often called the **articulators.** The divisions used here are arbitrary, but were made on the basis of frequently useful distinctions.

The various parts of the tongue important to speech sounds are labeled in Figure 1. The **tip** of the tongue is also called the **apex,** and articulations in which it plays an important role are called **apical.** The combining form of "apex" is **apico-,** as in an expression like **apico-**

alveolar, which indicates that the tip of the tongue contacts the gum ridge behind the teeth, called the **alveoli.** Next is the **blade,** and behind that the **middle** (often called the **front**) of the tongue. The next division is the **back,** or **dorsum,** and the section furthest from the tip is the **root.** Articulations involving the front (and often the blade) of the tongue are called **frontal,** and those involving the back, **dorsal.**

Another important point of articulation involves the lips, called the **labial** area. The combining form for describing articulations involving the lips is **labio-,** as in **labio-dental,** indicating that the lower lip contacts the upper teeth. Articulations involving the teeth are called **dental.** Behind the teeth is the **gum ridge,** or **alveoli,** and articulations in which it is important are called **alveolar,** the combining form for **alveo-,** as in **alveo-palatal,** indicating the overlapping contact between the alveolae and the **palate,** the hard section of the mouth behind the alveolae. The alveo-palatal region is also called the **cacuminal** area. Instead of referring, as the popular terminology does, to the hard and soft palate, the phonetician discusses the **palate** and the **velum,** respectively. Articulations in these areas are called **palatal** and **velar,** and each can be divided into **pre-, medio-,** and **post-** positions. The tonguelike appendage at the end of the soft palate or velum is the **uvula,** and articulations involving it are called **uvular.**

Manners of Articulation: Consonants

Because it is fairly easy to feel the approach of a movable organ to an immovable one, or their contact, consonantal articulations are easier to describe than vocalic. If we define a **vowel** as a sound resulting from the unrestricted passage of the air stream through the mouth or nasal cavity without audible friction or stoppage, we can define a **consonant** as the opposite—a sound that involves stoppage, preventing the air stream from escaping through the mouth, or a constriction of the air stream that results in audible friction. Since no stream of air through the passages is wholly without friction, this is a relative matter. While vowel sounds are generally voiced, they need not be, as whispering shows. Some languages regularly employ both voiced and whispered vowels.

Some Phonetic Characteristics of English Consonants

In articulatory phonetics the composition of speech sounds can be assigned by listing the **place** and **manner of articulation** and adding the other constant features that co-occur. Because of their manner of articulation, English consonants can be described as stops, fricatives, nasals, laterals, and affricates.

A **stop** is a sound that involves the complete (if momentary) halting of the passage of the air stream through the mouth. In English there are three main places where this manner of articulation is found—in the labial, alveolar, and velar areas. Examples are heard in the initial sounds of *pill, till,* and *kill.* The first can be described as a bilabial stop, the second as an apico-alveolar stop, and the third as a dorso-velar stop. Three other common English consonants can be described in the same terms, the sounds found in the beginning of *bill, dill,* and *gill.* The difference between the first and the second set of examples is the absence of vibration in the vocal cords for the first set (**voiceless stops**) and the presence of this vibration in the second (**voiced stops**). Besides this obvious difference, there are two others that may not be as immediately evident to the ordinary speaker. First, **aspiration,** or the expelling of a noticeable amount of breath, is associated with the voiceless stops, but not the voiced. Second, the muscular tension involved in forming the initial sounds of the voiceless stops is more marked than for the voiced.

The phonetic components that we have been able to analyze out of the English stops so far include the lips, the alveoli, the velum, the tip and the back of the tongue, stoppage, presence or absence of voicing, presence or absence of aspiration, and degree of muscular tension. While additional components can be isolated when these same stops are associated with other sounds, the ones mentioned so far should illustrate how the phonetician would identify the factors relevant to listing the articulatory components of a sound.

A **fricative,** or **spirant** consonant, is one produced by forcing the air stream through a passage which has been so narrowed that audible hissing, buzzing, or scraping results. In English it is useful to distinguish such passages as **slits** or **grooves. Slit fricatives** are heard in English in the initial sounds of *fan, van, thigh, thy,* and *hot.* The manner of articulation is the same for all of these sounds, but the place varies. The initial fricatives of *fan* and *van* are produced by making a narrow slit between the upper teeth and lower lip and are described as **labio-dental fricatives.** The initial fricatives of *thigh* and *thy* are made by forcing the air through a slit formed between the blade of the tongue and the upper teeth, although these fricatives are often called **apico-dental fricatives.** The friction in the initial sound of *hot* is caused by the air passing through the **glottis,** and the consonant formed is called a **glottal fricative.**

Groove fricatives are heard in the initial sounds of *sue* and *zoo* and in the medial consonants of *Asher* and *azure.* The first pair is made by placing the tip of the tongue directly behind the teeth, with the blade of the tongue under the alveolae, the tongue being slightly grooved so that the air stream escapes only through this central channel. These fricatives are called **apico-alveolar.** To produce the medial sounds of

Asher and *azure* the tongue is retracted slightly from the forward alveolar position and is curled more toward the center, so that the groove is under the alveo-palatal area. Thus these fricatives are described as **alveo-palatal.** Compared to the alveolar type, they involve some protrusion or rounding of the lips. As with the stops discussed above, all of the types of fricatives represent contrasting pairs of voiced and voiceless sounds, except for the glottal fricative, which is voiceless.

In addition to the components isolated in describing the stops, we can now add the factors of friction (produced by a slit or groove), involving the dental, alveo-palatal, and glottal areas, and the degree of lip rounding.

A **nasal consonant** is produced when the soft palate or velum is lowered, so that there is no velic closure, permitting the air to pass through the nasal cavity, but preventing it from issuing through the mouth, or **oral** cavity. A velar stop involves an oral occlusion, while a velic closure concerns nasal occlusion. The closure in the mouth for English nasals is effected at three places of articulation—the labial, alveolar, and velar areas. Examples are heard in the final consonants of *Kim, kin,* and *king.* The first of these sounds is described as a **bilabial nasal,** the second as an **apico-alveolar nasal,** and the third as a **dorso-velar nasal.** All three are commonly voiced, but they are not opposed by voiceless varieties. These consonants add only features of nasality and absence of velic closure to our list of components.

A **lateral consonant** is produced by the air stream passing through the mouth, but only around the sides of the tongue, which otherwise blocks its passage. In English such a consonant is heard in the initial and final sounds of *little.* The sound is usually voiced and is described as an **apico-alveolar lateral.**

An **affricate** is a consonant that consists of a momentary stoppage of the air stream in the mouth, immediately followed by friction at the same, or at an immediately adjacent, point of articulation. English has two affricates, heard in the first and last sounds of *church* and *judge.* These are described as **alveo-palatal affricates** and consist of (1) an apico-alveolar stop immediately followed by (2) friction between the blade of the tongue and the alveo-palatal area. There are voiced and voiceless pairs, illustrated in these two words. These articulations are composed of factors already listed.

Manners of Articulation: Vowels

Vowels have been described as sounds resulting from the unrestricted passage of the air stream through the mouth or nasal cavity. More than the consonants, they approximate the phonetic ideal of sounds describable in terms of purely simultaneous components, since their production should involve no movement of the tongue or lips, and only the vocal cords in vibration or in a whispering position introduce a variable factor.

The usual criteria for the articulatory description of vowel sounds include (1) the relative position of the tongue in the mouth (for example, front, central or back); (2) the relative height of the tongue in the mouth (for example, high, mid, or low); and (3) the relative shape of the lips (for example, spread, unrounded, or rounded). These criteria serve to describe simple vowels because the three components do not change during the production of the vowel. Additional information is required to describe **diphthongs,** which involve the succession of vocalic sounds.

The terms "front," "central," and "back" and "high," "mid," and "low" refer to the position of the highest part of the tongue relative to the roof of the mouth during the production of vowels. One scheme for representing the relations among the simple vowels of English in these terms is as follows:

	Front	**Central**	**Back**
High	i	ɨ	u
Mid	e	ə	o
Low	æ	a	ɔ

This diagram is not, strictly speaking, a phonetic chart, which usually gives the positions that are invariably assumed to produce the sounds symbolized. The symbols used here are taken from standard phonetic sources, where they correspond to articulatory components that produce slightly different sounds from the English set. One way of keeping the phonetic and phonemic use of such symbols separate is to use the convention of placing symbols to be interpreted in terms of phonetic composition in brackets for example [i], and those to be interpreted phonemically between slanted lines, for example /i/. The term "phoneme" will be explained shortly, but for the present it should be understood that the symbols in our chart represent certain ranges of sounds that contrast with each other and not single, invariable sounds produced by sharply differentiated articulatory positions. Some of the sounds symbolized are heard in the following forms: /i/ as in *hit,* /e/ as in *get,* /æ/ as in *cat,* /a/ as in *hot,* /ə/ as in *but,* and /u/ as in *book.* /ɨ/ does not occur in everyone's pronunciation, but is often heard in some pronunciations in unstressed words like *just* in relaxed sentences like "he just came in," or the final syllable of words like *gorgeous* and *business.* /o/ and /ɔ/ occur in most American pronunciations only as the first vocalic element of diphthongs, as in *boat* and *bought.*

Diphthongs have been described as sequences of vocalic sounds. In

English they are profitably discussed in terms of **syllables.** In such a sequence one sound is generally more prominent than the others (that is, one is generally more prominent since it is louder, more audible, or more stressed). This sound can be called a "peak of prominence," or a **syllabic,** in which case we can say that there are as many syllables as there are syllabics in a sequence of sounds. A diphthong in English, therefore, can be defined as a sequence of two vocalic sounds, only one of which is syllabic.

Typical examples of diphthongs in English are heard in *bite, boy, bout,* and *boat.* In these words the first vocalic elements are identifiable with /a/ and /o/, which are simple vowels, while the second elements are **glides.** Glides are vocalic sounds produced when the tongue moves from one position to another. For example, in *bite* and *boy* the tongue moves from a lower to a higher and more fronted position, or, in pronouncing *bout* and *boy,* the tongue moves from the position for pronouncing /a/ to a higher, backed position, during which the lips are progressively rounded. The first movement involved in the glides in *bite* and *boy* is called a **palatal glide,** because it involves a movement from a lower to a higher, fronted position in the palatal area. The glide from the simple vocalic positions in *bout* and *boy* is called a **labio-velar glide,** because of the rounding of the lips and the velar direction of the tongue movement. These glides are transcribable as /y/ and /w/, respectively, to represent the ñonsyllabic occurrence of /i/ and /u/. The words cited above would be represented, according to these conventions, as /bayt/, /boy/, /bawt/, and /bowt/. Another glide is also heard in some pronunciations and distinguishes many expressions, for example (a tin) *can,* /kæhn/ and (we) *can,* /kæn/. This glide, which can be transcribed /H/, is either a glide to a more central position or an increase in length or both.

The introduction of sounds represented by /w/ and /y/ under the section on vowels brings us to a consideration of **semivowels.** Earlier in this section vowels and consonants were distinguished phonetically on the basis of the possibility of friction or stoppage in the former and its absence in the latter. There is no notable friction in the pronunciation of /w/ or /y/ or in the /r/ of *red* or *car* (which in some pronunciations could be transcribed as /kaH/). We have seen, however, that items in parallel, or contrastive, distribution tend to have similar functions. While these sounds are vocalic in composition (that is, there is no notable friction or stoppage in their production), they are characteristically consonantal in distribution. For example, all of these semivowels contrast in environments like /—æk/ or /ba—/, as in the expressions *yak, WAC, rack,* (/yæk/, /wæk/, /ræk/) and in *buy, bow, bar* (/bay/, /baw/, /bar/). Most of the other consonants also contrast with the semivowels in the same environment, as in *pack, tack, knack, shack* and in *bomb, Bob, bog, bosh, botch*.

For these reasons, among others, /y/, /w/, and /r/ can be classified as semivowels: /y/ is palatal and /w/ is bilabial. /r/ is also describable as palatal, but is characterized in most pronunciations by a turning back, or **retroflection** of the tip of the tongue, which approaches the palatal area; it is not a glide from other positions to a higher, fronted one. All of these semivowels are typically voiced, although one hears a voiceless /r/ frequently when it occurs with voiceless stops, as in expressions like *pray, try,* or *crash*.

It was suggested earlier in this chapter in the section "Manners of Articulation: Vowels" that the English vowels that were represented in the chart represented ranges of sounds we produce in certain areas, rather than determinate phonetically describable articulations. It will be helpful to recall that one of the basic characteristics of language is that it is a pattern of contrast (see Chapter 1, "Language Is a System of Contrasts"), which makes the actual composition of units of less importance than the contrasts. This can be appreciated by first producing the vowels of English according to the articulatory descriptions given above, and seeing that they are reasonably accurate. Then clamp the tip of your tongue between your teeth, or put the tip of the tongue firmly against the roof of the mouth. You will still be able to produce the same number of vowel *differences* as have been ascribed to English, although the composition of their sounds will necessarily be quite different. This is analogous to playing a piece on the piano in several different keys: the composition of the various notes will be different, but the relational patterns among them are identical.

The phonetic components that we have discussed for the vowels have added nothing to the inventory selected from the consonants. It should be noted, however, that while consonantal articulations produced in certain areas involve contacts or constrictions, the vowels that are produced in similar areas do not involve constriction.

Some Phonetic Characteristics of English Vowels

The basic components in the production of the vowels have been discussed in terms of the relative height and position of the tongue. The position of the lips is also a factor that determines their characteristic qualities. The front vowels are pronounced with the lips typically more or less spread, the central vowels with the lips unrounded, and the back vowels with the lips more or less rounded.

Although these are the most frequently cited characteristics in the production of the vowels, others are observable, depending on the other sounds with which the vowels are pronounced. For example, even front and central vowels are pronounced with the lips **rounded** when /r/ is in the same syllable of many pronunciations, as in *rid* and *fir* (/rid/ and /fer/). The relative position of the lips can also vary, as is readily appreciated in /fer/, where the /e/ is less fronted than in /get/.

None of the English vowels is characterized as such by a **nasal** articulation as are vowels in many languages, for example, as in French *pain, bain,* but all are nasalized when found in the same syllable as one of the nasal consonants, as in *mat, man,* or *sang.*

Differences in **length** are noticeable in all of the vowels, depending on the kind of consonants that follow them in the same syllable or whether or not the vowel is followed by consonants in the same syllable. In the first instance we speak of **closed syllables,** and in the second, of **open syllables.** English vowels are **short** in closed syllables before voiceless stops, as in *hit, hat, hot;* **longer** in closed syllables before voiced stops, before voiceless spirants, and in open syllables, as in *hid, had, hod, hiss, pass, moss* or *tabu, hurrah;* and **longest** before voiced spirants, as in *his, has, badge.* Differences in relative **loudness** can be heard, depending on the degree of stress, as can be heard when comparing the sounds in *dig* and *he* with *dignity* and *digit* or the series *post, postman, postmaster, postgraduate.*

This brief discussion is not intended to take the place of the detailed treatments of English phonemics that are readily available in other specialized works, but only to illustrate the kind of information the formal analysis of language readily brings to light. Subsequent chapters will examine what various scholars have discovered about similar aspects of language, and the preliminary information given here can help us make a more informed judgment about their accomplishments.

It will be useful at this point, too, to inquire about the scientific standing of the methods described so far. It should be evident that little of what impressionistic phonetics discusses, and much of what articulatory phonetics describes, is not apparent. Despite the comparatively high degree of practical agreement that is reached in articulatory phonetics, we must rely largely on the sense of touch to describe to each other what we feel in making the articulations we describe. No one else can readily detect, for example, how another person articulates sounds with the uvula, tongue, or glottis when the lips remain closed. Little of what is relevant to the production and discrimination of many sounds is publicly visible, and individuals vary greatly in their ability to hear and feel the important differences.

Some of the factors that are not immediately apparent can be made mediately available through the use of mechanical and electrical aids. X-rays can inform us about many articulatory movements. The **palato-**

gram can show what sort of contacts the tongue makes in the upper, forward part of the mouth. This is done by using an artificial palate coated with a substance that comes off when the tongue contacts it.

Another mechanical aid is the **kymograph,** which can show differences of voicing, duration, aspiration, and nasality. This machine uses a roll of paper coated with soot that is easily removed by the light pressure of a needle set on a diaphragm at the end of a tube. When we speak into the tube, the sound waves we produce cause the diaphragm stretched over a cup at the other end to vibrate, so that the needle can trace a "picture" of the vibrations caused by voicing, and the jumps caused by aspiration, on the coated paper that is passed under it. A timer linked to this device can trace the fractions of seconds that these movements require. An additional tube attached to the nose can record the exit of air involved in nasality.

The nature of sound waves can be appreciated when we consider what happens when we strike a tuning fork. The two tines of the fork swing from a position of rest on one side to the other side and back again. If the swings from the rest position and back again occur in a short time, the wave produced by the disturbance of the air is of **high frequency.** If they take a longer time, the wave will be of **lower frequency.** Depending on how hard the fork is struck, the swings will be shorter or wider, and these will correspond to the **amplitude** of the wave. The same fork will always have the same frequency, regardless of the amplitude.

The sound produced by a tuning fork is a relatively simple one since it results from a simple sound wave. Other sounds are more complex in their origin and in their effect on the air because of the **resonance** of other objects about them. Striking a piano key causes one of the strings to vibrate in much the same way as a tuning fork, but there are several important differences. While the tuning fork vibrates only from side to side, the piano string will vibrate in more than one direction. In addition, there will be sympathetic vibrations set up in the other strings, in the piano frame, and in the sounding board, and all of the sound waves produced will depend on the structure of these elements and on the shape of the instrument. The analogies for speech sounds are obvious—the sounds we make will depend on the length, position, and tension of the vocal cords and how quickly they vibrate, as well as on the number, qualities, and shape of the resonating cavities through which the air stream passes.

A much more reliable and sensitive "picture" of the sounds of language is provided by the **sound spectrograph.** This is an electronic device that registers the disturbances in the air, which we call sound. These disturbances can be thought of as similar to waves made when water is disturbed by a pebble that is thrown into it. Similar disturbances in the air are caused by the air stream we emit when we speak.

This kind of machine gives objective correlates to the properties of sound we perceive subjectively. What we perceive as sounds of high or low pitch correspond to the **frequency** of sound waves. The apparent loudness of sounds is related to their **amplitude** or **intensity,** as registered by the machine. The length of time during which we hear sounds can be compared to the **duration** indicated by the machine.

The sound spectrograph gives us a "picture" of sound waves in much the same way that photographs are reproduced in newspapers and magazines by using a fine screen to break up continuous tones, often into hundreds of fine dots per square inch. Since the dots are so tiny, the eye perceives the result as a continuous image. Similarly, the sound spectrograph has a drum on which there are thousands of tiny points that are made sensitive to differences in both the frequency and intensity of sound waves. The row of dots that are arranged from the top to the bottom of the drum form the highest to the lowest perceptible frequencies; the dots that are sensitive to the same frequency extend around the drum. This arrangement thus provides a way of measuring the duration of frequencies, although only stretches of speech that last a few seconds can be analyzed by most such machines.

After a stretch of speech has been recorded by the machine, in much the same way as on magnetic tapes, the drum is covered with a piece of paper, and an electric arc passes over the drum as it revolves, "scanning" it for sensitized points. The arc is activated to burn a dot on the paper at each point that corresponds to a detected frequency, and the intensity of the dot burned on the paper is proportioned to the intensity with which it was recorded by the machine. Reading from top to bottom on the paper we can tell what frequencies were recorded and judge their relative intensity by the relative density of the impression. Reading from left to right, we can determine within hundredths of seconds how long a given frequency was present at a particular intensity. It is then possible to correlate these objective findings both with our impression of the sounds and with the articulatory descriptions we have given them.

While there are certain problems connected with the use of such machines (for example, volume adjustments can bring out a finer discrimination of sounds with less intensity, but only at the expense of obscuring differences among sounds of higher intensity, and vice versa), they give promise of providing extremely accurate and verifiable results. An interesting consequence of this procedure is the process of reversing and synthesizing speech. That is, the characteristic "picture" of sounds as presented can be fed into devices that will produce, rather than analyze, sound waves. This analysis by synthesis is one of the ways in which we can learn what is linguistically significant in the representations of the sound. It should be clear that such machines do not provide automatic answers to linguistic problems, but they do tell us the composition of sounds. The linguist must then interpret the significance of the distributions and contrasts.

THE DISTRIBUTION AND FUNCTION OF LANGUAGE SOUNDS

Distribution

The basically systematic nature of language has already been discussed, and one consequence of this property is that distinguishable components of the sounds of a language will combine only in a limited number of ways, and not according to the number that is mathematically possible. This should be seen from our list of phonetic components in English sounds: we do not find bilabial fricatives, velar spirants, or dental affricates, among many other possible combinations, in English. When we discussed some of the phonetic properties of English vowels and consonants we found that many of them could have alternative lists of phonetic components, although they would be called the "same" sounds. For example, the first and last sounds (the voiced, lateral consonants) of *little* are clearly different (the second involves raising the back of the tongue, while the first does not), but we would say that they are the "same" sound in English.

These "same" sounds that most speakers of a language would identify are called **phonemes,** and the study that deals with them, **phonemics.** Methods used to isolate phonetic units differ from those used to discover phonemic units. In phonetics we are primarily concerned with the composition of sounds. In phonemics we must also include information about the composition of sounds, but we are more interested in their **distribution** and **function.** Another difference between the phonetic and phonemic study of language sounds is that we need have no information about the meanings (the differential or referential function) of the sounds we analyze in phonetics, but establishing phonemes as functional units in the language requires some knowledge of the meanings involved. In studying the distribution of sounds in phonemics we find that some sounds are in contrastive or parallel distribution with each other, since they can occur in the same linguistic environments, while other sounds cannot occur in certain combinations or positions and, therefore, are in complementary distribution with those that can occur there.

Function

When the sounds of a language are in parallel distribution in some environments we are given a **choice** between them, and it is for that reason that they are said to contrast. Since they do contrast they can have a **differential function** in that position. When sounds are in complementary distribution in a given environment we are never offered a choice between them, and so they do not contrast; while the sounds may be different, the differences will not be functional. Thus there is an important relation between the distribution and function of sounds in language. Because the phonemes serve to distinguish meanings, they are said to have a differential function. On the other hand, the whole word *cat,* for example, has a referential function, but the individual sounds or phonemes in the word do not, since they are not conventional symbols for nonlinguistic items. It is ultimately on the basis of their differential function and nonfunctional differences that we consider the sounds of a language "the same."

The Phoneme

It is rarely true that a language is pronounced as it is written, since single letters often appear for more than one sound, and the same sound is often represented by more than a single letter. A phonemic transcription aims at employing a single symbol for each contrastive sound of the language. We know already that the "same" sound is variously pronounced, although it can be unambiguously represented by a single symbol for the native speaker. The criterion of "sameness" cannot, therefore, be phonetic composition. Some sound differences are produced automatically by speakers, as are, for example, the differences in the /p/ of *pin, spin,* and *tip.* We do not choose to produce these differences. We would choose between the initial sounds of *pin* and *bin,* depending on which word we wanted to use, because /p/ and /b/ differentiate meaning. /p/ and /b/ are phonemes in English, and phonemes are sounds that signal the difference in meaning between otherwise identical expressions. A single phoneme (for example, /p/ in *pin, spin,* and *tip*) may be variously realized, but cannot actually be pronounced; that is, we cannot simultaneously produce a voiceless bilabial stop that is both aspirated and nonaspirated, made with the lips both rounded and unrounded, and so on. For this reason we can describe a single phoneme in a language as a **class** of sounds (for example, the sounds represented by the *p* in *pin, spin,* and *tip*) whose phonetic differences are not functional. That is, the presence or absence of features like aspiration in

English does not distinguish words, whereas the phonetic components of bilabiality, stoppage, and voicing or voicelessness do distinguish meanings. Other contrasts of phonetic components that distinguish meanings in English are seen in *tin* (voicelessness, stoppage, apico-alveolarity) and *kin* (voicelessness, stoppage, but dorso-velarity).

Phonemes are, therefore, classes of sounds that contrast with other classes of sounds, and a single phoneme can be defined as a class of sounds whose phonetic differences are incapable of distinguishing one meaning from another. The elements of the definition are worth expanding.

1. The members of a phoneme not only differ from each other but, as can be seen in the examples using /p/, are also phonetically similar in composition, whether we consider the sound as a wave form in the air, something perceived by the ear, or in terms of the movements that produce it.

2. The differences among the members of a phoneme class are called **allophonic differences,** and the members of the phoneme class are called **allophones.** The prefix *allo-* derives from a Greek word meaning "other, different." These differences concern composition and can be heard or produced. They are generally predictable differences in terms of the distribution of the sound—that is, where the sound occurs and the other sounds with which it occurs.

3. Allophonic differences in English include the presence or absence of aspiration, degree of lip rounding, degree of muscular tension or laxness, length, and some degrees of fronting or backing according to certain environments. Phonetic components that are required to distinguish meanings are called distinctive features, and phonemes are sometimes defined as **bundles of distinctive features.** These include, in English, the presence or absence of voicing and contrasts in the various places and manners of articulation. While each of the phonemes of the language has a characteristic phonetic composition by which it can be recognized and produced, the most important factor is the contrast by which each phoneme is distinguished from another. Foreign speakers often have difficulty hearing the phonemes that differ through contrasts not found in their own language.

4. The phoneme is, therefore, a unit of contrast in a language. It has only differential function. That is, it merely signals a difference in meaning, without carrying a meaning of its own. The most obvious example is the difference between two names, for example, *pat* and *bat.* While this explanation may suggest that the linguist is just as dependent on meaning for his analysis as the traditionalists, it may be noted that linguists do not and need not examine in detail the meaning of these two

words. It is sufficient that they know that the two words are meaningful and that they mean something different in order to establish the signal for the difference between the sounds represented by *p* and *b*.

Minimal Pairs: Parallel Distribution of Sounds

An initial step in isolating the phonemes of a language is to compare expressions that, ideally, are alike in all but a single phonetic feature. If such a difference is correlated with a difference in meaning, the phonetic feature is established as functional or phonemic. In English we are fortunate in having many pairs of short words that differ in this way; in other languages that do not have monosyllabic words it is much more difficult to be sure of the distinctive features involved. Often we can be misled in those circumstances where it is difficult to compare truly minimal pairs by not taking sufficient factors into account. Such factors would be, for example, the position of the sound, the presence of other sounds with it, and the role that stress or pitch may play. In other words we must be sure that we have identified all the variables actually involved in the contrast. A list of a few minimal pairs in English will be useful to illustrate the systematic and arbitrary nature of the sound system (Table 1).

The procedure of comparing minimal pairs is analogous to the use of controlled experiments in the physical sciences, in which an effort is made to identify all the possible variables and to distinguish those that are predictable in terms of the environments in which they are found and those that are correlated with a particular function when they are present or absent. The existence in English of a large number of short words provides ready material for listing minimal pairs.

But it has been found that all languages are systematic and that the regularities, both of functional distinctions and allophonic differences, can be precisely stated. The list of forms in Table I will illustrate the arbitrary nature of a sound system: not all of the distinguishable phonemes of the language can appear in all positions. A list such as the one given here would be sufficient to convince a native speaker that we have to do with phonemically minimal pairs, but it should be remembered that in a language with which we are unfamiliar, an exhaustive examination of the conditions that make phonetic differences predictable in terms of the environment in which they occur would have to be made.

Since the pairs listed in Table 1 illustrate principally how some of the sounds of English can be found in parallel, and, therefore, contrastive, distribution in a small number of environments, such a list is not a completely convincing proof of the arbitrary, systematic organization of sounds in the language. Many of the combinations that do not occur in the list are readily pronounceable, and, therefore, give leeway to those who want to coin new words without doing violence to the sound system of the language. However, there are two slots that contain no examples at all, and it should be pointed out that this situation is not a consequence of the particular environments selected. Neither /ž/ nor /ŋ/ occur in word-initial position in any environment in English. There are a few foreign borrowings that can be pronounced with these sounds, such as the native pronunciation of *Zsa Zsa* and *Jean* for /ž/ and *Ngaio* (Marsh, the detective story writer) for /ŋ/.

Allophones: Complementary Distribution of Sounds

Another illustration of the systematic nature of language is found in the distribution of features that are not contrastive, and, therefore, not in parallel distribution. This situation is found in the allophonic variation of related phonemes. It has been noted that voiceless stops in English are aspirated in initial position and before stressed syllables. This pattern is found to be true of all the voiceless stops in similar environments and also of the voiceless affricate, while it is not true of the voiced stops nor of the voiced affricate.

Similarly, an allophonic feature of lip rounding is connected with all of the consonants found in the same syllable with a back vowel. In words like *poor, boor, tour, dour, cure, good, fool, vocal, thole, though, sue, zoo, shoe, chew, jewel, moor, noon, loop,* and *you* all of the initial consonants are pronounced with the lips rounded. The lips will also be rounded in pronouncing the final consonant of a syllable involving a back vowel, but not with one involving central or front vowels, whether the consonant is in initial or final position. The two other phonemes not mentioned in this list were /w/ and /r/, which are usually pronounced with the lips rounded, regardless of whether they are in the same syllable with a front, central, or back vowel.

A similar pattern of allophonic differences is found in the velar consonants; /k/, /g/, and /ŋ/ will be articulated as pre-, medio-, or postvelars when in the same syllable with a front, central, or back vowel. The regular, but allophonic, nasalization of vowels in the same syllable with the nasal consonants has also been mentioned.

In some instances the phonetic composition of the allophones will not be predictable in terms of their environment, and such unpredictable differences are considered instances of **free variation**. For example, the phonemes /l/ and /r/ have no contrast with voiceless pairs of consonants made in the same place and manner of articulation. Often in the environment of a preceding voiceless stop both of these normally voiced phonemes will be found to have voiceless allophones, for example, in *please* and *pray*.

Table 1: Some Minimal Pairs in English

Stops										
/p/	pay	pie	Pee	pooh	pow	ape				
/b/	bay	buy	bee	boo	bow	Abe				
/t/	Tey	tie	tea	too	Tau	ate		eat		out
/d/	day	die	Dee	do	dhow	aid				
/k/	Kay	Chi	key	coo	cow	ache	Ike	eke		
/g/	gay	guy	ghee	goo		ague				
Spirants										
/f/	Fay	fie	fee	foo					oof	
/v/		vie	Vee		vow			Eve		
/θ/		thigh		thew						
/ð/	they	thy	thee		thou					
/s/	say	sigh	see	sue	sow	ace	ice			
/z/			Zee	zoo				ease	ooze	
/š/	shay	shy	she	shoo						
/ž/										
/h/	hay	high	he	who	how					
Affricates										
/č/	Che	Chi		chew	chow	aitch				ouch
/ǰ/	jay		gee	Jew		age				
Nasals										
/m/	may	my	me	moo	mow	aim	I'm	eme		
/n/	nay	nigh	knee	knew	now	ain				
/ŋ/										
Lateral										
/l/	lay	lie	lea	Lou	low	ail	I'll	eel		owl
Semivowels										
/w/	way	why	whee	woo	wow					
/y/	yea	yi	ye	you	yow					

Stops

	-ap	-ip	-eep	-ep	-ape	-ass	-atch	-adge	-am	-an	-ale	-air
/ p /	pap	pip	peep	pep	pape	pass	patch		pam	pan	pale	pair
/ b /			beep			bass	batch	badge	bam	ban	bale	bear
/ t /	tap	tip			tape	Tass			tam	tan	tale	tear
/ d /		dip	deep						dam	Dan	dale	dare
/ k /	cap	kip	keep		cape	Cass	catch	cadge	cam	can	kale	care
/ g /	gap	Gip			gape	gas			gam	gan	gale	

Spirants

	-ap	-ip	-eep	-ep	-ape	-ass	-atch	-adge	-am	-an	-ale	-air
/ f /	fap									fan	fail	fair
/ v /			Veep							van	vale	
/ đ /										than		there
/ θ /							thatch					Sayre
/ s /	sap	sip	seep			sass	Satch		Sam		sale	
/ z /	zap	zip		Zep							Zale	
/ š /		ship	sheep	Shep	shape				sham	shan	shale	share
/ ž /												
/ h /	Hap	hip	heap	hep			hatch		ham		hale	hair

Affricates

	-ap	-ip	-eep	-ep	-ape	-ass	-atch	-adge	-am	-an	-ale	-air
/ č /	chap	chip	cheap							Chan		chair
/ ǰ /	Jap	gyp	jeep		jape				jam	Jan	jail	

Nasals

	-ap	-ip	-eep	-ep	-ape	-ass	-atch	-adge	-am	-an	-ale	-air
/ m /	map					mass	match	Madge	Ma'am	man	mail	mare
/ n /	nap	nip			nape		natch			Nan	nail	Nair
/ ŋ /												

Lateral

	-ap	-ip	-eep	-ep	-ape	-ass	-atch	-adge	-am	-an	-ale	-air
/ l /	lap	lip	leap			lass	latch		lamb			lair

Semivowels

	-ap	-ip	-eep	-ep	-ape	-ass	-atch	-adge	-am	-an	-ale	-air
/ w /		whip	weep						wham		wail	wear
/ y /	yap	yip		yep					yam		Yale	
/ r /	rap	rip	reap	rep	rape				ram	ran	rail	rare

Classifying Allophones as Members of the Same Phoneme

There are three basic criteria by which phonetically different sounds in a language are classified together as instances of the same functional sound units:

1. The allophones should be phonetically similar to each other.
2. Their differences in phonetic composition should be in complementary distribution or free variation.
3. There should be pattern congruity among the allophonic differences of the phonemes with a similar manner or place of articulation.

The criterion of phonetic similarity is often satisfied in English because the allophones have a similar place or manner of articulation, but this is not always the case. A familiar allophone of the voiceless apico-alveolar stop /t/ is a voiceless glottal stop, which is frequently heard in words like *sentence, pittance,* and *mutton* and in some dialectal pronunciations of words like *butter* and *daughter.* Here, the basis of phonetic similarity is impressionistic rather than articulatory.

The manifestation of complementary distribution and pattern congruity of allophonic differences was earlier illustrated for the consonants. A similar phenomenon among the vocalic sounds will serve to illustrate the requirements for classifying sounds as allophones of the same phoneme.

The phonetic components of the semivowels /y/ and /w/ both resemble and differ from those ascribed to the vocalic off-glides of the diphthongs. They are similar because they are all glides in the palatal or velar areas, but phonetically different because the directions of the glides and the lip rounding involved occur in reverse orders. In /yes/, for the semivowel /y/ the tongue starts in a high, front position and then glides to the lower, backer position of /e/. In *say,* which we can transcribe as /sey/, for the vocalic off-glide of the diphthong the tongue starts at the level of /e/ and goes to a higher, fronter position. Both the semivowel /w/ and the labio-velar off-glide of diphthongs can be illustrated in *wow,* which can be transcribed /waw/. The semivowel is articulated with the lips initially rounded and the tongue in a high, back position; then follows a glide of the tongue to the lower, central position of /a/, while the lips are unrounded; the off-glide of the diphthong reverses this procedure, the tongue gliding from the level of /a/ to a higher, backer position, while the lips are progressively rounded.

In other words the glides in initial and final position are mirror images of each other and show (1) phonetic similarity because of the areas involved; (2) complementary distribution of their differences in the direction of the glides; and (3) pattern congruity because of their initial and terminal relations to the level of the vowel preceding or following them. According to the criteria proposed earlier in this section they are clearly allophones of the same phonemes and, therefore, can be transcribed with the single symbols /y/ and /w/.

A similar argument has been proposed to recognize the centering glide, transcribed /H/, and the glottal fricative /h/. These two sounds show complementary distribution of their phonetic differences, since /h/ is always initial and /H/ is always final in syllables, but the criteria of phonetic similarity and pattern congruity are not convincingly applicable.

Suprasegmental Phonemes

So far, we have discussed English in terms of its consonants and vowels. These can be called **segmental phonemes** of the language, since they are the discrete parts of the line by which we represent speech. But no one speaks in the perfectly level tone that such a line could suggest. There are differences in pitch and stress in different syllables, and both during utterances and at their end the voice usually rises or falls. The meanings of messages vary according to these features, as well as a result of contrasts of consonants and vowels. Because they are usually written over the segments, and because such features as stress, intonational contours, and different pitch levels affect more than a single consonant or vowel, such phonemes are called **suprasegmental.**

Since a language is a system of systems, there will usually be more than one set of regularities that will enable us to discriminate messages. In English one signal that is capable of distinguishing meanings is **stress.** While it is not the only way of distinguishing nouns and verbs, stress is an integral part of the sound system of English and often serves as the sole means of distinguishing among different utterances. One example of stress distinguishes the nouns, on the left in the following list, from the verbs, on the right:

présent	presént
pérmit	permít
cóntract	contráct
ímport	impórt

"Stress" as used here means the impression of more energy in the articulation of the stressed syllable, which usually results in its sounding louder and longer than other syllables in the same word. In the words given above, two degrees of stress can be distinguished, the stronger, called **primary stress,** and symbolized as / ˊ/, and the other, called **weak stress,** symbolized as / ˘/. By convention the absence of a stress marking is interpreted to indicate weak stress. The last word of the list can, therefore, be transcribed as /ímpɔrt/, /impɔ́rt/, or /ímpɔ̆rt/, ĭmpɔ́rt/.

Another degree of stress is perceptible when we compare the verb *contents* and the noun *contents,* comparing the latter with *conscience.* The verb is transcribed with the two degrees of stress already distinguished, /kanténts/. The word *conscience* requires no added degree of stress, /kánšins/, but the noun *contents* cannot be pronounced on the pattern of *conscience.* Instead, it requires the notation of **tertiary stress,** transcribed as / ˋ/, therefore, /kántènts/.

In a sentence like "They examined the contents of the Kahn tents" we find there is an additional level of stress in the last two syllables, as will appear if they are pronounced on the pattern of the noun *contents.* This requires the addition of another degree of stress, which some speakers find difficult to discriminate from tertiary stress, called **secondary stress** and symbolized as / ˆ/. *Kahn tents* from this sentence is, therefore, written as /káHn + tênts/.

Notice that an additional symbol, /+/, was also required. This implies that there is a contrast in the transition between the first and second syllables of *Kahn tents* and *contents,* which is called **open,** or **plus, juncture.** The same phenomenon would account for our ability to differentiate between the following pairs of sentences when they are spoken:

We are fortunate in having General Drum right here.	(/drə́m + rayt/)
We are fortunate in having General Drumwright here.	(/drə́mrayt/
If I had to, I'd lend him one.	(/hæ̀d + tùw/)
If I had two, I'd lend him one.	(/hæ̀d + túw/)
They tried to shoot the black bird.	(/blæ̀k + bérd/)
They tried to shoot the blackbird.	(/blǽkbèrd/)
They inquired about the night rate.	(/náyt + rèyt/)
They inquired about the nitrate.	(/náytrèyt/)

Since they are phonemes, the stresses have phonetically different impressions of loudness, but the ranges contrast. The allophones of plus juncture are more complex, including differences in the length, voicing, and degree of aspiration of the vowels and consonants involved in the syllables between which there is the open transition, or plus juncture.

The examples "If I had to, I'd lend him one" and "If I had two, I'd lend him one" contrast in ways other than the degrees of stress and juncture: there is a difference in **pitch** and in the **terminal contours** as well. The terminal contours are the changes in pitch at the end of phrases, clauses, or sentences. Familiar examples of terminal contours are the typical endings of contrastive sentences like

He's my friend.	/²hiyz + may + frénd³¹↘/
He's my friend?	/²hiyz + may + frénd³⁴↗/
He's my friend . . .	/²hiyz + may + frénd³⟶/

The first example would usually be interpreted as a simple statement, the second as a surprised question, and the last would indicate that more is to follow. Terminal contours, therefore, have a differential function; that is, they discriminate meanings, but have no conventional meaning of their own, since the level of tone used in speaking the statements or questions can fall, or, particularly in questions, remain level.

The numbers written slightly above the segmental phonemes in the above list indicate the **pitch levels**. /²/ is taken to be "normal," that is, the tone a speaker employs for most of his utterance; /³/ is the high tone of a normal utterance, which can fall to /¹/, the lowest tone, commonly found at the end of statements; /⁴/ is "extra high" and usually indicates surprise, contradiction, commands, and the like. Not every syllable is marked for pitch, the convention being that only the contrast of pitch levels is indicated. Since the range of individual voices varies greatly, there will be numerous allophones of each pitch level, but the ranges contrast with each other in the same way as the stress ranges.

The Phonemes of English

The ideal phonemic transcription should mark each sound contrast by which each utterance of the language is distinguished. The ideal phonetic description should use a single symbol for each distinguishable articulatory movement involved in the production of an utterance. The first goal, as defined here, does not seem impossible, but the second seems either impossible or impractical, since the phonetician, transcribing another person's speech, cannot check all the nervous and muscular activity associated with the production of an utterance; and if he were transcribing his own speech, the task would be so complex, even for a short utterance, as to be impractical.

If the phonetic contrasts discussed here are valid for most speakers of English, then any native speaker could give an intelligible reading of a phonemic transcription, once he has been informed about the phonetic values typically associated with the symbols. The allophonic differences characteristic of English would be automatically supplied, and the reader would only have to pay careful attention to phonemic transcription of dialects other than his own, where the distribution of the phonemes could be different. Bearing in mind that there are some minor disagreements about the assignment of certain sounds, and particularly about the number of stress phonemes, we can give the following list of the sound contrasts by which utterances in English can be identified and distinguished:

21 Consonants	/ p b t d k g f v θ đ s z š ž č ǰ h m n ŋ l /
3 Semivowels	/ y w r /
9 Vowels	/ i e æ a ɨ ɘ ɔ o u /
4 Stresses	/ ´ / / ^ / / ` / / ˇ /
4 Pitches	/ ^{1} / / ^{2} / / ^{3} / / ^{4} /
1 Plus juncture	/ + /
3 Terminal contours	/ ↘ ↗ → /
45 Phonemes (not including /H/)	

Phonemic Transcription and Traditional Orthography

In the English-speaking world there are periodic campaigns to reform the spelling system of the language. Would a phonemic transcription be a solution to the problems associated with our traditional orthography? It is clear that phonemic transcription comes close to the ideal of writing— to use a single symbol to identify each sound difference of a language. The Eng:ish writing system does not do this. It can be seen how inconsistent the system is by comparing the traditional five vowels of writing, *a, e, i, o, u,* with the simple phonemes and diphthongs for which they can stand. The letter *a* stands for the phonemes /a, æ, e, ɔ,/ and /ə/ in *car, cat, any, all,* and *sofa.* The letter *e* represents the phonemes /e, i,/ and /ə/ in *bell, been,* and *senility,* the diphthongs /ey/ and /iy/ in *café* and *be,* and nothing in *gate.* The letter *i* stands for the phonemes /e/ and /i/ in *bird* and *bin* and the diphthongs /iy/ and /ay/ in *machine* and *life. o* represents the phonemes /a, e, u, ɔ/ and /ə/ in *dock, worm, book, cost,* and *come* and the diphthongs /ow/ and /uw/ in *comb* and *do. u* is pronounced as /u, e, ə/ in *bull, fur,* and *just,* but for some speakers, *just,* when unstressed, is pronounced as /ɨ/. *u* is also pronounced as /uw/ and /yuw/ in *rude* and *pure,* but is not pronounced at all in *guard.*

Not all dialects of English have been sufficiently investigated to guarantee that the phonemic distinctions proposed above would serve as the perfect means of writing the language. If the only difference among dialects were the distribution, and not the number, of phonetic qualities, substitution of phonemic writing would have some obvious advantages, but some obvious disadvantages as well. While traditional orthography is inconsistent, it enables any speaker of any dialect to read the writing of people who speak other dialects without difficulty. A phonemic transcription might have the advantage of bringing us closer to the original pronunciation in some instances, and this would be a boon to poetry, perhaps. But it would also mean that children who learn only phonemic transcription would be cut off to a large degree from the usual literature of the language.

One clear advantage of phonemic writing over the traditional system is that it can represent the intonational features of a language. Punctuation in traditional writing is more closely tied to grammatical distinctions of coordination, subordination, and modification than to mere phonological differences. Symbolizing the pitches, stresses, and terminal contours would bring us closer to the melody of different English dialects. The viable solution to the problems of orthography, however, is more social and political than linguistic. It is unlikely that the accuracy claimed for phonemic writing will much affect those who have the authority to bring about changes in our educational practices. It would seem, however, that knowledge of phonemics and a combination of phonetic and phonemic transcriptions would be of great use in teaching native children to read and in helping foreigners to acquire the pronunciation of the language.

Review Questions

1. Give three definitions of "sound" as the linguist might study it, and the reasons for using articulatory phonetics.
2. Describe the basic physical movements involved in the production of sound.
3. Distinguish the basic points and manner of articulation in English.
4. Be prepared to label an outline sketch of the basic points of articulation.
5. Give an articulatory description of the following: consonant, vowel, stop, fricative, affricate, nasal, lateral.
6. Explain the difficulty in defining vowels in articulatory terms.
7. Describe the nine vowel distinctions proposed for English in articulatory terms.
8. Define "diphthong" and "semivowel."
9. List some of the ways in which English consonants and vowels can vary in their pronunciation.
10. Distinguish the composition, distribution, and function of speech sounds.
11. Distinguish complementary and parallel, or contrastive, distribution.
12. Define "phoneme" and "allophone."
13. Explain the relevance of the distinction between parallel and complementary distribution to the distinction of phonemes and their allophones.
14. Define "minimal pair" and explain its importance in linguistic analysis.

15. Explain the criteria used for classifying allophones as members of a phoneme.
16. Explain the reasons for classifying the semivowels and vocalic off-glides of diphthongs in English as allophones of the same phoneme.
17. Define "segmental" and "suprasegmental" phonemes.
18. List and illustrate the suprasegmental phonemes of English.
19. List the phonemes of English and comment on the number you give in view of alternatives taken.
20. Explain the advantages and disadvantages of phonemic transcription and traditional orthography in English.

Suggested Readings

Bloch, B., "A Set of Postulates for Phonemic Analysis," *Language,* 24 (1948), 3–46.

Harris, Z. S., Review of N. S. Troubetzkoy's *"Grundzüge der Phonologie"* (Prague, 1949), *Language,* 17 (1941), 345–349.

Heffner, R., *General Phonetics* (Madison, Wisc., 1949).

Hockett, C. F., *A Manual of Phonology,* Indiana University Publications in Anthropology and Linguistics, Memoire II (Bloomington, Ind., 1955).

Jakobson, R., and M. Halle, *Fundamentals of Language* (The Hague, 1956).

Joos, M., *Acoustic Phonetics,* Language Monograph No. 23, Linguistic Society of America (Baltimore, Md., 1948).

Ladefoged, P., *Elements of Acoustic Phonetics* (Chicago, 1962).

Martinet, A., *La Description phonologique* (Geneva, 1956).

Pike, K. L., *The Intonation of American English* (Ann Arbor, Mich., 1945).

——, *Phonemics* (Ann Arbor, Mich., 1947).

——, *Phonetics* (Ann Arbor, Mich., 1943).

——, *Tone Languages* (Ann Arbor, Mich., 1948).

Potter, R., G. Kopp, and H. Green, *Visible Speech* (New York, 1947).

Smalley, W. A., *Manual of Articulatory Phonetics* (Tarrytown, N.Y., 1961).

Swadesh, M., "The Phonemic Principle," *Language,* 10 (1934), 117–129.

Troubetzkoy, N. S., *Grundzüge der Phonologie* (Prague, 1939); French edition, *Principes de phonologie,* trans. J. Cantineau (Paris, 1949).

Twaddell, W. F., "On Defining the Phoneme," Language Monograph No. 16, Linguistic Society of America (Baltimore, Md., 1935).

Wells, R. S., "The Pitch Phonemes of English," *Language,* 21 (1945), 27–39.

Westermann, D., and I. Ward, *Practical Phonetics for Students of African Languages* (London, 1933; paperback reprint, London, 1964).

3

Grammar As a Formal System

One characteristic that linguists assume all languages have in common is a systematic nature. By "systematic" it is meant that language consists of a finite number of units that combine in a finite number of ways and in which not all of the mathematically possible combinations occur. We have seen that language is actually a system of interdependent and independent systems. The phonological and grammatical systems of language can be seen to be independent when we consider the criteria used to establish the units in each.

The over-all function of language is to communicate and discriminate meanings. Every unit in a language, therefore, has at least a differential function. On the level of phonology units were established by virtue of their differential function alone, but on the grammatical level, both the differential and the referential functions must be considered. The referential function is roughly what has been called "meaning," and the simplest example of this function is the use of words to name things. A distinction has already been drawn between referential, or denotational, meaning and connotational meaning. But even these notions will have to be further refined, since some of the criteria we must use in the study of grammar involve meaning more directly than those applied in phonology.

MEANING AND GRAMMAR

Meaning Functions of Language

Traditional studies of language have pointed out that language serves to communicate several kinds of messages: ideas, emotions, and desires. In this view language has three functions, which can be called cognitive, effective, and affective, depending on the kind of message to be communicated.

Sometimes observable responses in the listener can serve to distinguish these three uses of language. When a question is asked or a command is given, the listener may respond immediately by some sort of linguistic or physical activity. Language used in this way serves the **effective function.** When a speaker makes a statement there may be no obvious immediate response, except signs of agreement or disagreement, but it may later be determined that the listener's actions have been shaped by the information communicated. This use of language can be called its **cognitive function.** When a speaker utters an exclamation of pleasure or anger there is often an observable difference in the response of the listener with respect to the message communicated either immediately or subsequently. Communications of such attitudes illustrate the **affective function.**

These different uses of language are of varying importance for establishing the grammatical and phonological units of a language like English. Some languages, often called "tone languages," depend on pitch or other suprasegmental features to distinguish lexical and grammatical meanings. Such a use pertains to the cognitive function of language. English, as we have seen from the examples of minimal pairs given, rarely does this; the segmental phonemes are the ordinary and necessary signals for distinguishing cognitive meanings, as illustrated in the minimal pair "I just bought a cat" and "I just bought a gat." The English suprasegmental phonemes show contrasts in meanings between otherwise identical sequences of segmental phonemes and are most commonly used in the affective (for example, through stress and pitch contrasts possible in "I just bought you a new hat") and effective (for example, through pitch and terminal contours as distinctive of questions, statements, and commands) functions. Junctural features in English distinguish words from phrases or a phrase from a compound word, and not one word from another, as do the segmental phonemes. But whatever their role in distinguishing various kinds of meaning, because of the fact that they have a differential, and not a referential, function, we establish such contrasts as phonemic. That is, we do not equate the role of /s/ in *slip* with the function of /s/ in *lips*. In both cases /s/ has a differential function (for example, it distinguishes both *slip* and *lips* from *lip*), but the final /s/ of *lips* can be said to have referential function as well (that is, it signals plurality).

Meaning Functions in Grammar

All language study is concerned in some way with correct combinations, but since language is a system of systems, there can be more than one single norm of correctness for any combination. On the level of phonology this norm is established by observing and tabulating the combinations that occur, since a single relation is involved, that between the composition of a sound in a particular environment and its ability to distinguish meaning in that environment.

Grammar deals, however, with the correct combinations of language units that have meaning, and meaning is not simply a relation between two terms but a very complex set of relations. That is, combinations that have some connection with nonlinguistic aspects of the environment in which they are uttered can be "correct" for reasons such as the following:

1. They accurately refer to the nonlinguistic situation.
2. They are the correct choice of alternative, accurate referents.
3. They are true.
4. They are not pretentious or affected.
5. They are not vulgar.
6. They are not based on false etymology or incomplete analogy with derivational processes.
7. They are not from the wrong dialect.
8. They make sense to the hearer.

The reasons for distinguishing "correct" and "incorrect" combinations are many more than the ones listed, but they might all be summarized by classifying them under two systems, the lexical (or semantic) and the stylistic. Both systems are important and operative considerations in the study of language, but in the study of grammar, we need some more basic way of discussing the regularities we find in actually observed (and, therefore, presumably "correct") utterances. Working backward, we try to find some basis for correct combinations that is independent of stylistic or lexical considerations or both. This is difficult, since actual sentences do and must occur with particular lexical items and, therefore, have a particular style. But what we are obviously concerned with is discovering combinatory rules that are *independent* of, though *illustrated* in, the particular instances. One possible approach will consist of classifying forms and studying the relations among these classes. The classes can be assigned some generic sort of function common to, but still independent of, the actual lexical items that represent them. From this very general basis we can then descend to more particular combinations, where it will be found that subclasses of lexical forms must be regarded as grammatically significant.

FORMAL UNITS IN GRAMMAR

Since the linguist takes the basic manifestation of language to be sound, the basic unit of grammatical study will be found by defining and classifying the sounds or sound sequences that are meaningful in the language. The first step is to look to the actual forms of the language for some clue that will aid in classifying them accurately. The basic image of language that we are using derives from the nature of sound: it is linear, in terms of which we can define linguistic items through their composition and distribution. We may also classify linguistic items according to function. Within the framework of this linear image of language, distribution can be described according to the possible combinations that can precede or follow a given unit in the linear sequence and the items that may or may not substitute for it at that part of the sequence.

The Minimal Unit of Grammar

If we view grammar as a study of the correct combinations of the form classes of a language, we have already determined what kind of unit we will consider minimal in our analysis. This will not be a sentence, since sentences most often consist of more than one meaningful part, and just as in phonology, we would be well advised to look for some minimally definable unit of grammar that occurs in many combinations rather than to work with combinations that can be further broken up by the same principle of analysis. We take as our minimal unit, therefore, the **minimal meaningful unit,** which is called a **morpheme.** Since a morpheme is a unit of language, it will have a differential function, but it is distinguishable from the phonemes because it can also have a referential function; that is, it has some conventional and recurrent connection with the nonlinguistic circumstances in which it occurs. A morpheme may "refer" to an object or situation or some sort of relation between the two. In the earliest stages of examining an unfamiliar language the linguist may not be sure just what kind of reference the morphemes have, but the formal methods of his analysis will be helpful in sidestepping these problems until further information is available.

Types of Linguistic Forms

When we start analyzing a language like English we find that there are many kinds of linguistic forms. If a **linguistic form** is described as a recognizable phoneme or sequence of phonemes in a language that has a meaning, we suggest that the forms we are interested in have a referential function. This function is readily seen in words that are names. Expressions in English such as *cat, dog, hats, locker,* and *coathanger* allow us to separate out different kinds of linguistic forms: *cat* and *dog* cannot be further analyzed into meaningful parts; *hats, locker,* and *coathanger* can, as *hat + s, lock + er,* and *coat + hang + er,* by breaking them up according to the familiar orthography.

Parts of words, as well as simple words themselves, meet our definition of **morphemes.** All are minimal, meaningful parts of the English language. They are minimal since they cannot be broken down further on the basis of meaning. They are meaningful because we can specify the kind of connection they have with the nonlinguistic circumstances in which they are used: the *-s* commonly stands for the plural when used with nouns, the *-er* combines with the preceding form to stand for things or persons with a function describable in terms of the meaning of the preceding morpheme, and the references of *cat, dog, coat,* and *hang* can be explained by pointing or acting out the meaning.

On the basis of their occurrence in language we can distinguish two kinds of morphemes. A **free morpheme** is one that does not require the presence of another morpheme to occur. A **bound morpheme** is one that can occur only with another morpheme, bound or free. On this basis the forms represented by *-s* and *-er* are bound morphemes, while those represented by *cat, dog, lock, coat,* and *hang* are free morphemes. We can use similar norms to classify different types of linguistic forms. A **simple form** consists of a single morpheme, bound or free. It need not be a single syllable, as is seen in the simple free form *asparagus* or in the bound form represented by the *-ity* in *civility.* A **complex form** consists of no more than a single free form and one or more bound forms or of several bound forms, as in *unquenchable* and *ineluctably.* A **compound form** consists of at least two otherwise free forms, for example *coathanger.* A **word** can be defined as a minimum free form, which can either be simple, complex, or compound.

We have distinguished simple, complex, and compound forms on the basis of their composition. Some of these forms are in parallel distribution with each other and some are not. In English complex and compound forms in parallel distribution with simple ones can be called **derived forms,** since it can be considered that their distribution is explainable in the same fashion as the simple forms and, therefore, "derived" from them. Complex and compound forms that are not in parallel distribution with simple forms can be called **inflected forms.** For example, *boyish, gentlemanly,* and *helpless* are complex forms consisting of either bound or free forms or constructions of bound forms. In an environment like "We always considered him . . . ." any of the complex forms mentioned could appear, and so could simple forms like *gay, polite,* or *lost.* Compound forms like *doorknob, flatiron,* or *fireman* are in parallel distribution with simple forms like *man, bird,* or *desk* in environments like "I just saw another. . . ."

Complex forms that cannot substitute for simple forms grammatically are found in examples like *get, got, getting,* and *gotten* in sentences like:

He *gets* (or *got*) money from home through the mail.
He is *getting* stouter all the time.
He has *gotten* so much attention, he's spoiled.

For the italicized forms we can grammatically substitute only other complex forms, such as *receives, received, becoming* or *grown,* and not forms like "He get money through the mail."

The inclusion of *got* among the complex forms that are called inflected indicates that more than apparent composition, through the addition of phonemes or sequences, is involved. When a form cannot be analyzed into succeeding sequences like *heat-ed,* there are several ways in which the equivalence of inflection with complexity is discussed. One is to posit a zero (∅) sequential unit, so that the plural of *sheep* (/šiyp/) could be considered *sheep* + ∅, on the model of the overwhelmingly more common pattern of *cat* + *s,* and so on. Another way is to discuss the formation of the plural form from the singular as a process that does not involve the addition of a phoneme or phoneme sequence, but as an **internal change** of phonemes, as in *mouse, mice* (/maws/, /mays/), where a palatal glide is substituted for the velar. Similarly, the formation of the irregular past tense in English can be described as a process of internal change, as when the past tense of *get* (/get/) is formed by the internal change of /e/ to /a/ in *got* (/gat/). In each case the process is discussed in terms of a basic form plus some process, either of addition, zero modification, or internal change. When there is insufficient resemblance among the phoneme sequences involved in such relations to show a basic form, the process of **suppletion,** or substitution of another base, is discussed. In this way the relations among *good, better, best; go, went, gone;* or *be, am, is, are, were, was,* can be described.

Such sets of related forms are called **paradigms.** In the sets discussed the bases for grouping the forms in the same paradigm included semantic similarity among the forms of the same set and parallel syntactic distribution among the members of similar sets. The reason for setting up these particular paradigms is to show some of the systematic aspects of the language, but it is possible to compile sets of forms that are related in many other ways, such as in similarity or difference in meaning (synonyms and antonyms), similarity of form (alphabetical list, rhyming words), or similarity of difference in formation (inflectional or derivational sets).

Within a paradigm the relations are most clearly revealed when the form selected as basic meets certain requirements: it should be most like the other forms to which it is related by the process involved and it should be most different from the basic form of other paradigms from which we want to distinguish it. When a paradigm consists of a simple free form, to which affixes are added in a regular way, the choice of the basic form is not difficult. It becomes more difficult when the paradigm consists of complex forms, whose constituents are both bound, and which are not always found in the same phonemic sequences, or when the free form to which we would most naturally relate them on a semantic or syntactic basis does not have the same phonemic shape as the bound forms. The choice of the basic form in a derivational paradigm like *rational, rationalize, rationalizer, rationalization, rationalizable* does not present any difficulty until we try to include *reason,* since the principle that relates the other forms to each other does not apply for the inclusion of *reason.* Since our purpose in such situations is to show the regular or systematic patterns of the language, we would not make our choice after considering only a single set, but would investigate many similar sets to find the most economical way of explaining the relations.

Morphemes and Allomorphs

Most of the examples given so far have been quoted in the usual orthography, but it is obvious that writing can conceal both similarities and differences in sound. When we attend to the pronunciation of forms, or represent them consistently in a phonemic transcription, we find a similar relation between the morpheme and its variant representations in allomorphs, as we found in considering phonemes and their allophones. Both phonemes and morphemes can be considered classes or classifications of sounds or sound sequences that have a single function in common, and the individual instances can be considered as members of these classes. All the allophones of a single phoneme are classified together because they have a similar composition, which enables us to identify them, because their differences are in complementary distribution or free variation, and because they all have the same function—to distinguish meaning by contrasting with other phonemes (or with their comparable allophones) in minimally identical environments. The allomorphs of morphemes are classified together on the basis of similar norms.

Besides having a differential function, the morphemes also have a referential function. Allomorphs of the same morpheme will, therefore, have both the role of making the same difference in meaning and having the same meaning, wherever they are found. The difference in the composition of the phoneme sequences that enable us to recognize the same morphemes will be partially explainable in terms of their distribution.

There are three basic situations in which we can be sure, or can decide, that two or more allomorphs are instances of the same morpheme: (1) when the phoneme or phoneme sequences and the meanings are identical; (2) when the meanings are the same, but the phonemic sequences differ in composition according to the composition of the other allomorphs with which they are joined; and (3) when the meanings are the same, but the phonemic sequences are very different, although regularly associated with another particular morpheme. In the case of irregular correspondences between the allomorphs and the morphemes, we can identify the unpredictable forms on the basis of their distribution.

1. Recurring, identical sequences of phonemes, which are associated conventionally with the same meaning, are instances of the same morpheme, for example, *cat, boy,* and *man* and *prevaricate, get,* and *rent* in the following groups, given in the usual writing, since the sounds are the same: *cat, catty, catfish, catlike, catnap, catnip; boy, boylike, boyish, boyhood; man, manlike, mannish, manhood; prevaricate, prevaricator, prevaricates, prevaricated, prevaricating; get, gets, getting; rent, renter, rents, rented, renting.*

2. Different sequences of phonemes that recur with the same meaning are instances of the same morpheme if the phonetic differences in composition are predictable in terms of their association with a particular place or manner of articulation, for example, the plural morphemes in the following words:

cats	/kǽts/	dogs	/dɔ́gz/	roses	/rówziz/
puffs	/pə́fs/	gloves	/glɔ́vz/	passes	/pǽsiz/
piths	/píθs/	boons	/búwnz/	fizzes	/fíziz/
		booms	/búwmz/	churches	/čérčiz/
		bangs	/bǽŋz/	judges	/jɔ́jiz/
		toes	/tówz/	hashes	/hǽšiz/
		baas	/báHz/		

The predictable difference in the phonemic shape is due to **phonological conditioning,** which can be expressed for the regular noun plurals in these terms:

/-s/ occurs in voiceless environments where there is no friction.

/-z/ occurs in voiced environments where there is no friction.

/-iz/ occurs in voiced or voiceless environments where there is friction.

The same sort of conditioning is found in the third person of verbs in the present tense, with some differences in the past tense, since a different manner of articulation is involved:

heaps	/híyps/	heaped	/híypt/
flits	/flíts/	flitted	/flítid/
rids	/rídz/	ridded	/rídid/
rigs	/rígz/	rigged	/rígd/
moves	/múwvz/	moved	/múwvd/
hisses	/hísiz/	hissed	/híst/
rushes	/rǝšiz/	rushed	/rǝšt/
rooms	/rúwmz/	roomed	/rúwmd/
rings	/ríŋz/	ringed	/ríŋd/
ribs	/ríbs/	ribbed	/ríbd/
kids	/kídz/	kidded	/kídid/
kicks	/kíks/	kicked	/kíkt/
riffs	/rífs/	riffed	/ríft/
mouths	/mawđz/	mouthed	/mawđd/
buzzes	/bǝ́ziz/	buzzed	/bǝ́zd/
rouges	/rúwžiz/	rouged	/rúwžd/
guns	/gǝ́nz/	gunned	/gǝ́nd/
fills	/fílz/	filled	/fíld/

Here the phonological conditioning for the third person singular is identical with the predictable changes for the plural. The conditioning in the past tense can be expressed as:

/-t/ occurs in all voiceless environments except after /t-/.

/-d/ occurs in all voiced environments except after /d-/.

/-id/ occurs after /t-/ and /d-/.

The syllabic allomorphs /iz/ and /-id/ occur in environments where there would otherwise be consonantal clusters not found in English.

3. Phonemes or sequences of phonemes conventionally associated with the same meaning are taken to manifest the same morpheme, even when they are not phonologically conditioned, as long as the differences are in complementary distribution or free variation.

Examples of free variation in the phonemic representation of the same morpheme are found (in some dialects) for *dived* ~ *dove* (/dáyvd/ ~ /dówv/), *older* ~ *elder* (/ówldir/ ~ /eldir/), and different pronunciations of *with* (/wíθ/ ~ /wíd/) or *toward* ~ *towards* (/tɔHrd/ ~ /tɔHrdz/).

Examples of allomorphs whose differences are in complementary distribution are found in the indefinite and definite articles. Before consonants the indefinite article is usually /ə/, as in *a man,* and before vowels, /æn/, as in *an apple.* Before consonants the definite article is usually /ðə/, as in *the man,* and before vowels, usually /ðiy/, as in *the apple.*

Phonemes or phoneme sequences that are conventionally associated with the same meaning are considered manifestations of the same morpheme, even if their differences cannot be predicted in terms of phonological conditioning; they are neither in free variation nor complementary distribution, but are predictably associated with certain morphemes. These are the familiar "irregular plurals," for example, *ox, oxen; child, children; foot, feet.*

Notation for Morphemes and Allomorphs

When a morpheme has many allomorphs, as does the third person singular of the verbs and the plural of the nouns, we cannot conveniently use a single phonemic symbol to represent it. Just as there is a convention by which phonetic symbols are included in brackets and phonemic symbols within slanted lines, morphemes are conventionally written within braces { }. Any symbols would serve, but, just as the phonemic symbols are generally selected from the phonetic charts to suggest the nearest phonetic realization, morphemic symbols are more useful when they suggest something about the typical phonemic representation. For the English plurals the symbol $\{Z_1\}$ is often used. This could be distinguished from other morphemes that have a similar shape, for example, the third person, by agreeing to symbolize that as $\{Z_2\}$.

To indicate alternation in the phonemic representation of allomorphs we could agree to make the symbol in braces equivalent to an expression of the different allomorphs, such as /-s ~ -z ~ -iz ~ -in ~ -rin . . ./, where ~ is to be read as "alternates with."

It will be worth distinguishing the two commonly discussed aspects of grammar at this point, morphology and syntax. Traditionally, morphology has concerned words, and syntax, groups of words. Grammar studies grammatical constructions, a "construction" having already been defined as a grammatical unit composed of a minimum of two linguistic forms. Both *cats* and *two catnaps* meet this description. The linguistic forms represented by *cat + s* and *two + cat + nap + s* can be called the **constituents** of the constructions, and the order in which we analyze them determines whether they are **immediate, mediate, or ultimate constituents.**

Since we can analyze only two constituents of *cats, cat + s,* these are the immediate constituents (ICs) of the construction. They are obtained immediately by our first cut. In *two catnaps,* however, we would first analyze *two + catnaps,* so that this pair represents the ICs of the construction. But *catnaps* can be broken down into further parts, so that the ICs of *catnaps* are called the mediate constituents, or **parts,** of the construction two *catnaps.* The ICs of *catnaps* are *cat + naps,* and *naps* can be analyzed into the ICs *nap + s,* the mediate constituents of *catnaps.* All of the constituents, considered apart from their order, are the ultimate constituents of *two catnaps.* We can, therefore, distinguish morphology from syntax by saying that morphology studies constructions whose ICs can be bound forms (for example, *-s*), while syntax studies constructions all of whose ICs must be free forms (for example, *two, catnaps*). Syntactic constructions, of course, may contain bound forms as their mediate or ultimate constituents (for example, the *-s* in *two catnaps*).

FORM CLASSES

Since words consist of either free forms or combinations of free and bound forms, and each form has its characteristic meaning, we are offered three ways of classifying forms: (1) morphologically, according to the composition of complex or compound forms; (2) syntactically, according to the distribution of simple, complex, or compound forms; and (3) according to the function of the forms.

In English there are a comparatively small number of bound forms that are found only with a larger group of forms. Since the latter are required for the presence of the bound forms, we can use this feature of composition to set up a form class. In English as well as in other languages not all forms can be mutually substituted in a given environment, and this restriction on their distribution can provide another criterion for establishing form classes. If there is some function that all the forms of a class have in common, this feature can be another basis for setting up form classes.

Form Classes Defined through Composition

In English the class of **nouns** can be said to consist of forms that can enter into composition with the bound forms usually glossed as **plural** and **possession,** as in *ox, ox's, oxen, oxen's.* The class of **verbs** can be defined as made up of forms that can be combined with the bound forms identifiable as third person singular, present participle, past participle, and past tense, as in *grow, grows, growing, grown, grew.* The class of **adjectives** can be defined as consisting of forms that can enter into composition with the bound forms glossed as **comparative** and **superlative,** as in *hot, hotter, hottest.* **Adverbs** can be defined on the basis of their composition with the bound form *-ly,* as *hotly,* and the meaning of the bound form can be glossed as "in the manner of the preceding form." An additional negative norm must be used to distinguish adjectives and adverbs with similar terminations, the requirement that adverbs do not combine with the comparative bound forms, *er, est,* since we do not find words like **hotlier, *hotliest.* (The asterisk is used to indicate forms that are not attested.)

Since the definitions proposed here are based on their composition, many forms traditionally assigned to one or another of the classes because of distribution or function may be excluded.

Form Classes Defined through Distribution

If we consider only their composition, the allophones of phonemes, the allomorphs of morphemes, and the form classes as defined above are simply different from each other. If we consider their distribution, all three items can be classified together. We have distinguished parallel and complementary distribution. Some of the form classes defined as different in terms of their composition are in parallel distribution (that is, can substitute contrastively for each other).

To distinguish these two points of view we can call the compositional definition of the form classes **morphological** and the distributional definition **syntactic,** for the reasons explained above. Again, to keep the points of view distinct, we can restrict the use of the terms "noun," "adjective," "verb," and "adverb" to the morphological level and use the terms "nominal," "adjectival," "verbal," and "adverbial" to refer to linguistic forms that do not meet the morphological requirements defining form classes, but which are in parallel distribution with the forms that do.

There are several factors to be considered about a unit when we define it on the basis of its distribution: (1) its possibilities of substituting for a form; (2) its possibilities of occurring with a form, either as grammatically required or as grammatically permitted; and (3) its possibilities of excluding or being excluded by another form. In each case we must try to specify the precise linguistic environment in which these relations hold.

The forms defined morphologically as verbs, adjectives, and adverbs can substitute for the nouns: for example, "*Work* is fun"; "*Singing* is fun"; "*Perseverance* does it"; "*Easy* does it"; "*Money* is the answer"; "*Beautifully* is the word." The last example differs from the others in that it represents the metalinguistic use of language—that is, the use of language to talk about language instead of nonlinguistic items; the word *beautifully* does not refer outside language but to itself in a previous use.

The most familiar substitute for the nouns are the pronouns, which require a formal distinction not found in the nouns. The form of the pronoun differs in the preverbal (subject) and postverbal (object) positions: while we can say either *Bill hit John* or *John hit Bill* we can say only *He hit him.* Other common substitutes for the nouns are prepositional phrases and relative clauses. All of these substitutes can be called **nominals.** Nouns and verbs both have forms that can substitute for adjectives, but an example like "The bereaved widow and the singing waiter" points out that only participial forms of the verbs can substitute, while all the forms of the nouns are possible in place of adjectives.

Pronouns substitute for adjectives, as in *The stone house; their house. He looked rich; he looked it.* Prepositional phrases and relative clauses (which can be called **adjectivals**) are also common substitutes for adjectives. The nonparticipial forms of the verb can be replaced only by verbal phrases or clauses, and these substitutes are therefore called **verbals.** The only substitutes for adverbs are prepositional phrases and subordinate clauses, and they are identified as **adverbials.**

Many forms in English are best defined on the basis of their syntactic distribution or combinatory possibilities, either because they are invariable (prepositions and conjunctions) or because a morphological definition would be less clear (the pronouns). The most common prepositions in English, are *at, by, for, from, in, of, on, to,* and *with.* These are best defined distributionally, since they are used to express relations of such a nature that the kind of lexical items they link largely determines their grammatical employment.

In order to establish the grammatical standing of a linguistic form through its distribution we generally require three linguistic forms: (1) the form whose substitutional or combinatory relations we are interested in; (2) the form with which it is to combine; and (3) another form (or several forms) that is constructed with the second, in order to establish the particular linguistic environment defining the combination as grammatical or ungrammatical. This other form that is constructed with the second may be a feature of intonation, but we will consider primarily grammatical forms.

A **construction** can be said to consist of at least a pair of linguistic forms related to a linguistic environment as a single form.

For descriptive convenience we can assume that the cognitive function of language is presupposed for the successful use of affective and effective communication. By considering the constructions that are required or permitted in statements, we can restrict our discussion to an examination of how nouns, verbs, adjectives, and adverbs combine grammatically; such a study helps establish the grammatical standing of the nominals, verbals, adjectivals, and adverbials, no matter how complex.

The minimal grammatical form of conversation-initiating statements in English (that is, not answers to questions) requires a nominal and a verbal. For convenience of symbolization we can use the following abbreviations:

N	Nominal
V	Verbal
Adj	Adjectival
Adv	Adverbial

The system enables us to symbolize *Men work* as N + V and also to indicate that a sentence like *Perhaps all the five very dangerous criminals immediately escaped safely in a car to Philadelphia* can also be symbolized accurately as N + V, though perhaps not as clearly for other purposes.

In English neither the adverbials nor the adjectivals are grammatically required for a minimal statement, but at least the nominal and the verbal are necessary. This difference in what is grammatically required for a construction illustrates two basic construction types, the **endocentric** and the **exocentric.** An endocentric construction consists of a **head,** or **center,** and an optional addition, or **expansion.** An endocentric construction like *Crazy Harry* (Adj + N) has the noun as its head, and the construction is related to a defining environment (for example, -*sings*) in the same way as its head, so that the minimal grammatical elements of the construction *Crazy Harry sings* (N + V, or Adjective + Noun + Verb) are, morphologically, the noun and the verb, or, syntactically, the nominal and the verbal.

An exocentric construction does not have a center, or head, so that neither of the members can be considered an expansion of the other; either both of the constituents are present or there is no construction. As a consequence, neither of the constituents of an exocentric construction is related to the rest of the linguistic environment in the same way as one of the constituents. The construction forms a unity that is syntactically related to the defining environment as an undivided whole. The construction *Crazy Harry sings beautifully* consists of three distinguishable constructions: two are endocentric (contain optional expansions of a head or center) and one is exocentric (contains no optional expansions, so that both constituents are grammatically required). The endocentric constructions are *Crazy Harry* and *sings beautifully* and the exocentric construction is *Harry sings.*

Besides the N + V construction for statements, other examples of exocentric constructions in English would include prepositions + nouns (for example, *Harry sang to the crowd,* since we can have neither *Harry sang the crowd* nor *Harry sang to crowd*) and article + count noun (as opposed to mass noun, for example *sugar, wheat, milk, honesty*). The example illustrates the distinction between mass and count nouns, since we can have *Harry sang to Beauty,* but not *Harry sang to cat.*

Examples of endocentric constructions that involve optional expansions of an element considered the head of the construction are:

Adjective + Noun	*Old Ned* died.
Noun + Noun	*Ned Smith* died.
Verb + Adverb	Ned Smith *died recently.*
Adverb + Adverb	Ned Smith died *unexpectedly recently.*
Adverb + Adjective	Ned Smith died *unexpectedly rich.*
Noun + relative clause	Ned, *who was sick,* died.
Noun + adjectival phrase	Ned, *at the bar,* paid.
Noun + adverbial phrase	Ned paid *at the bar.*

Not all possibilities have been illustrated, but two things are worth noticing from the examples. First, while there are fewer *types* of exocentric constructions, they occur frequently. Second, we can distinguish coordinate endocentrics, where either member of the construction can be the head ("*Ned Smith* died") and subordinate endocentrics, where only one member can be the head ("*Old Ned* died").

A relation of **exclusion** among forms in a given environment is another way of expressing the facts elsewhere discussed in terms of necessary accompaniment. This relation is illustrated in the familiar concepts of **concord** or **agreement,** and **government** on the grammatical level. There are also systems of exclusion and inclusion on the lexical and stylistic levels. English has concord of person, number, and gender, with more complex relations of tense and mood between sentences. The form of the pronouns in subjective and objective positions can be considered concord or government. All of these relations are indicated by differences in the composition or distribution of the items involved.

Form Classes Defined through Function

Since form classes are grammatical units, it should be possible to characterize them on the basis of their referential as well as their differential function. But since the members of form classes are lexical items whose meanings vary widely, it is not possible to make a statement about their meanings that can approach in specificity those that can be made about the lexical items themselves. A formal approach to classifying the meanings of form classes includes gathering positive information about the typical reference type of the class as well as the major contrasts in meaning among classes. Such information would probably be based on considerations concerning meanings and meaning contrasts that the members of the class contract because of (1) their characteristic bound morphemes of inflection; (2) their characteristic bound morphemes of derivation; (3) the exocentric construction into which they enter; (4) their endocentric constructions; and, (5) their respective distributional possibilities in one of the different syntactic functions.

As will be seen from the discussion of syntactic constructions, the most general statement about the syntactic functions of form classes in English will be derived from an examination of the basic structure of statements: required are at least a nominal and a verbal; permitted are adjectivals and adverbials. The traditional labels of "subject," "predication," and "modification" can serve to characterize the three basic syntactic functions until these have been further specified.

SYNTACTIC CONSTRUCTIONS

Since we are trying to show how we could formally identify the basic grammatical requirements and restrictions of a language, it will be useful to start with the most elementary patterns. In English these can be seen by using the pronouns instead of the nouns, since they have the same syntactic properties as the nouns, but unlike individual nouns they do not contract lexical restrictions. Forms of *he, it,* and *they* can be used to suggest the subjective and objective functions, and since *they* is independent of the subdistinction between count and mass nouns, it can give greater generality to the statements about grammatical patterns. We can thus see more clearly whether the addition of other lexical items is a consequence of the grammatical patterns of a particular language or of free lexical choice (that is, because we are talking about *this*).

Individual verbs will be used in the illustrations of the patterns, but they should be considered primarily as the verbs that fit the patterns instead of as means of determining the patterns as a consequence of their lexical relations. The abbreviation LV will be used for linking verb, which will be explained, and TV for transitive verb. *Be* stands for any of the forms of *be* required, and ± before a symbol indicates that the form is optional.

A supplementary formula will also be used to illustrate the grammatical patterns in which X, Y, and Z will stand for nouns or nominals, and y and z for adjectives or adjectivals. The patterns are those of statements, which are not answers to questions and so are supposed to be the sole linguistic signal of meaning. Since such generalized terms are used, the "sentences" sound odd, but they are meant to illustrate grammatical and not lexical or stylistic systems.

Basic Forms of English Sentences

The following appear to be basic forms of English statements:

(1)	N + V	They happened.	(X happened)
(2)	N + LV + N	They became it.	(X became Y or y)
(3)	N + TV + N	They made it.	(X made Y)
(3a)	N + TV + N ± N	They made it (for him).	(X made Y for Z)
(3b)	N + TV + N + N	They made him (it).	(X made Y into Z or z)
(4)	N + Be + N	They were it.	(X were Y or y)

Set (1) is the most characteristic of the intransitive use of verbs such as *happen, occur,* or *exist* and their synonymous equivalents, but almost any verb which might also be found in set (3) can be used in the pattern, as in *It rained, They shot.* This pattern is found more commonly with adverbial and other expansions, as in *Almost all the invited guests arrived at eight o'clock sharp.*

Set (2) is distinguishable from (1) and (3) because of the use of a linking verb, but will be listed apart from set (4) because this pattern is related in a different way to other sentence patterns to be mentioned. Both *be* and linking verbs can be considered as alternative ways of constructing *Noun + Noun* or *Noun + Adjective,* as can be seen by comparing statements like *Washington became the first President* and *The planter was rich* with endocentric constructions like *Washington, the first President* and *The rich planter.* Verbs frequently used with linking functions include *seem, appear, smell, taste, grow, sound, cost, weigh, resemble, feel,* and so on.

Set (3) is distinct from the others because it uses a transitive verb and has two frequently occurring optional expansions. In all the cases there can be an optional expression of *for whom* something is done, and with sets involving verbs such as *name,* there is an optional specification of the "naming." Set (3) has the most numerous examples, as in *They bought a new car, The enemy started the hostilities.* Set (3a) is illustrated in sentences like *They shot him a deer* (or, *They shot a deer for him*), *They gave him the prize* (or, *They gave the prize to him*), *She baked him a cake* (or, *She baked a cake for him*). Set (3b) is illustrated in examples like *They soon made themselves wealthy* (*diamond merchants*) and *The majority of the people elected Washington* (*the President*). In these examples the combinations of Adjectival + Nominal or Nominal + Nominal are coordinate endocentric constructions, since any element can be considered as the head, or center, of their constructions. Verbs that would appear most frequently in (3b) would include *choose, elect, proclaim, consider, crown, believe, call, suppose, name.*

Set (4) differs from (2) in that adverbials cannot form one of the elements of the construction in its basic form. Any adverbials that appear will be expansions of the adjectivals, as in *He was completely loyal,* compared to *He quickly became rich* (2). We do not find **He is completely,* and expressions like *He was there,* since they are not in parallel distribution with a possible **He is completely,* and are better considered adjectivals. This distinguishes them from other constructions in which *there* can be an adverbial or an adjectival, as in *The man there paid the bill* or *The man paid the bill there* (3).

Examples of (4) would include *They were rich men,* which involves a coordinate endocentric construction, since *They were rich* and *They were men* are both possible. Set (4) contrasts with (1), since adjectivals in the first set are optional expansions, as in *They arrived safe,* and adverbial expansions are permitted, as in *They arrived safely,* whereas in (4) either an adjectival or a nominal is an integral part of the construction and adverbials are not. *They were* is not an instance of (4) as a conversation-initiating statement but of (1), as in *They existed.*

Systematic Relations among Sentence Types

All of the examples given here are positive statements. The statement form was selected for descriptive convenience, since it is possible to show that this pattern type is systematically related to the others. Both positive and negative statements are typical of the cognitive function of language, while questions and commands are more frequently used in the effective function, and exclamations in the affective.

Since /231\/ is the typical intonation pattern of statements and negations, these can be systematically related to exclamations involving the same sequence of morphemes through the contrast of intonation patterns, which is typically /241\/ in exclamations. Statements can be systematically related to questions that do not involve an interrogative word when the intonation patterns for the same morpheme sequences contrast, with $/231\searrow/$ for the statement and $/23\nearrow/$ for the question.

For the examples cited the following systematic relations among sentence types can be given in the form of transformations. By **transformation** is meant here the addition, deletion, or change in order or form of the morphemes involved, which enables us to relate many utterances that appear, on the surface, to be simply different. The symbol → is used here, which can be read as "rewrite."

Negative Statements

The positive statements in sets (1), (2), and (3) are systematically related to their negative form as presented in the formula

(1) $N + V \longrightarrow N + do + \text{not} + V_{\text{inf}}$

which can be read as "rewrite the positive statements as nominal + the required form of *do* (the proper person and tense) + the verb in the infinitive form." This rewrites *They happened* as *They did not happen,* or *They arrived safely* as *They did not arrive safely.* When the additional elements involved in patterns (2) and (3) are added, there are similar systematic relations, giving *They did not become rich men* (2), *They did not buy a new car, They did not shoot him a deer, They did not make themselves wealthy diamond merchants,* and so on (3). Set (4) was not included under (2) because it requires a different formula for negatives and questions. The negative formula would be:

(4) $N + be + N \longrightarrow N + be + \text{not} + N$

which can be read as "rewrite the positive statement as nominal + *be* in the required form + negative + nominal." This rewrites *They were rich men* as *They were not rich men.*

Questions

The positive statements in sets (1), (2), and (3) are systematically related to their question form as presented in this formula:

(1) $N + V \longrightarrow do + N + V_{\text{inf}}$

which can be read as "rewrite the positive statement as the required form of do + nominal + verb in the infinitive form." This rewrites *They happened* as *Did they happen?* or *They arrived safely* as *Did they arrive safely?* When the additional elements involved in patterns (2) and (3) are added, there are similar systematic relations, giving *Did they become rich men?* (2), *Did they buy a new car? Did they shoot him a deer? Did they make themselves wealthy diamond merchants?* (3). Set (4) requires a different formula:

(4) $N_1 + be + N_2 \longrightarrow be + N_1 + N_2$

which can be read as "rewrite the positive statement as the required form of *be* + the subject nominal and the predicate nominal." This rewrites *They were rich men* as *Were they rich men?*

Commands

The statements given as illustrations are all in the third person. The most common commands involve the second person, so leaving aside the use of forms like *let* with the first and third persons, whose systematic correspondences could also be formulated, the correspondences here will be illustrated for the second person forms, in the following formula:

(1) $N + V \longrightarrow N + V_{inf}$[41]

which can be read as "rewrite the positive statement by deleting the nominal and use the infinitive form of the verb with a /41/ intonation pattern." This rewrites *You happened* as *Happen!* or *You arrived safely* as *Arrive safely!* When the additional elements involved in patterns (2) and (3) are added there are similar systematic relations, giving *Become rich men! (2) Buy a new car! Shoot him a deer! Make yourselves wealthy diamond merchants!* (3). Set (4) follows the same system, as in *Be rich men!*

Passives

Passive transformations apply only to set (3), which involves the transitive use of verbs, and this fact provides a formal definition of **transitive verb**. The basic formula for set (3) could be expressed as:

(3) $N_1 + VT + N_2 \longrightarrow N_2 + Aux + V_{part\ 2} + by + N_1$

which can be read as "rewrite the active statement as: use the subjective form of the nominal, which is objective in the active statement, + the proper auxiliary (for example, *is, were*) + the past participial form of the verb + *by* + the objective form of the nominal, which is subjective in the active statement." This rewrites *They bought a new car* as *A new car was bought by them* or *He chose her* as *She was chosen by him. The judges gave him the prize* becomes *He was given the prize by the judges* by a slightly different formula:

(3a) $N_1 + VT + N_2 + N_3 \longrightarrow N_2 + Aux + V_{part\ 2} + N_3 + by + N_1$

This formula applies equally to set (3b), and rewrites *The majority of the people elected Washington (the) President* as *Washington was elected (the) President by the majority of the people.*

Other Systematic Relations

Many other systematic relations have not even been alluded to here, for example, the forms to be used when different tenses are involved, which may change the patterns of the questions; the possibility of two passive transformations in (3a), which could produce *He was given the prize by the judges* or *The prize was given him by the judges;* and the fact that sentences like *I want you to go* are best considered as transforms of *I want it, You go,* and so on. The latter example also suggests that the symbols for the various elements involved in the constructions would have to be chosen with much more care in order to avoid ambiguities. Designations such as "singular" and "plural" or "present participle" and "past participle" are insufficient to indicate the role that the forms designated in this manner actually play in many sentences.

This transformational approach to language should also indicate that the simplistic definition of "linguistic system" as "a finite number of units that combine only in a limited number of ways" given in Chapter 1 will have to be reconsidered. Part of the system of a language consists of the transformational potential of its units and constructions.

GRAMMAR AS A FORMAL SYSTEM

The linguistic study of language has sometimes been compared to mathematics, and the examples of the formal treatment of linguistic items given so far may indicate some of the points of comparison. Both studies are interested in **formal systems,** that is, relations which hold among many entities. Part of the power of a mathematical formalization of systems is our ability to interrelate things that differ from each other in many ways.

The linguist is trying to do something similar in the study of language and some of the difficulties have already been seen. Language is considered as a system of systems, many of which are interdependent. But language is not merely an abstract system of systems but a means used by human beings, who are even more complex than linguistic systems, to communicate with each other about a world that is constantly changing as they experience it, and which they change, largely through the use of language. The linguist thinks that it is a verifiable hypothesis that the systems of language can be described apart from the individual characteristics of the users.

The traditional study of language has been largely concerned with the use of language by people and has based much of its description on considerations that intimately involve the users. This kind of study is clearly important and valuable, but the linguist believes that it has led to a certain amount of confusion because of its orientation. One way to bring rigor into the study of language is to assume a more abstract point of view and to look for patterns and units that are presupposed by any particular use or user. Another way is to view each language as unique. Such a recognition need not ignore or deny the assumption of traditional study, that languages are very much alike. But instead of a subjective "very much," linguistic science prefers to be able to specify objectively "how much" languages resemble and differ from each other. Instead of taking the systems of Latin and Greek as models of linguistic structure, the linguistic approach prefers to discover the autonomous system of each language.

The following chapters will consider how various scholars at different periods treated these problems. Seeing how these studies resemble and differ from each other in their conceptions of language, its parts and uses, and how these are best to be described and explained should make us more aware of the dimensions of linguistic study. It should enable us, in however general terms, to formulate the conditions under which progress has been made in linguistic study. These general conditions appear to involve the clear definition of linguistic units at different levels and the ability to show systematic relations among the units on a given level and among different levels.

Review Questions

1. Distinguish: referential and connotational meaning; the cognitive, affective, and effective functions of language.
2. Distinguish phonology and grammar.
3. List some of the criteria for "correct" linguistic combinations and give examples of each.
4. Give a basic unit of grammar; the minimal unit of grammar.
5. Distinguish, with examples, free and bound morphemes; simple, complex, and compound forms; inflected and derived forms.
6. List, with examples, four morphological processes.
7. Transcribe phonemically, and give the base form, with your criterion of choice, for the following paradigms: (a) *enter, entry, entrance, entrant;* (b) *introduce, introduction, introducer, introductory.*

8. Give four criteria for considering different items as instances of the same morpheme and illustrate them with examples.
9. List the immediate, mediate, and ultimate constituents of *three gentlemen* and *simply delicious*. Give your criteria.
10. List the form classes you would recognize for English and give your criteria. Distinguish nouns and nominals.
11. Distinguish endocentric and exocentric constructions and give examples of each.
12. List six basic constructions in English syntax and give your criteria for distinguishing them.
13. Give some reasons for studying grammar formally.

Suggested Readings

Chomsky, N., *Syntactic Structures* (The Hague, 1957).

Elson, B., and V. Pickett, *Beginning Morphology and Syntax* (Santa Ana, Calif., 1960).

Francis, W. N., *The Structure of American English* (New York, 1958).

Fries, C. C., *The Structure of English* (New York, 1952).

Joos, M., *The English Verb, Form and Meanings* (Madison, Wisc., 1964).

Lees, R. B., *The Grammar of English Nominalizations* (Bloomington, Ind., 1960).

Nida, E., *Morphology*, 2d. ed. (Ann Arbor, Mich., 1949).

————, *Synopsis of English Syntax* (Norman, Okla., 1960).

Roberts, P., *English Sentences* (New York, 1962).

————, *English Syntax* (New York, 1964).

————, *Patterns of English* (New York, 1956).

Sledd, J., *A Short Introduction to English Grammar* (Chicago, 1959).

Strang, B., *Modern English Structure* (New York, 1962).

4

The Development of Language
Study in the West

One of the sources of cultural unity in the West is our common educational inheritance from the ancient Greeks. One influence is reflected in the way we ask and answer questions. More than most people realize, it was the Greeks who set the norms for asking and answering questions for many centuries. In modern times, however, science has learned to ask questions quite different in nature from those asked by the Greeks and demands the kind of answers that would not have occurred to the ancients or to the generations educated through the study of their wisdom.

Although our schools have learned to ask scientific questions about many things, the vast majority of them are still asking the same sorts of questions about language that the Greeks first raised about their own language—questions concerned with, for example, person, number, gender, case, voice, mood. Our schools accept as the "correct" answer one that uses the same vocabulary that the Greeks used to describe Greek: "third person," "plural number," "neuter gender," "dative case," "subjunctive mood," "declarative sentence," and so on.

We have already noted that many sets of different data can be called "language" and that the linguist selects from among them sounds and sequences of sounds that can be structurally described. It is possible that questions about voice, case, mood, and so on, when raised about Greek, could be answered for Greek only by giving details of Greek morphology, but in English would require information concerning either lexical or syntactic distinctions. The association between form and meaning is arbitrary and differs from language to language. The linguistic scientist asks questions that are different from those raised by the Greeks, and the methods he uses to ask them are not the same; it is hardly surprising that the answers he finds acceptable are also different.

Often the terminology used by linguists and traditional grammarians is the same. For that reason, among others, it is useful in a course in general linguistics to investigate the origin and development of these terms; it is useful as well to see the presuppositions—especially the semantic theory—behind traditional work, since it is often concerning the role of meaning that traditionalists see the greatest difference between their work and that of structural linguists. From the examples of formal analysis of language that we have seen it should be clear that this statement does not mean that the linguist ignores the question of meaning in language. It does mean that he does not assume that the meaning categories of the classical languages, which were established first on the basis of formal distinctions in Greek, must also find a formally distinct expression in the grammatical system of every language. It might also be said that no linguist has as yet proposed a theory of meaning as comprehensive as the traditional one, even though the latter can be shown to be inadequate on several counts.

The terminology of traditional grammar, inherited from the Greeks, comprises the most widespread, best understood, and most generally applied grammatical distinctions in the world. However, many teachers of school grammar today—and many linguists—do not have an adequate understanding of the background of this terminology. To communicate with others about language or anything else we require shared experience. And in order to judge which of two ways of talking about language is superior in view of a stated goal, we must understand the presuppositions of each. For the past thirty years or so linguistics has been identified as descriptive linguistics, since it was the conviction of many workers in the field that description, and not explanation, of languages was the legitimate purpose of their discipline. Recently many linguists have concluded that mere description is not a satisfactory goal and that we now have within our means the tools for explaining language in linguistic terms. One goal of traditional grammar has been to present the facts of language in an explanatory, and not merely a descriptive, way. By examining the development of this work we can learn from both its successes and failures.

In studying traditional work we have to consider a certain amount of material that is nonlinguistic, since much of traditional language study has treated the question of how a man knows the things he talks about, as well as what there is for him to know. We must have, therefore, an elementary understanding of the psychology and logic of antiquity and the medieval period. Our focus, of course, remains on the linguistic facts proposed: against the background of the first three chapters, we can judge the kinds of statements made by the ancients about the forms of language.

One reason for studying the ancient and medieval work on language has already been mentioned: its outlook is the point of view basic to traditional grammar, much of which makes sense only when we put it into such a framework. A structural reason for such study is that we cannot fully know something until we know what it is not. This review will, therefore, clarify our understanding of the nature and scope of traditional grammar as well as of modern structural work. Finally, much of the work of the ancients had rigor and consistency, which accounts for their satisfaction with the answers they obtained. To the extent that linguists do not ask the same questions they cannot give equally satisfying answers. The study of language progresses in the same way as other sciences. We start with one problem, and the solution proposed for it gives rise to another problem, usually more fundamental than the first. Theories are developed to organize the answers we get, but it is possible that ambiguities which we inherit unresolved from earlier stages of investigation can weaken descriptive accuracy and explanatory power. As a result, our "explanations" can become unwieldly and overcomplex, since they sometimes confuse things that should be distinguished. At the same time it is possible to attain a more accurate description of the elements involved in a problem dealt with in the past and produce explanations demonstrably superior to those once offered without meeting the precise problem that led to the original formulation. Such is the relation between much of modern linguistics and some traditional grammatical views.

THE ANCIENT GREEKS

The first problems that interested the ancient Greek thinkers were concerned not with language but with the composition of the physical world about them. Over a long period of time contradictory opinions were advanced about the basic elements underlying the various natural phenomena. Principally because the ancients did not have a common system of logic, these disagreements remained unresolved. During the pre-Socratic period that preceded the development of a more systematic investigation of the role of language in thought, many thinkers were convinced that there was no way to attain answers with certainty. Another factor that distracted the Greeks from these speculative problems was the spread of Greek trade and influence. The practical need of that era was the training of men of politics and business rather than speculative thinkers. Training in citizenship was especially in demand, and teachers who offered themselves to instruct others in the art of winning victories in debate were considered teachers of the only worthwhile "wisdom." Such were the **Sophists.** The original meaning of the word "sophist" was "a wise man," since training in rhetoric was equated with wisdom. It was Socrates who showed the shallowness of this claim and attached to the word "sophist" the notion of "false appearance of wisdom," pointing out that the Sophists trained their students to move others to action regardless of the cause advocated. They made no attempt to convince an audience of the "truth" of a cause, since its very existence was in doubt.

The Sophists

Considering the stress given to empirical procedures in modern science, it is interesting to note that there was a strong empirical tendency among the Sophists of the fifth century B.C. They attempted to subject everything to measurement—music, geometry, astronomy, and even language study. In their teaching of rhetoric, for example, they recommended the use of rounded sentences, in which phrases and clauses of successive sentences would be of equal length, right down to the last syllable. The reaction in their day against such proceedings was similar to the humanistic distaste in modern times for the empirical tendencies of linguistics. The methods of the Sophists were satirized by Aristophanes in *The Frogs,* where he describes a contest that Dionysus witnesses upon his arrival in the Underworld. Aeschylus and Euripides, a disciple of the Sophists, have been disputing each other's literary merits. They agree to submit their quarrel to the judgment of Pluto, but Euripides asks Pluto's servants to bring scales, rules, and circles so that he can render an objective, and not just an emotional, evaluation.

The Sophists laid the groundwork for the technical vocabulary of rhetoric, much of which, in translation, is still current today. One reason for their success was certainly their empirical method. They did not merely theorize about what constituted a successful rhetorical composition but observed men in action who were acknowledged masters of the art. They analyzed the speeches of the masters in terms of a certain number of units and then instructed their students to construct speeches of similar units in similar arrangements. Protagoras is credited with being the first to distinguish sentence types. According to some sources, he listed four—prayer, question, statement, and command—and according to others, seven—narration, question, answer, command, report, prayer, and invitation. According to Aristotle, Protagoras was also the first to call attention to the distinctions between gender and tense. The Sophist Gorgias was a contemporary of Socrates and was one of the first to name and recommend the use of various figures of speech, still current in rhetoric, such as "antithesis," "assonance," "analogy," "apostrophe," "allegory," "hypallage," "similar endings," "repetition," "metaphor," "puns," and "rounded sentences." Prodicus is chiefly remembered for his work in distinguishing words that were thought to be synonyms from true synonyms, and Hippias made a more detailed study of sounds than his predecessors.

Although the Sophists made other distinctions about the operative elements of rhetoric, it would not be unfair, for our purposes, to examine their analysis of language on the basis of the units mentioned so far. As units they explicitly discussed syllables (but not individual phonemes), and sentences of different kinds. We are not accurately informed about how they defined "syllables," but they could apparently agree on how many there were in rounded sentences. There is no explicit distinction of levels of analysis or different systems in their work, but they implicitly recognized the difference between the phonological (in their discussion of syllables and sounds), the grammatical (in their tense and gender distinctions), the lexical (in distinguishing synonyms), and the stylistic levels (through their distinctions of various rhetorical devices). Their sole purpose in all of this was to teach their students how to convince others and not to discuss "grammar." For that purpose their units were certainly apt compared to the complete lack of system and technical terminology before them, but for our present purposes, their work is not linguistically useful, since it lacks universality, being concerned with a single use of language and not with the fundamentals of language that are presupposed by any use of it. The Sophists gave us no formal criteria for distinguishing the various units discussed.

The *Physis-Nomos* Controversy

In the preceding section we considered the initial vocabulary available to the Greeks for talking about language in the fifth century B.C. In line with Prodicus' discussion of synonyms, real and apparent, a more fundamental question was being raised about how words in particular, and language in- general, acquired meaning. This was discussed in Plato's dialogue *Cratylus,* where the two positions argued hold that language has meaning arbitrarily and through convention, or that language has some natural connection with the things it is used to discuss.

In the dialogue Socrates is asked to settle the dispute between Hermogenes and Cratylus. Cratylus believes that the name of a thing is a consequence of the nature of the thing named, and thus that language has meaning naturally (*physei*). The phonetic composition of the name, therefore, should mirror the composition of the thing named, so that isolated words can be examined as being true or false in themselves. There should thus be only one correct name for anything, and this should be common both to Greek and barbarian.

Hermogenes denies this assumption and holds that names stand for things only through convention—agreement among the speakers— (*nomō*). Since this agreement is subject to change, any word is the correct word as long as there is agreement about its reference.

Socrates then proceeds to argue the merits and defects of both views. He points out that the *onoma* ("name" or "noun" or "subject") is the smallest part of a *logos* ("phrase" or "clause" or "sentence" or "argument") and, therefore, an important tool for teaching and for distinguishing things. Names should thus be apt for their purpose. Some people are skilled in making names, while others are not, so we must hope that the one who first makes up a name knows well the nature of the thing named. Socrates discusses two sorts of names in the dialogue, those that are complex, or compound, and those that are simple, and he points out that we must use a different method in analyzing the two types.

A compound word, which he exemplifies with the name of the sea god Poseidon, can be examined by first breaking it into its constituents. These, he suggests, could be *posi* ("for the feet," dative of the word *pous,* "foot") and *desmos* ("a fetter"), since the one who first assigned the name might have thought that walking through the water would be difficult for Poseidon. He notes that the name is not exactly a simple combination of these two parts, but some letters may have been added or dropped for the sake of euphony. It is by no means clear that Socrates is serious in this, but apparently this is the method used by those who favored the natural theory of language correspondence.

In the case of simple forms Socrates says we must proceed differently, since we cannot inquire about the correct combination of two meaningful parts to name a single thing. Here we must ask what the single letters imitate. We can classify letters into vowels, consonants (occlusives and mutes), and semivowels (*hēmiphōna,* a consonant that is neither occlusive nor mute) and examine their qualities, much in the fashion that an artist would examine the colors he could use to imitate a natural scene. A letter like *rho* seems apt to express motion, since the tongue moves rapidly when producing it (probably an apico-alveolar trill); it would, therefore, be a good sound to use in a word like *rhoein* ("to flow"). *Sigma, phi,* and *ksi* are pronounced with a great expenditure of breath, and so are well used in *psychron* ("shivering"), *kseon* ("seething"), and *seiesthai* ("shaking"). The *l* sound of Greek, *lambda,* "because of its liquid movements causes the tongue to slip," is aptly used in *leios* ("slippery") and *olisthanei* ("slips"). Socrates then cites quite opposite examples, such as the oddity of finding a *lambda* in the word for "hardness" (*sklērotes*), which is compounded by discovering that this word, in the Eritrian dialect, is *sklēroter,* suggesting an unexplainable equivalence of *sigma* and *rho.* Cratylus' answer to this is that it is just a matter of custom, but Socrates shows him that custom is convention or agreement, and since letters both alike and different can represent things that resemble or differ from each other, it would appear that language is fundamentally conventional. He concludes, "we must admit that both convention and usage contribute to the manifestation of what we have in mind when we speak."

Plato

Besides in the dialogue *Cratylus,* we find Plato's views about language in the *Theatetus* and *Sophists.* In these other dialogues he was more concerned about the relation of thought, language, and the things talked about than the etymology of individual expressions. He saw that just as some things in nature can go together and others cannot, so too certain words can be correctly combined and others cannot. He appeared to see the reason for this in the conventional restrictions of language, in the way we think about things, and in the nature of the things themselves. He was interested, therefore, in finding some way of describing correct combinations that would lead to true statements or definitions. His attempt to establish a discipline that could deal with such rules was a first attempt to found a formal logic, that is, a system by which we can tell whether combinations are correct or not merely by inspecting the relations among the terms used. He did not distinguish sufficiently among the various sources of limitation on linguistic constructions (grammatical, stylistic, truth-functional), but he did devise a technique that leads later to the formulation of syllogistic rules.

This technique is called the **division.** In the dialogue *Sophists,* Socrates started by discussing the problem of whether three names for a Sophist—"sophist," "statesman," or "philosopher"—are synonyms for the same person, names for two different types of person, or different names for three different types of person. Before the question can be resolved a definition of these three activities has to be framed, and a method of dividing a genus into its species is developed. The example that is used is hardly a serious one, but since it is meant to be an illustration of method, this is unimportant.

The method is as follows: If we wish to define some species, *x,* we start by taking a more inclusive and familiar class, *a,* of which we know *x* is a member. Then class *a* is divided into two mutually exclusive subclasses, *b* and *c*, making sure that only one of them still contains the property *X*, which we know belongs to the class *x* we are trying to define. Using a kind of tree diagram we can put class *b* on the right and class *c* on the left, so that *b* contains our property *X* and *c* does not. We then divide *b* into two mutually exclusive subclasses in the same way and continue dividing the classes on the right-hand side until we no longer need to divide. We should then arrive at some ultimate division whereby we can perceive, by simple inspection of all the terms on the right-hand side, from *a* to whatever is the final subclass, that we have a satisfactory definition of *x*.

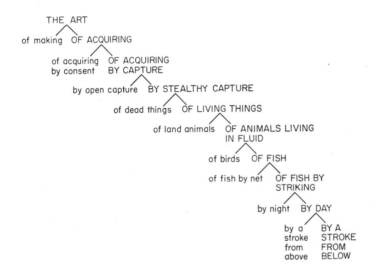

Fig. 2. Using Plato's Method to Define the Term "Fishing."

As shown in Figure 2, the definition of "fishing" is, therefore, "the art of acquiring, by capture, live animals living in fluid, namely fish, by striking with a stroke from below by day."

Anyone could find fault with this definition, and it was Aristotle's dissatisfaction with the technique (essentially that of good guesses illustrated in "Twenty Questions") that led him to invent the deductive syllogism. His objections included the fact that we must know the first and fundamental notion of the series, class *a*, and then have a good deal of ingenuity to select the proper division in each case in order to assure a true dichotomy, since there are no real rules to guide our choice. Besides, this technique can work only with items that are necessarily related, whereas a logic should be able to handle factors that are both necessary and contingent.

In the *Theatetus* Plato put this definition of language into the mouth of Socrates: "the expression of one's thoughts by means of *onomata* and *rhēmata* which, as it were, mirror or reflect one's ideas in the stream [of air] which passes through the mouth."

The expressions *onomata* and *rhēmata,* plurals of *onoma* and *rhēma,* are left untranslated in the definition because they correspond to many expressions we use in ordinary language and in the technical vocabulary of both grammar and logic. In ordinary language *onoma* can mean "name"; in the vocabulary of grammar it can mean "noun," "nominal," or "subject," and in logic it corresponds to "logical subject." In ordinary language *rhēma* can mean "phrase" or "saying"; in grammar it may mean "verb," "verbal," or "predicate," and in logic it corresponds to "logical predicate." The *onoma* and *rhēma* were, in Plato's usage, the basic members of a *logos,* which is often translated as "sentence." But Plato and the ancients did not distinguish the vocabulary of ordinary language, grammar, or logic, so that such a translation must be viewed with caution. *Logos* has many meanings, such as "nature," "plan," "argument," "phrase," "clause," "sentence," and "proposition," depending on the universe of discourse we would assign it. Later, in the *Sophists,* Plato defined the *rhēma* as "the name of an action" and *onoma* as "the name of the one who performs the action." These definitions come closer to our understanding of "noun" and "verb" in traditional grammar.

Plato had the advantage of knowing all the units distinguished by his predecessors, and he showed that he was aware of other differences they did not discuss explicitly. He distinguished, for example, different dialects of Greek; a sound sequence as a word or as a sentence, depending on the accent; native Greek words from those borrowed from other languages; letters from their names; and Greek vowels, consonants, mutes, and semivowels. Very likely Plato owed a good deal to Hippias for these distinctions.

For our present purpose of offering a linguistic criticism of his work, we can consider only the principal new units of language that Plato seems to have distinguished for the first time, the *onoma* and *rhēma* as constituents of *logos,* since these distinctions represent a clear advance over the work of the Sophists, who discussed sentences, but only their phonological and lexical constituents. The criteria that Plato used to distinguish these new units (*onoma, rhēma, logos*) are purely semantic. Although he was capable of observing formal differences, he did not use these to distinguish language units. He did not advance over his contemporaries in the number of systems he discussed in language. He did not distinguish between the phonetic and phonological levels, for instance, in his examination of sound-meaning correspondences, and he seemed to assume that a single sound corresponds to a single letter. While he saw clearly that some expressions could and other expressions could not be correctly linked, he did not clearly distinguish the lexical, grammatical, and stylistic sources of these restrictions. Above all, he did not distinguish grammar and logic. In his day the expression *grammatikē techne*, which is sometimes translated "grammar," was not a study of morphological or syntactic constructions but of letters and their arrangement in words. His study, therefore, was focused on the lexical system of Greek. This is a consequence of his purpose in discussing language, the possibility of learning something about things through a study of their names and the correct combinations of expressions dealing with them. He rejected the hypothesis that things and their names are naturally connected, apparently, and held that there is only a conventional connection, but he did not investigate the arbitrary, conventional system of language. In view of his logical purpose, the units and methods he devised were not apt. Nor were the factors he distinguished in his logical studies universal in languages or language uses, since he was concerned principally with the true and false use of language, and human languages are used for far more than this. It is also quite clear to anyone who does not know Greek that the criteria he used to identify the *onoma*, *rhēma*, and *logos* are not formal, since, given a pair of expressions, we could apply his terms only if we knew both his definitions and the meanings of the expressions. In Plato's writings there are many complete utterances in which neither an *onoma* nor a *rhēma* appears.

Aristotle

Although Aristotle is represented as having objected to most of Plato's work, it is obvious that he accepted the bulk of his master's ideas and then developed them with further insights of his own. Since Aristotle dealt more consciously and extensively with language facts, it will be worthwhile to quote a number of passages from his works, although many cannot be cited. In these selections we will see that Aristotle had a general theory about what there is to know, how men know it, and how they express it in language. He saw several levels on which language can be studied and distinguished the forms of words and of sentences, the meaning of words in isolation and in constructions, and differences between the written and spoken styles of language.

ON INTERPRETATION

I. Let us first define *onoma* and *rhēma*, then explain what is meant by "denial," "affirmation," "proposition," and "sentence" (*logos*).

Words are spoken symbols or signs of affections or impressions of the soul; written words are signs of words spoken. As writing, so also speech is not the same for all races of men. But the mental affections themselves, of which these words are primarily signs, are the same for the whole of mankind, as are also the objects of which those affections are representations or likenesses, images, copies. With these points, however, I deal in my treatise concerning the soul; they belong to a different inquiry from that which we now have in hand.

As at times there are thoughts in our minds unaccompanied by truth or falsity, while there are others at times that have necessarily one or the other, so also in our speech, for combination and division are essential before you can have truth or falsity. An *onoma* or a *rhēma* by itself resembles a concept that is neither combined nor disjoined. Such is "man," for example, or "white," if pronounced without any addition. As yet, it is not true or false.

II. An *onoma* is a sound having meaning established through convention alone but no reference whatever to time, while no part of it has any meaning, considered apart from the whole. Take the proper name "Goodsteed," for instance. The "steed" has no meaning apart, as it has in the phrase, "a good steed." It is necessary to notice, however, that simple *onomata* differ from composites. While in the case of the former, the parts have no meaning at all, in the latter they have a certain meaning, but not as apart from the whole. Let us take the expression "pirate vessel," for instance. [In Greek, this is one word, *epaktokelēs*, and the free form *kelēs* means "vessel."] The "vessel" part has no sense whatever except as part of the whole.

We have already seen that an *onoma* signifies this or that by *convention*. No sound is by nature an *onoma:* it becomes one, becoming a symbol. Inarticulate noises mean something—for instance, those made by brute beasts. But no such noises of that kind are *onomata* . . . "of Philo" or "to Philo" [in Greek, *Philonos, Philoni,* genitive and dative of the proper name *Philo,* respectively] and so on are not *onomata,* but cases [Greek, *ptōseis*] of the *onoma.* Otherwise we define all these cases as the *onoma* itself is defined; but when "is" or "was" or "will be" is added, they do not then form propositions, which are either true or false, as the *onoma* itself always does then. For "of Philo is" cannot of itself constitute a true or false proposition. Nor yet can "of Philo is not."

III. A *rhēma* is a sound that not only conveys a particular meaning but has a time reference as well. No part of itself has a meaning. It indicates always that something is said or asserted of something else. Let me explain what I mean by "it has a time reference also." Now "health" [Greek, *hygeia*] is an *onoma,* but "is healthy" [Greek, *hygeiainei*] is a *rhēma,* not an *onoma.* For the latter conveys, besides its own meaning, that the state signified (namely, health) now exists. Then "a *rhēma* is an indication of something asserted of something else"; by this I mean, of something predicated of a subject, found in a subject. . . .

"He was healthy" or "he will be healthy" I would likewise not call a *rhēma.* I would call it a case of the *rhēma.* [Greek for "case" is *ptōsis,* the same expression used for the *onoma's* "cases."] The *rhēma* and its cases differ in this respect: the *rhēma* indicates present time, but the cases, all other times except the present.

Rhēmata by themselves, then, are *onomata,* and they stand for, or signify something, for the speaker stops his process of thinking and the mind of the hearer acquiesces. However, they do not as yet express positive or negative judgments. For even the infinitives and participles "to be" and "being" are indicative of fact, if and when something further is added to them. . . .

IV. A *logos* is a significant speech, of which this or that part may have meaning—as something, that is, that is uttered, but not as expressing a judgment of a positive or negative character. Let me explain: take "mortal." This doubtless has a meaning, but neither affirms nor denies anything; some addition or other is needed before it can affirm or deny. But the syllables of "mortal" are meaningless. So it is also with "mouse," of which the "-ouse" has no meaning whatever and is but a meaningless sound. But we saw that in composite *onomata*, the particular parts have meaning, although not apart from the whole.

While every *logos* has meaning, though not as an instrument of nature but, as we have observed, by convention, not all can be called propositions. A prayer, for instance, is a *logos*, but has neither truth nor falsity. . . . Let us pass over all such examples, their study being more properly taken up in the province of rhetoric or poetry. . . .

Before quoting more of the texts of Aristotle on language, which had an unparalleled influence on the study of language in the Western world, it will be helpful to clarify some of the ideas that are not explained in the foregoing passages. The first, perhaps the most difficult, and certainly the most important, idea that requires examination is Aristotle's notion of meaning. In his work on the soul he defines "voice," as opposed to other kinds of noises, as "a sound uttered by an animal, in association with an image." Aristotle's notion of what language can express is actually much more complex than this, but in the passages quoted it is obvious that he is restricting himself to an extremely naïve referential-meaning definition of "meaning." When he says that an expression either does or does not have a meaning he is saying that the noises we make are or are not associated with some kind of an image—visual, tactile, or of another sense. A word like "steed" is capable of summoning up an image of a horse; but in the compound "Goodsteed," he claims that we have only one image, of the person whose name the word represents, and not a separate image of a horse ("steed") and something else ("good"). Just what an image of "good" would be is a bit of a puzzle: his example of "pirate vessel" is better adapted to this image theory. It is for this reason that Aristotle would say that the noises animals make do have a meaning, since they are presumably associated with images of pain, hunger, anger, and so on, in much the same way as the sighs and groans of men in pain. His use of the term "case" (*ptōsis*) is also peculiar. In these passages he is discussing propositions that we can decide to be true or false by looking at the states of affairs they represent. In his view states of affairs in the past are already determinately true or false, while those in the future cannot be decided as true or false. He wants to work only with statements whose truth or falsity can be determined from present experience, and, therefore, he excludes the others from his study—hence the declaration that the past and future tenses will be called "cases" of the verb, while the "real" verb is the form in the present indicative. Similarly, in discussing the nouns Aristotle employs sentences in which all nouns appear only in the nominative case and so decides that this form is the "real" *onoma,* while the oblique forms (genitive, dative, accusative) are "cases," since they do not produce sentences that are true or false when used with the verb "is." However, in ordinary Greek we find sentences like *tou de agathou politou esti ta arista kai legein kai prattein* (literally, "of the good citizens *is* to do and say the best," which could be rendered as, "It is expected of the good citizen that he will both do and say what is best"). Such a statement can be declared true or false. Besides the genitive with "is," we find dative forms, as in *phylakē ouk ēn tē kōmē* (literally, "garrison not was to the village," which could be translated as, "There was no garrison in the village").

These examples, of course, contain constructions that are not precisely the type Aristotle was discussing, since they contain *onomata* used as complements or parts of the predicate, whereas the *onomata* he had in mind stand as subjects in the sentences discussed so far. This shows that he was attempting to establish a technical, restricted language that would be maximally free of the ambiguities and irregularities of conversational language. This seems to be not only a sensible procedure in logic but also an effective means of pointing out one of the needs for such a discipline. It is unfortunate, however, as will be seen of later authors, that while the logicians always seemed to be quite clear about what they were doing, the grammarians did not always sufficiently distinguish between the regularities that are defensible in logic and those acceptable in ordinary language.

Aristotle distinguished, in the passages quoted, the same units as Plato—the *onoma,* the *rhēma,* and the *logos.* There is another word type discussed, but not named, in *On Interpretation,* which he treats explicitly in two other sources, *Rhetoric* and *Poetics.* The relevant chapter of the latter work is not considered by some commentators to be the authentic work of Aristotle, but it is worth including in the Aristotelian account of language, since it is consonant with the rest of his work and represents one of his clearest advances over the work of Plato. The forms that make up this class are called *syndesmoi,* which has been variously translated as "conjunctions" or "linking particles." Since the term *syndesmos* has a technical meaning in logic, as opposed to a more general meaning in ordinary language, the latter translation, being more vague, is preferable.

But the purity of speech, which is the foundation of style, depends on five rules: first, linking particles [Greek, *syndesmoi*] should be introduced in their natural order, before and after, as they are required . . . they should also be made to correspond while the hearer still recollects. . . .

[*Rhetoric* III.iv.5]

We must not lose sight of the fact that a different style is suitable to each kind of rhetoric. . . . The style of written compositions is most precise, that of debate most suitable for oral delivery, and so speeches that have been written to be spoken sound silly when they are not delivered orally, and do not fulfill their proper function. For instance, *asyndeta* [omissions of connectives, *syndesmoi*] and repetition of the same word are rightly disapproved in written speech, but in public debate, even rhetoricians make use of them. . . .

[*Rhetoric* III.xii.1]

In another passage in *On Interpretation* Aristotle discusses the meaning of expressions that are not explicitly called *syndesmoi,* but that clearly have that function and that later logicians assigned to that class. In discussing sentences like "Man is healthy" or "Every man is healthy" or "No man is healthy" he says, "the expressions 'every' and 'no' signify nothing more than the fact, be the statement affirmative or negative, that the subject itself is distributed."

By saying that these expressions signify the fact that the subject is "distributed," Aristotle means that they tell us how many of the subject class belong to the predicate class. This qualification avoids the difficulties of the Platonic either-or, all-or-nothing dichotomies. In view of his elementary image theory of meaning, we can understand the definition of *syndesmoi:*

A *syndesmos* is a sound without a meaning, which neither hinders nor causes the formation of a single significant sound or phrase out of several sounds, and which, if the phrase stands by itself, cannot properly stand at the beginning of it, for example, *men. . .de, toi. . .de;* or else it is a sound without a meaning, capable of forming one significant sound or phrase out of several sounds, each having a meaning of their own, for example, *amphi, peri. . . .*

[*Poetics* xx]

Greek participles like *men* and *de* indicate connections between the words they generally follow immediately and would supply the function that intonation serves in a sentence like "*We* did, but *they* didn't." The words *amphi* and *peri* are used like our prepositions "about," "near."

Some passages from Aristotle's *Categories* must be included to indicate another point of view that has had a lasting effect on Western linguistic thought. This little book, which concerns, ostensibly, the typical meanings of isolated forms in Greek, has been of incalculable influence in Western grammar, logic, and philosophy. Numerous commentaries were written on it by those Greeks, Romans, and medieval

Europeans who considered that the *Organon* was a cornerstone of education. The *Organon,* or "tool of science," consisted of three short works, the first of which was the *Categories,* the second, *On Interpretation,* a study of propositions, and the third, *Prior Analytics,* on the theory of the syllogism. A little reflection will show that the traditional distinctions of the eight parts of speech were made from the point of view first systematically assumed here.

The first section of the *Categories* distinguishes **equivocal** and **univocal** expressions. Expressions are called equivocal that have nothing in common but their sound and correspond to different meanings, as when we apply the term "animal" to a man and to his portrait. A univocal expression is one that is always used with the same meaning, as when we employ the term "animal" for a man and an ox. A term that is similar to and different from another term in form and meaning is called **derivative,** as "grammarian" and "grammar" or "heroism" and "hero." In this text derivation is discussed as a form of *ptōsis,* which has already been translated as "case." Comparing the uses of the term *ptōsis* shows that it includes what we distinguish as inflection and derivation, and, therefore, is a generic term referring to any grammatically significant form of morphological relation.

In the second section Aristotle distinguishes between combined and uncombined expressions. The uncombined, like "man, "walks" or "ox," do not represent propositions, he says, as the combined do, as in "the man walks." The section continues with a compressed and difficult distinction between predicating things *of* a subject that are not *in* a subject, but the difficulties need not detain us beyond remarking that the discussion shows that Aristotle was fully aware of the differences between grammatical combinations and actual states of affairs.

In the third section he states, with disarming simplicity, the basic idea of the deductive syllogism, probably the most ingenious insight of antiquity:

III. When you predicate this thing or that of another thing as of a subject, the predicate then of the predicate will also hold good of the subject. We predicate "man" of "a man," so also of "man" do we predicate "animal." Therefore of this or that man, we can predicate "animal" too. For a man is both "animal" and "man." . . .

Aristotle then goes on to assign typical meanings of uncombined expressions in the form of Greek he used. These are stated positively, not negatively, so it is not necessary to assume that Aristotle considered his *Categories* as exclusive. Commentators have drawn the conclusion that the *Categories* represents all the meanings of Greek—possibly of any language. If this claim were taken at face value, the implications would

Stylistic: logical, rhetorical, poetic, written, spoken, and ordinary words.

The grammatical distinctions, it is worth pointing out, are not explicitly grammatical as opposed to logical in Aristotle's works, since he did not know of this distinction. The purpose he had in mind was logical, but the definitions he gives of the forms he uses in his logic, as well as the examples he uses, justify our considering these distinctions as grammatical. The restrictions that Aristotle discusses, however, are those which prevent statements from being determinately true or false and are, therefore, logical and not grammatical distinctions. The source of Aristotle's restrictions is then to be sought not in the language in which they are discussed but in the things discussed in the language.

The criteria he uses to distinguish most items are semantic and usually are based on a naïve referential-meaning theory. It is on this basis that the *onoma* and *rhēma* are distinguished from the *syndesmoi*, although the latter, along with the *arthron*, is also referred to in terms of its syntactic position and function. The different word types are distinguished according to meaning by a kind of paraphrase, and a vague type of morphological characterization is used to distinguish the derived from the original word types. Examples of the *syndesmoi* that he gives include the particles, untranslatable in English in isolation, *men* and *de*. These are expressions that "do not have meaning [that is, referential meaning] but link those that do." An expression like *egō men, su de* would render the italicized words in the following English sentence: "*I* never liked him *but you* did." This same function is very often fulfilled in English by varying the stresses on "I" and "you."

The *arthra* are discussed in the *Poetics* in terms of meaning (they do not mean anything) and formally, according to their syntactic function, to indicate the beginning, middle, or end of a phrase or sentence. Gender is discussed formally, and in this case, by means of phonetic criteria, since the genders are to be distinguished according to the final letter of the words. Masculines are words that end with *n* and *r*, *ksi* and *psi*; feminines are all those that end with *omega*, *eta*, and *alpha*, and neuters end with these letters as well as with *sigma*. This is excellent formal procedure, since one need not know Greek in order to discover the genders of words according to these rules. The fact that the rules are unsatisfactory is, in a sense, beside the point. The statement of the genders is a scientific statement, one that can be verified, or, as in this case, shown to be false; the distinctions of the other units are not verifiable except for those who know the language. There are masculines that, contrary to these rules, end in *s* (*ho neanias*, "the young man"), feminines that end in *s* (*hē hodos*, "the road"), and neuters that end in alpha (*to drama*, "the drama"). Having seen these examples, even the student who knows no Greek would probably suspect that genders should be defined syntactically and not phonetically, since the sign of the genders is the article which precedes the forms. It also happens that the selection of the final letter in Greek is unfortunate, since the final letter does not always represent a morpheme, because Greek inflections usually contain more than one letter. The emphasis given to the final letters in these early examples of language description was imitated for centuries and impeded the recognition of some obvious facts about the morphological structure of Latin and Greek.

We find a vague approximation of the phonemic principle in Aristotle's distinction of noises, which can be used to construct a meaningful expression out of sounds that do not form meaningful expressions. The "letters" he discussed appear to be universal in languages—that is, languages can presumably be analyzed according to a limited number of phonemic distinctions—but many of his other units do not appear to be universal. Aristotle's interest in language was logical, and this constitutes only one of many uses of language; nouns, verbs, syllables, and different kinds of words are certainly quite general, if not universal. Case, as Aristotle defined it, is a peculiarity of his treatment and not a peculiarity of Greek. What he pointed out for the most part is of no use to us linguistically, considering the norms on which he based his definitions, although the kinds of units he discussed have to be considered. In present-day work phonology would obviously deal more expeditely with the doctrine Aristotle handled under "letters," morphology could distinguish more neatly the complex and compound words and separate the original from the derived forms, and syntax would handle his words, phrases, and sentences both more concretely and more convincingly.

The Stoics

The Stoics were a group of philosophers and logicians who flourished from about the beginning of the fourth century B.C. The last notable author in the Stoic tradition was the Roman Emperor Marcus Aurelius, who reigned from A.D. 161 to 180. In their logical work the Stoics were the chief opponents of Aristotle's successors, who were called Peripatetics. In summarizing the Stoic contribution to language we will see that (1) they made a clear advance in the distinctions drawn between the logical and grammatical study of languages; (2) there is an increased precision in the technical terminology they used to discuss language; and (3) both of these advances are correlated with the difference between Stoic and Peripatetic logic.

The first step the Stoics took in examining the meaningful forms of language was to distinguish three intimately related aspects of "language": (1) the symbol or sign was called the *sēmainon,* and this was "sound," or "material"; (2) the significate or meaning was called the *sēmainomenon,* or *lekton* ("that which is said"); and (3) the external thing named by the sign was called a "thing" or "situation" (*to pragma* or *to tungchanon*). The "thing" and the "symbol" were considered to be bodies, but the meaning was not. The Stoics would say that when we pronounce the name "Dion" we have produced a material symbol; Dion himself is an external body, but the meaning of "Dion" is "the thing we perceive as subsisting within our thought," or, "what the barbarians do not understand when they hear the Greek words spoken." The *lekton* was also defined as "what consists in conformity with a rational presentation" and, therefore, the "object as conceived" rather than the object itself or our name for it. In a similar fashion the Stoics distinguished three meanings of the Greek word *gramma* ("letter"): "Language consists of 24 letters. But 'letter' can have three meanings, the letter itself, the written sign for the letter, and the name of the letter." Considering their attention to technical terms, it is regrettable that the Stoics did not reserve special expressions for the "letter itself" (that is, a sound), the written symbol, and the name for the letter. They did nothing to alleviate the confusion between sound and writing, which has misled many people for centuries.

But the Stoics were interested in the study of sound, *phonē,* in and for itself. They distinguished the expression *legein,* the uttering of sounds that can be part of the phonology of a language but have no meaning, from *propheresthai,* the utterance of sounds that do have a meaning in the language. This distinction was useful to phonetic study, since it made it possible to deal with permissible sequences that have no meaning (phonetic "nonsense"), a technique which is still useful in general phonetic training.

Their subdivisions of the *lekton* (Fig. 3) will show how carefully the Stoics kept separate those aspects of language that had caused some confusion in Aristotle's writings and will also enable us to pinpoint the difference between Stoic and Aristotelian logic, and, therefore, the reasons for the Stoic advances over Aristotle.

We are not particularly concerned here with the complete list of logical distinctions; it is sufficient for our purposes to call attention to the Stoic practice of dividing their data into as many distinguishable parts as they could and of assigning a technical term to each division. From these and the previous distinctions we can find the following advances: (1) in Aristotle's writings it is not always clear, when he is discussing a proposition, whether we are to deal with a combination of sounds only (the Stoic *sēmainon*), a concept (the Stoic *lekton*), or an objective structure in reality (the Stoic *tungchanon*). (2) On the basis

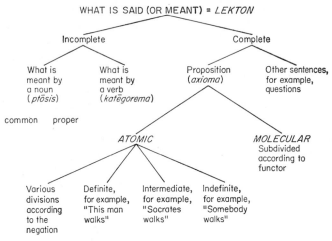

Fig. 3.

of these distinctions we can see that there would be three sets of technical terms for the kind of things grammar and logic could study: grammar or logic could study the combinations of symbols (*sēmainonta*) alone, a fair description of formal grammar or formal logic, and the two studies would be distinguished according to the source of "correctness" in each; or they could study *lekta* or combinations of *lekta* and *sēmainonta*. In any case the technical terms would be there to keep the different studies distinct. (3) The difference between Aristotelian and Stoic logic can also be explained through these distinctions. This difference is linguistically significant, because a more extended sample of the forms of Greek is included in the Stoic logical works than in the Aristotelian. Briefly the typical units of Aristotelian logic, as practiced by Aristotle's successors, were combinations of incomplete *lekta,* whereas the Stoics dealt only with correct combinations of complete *lekta.* This will be illustrated with typical forms of the syllogisms the two schools dealt with most frequently. The typical Aristotelian syllogism contains three propositions or declarative sentences, the third of which is called the **conclusion,** which is derived from its relations to the other two, called the **major** and **minor premises.** When all three are related according to the rules, the conclusion is "correct." If the major and minor premises are true, the conclusion will also be true, but this will depend on the states of affairs discussed. The "correctness" involved here is not grammatical, since grammatical sentences can be false; neither is it a "correctness" of style, which is also independent of states of affairs. But the conclusions can be pronounced formally correct by investigating the regulated use of linguistic forms in the sentences. Paradoxically, the most important forms in this kind of logic would be listed by Aristotle among the *syndesmoi*, since they correspond to the items called "logical constants" today. This is because syllogisms that have the same constants have the same form in the same relations, regardless of the logical variables (the *onomata* and *rhēmata*, subjects and predicates) involved. That is why Aristotle early started using symbols like A and B instead of actual nouns in a typical syllogism like

> If all A belong to some B,
> And some C belong to all B,
> Then some C belong to all A.

If we are trying to say something about familiar situations in a syllogistic way, we will find that the expressions become rather awkward. This is one reason for formalizing the logical language rather than letting demands of style obscure the relations involved. For example, if we wanted to say that women who want to join the Waves have to be Americans, we would have the three terms required by a deductive syllogism: A = Waves, B = Americans, and C = women. Put into the syllogistic form above, the statement would read:

> If all Waves belong to some Americans,
> And some women belong to all Americans,
> Then some women belong to all Waves.

This is the form of the syllogism with which Aristotle began his study. Since it involved the use of *onomata* in cases other than the nominative, he soon adopted an alternative expression that avoided this and made the purely formal relations clearer, since he could use A, B, and C instead of actual nouns for the subjects and predicate nominatives:

> All A are some B.
> But some C are all B.
> Therefore, some C are all A.

This is the form most frequently used by the Peripatetics, the followers of Aristotle, and it has been thought of as the typical Aristotelian syllogism. It contrasts with the only form of the syllogism the Stoics investigated:

> If the first, then the second.
> The first,
> Therefore, the second.

Here the variables are symbolized not by letters but by numbers; not only that, the variables of the Stoic logic are complete *lekta*, propositions, whereas the variables of the Peripatetic syllogisms were incomplete *lekta*, terms. An accidental by-product of this difference for the grammatical examination of language is that the nouns studied by the Peripatetics would all be in the nominative case, and the verbs all in the present indicative, whereas other cases of the nouns, and many forms of the verbs, could appear in the Stoic syllogisms, as would be the case in a syllogism like the following:

> If I buy this from you, I might be cheated.
> I buy this from you.
> Therefore, I might be cheated.

It was this sort of difference that enabled the Stoics to bring some order into the confused Aristotelian notion of "case" (ptōsis). Aristotle's use of the term and many fanciful reasons for it were defended by the Peripatetics, leading to a long confusion between form and meaning, even in grammar in considering the question of case. The Stoics first restricted the use of this term to forms with case endings, such as are found in the inflection of nouns, adjectives, and participles (although they could not delimit the boundaries of root and inflectional morphemes). The nominative as well as the oblique forms were then equally cases. The term was then no longer applicable to the verbs, and Aristotle's general expression rhēma was restricted by the Stoics to label the infinitive form, while the finite forms were called katēgorhēmata.

The Stoics discussed first four, then five, "parts of speech." This expression is a misleading translation of the Greek merē tou logou, "parts of a sentence or phrase" (noun, verb, syndesmos, and arthron). They determined these parts on a mixed basis of form and meaning. Nouns were identified morphologically because they had case inflections, and were then subdivided semantically into proper and common nouns. Proper nouns were those that signified a "proper quality," such as the quality of being Socrates, while common nouns were those that signified a "common quality," such as the quality of being a man. While in English we might be able to distinguish proper and common nouns formally, because of their combinations with articles and the like, this distinction is not accurate for Greek. The verb was defined as "a part of a sentence that states something when not in construction." This definition is more accurate than Aristotle's, since it points out that the noun-verb construction in Greek is endocentric and that the verb, by itself, can make a statement that is true or false. Another definition, closer to Aristotle's idea that the rhēma was always a predicate, was "an element of a sentence without case inflection that in constructions signifies something about one person or more, such as graphō ["I write"] or legō ["I speak"]." In Stoic terminology these elements would not be called rhēmata but katēgorhēmata. The syndesmos is defined as "a part of a sentence without case endings which links up the parts of the sentence," and the *arthron* as "an element of a sentence with case endings which distinguishes gender and number of nouns, such as *ho, hē, to* and *hoi, hai, ta*" (the masculine, feminine, and neuter nominative articles, singular and plural, respectively). What were later distinguished as articles and relative pronouns were included here in the same class, *arthron*.

The Stoics used syntactic criteria to distinguish the active, middle, and passive voices:

> The active forms are those that construct with the oblique cases [that is, other than the nominative] and according to the type of the verb, such as *akouei* ["he hears"] . . . ; passives are those that construct with the particle of passivity [*hypo*, "by"] and these are verbs like *akouomai* ["I am heard"]; the middles are those that do neither of these things, such as *phronein, peripatein.*

Since the Stoics were able to distinguish some forms of the verb according to their syntactic behavior and morphological construction, it is odd that they did not classify the tense forms of the verbs in the same way. However, they were the first to recognize the two major semantic dimensions of the Greek verbal system: time reference and completed vs. incompleted action:

Present continuing	*baino*	("I am going")
Present completed	*bebēka*	("I have gone")
Past continuing	*ebainon*	("I was going")
Past completed	*ebebēkein*	("I had gone")

THE GENERAL LINGUISTIC THEORY OF THE STOICS   As in the case of Aristotle, the ideas of the Stoics have to be patched together from various sources. Their basic view was expressed by one of them in this way: "When a man is born, his spirit is like a piece of paper which is well adapted to be written on." This is the familiar *tabula rasa,* or "blank page," which is "written on" through our sensory and intellectual experiences, and the latter in turn are what language expresses. Speech itself is not intellection but its expression. The medium of this expression is *phonē,* "the voice." As we have seen, this idea led to a more careful investigation of phonetics, although not much progress was made. One of the factors that impeded the work of the Stoics was their conviction that the tongue is the initiator of sounds. Because they were not aware of the role played by the vocal cords, the phonological study of Greek and other languages was hindered for a long time. In Aristotle's basic system what is conveyed immediately by vocal expression is a sensory image, although there is reason to believe from some of his writings that he would not have disagreed with the Stoic position that what is conveyed is a concept, the *lekton.* Unlike Aristotle, the Stoics held that there is, in the remote history of the language, a natural, necessary connection between the sounds of the language and the things for which the sounds stand, although they could see that the present forms of their language did not justify this claim. They undertook, therefore, to search for the original forms, the roots, or *etyma,* of current expressions, thus starting the study called etymology.

The Alexandrians: Anomaly versus Analogy

The next important stage in the Greek study of language can be thought of as another attempt to solve an old problem, but with better tools, as a consequence of studying a different kind of language use. The old problem was that of how language is related to the universe—a question that had been discussed in the early *Physis-Nomos* controversy. The new tools were a more sophisticated set of grammatical distinctions and a more detailed understanding of the working of language and its parts. One of the occasions for bringing language into this discussion was the study of literature. In the *Physis-Nomos* period the discussion had centered around words in isolation. Although literature, particularly the study of Homer, had never been wholly neglected, the Greeks of the next period had more compelling reasons to examine Homer, as well as later authors, from a grammatical rather than a literary perspective.

One of the chief reasons was the political downfall of Athens and the rise to power of expatriate Greek centers. After his conquests Alexander founded several colonies and put his favorite lieutenants over them as kings. Two of the most famous were Alexandria in Egypt, governed by Ptolemy, and Pergamon, given to Eumenes. These two cities soon emerged as the centers of Greek culture and were political as well as cultural rivals. Both were famed for their libraries, an invaluable possession in ancient times, and for the universities that grew up around them. Alexandria followed the Aristotelian tradition, and Aristotle's own library was the foundation of the Alexandrian collection. Many scholars settled in Alexandria and conducted research in varied fields; from this school came two of the most famous and influential books in the world, the *Elements* of Euclid and the *Grammar* of Dionysius Thrax.

ANOMALY VERSUS ANALOGY   An important influence on language study came out of a dispute that was not primarily concerned with language. It was based first of all on a difference of opinion about the constitution of the universe and secondarily on how the workings of nature are reflected in language. Some scholars thought that there are no laws or regularities (analogies) to be discovered in nature; others thought that the movements of the stars and the regularities of the seasons are not haphazard (anomalous) but the consequence of inexorable laws. The latter opinion had been Aristotle's and was held by the Alexandrians, while Pergamon favored the first view. Whatever the state of natural entities, of course, language could still be considered to mirror natural chaos or regularity or to be independent of it. In general it was the view of the Alexandrians that both the natural processes and the constructions of language are subject to regular rules, patterns which could be discovered and described. If this were the case, then grammars could be written; otherwise one could only give lists of expressions, and no pattern or connection could be shown to exist among them.

The consequences of this dispute were most fortunate for the study of Greek, since the analogists of Alexandria took great pains to construct *kanones,* or lists of regularities discovered in the forms of Greek. These lists were principally made up of paradigms of Greek nouns and verbs that showed similar conjugation or declension. Because they followed the unfortunate example of Aristotle in concentrating on the final, single letter of forms, they were unable to show the complete regularities of the declensions and conjugations, so that their lists were always subject to the attack of the Pergamon anomalists. This spurred them on to find other factors to account for the regularities they were sure were there, resulting in a more and more accurate cataloguing of the rich variety of forms in the Greek language. As an example of what the Alexandrians admitted to be an exception, we can give the parallel declension of two Greek forms:

Nom.	*bias*	*lysias*
Gen.	*biantos*	*lysiou*
Dat.	*bianti*	*lysiō*
Acc.	*bianta*	*lysion*

Since the nominative of these forms ends in the same letter, *s* (*sigma*), the analogists as well as the anomalists thought that they should be the "same" form and, therefore, be declined alike. Notice that the Aristotelian idea about the primacy of the nominative case has been at work here, since the best selection of the root morpheme is obviously one of the oblique cases for *bias,* whereas it makes little difference for *lysias.*

The anomaly-analogy controversy lasted for several centuries in the grammatical field, beginning with the work of Xenodotus Philadelphus (284–257 B.C.) and culminating in the work of Apollonius Dyscolus and his son Herodian (fl. A.D. 180). The authoritative codification of the work of the Alexandrians is the grammar of Dionysius Thrax (100 B.C.). This was translated into Latin as the *Ars Grammatica* by Remmius Palaemon in the first century A.D. and has served as a model, both in the sequence of topics and in terminology, for grammars right up to our own day.

THE NOTION OF ANALOGY In his definition of grammar, Dionysius Thrax lists six things the grammarian ought to do, and one of them is to list the analogies of the language. This, of course, states at the outset where he stood in the anomaly-analogy dispute. Analogy is an Aristotelian notion, and investigation of the descriptive method it implies will show why the Alexandrians failed to attain complete success in their work, as well as the interesting fact that it approaches the structural linguist's distinction between the composition and distribution of linguistic items. Understanding this notion will also make clear why subsequent grammarians did not make the progress that these promising beginnings could have produced, because they shifted their attention from the distribution to the composition of forms.

An analogy can be defined as "similar proportions or relations between terms." The significant factor is that the terms can differ greatly in their composition. An abstract formula for an analogy would be:

$$A:B = C:D$$

which was verbalized by Aristotle as "A is to B (or is in B) in the same way as C is to D (or is in D)." Terms that enter into such relations are analogous terms. For example, since there is a similarity in the relation between various parents and their offspring, we can speak of an analogy that makes all the members of this relation the "same," and say that the terms "parent," "offspring," and the like are analogous terms:

Human Being	Human Being		Other	Other
parent	: offspring	=	parent:	offspring
father	: child	=	dog	: puppy
mother	: son		hen	: chick
	etc.		tree	: blossom
			cell A	: cell B
			store	: branch store

In these examples we can see that for the sake of classification, obvious and undenied differences are declared irrelevant to the classification. The principle of classification is a relation of origin. The differences can be in composition or distribution or both. The same kind of reasoning and descriptive procedure has been illustrated in linguistic analysis: the compositional differences that distinguish the allophones of phonemes or the allomorphs of morphemes are, at a particular level of analysis, declared irrelevant, since they are an automatic consequence of their distribution, and we prefer to consider them the "same" unit since this reduces the complexity of our analysis and notation. In the same way the method of origin in the various entities listed above can be considered irrelevant and all of the entities, therefore, can be said to be the "same" from a particular point of view. Notice that the word "same" is itself an analogous term. We have to specify, of course, the precise point of view according to which the different terms will be declared the same. For example,

$A : B = 1 : 2$
  (based on order, the first and second members of two familiar, invariable lists)
1 inch : 1 foot = 1 millimeter : 1 centimeter
  (based on relation to next size level in two systems of measurement)
President : Americans = King : Belgians
  (relation of governor to governed)

From these simple examples it is obvious that the same terms can be "the same" from one point of view, and, at the same time, "different" from another. "Sameness" and "difference" in linguistic analysis are consequences of the "level of analysis," which is a technical expression for "different point of view" with respect to the same materials. It is important, therefore, to state clearly both the nature or composition of the terms in the analogy and the precise point of view according to which they are considered the same or different. In the early stages of the anomaly-analogy dispute about language the terms were discussed from a semantic and a "morphological" point of view, with the morphological idea that words ending in the same letter should belong to similar inflectional paradigms. That *bias* and *lusias* were considered irregularities shows that the Alexandrians did not appeal to a sufficiently inclusive environment, since these forms have the same syntactic behavior, and, from *that* point of view, are the same. This example suggests one of the sources of difficulty one encounters in syntactic analysis. At that level there are phonological, lexical, morphological, and syntactic factors in the composition of two constructions we compare. One of the difficulties is to decide which, and how many, of these factors will be considered relevant to the definition of different syntactic structures. For example, English constructions can be active or passive, regardless of the number, person, tense, or mood of the verbs involved. Gender is irrelevant to distinctions of singularity or plurality, and vice versa; voice, person, number, and tense are irrelevant to distinctions of mood, and so on. The statement of such structures follows the same lines as the statement of the analogies in a language, as recommended by Thrax. In order to give a complete grammatical account of a language we should take into account all the analogies—all the structures of the language. But there does not seem to be any factor in the composition of the data itself that impresses itself upon us as signally relevant. For this reason it would appear that the best method of selecting the "relevant" structures or analogies of a language is frequency of use.

THE *GRAMMAR* OF DIONYSIUS THRAX   The entire text of Thrax's grammar will not be quoted here, even though it consists of only twenty-five brief paragraphs, since we are more interested in the method it employs than in the actual description of Greek. In the grammar Thrax dealt with what we would call the phonology and morphology of the language. He did not treat syntax. In the phonology section he discussed *grammata*, "letters," a terminological confusion we have already considered, which does not explicitly distinguish the sounds, symbols, and names for them.

When Greek children learned their "letters" (*grammatikē* was first of all a study of the letters) it was quite a painful process. No account was taken of the pupil's difficulties, but the twenty-four letters of Greek were taught in strict "logical" order (that is, the order in which the alphabet was recited). They were first learned by name and then by phonetic value, and often in hexameter verses. Learning the letters was important in those days, since the letters were also used for musical notes and counting. After the names and phonetic values had been learned the children were taught all the possible syllables, with no thought as yet to learning words: all two-letter syllables, three-letter syllables, and so on were practiced. In the study of words, which then followed, the same "logical" order was followed: first, monosyllabic words, then polysyllabic tongue twisters were learned. When texts were examined the first step was to separate out the syllables and then the words, a practice required by the Greek fashion of continuous writing, which did not distinguish "institutionalized words."

Excerpts from Thrax's *Art of Grammar*

1. GRAMMAR

Grammar is the technical knowledge of the language generally employed by poets and writers. It has six parts: (1) correct pronunciation, (2) explanation of the principal poetic tropes, (3) preservation and explanation of glosses and mythological examples, (4) the discovery of etymologies, (5) the discovery of analogies, and (6) a critical consideration of the compositions of poets, which is the most noble part of this science.

6. ON THE LETTERS

There are twenty-four letters, from alpha to omega. . . . Of these, seven are vowels, and they are *a, e, ē, i, o, y, ō*: they are called *self-sounding* because they produce a sound by themselves. Of the vowels, two are long (*ē* and *ō*), two are short (*e* and *o*), and three are either long or short (*a, i, y*). There are five prefixed vowels (*a, e, ē, o,* and *ō*) and they are so-called because they are prefixed to *i* and *y* to form one syllable, such as *ai* and *ay*. Postponed vowels are *i* and *y*. Sometimes the *y* can stand before the *i* as in *myia* and *harpyia*. There are six diphthongs: *ai, ay, ei, ey, oi, oy*. The rest of the seventeen letters are consonants: *b, d, g, dz, th, l, m, n, ks, p, r, s, t, ph, ch, ps*. They are called consonants because of themselves they have no resonance, but combine with vowels to produce a single sound. Of these, eight are semivowels: *dz, ks, ps, l, m, n, r, s*. They are so-called because they are less resonant than the vowels. There are nine mutes, *b, d, g, k, p, t, th, ph, ch*, and they are so-called because they sound less well than the rest. Of these, three are smooth, *k, p, t*, and three are rough, *th, ph, ch;* three are medium, *b, d, g*, and are so-called because they are smoother than the rough and rougher than the smooth sounds. . . . Of the consonants, three are double sounds, *dz, ks*, and *ps*, and they are so-called because they consist of two consonants, the *dz*, out of *d* and *s*, the *ks* out of *k* and *s*, and the *ps* out of *p* and *s*. There are four unalterable consonants, *l, m, n, r*. They are so-called because in the inflection of nouns and verbs they are not altered. They are also called liquids or fluid sounds.

7. ON THE SYLLABLE

The syllable is the linking of vowels and consonants or several vowels with consonants, as in *gar, bous*. This is the syllable properly so-called; improperly, a single vowel as *a* or *o* can be called a syllable.

11. ON THE PARTS OF A SENTENCE [THE "PARTS OF SPEECH"]

The word is the smallest part of a sentence, which requires composition. The sentence is a combination of words that have a complete meaning in themselves. There are eight parts of a sentence: noun, verb, participle, article, pronoun, preposition, adverb, conjunction. . . .

12. ON THE NOUN

The noun is a part of a sentence having case inflections, signifying a person or a thing, and it is general or particular, for example, "stone," "education," "man," "horse," "Socrates." It has five simultaneous features [grammatical accidents]: gender, type, form, number, and case.

There are three genders: masculine, feminine, and neuter. Some have in addition common gender, for example, *hippos, hē* or *ho* [horse," m, f.] . . . there are two types, original and derived; the original is that which is first characterized, for example, "earth," and the derived is that which takes its origin from another word, for example, "earthly." There are seven types of derivation: patronymic, possessive, comparative, superlative, diminutive, denominative, and verbal.

There are three numbers, singular, dual, and plural

The noun has five cases, nominative [*orthē*, "upright"], genitive [*gēnikē*, "origin"], dative [*dōtikē*, "giving"], accusative [*aitiātikē*, indicating that upon which some force or effect has been operated: the Latin-English "accusative" is a mistranslation of a similar Greek word meaning "accuse"], and vocative [*klētike,* "calling"].

The nominative is also called the name form, or the upright case, the genitive, the possessive, or father case, the dative, also the case of address, the accusative, the effective case, and the vocative, the case of address.

13. ON THE VERB

The verb is a part of a sentence without case inflection, susceptible of tenses, persons, number, activity, and passivity as its meaning.

The verb has eight simultaneous features: moods, kind, types, forms, number, person, tense, conjugation. There are five moods: indicative, imperative, optative, subjunctive, and infinitive.

There are three kinds, active, middle, and passive: active, "I strike"; passive, "I am struck"; the middle expresses both activity and passivity. [The English gives only the meanings of these forms: the active is clearly distinct in form from the middle/passive; the middle/passive are distinct formally only in some forms: "I wash myself," "I do it for myself."]

There are two types, original and derived.

There are three forms, simple, compound, and derivative [formed from a compound: the "derived" type is formed from a simple form for Thrax].

There are three numbers, singular ("I strike"), dual ("we strike"), and plural ("we strike"). [In Greek these are three obviously different forms, complex forms with different meanings than the English syntactic constructions render.]

There are three persons, first, second, and third; the first is the one who speaks, the second, the one to whom he speaks, the third, what (or of whom) one speaks.

There are three tenses, present, past, and future. There are four grades of the past, imperfect, perfect, pluperfect, and aorist. Of these, three are related: the present is related to the imperfect; the perfect is related to the pluperfect, and the future is related to the aorist.

The last paragraph is a vague appeal to formal rather than semantic similarity. The regular forms discussed for the verb "loose" would be: present, *luo;* imperfect *eluon;* aorist, *elusa;* future, *luso;* perfect, *leluka;* pluperfect, *elelukē.* This means that the present and imperfect have the same stem but differ in endings and in the presence of the augment $e-$; future and aorist have the same stem but differ in endings; perfect and pluperfect have the same reduplicated stem but differ in endings and in the presence of the augment $e-$.

15. ON THE PARTICIPLE

The participle is a word type that shares the properties of verb and noun. It has the same simultaneous features as the noun and verb, except for person and mood.

16. ON THE ARTICLE

The article is a case-forming part of a sentence that precedes or follows nouns. The one that precedes is *ho* (and so, implicitly, *hē* and *to*) and the one that follows is *hos* (hence, implicitly, the other relatives, *hē, ho*). Its simultaneous features are gender, number, and case.

17. ON THE PRONOUN

The pronoun is a part of a sentence that is used in place of a noun and indicates a determined person. It has six simultaneous features, person, number, gender, case, form, and type. . . .

18. ON THE PREPOSITION

The preposition is a kind of word that can occur before all parts of a sentence, either in direct composition or in combination.

19. ON THE ADVERB

The adverb is a part of a sentence without inflection, which says something about a verb or is joined to one. . . .

20. ON THE CONJUNCTION

The conjunction is a kind of word that links together our thoughts in a determined order and fills in the gaps of speech. . . . These are distinguishable into copulative, disjunctive, conditional, causal, final, dubitative, ratiocinative, expletive.

a. The copulatives link continuous speech, for example, "and," "also," "but."
b. The disjunctives link sentences, but separate their matter, for example "or."
c. The conditionals indicate an unreal consequence, for example, "if," "even," "though," "otherwise."
d. The causals express a real consequence, for example, "when," "consequently," "since," "in order that," "because of."
e. The finals are used to indicate the presence of a cause, "so that," "in order that," "because of."
f. The dubitatives used in doubt, for example "whether," "perhaps."
g. The ratiocinatives are used for conclusions and assumptions apt for proofs, for example, "consequently," "therefore."
h. Expletives are used for the sake of meter or to decorate language, as a matter of usage, for example, "well," "of course," "indeed," "naturally." [Thrax's listed examples, of course, are Greek expressions, the English equivalents of which are given here. Most of the Greek forms are simple or complex forms, compared to the English syntactic constructions.]

Now that we have seen some typical excerpts from Dionysius' *Grammar*, we can make some observations about it.

DEFINITION OF "GRAMMAR"   Thrax's definition of "grammar" is translated as "technical knowledge." But in order to specify accurately what that means, we must know what other words it is opposed to and different from in Greek. In Thrax's day the Greeks discussed four kinds of "scientific knowledge," labeled *peira, empeiria, technē,* and *ēpistēmē.* The *Art of Grammar* translates the Greek *technē grammatikē.* The Greek *peira* is approximately "skill"; *empeiria,* "artisanship"; *technē,* "art"; and *ēpistēmē,* "demonstrable knowledge," from a standard Aristotelian division of knowledge. The first kind of knowledge is the sort the experienced workman has, the second is what the foreman must have, the third, what the engineer requires, and the fourth, the sort of knowledge the philosopher skilled in the other three degrees has attained. As far as language is concerned, the first kind of knowledge is what all mature speakers of a language have from its daily, practical employment. The second is what people who have reflected on their skills would have, but which they could not explain in very abstract terms, either because of their lack of information or because of the complexity of the material dealt with. The third is what a person has who sees the underlying principles and analogies that unite seeming irregularities. The fourth is the type of knowledge one attains when all the causes involved are known, so that any given element of a structure is seen to be necessarily the way that it is, that it could not be otherwise. The Greeks thought that this sort of knowledge was possible about anything. Thrax used *empeiria,* then, possibly to suggest that there are many regularities in language, although he may not have been able to list all of them.

Second, we note that the object of study is not just any use of language, but that of literary men. One of the reasons for this is the needs of the time: expatriate Greeks were not as familiar with their classic authors as native Greeks, for whom the ancient forms were also a problem. Perhaps the most esteemed and quoted author for all Greeks was Homer. But by the time of Alexander and the Alexandrians, the forms Homer used were as opaque to the Greeks as Chaucer's English is to us. Thrax hoped to make clear that there was a correspondence in forms and usage between contemporary and Homeric Greek. Such an analogy might be stated as follows:

In situation *A,* where Homer uses form *X,*
In situation *A,* modern authors use form *Y.*

PARTITION OF GRAMMAR   Thrax did not discuss all six parts of grammar as he defined them, and the following gaps are apparent in his work. (1) Correct pronunciation and reading are not dealt with sufficiently by modern standards. The differences among letters are discussed, and only indirectly their acoustic or articulatory properties. (2)

There is no treatment of poetic tropes. (3) There is no discussion of translation or mythological examples. (4) There is no discussion of etymologies. (5) Only obvious morphological analogies, not syntactic ones, are considered. Such a discussion would have shown that *bias, biantos* and *lysias, lysiou,* though morphologically different, have similar syntactic behavior. (6) There is no discussion of poetic composition.

Despite these gaps, which are obviously deliberate, the field of "grammar" or philology was given a scope far wider than that encompassed by present-day linguistics. Commentators after Thrax took exception to his view that grammar is restricted to technical knowledge, since Thrax's own definition and later practice seemed to point beyond that. But in view of the formal method he codified, his tiny grammar had tremendous influence that was all the more remarkable because it was often so poorly understood.

ON THE LETTERS   We have seen the root confusion of sound-letter-letter-name already, despite the clear distinctions of Aristotle and the Stoics: neither invented separate technical terms that would force grammarians to keep the distinction in mind. Several confusions thus arose; for example, many modern scholars believe that the "diphthongs" *ei* and *ou* discussed by Thrax were really a single sound and not vowel sequences. It is also difficult to understand what Thrax meant by calling *b, d, g* "medium"—"medium" compared to what? Concerning *p, t, k* and *ph, th, ch,* the former are probably voiceless stops at the same point of articulation and the latter are probably voiceless, but aspirate, articulations (spirants, not stops) at the same points of articulation. It has already been noted that the Greeks could distinguish between aspirate and nonaspirate articulations, but not between voiced and voiceless sounds. Greek cannot be analyzed merely on the basis of the aspirate-nonaspirate distinction. Rather, a three-way distinction must be made: articulations are in a certain place, they are either voiced or voiceless, and they are either aspirate or nonaspirate. Thrax had a vague notion of "resonance," which he evidently employed to account for voice, but we can see how this involved him in confusion in defining "vowels," "semivowels," "syllables," and "consonants."

WORD AND SENTENCE   Thrax defined "word" formally, on the basis of syntax, as "the minimal unit of a sentence," but he defined "sentence" as "a complete thought." Sentences are complete if thoughts are complete, he said, but this does not assist us in deciding when thoughts are complete or incomplete. Evidently, the criterion would be greatly different for ordinary conversation, rhetoric, poetry, logic, and other uses of language.

ON THE NOUN   In identifying a noun the first criterion Thrax gave is formal (morphological, as we would say), although he was unable to distinguish the case endings as morphemes in their own right. One reason is that the morphemes of Greek have several functions, for example, to indicate gender, number, and case. Another reason is that Thrax and the other Greeks (later imitated by the Latins) insisted on talking about the last letter only, which rarely represents the complete morpheme.

SIMULTANEOUS FEATURES   The simultaneous features that Thrax discussed are the "accidents" of the later traditional grammars. A complete formal description of a language like Greek would require a statement of the regular correspondences, or analogies, among features of the language. These morphological distinctions take care of a good number of the simultaneous features of the language. Thrax's description was incomplete, however, since he did not treat the syntax of Greek explicitly. Some of the distinctions he did make, which he assigned to the morphology of the language, actually cannot be justified, except by appeal to the syntax. Such are the distinctions of gender and number. It is interesting to note that these distinctions are primarily formal (morphological or syntactic), while his subdistinctions are generally semantic or made on the basis of listing, another acceptable formal procedure for dealing with restricted classes that do not have clear-cut morphological or syntactic properties.

ON THE VERB   Again, Thrax's first criterion for identifying the verb is formal: absence of the typical noun endings and presence of the typical verbal endings. After this, the important class meaning (name of an action) is assigned. All of the subclasses, not mentioned here, are distinguished formally.

ON THE PARTICIPLE   The classification of the participle is again basically formal. The participle is a distinct part of a sentence according to Thrax, because it takes the number and gender agreements of the noun and the case-governing properties of the verb, as well as verbal tense distinctions. Note that a semantic definition is not given.

ON THE ARTICLE   Thrax classified the article exclusively on formal grounds—"morphologically," in that it is declined, and syntactically, in that it is shown to precede or follow certain forms. Thrax confused what we would distinguish as articles and relative pronouns, but in Greek the two are very similar in form and behavior. Thrax handled the members of this class by means of listing, a good formal procedure to apply with a closed, limited class such as this one.

ON THE PRONOUN   The pronoun was formally defined through its syntactic function: it substitutes for a noun. The semantic definition implies that the pronoun can substitute only for a predetermined person, a situation that is contrary to evident Greek usage, since in that language pronouns refer to things as well as persons. Again, we have to do here with a closed class, definable formally by means of listing.

ON THE PREPOSITION AND ADVERB   Thrax attempted a formal definition of the preposition and adverb (position for preposition, invariable form for the adverb) and indicated only in passing the meaning for the adverb. But this treatment is insufficient, since Greek adverbs also enter into constructions with adjectives (as in English; Thrax would classify our "adjectives" with his "nouns") and other adverbs.

ON THE CONJUNCTION   The conjunction is the only "part" that Thrax defined semantically alone, but note that he listed typical examples, so that from this list, even though incomplete and given here only in English translation, we can recognize the main Greek forms that he considered members of the class of conjunctions.

IN SUMMARY   We can say that the *Grammar* of Dionysius Thrax has had an influence in inverse proportion to its brevity and clarity. The questions he raised and the order in which he treated them have been little improved upon for more than twenty centuries. As we will see, it is not unfair to say that many traditional grammarians who do not employ structural methods are still, to a large extent, translating languages into Greek, even though they may know no Greek. That is, they discuss modern languages in terms of meaning categories that are important as a consequence of Greek structure, since they are the meanings of, or meaning differences between, formally different Greek structures, morphological or syntactic. Grammars are ways of talking about, and of describing, languages. What they discuss is the content of the formal grammatical distinctions—or should be. The content of Thrax's grammar is the frequent meaning categories associated regularly with the morphological distinctions of Greek. That languages as formally different as Attic Greek, Modern English, German, French and the like can be discussed in terms of the meaning differences of Greek structure is extremely significant: it indicates a continuity of world view, a solidarity of mutual understanding based on common cultural interests, which has united Western society. This unity is a consequence of our official educational system, which for centuries has required us to talk about our languages in the terms that Thrax found necessary to account for the differences of form—and meaning—in the Greek he spoke. The Indo-European (IE) languages are related historically as well as culturally to Greek. But it would be the height of folly, the same mistake made by the protagonists of the *Physis* view of language, to suppose that we must discover in every language the same form and content that characterize Greek.

THE METHOD OF THRAX   Thrax's meuiod is most instructive; to the best of his ability (which by modern standards, was extremely limited) he tried to tell us what to look for and listen to in order to identify structurally important pieces of his language. The "parts" are important because (1) they are formally different from each other; (2) the differences are correlated with meaning distinctions in his language; and (3) they are different elements of form and content that recur frequently, differing either in their morphological construction or syntactic behavior or both. As a consequence of their differences, the "parts" can be utilized in Greek to signal either different meanings or differences in meaning.

For native speakers of Greek it would perhaps be sufficient to point out the parts of a sentence on purely semantic grounds. Such a method presupposes an understanding of the sentences to be analyzed. We must, therefore, distinguish two entirely different kinds of criteria used in language study and evaluate the usefulness of each.

Grammars can enable us either to talk about a language or to talk the language. A purely formal grammar equips us only to talk accurately about a language. The ability to speak a language correctly comes only with a certain degree of enculturation, when we can make the noises that are correct in each distinguishable social situation. Through a knowledge of the semantic structure of a culture we can operate as members of that culture. Purely formal grammars, as defined, then, are a waste of time for one who wants to learn to use the language as the native speaker uses it.

On the other hand, if we reflect on the four kinds of knowledge the Greeks distinguished—practical mastery without reflection; mastery with the ability to compare techniques; intuitive mastery of art; and demonstrative knowledge of our subject—we can see that a "grammar" of meanings will be quite useless for getting us beyond the first degree of knowledge. Questions about language that are couched in terms of "meaning" will elicit no profitable answer from the unreflecting, unless the questioner is skilled in asking questions about language, because the association of form and content is quite arbitrary from one language to another. What we seek in linguistics is a method that will reveal the inner structure of each language, since (1) we know *a priori* that every language must differ from others because it is an arbitrary system and (2) we know that the fundamental technique for differentiating linguistic meanings, though varied in application, must be identical for all languages, whether we are discussing morphological, lexical, or syntactic differences.

The grammar of Dionysius Thrax was mainly concerned with the morphological paradigms of Greek, and a notable weakness of the work was a lack of information about syntactic constructions. The gap was partially filled by the grammar of Appollonius Dyscolus (fl. A.D. 100), which listed some of the features of grammatical agreement among form classes as well as rules for the case government of nouns in construction with prepositions.

Since Thrax was the first to identify linguistic units on the basis of their formal differences, and then to give a semantic correlate for each, we would expect that all his successors would have appreciated and followed the method. Not all did, and one reason was that the anomaly-analogy dispute ceased to be the live issue it was in Thrax's day. Once there was no dispute about the regular correspondence between form and meaning in language, grammarians could pay more attention to the semantic categories and less to the formal distinctions.

Varro

A contemporary of Dionysius Thrax, Marcus Terentius Varro, called the most learned man of his time, had been following the quarrel between the analogists of Alexandria and the anomalists of Pergamon. Crates of Mallos, ambassador of Pergamon to Rome, introduced the disputed question to the Romans, and it was widely discussed. Among those who followed the controversy with interest, and wrote on the subject, was Julius Caesar, who favored the analogist position.

Varro wrote a twenty-five volume work on the Latin language, *De Lingua Latina,* of which only books V–X have been preserved. The views he expressed there about the normal study of language are worth considering, even though they had little influence on his contemporaries, since they show a clear appreciation of some of the differences between form and meaning. The work was written as a consequence of the anomaly-analogy controversy, which is the subject of books V–X.

The views of the extreme partisans in the quarrel are illuminating: the Stoics, for example, had admitted that there was anomaly or irregularity in the *current* forms of their language, but claimed that by discovering the *original* forms, called the *etyma,* or "roots," the regular correspondence between language and reality could be established. This was the beginning of the study called etymology. The extreme anomalists, on the other hand, held that language was conventional, and since any word could signify anything, there was no norm except what people actually said. Other scholars, though convinced of the conventional nature of language, believed that the analytic Greek mind always had good reason for whatever terms and constructions it had developed, so that by examining the original forms the regularity of current forms could be discovered. In Varro's opinion the extremists of both camps were wrong. In Book VIII he argued for anomaly, and in Book XI for analogy. Book X is an attempt to reconcile the two views.

From his study of the irregular forms of Latin Varro concluded that those who hold that there is universal regularity in language must admit that anomaly has been proved against them. After treating the reasons for preferring the view that language is fundamentally a regular pattern, he noted that the view of the extreme anomalist is even more wrong, that "those who do not see regularity in language not only fail to see the nature of language but of the world as well."

Varro gave two reasons for holding a middle position between the view that language is chaotic and the one that holds it to be a system of absolute regularity. First, while we must admit that order and regularity are the most evident attributes of nature, we must see that human choice introduces an element of disorder and variety. But in language, there is not only room for order and regularity, the two are interdependent. Second, the whole discussion about whether language is regular or irregular should deal with resemblances between two like things. What are those two things, and how are we to decide whether they have something in common or whether they diverge? Varro says that the controversialists have long ignored the distinctions among the problems of whether things resemble other things, whether words resemble other words, or whether words resemble the things they name. These problems are quite different in nature and their solutions require different approaches.

Varro thought he could solve the problem of whether some words are like other words in Latin. He believed that he could show that Latin is regular and that apparent irregularities could be explained, especially apparent irregularities between words and the things they stand for.

In order to give this explanation, Varro offered his views about many features of the Latin language—what a word is, what variety and regularity are discoverable among the various forms of words, how these are to be accounted for, how differing styles and periods in a language are to be understood, whose task it is to study these various problems, and what kind of equipment is required to deal with these questions.

WORDS   Varro described a word as a minimum basic form that is not further analyzable into meaningful parts and that everyone uses in its different forms in the same way. (*Verbum dico orationis vocalis partem, quae sit indivisa et minima, si declinationem naturalem habet:*

DLL X.4.) There are many ways in which words can be studied, and one such study, etymology, concerns their origin. In discussing the problems of establishing etymologies, Varro made a fourfold distinction that can be applied to other aspects of language study as well.

He said that there are four levels on which the original forms of words can be sought: (1) a level of common sense, which would analyze forms like "Georgetown" and "Goodman" without need of expert information; (2) a level where more than common sense is required, since the analysis is based on the research of grammarians on earlier stages of the language. With this sort of information the grammarian could discuss the words that poets coin in an informative way. (3) A higher level requires knowledge of philosophy, so that causes can be assigned for words in common use in terms of that philosophy. (4) The highest and most difficult level requires both grammatical and philosophic skill to explain the origin of obscure words. Varro thought that this sort of study would be both speculative and experimental, much in the way a doctor deals with a puzzling case: his prescription is based on medical knowledge, but he cannot be certain that his treatment is the correct one until the patient has been cured. In language study Varro gave no assurance that he could offer much at this level, but he was confident that he could get past the second level. His position, therefore, is similar to that of the Stoics, as far as the ultimate correspondence between language and reality is concerned, though he differed from them in his estimation of the regularity of current forms.

DECLINATIO   In discussing both etymology and current forms Varro used the term *declinatio,* which appears to us to mean "declension"; for him it was a much more inclusive term, similar in scope to Aristotle's use of *ptosis.* It refers to some phonetic variation of some assumed basic form in a paradigm. In discussing etymology Varro assumed that time brings change with it in the original form of a word, either through the loss, change, or addition of "letters." In deciding whether forms are similar or not, he used this "letter" description, concerning himself principally with correspondences between the last letters of the words examined.

Varro used the single term *declinatio* for linguistic phenomena currently described in different terms: forms are said to be related in their *declinatio* when there is a phonetic difference between them, but some community of meaning. What would presently be called "derivation" (his example: "Rome" from "Romulus") is *declinatio* for him; so is the particular form, "conjugation," of "inflection" (his example: *legi,* the perfect tense, from *lego,* present), and "comparison" as well is called *declinatio* (his example: *candidus, candidius, candidissimus,* "bright," "brighter," "brightest"). Required for a relation of *declinatio,* then, is some basic form, with other forms related to it formally and in meaning. The choice in etymology is easy: the original form—or at least the earliest attested form. In analyzing words in current use Varro found the choice less obvious. He claimed that one way out of the difficulty is to rely on the Pythagorean notion:

> There are two elements, rest and motion: whatever is at rest or moves is a body; where it is moved is place, and while it is being moved, we have time; the fact of its movement is action. So it appears . . . there is a quadripartite division of all original things, body and place, time and action. And just as there are four prime *genera* of things, so too of words.
>
> [DLL V.1]

What Varro looked for, then, were binary oppositions, exactly in the same way as the linguist does in establishing the immediate constituents of constructions. Varro's reasons for so doing, of course, were evidently different from those of the linguists, and one suspects that the divisions he made were more a consequence of the obvious fact of the Latin language than of Pythagorean descriptions. It is particularly significant that in his analysis of language Varro worked first with binary oppositions in the forms themselves but not in the meanings of the forms. His proposed three steps for the analysis of Latin words are as follows:

1. Divide the language into variable and invariable words.

2. Of those words that vary, some do so regularly and others do not.

3. Those that vary regularly (*declinatio*) fall into four types: (a) those with case only, (b) those with tense only, (c) those with case and tense, and (d) those with neither case nor tense. As examples we find for the first type nouns; for the second, verbs; for the third, participles; and for the last, adverbs like *docte, facte,* which differ from the invariables because they can be compared (*declinatio*) *doctius, doctissime.*

Varro's point in making these divisions was to show part of the system of Latin. He distinguished what he called *declinatio voluntaria,* which corresponds roughly to one aspect of the modern term "derivation," by which new words are coined, and *declinatio naturalis,* which corresponds to the general notion of inflection. The discussion of regularity or irregularity, he said, can concern only these forms, not invariable ones. Varro held this view because he was concerned with the internal, formal regularities of language and not with the predictable or unpredictable correspondences between forms and meanings. He put it this way:

> In answer to the question of how a word should be considered similar to something else, whether on the basis of sound or meaning, I would say that it

should be studied on the basis of sound; so that when we say a word is masculine, it is not because it means a male, but that I can put *hic* and *hi* in front of it, and so too of the feminine, to which we can prefix *haec* or *hae*.

[DLL X.2]

The forms he cited are the masculine and feminine demonstratives, singular and plural, respectively. He also thought it pointless to discuss analogies between "citation forms," that is, single forms of the language without reference to the paradigmatic sets to which they belong. He noted that the Latin word *nox* ("night," declined *noctis, nocti, noctem*, and so on) and *mox* ("soon," an invariable adverb) may look alike, but they are incomparable, since one is a declinable form and the other is invariable.

Varro pointed out that while analogy requires regularity, one will find a different kind of regularity in the forms related by what he called *declinatio naturalis* and *declinatio voluntaria:*

I call variation by choice (*declinatio voluntaria*) the type of name anyone can derive from another name, as the name "Rome" from "Romulus." I call regular variation (*declinatio naturalis*) the type that everyone uses automatically, no matter who coined the word, without having to ask how he would want it declined; so that we say *hujus Romae, hanc Romam, hac Roma,* and so on. In these two cases the first type refers to usage, and the other to nature.

[DLL X.2]

It was his view that there are two sources for words, coining and declension, and that they are related "as the stream to the source"; he saw that there are many ways in which words can be coined, but few in which they are declined or inflected, so that even on hearing a new word for the first time, the native speaker knows how to decline it. Varro found another binary distinction in language: there are not only two sources for words but two kinds of words, productive and unproductive. The unproductive are the invariables like *vix* ("scarcely") and *cras* ("tomorrow"), and the productive are the declinables like *lego, legis, legam* ("I read," "you read," "I will read"). Only the productive words should be discussed under analogy, he said, and here he would exclude the derived forms from consideration (*nomen a nomine alio*), since this, being a matter of private whim, is common usage: we must take usage into account in order to speak correctly, however, since this is how we discover analogies.

ABSTRACT AND CONCRETE LANGUAGE   Besides distinguishing the levels of etymology and the various types of words, Varro drew a distinction that anticipated the famous *langue-parole* distinction of de Saussure. He pointed out the difference that is found between the language of the people in the abstract and the language of the people as spoken by individuals. He arrived at this distinction by calling attention to the different kinds of usage, that of the ancients, that of contemporary speakers, and that of the poets (DLL X.4).

Although we may not find this a very subtle distinction, it is one mark of Varro's originality, among many others, since he was the first to distinguish between the two kinds of language. In discussing the reasons for these variations he insisted that language is basically a pragmatic tool for the business of life and that it is as subject to change as are fashions in clothing, architecture, or art. Varro believed that it is current good usage that largely determines whether a form is acceptable or not, and the normative example of the ancients or poets is not the ultimate criterion of correctness; what was once right may now become wrong, and vice versa.

Above all, Varro said, it is the affairs of every day that call for particular sorts of words and for differences among them. He noted that even when there is an evident difference between things, it will not always be expressed in language unless there is a practical need for it. For example, he recorded that the Latin word *columba* ("dove") was used indiscriminately for male or female doves, but when the birds became domestically important, the formal difference, *columbus*, *columba*, was introduced to distinguish masculine and feminine. This principle enabled him to cite two sorts of norms in language, the pervasive regularities and the more individual and sporadic changes of individuals. Varro defined "analogy," therefore, as "the similar declension of similar words, consonant with common usage" (*analogia est verborum similium declinatio similis, non repugnante consuetudine communi* [DLL X.4]).

It is regrettable that the rest of Varro's work has been lost to us, particularly his treatment of Latin syntax. That it could be lost is an indication of the interests of his age, which focused on individual words and their typical meanings. His discussion of Latin was not intended as a grammar in the same sense as Thrax's, but because of the modern point of view they both assumed, it is instructive to compare their work. It is also valuable to compare Varro's writings with those of the later Roman grammarians, who were to become the authorities on the language.

Besides classifying words as variable or invariable and then subdividing the types of "variation," Varro had a second type of classification for the nominal class, which had four subordinate members: *provocabula* (perhaps, "words for other words"), like the relative or interrogative *quis* and *quae* ("who"); *vocabula* ("words"), like *scutum* ("shield") and *gladius* ("sword"); *nomina* ("names"), like *Romulus* and

Remus; and *Pronomina* (that is, substitutes for names), like *hic* ("he," "this") and *haec* ("she," "this"). Varro also considered these members to be distinct because of their comparative definiteness or indefiniteness in reference, and he applied the technical terms *infinitum* ("indefinite"), *ut infinitum* ("like the indefinite"), *effinitum* ("determinable"?), and *finitum* ("definite," "determinate"). These distinctions are not of equal validity: certainly it would be difficult to decide how definite these various "references" are. Of all the forms mentioned, only *quis* has notable syntactic restrictions, substituting for personal expressions only, while the other relatives substitute for both personal and nonpersonal expressions. Basing such distinctions on meaning alone would lead us to the kind of grammar suggested in passing by Quintillian, a Roman grammarian who recommended the admission of a seventh case in Latin and a sixth in Greek, since the Latin ablative and the Greek dative often have an "instrumental" meaning, different from the "usual" meaning of these cases. Were we to follow such a criterion, we would have to admit as many different cases in any language as there are important meanings. Importance is a purely relative matter, so that the list of such cases would be indefinite. Yet this is precisely the sort of terminology our school grammars use to discuss Latin ablatives ("agent," "instrument," "separation," and so on).

Remmius Palaemon

Remmius Palaemon was another Roman grammarian who deserves mention here, since he was the one who translated Thrax's *Grammar* into Latin and so set the order and terminology of subsequent grammars. Thrax had distinguished, quite legitimately, eight parts of a sentence; though Latin has no article, Palaemon found eight "parts of speech" by adding the Latin interjection to the list. One advance over Thrax is Palaemon's restriction that prepositions include only forms that construct with verbs and with the accusative or ablative noun forms. (The "prepositions" that construct with verbs are forms like the *di-* of *diducere*).

Donatus

Donatus was a fourth-century grammarian whose short work was the elementary text for schools. He also followed Palaemon's organization (and, therefore, Thrax's). One original advance over previous work is his discussion of definite and indefinite pronouns, on the basis of their ability to construct with verbs in all persons or only in the third person.

ROMAN ADAPTATION OF GREEK GRAMMAR

Priscian's Grammar

The most complete and authoritative description of the Latin language that has come down to us from antiquity is that of Priscian, a Latin who taught Greeks in Constantinople in the sixth century A.D. This grammar, Priscian said, is based explicitly upon the work of Apollonius Dyscolus for Greek. Priscian divided his work into eighteen books of unequal length, following the pattern of Dyscolus. The last two deal with syntax and were called *Priscianus Minor* by the medievals; the first sixteen, dealing with Latin morphology, were called *Priscianus Major*. Along with the shorter, didactic work of Donatus, Priscian was the authority not only for Latin but for the discussion of language among the scholars of the Middle Ages.

Priscian's work is important to us for two reasons: (1) it is the most complete and accurate description of Latin by a native speaker of the language; (2) his grammatical theory is one of the cornerstones of the traditional way of discussing language. While he claimed that semantic criteria are the basic norms for discussing language, Priscian made frequent use of formal criteria as well. The obscurity that results from the former, compared to the clarity of the latter, are convincing arguments for employing a distinct and ordered application of formal and semantic criteria for the description of any language. In Priscian we find no determined order in the application of these criteria. In direct contradiction of modern views he stated explicitly that semantic criteria are central to the distinction of the "parts of speech." In the Aristotelian tradition he gave the noun priority over the other parts, and the nominative form pride of place in nominal inflection. He was inconsistent in applying both of these fundamental principles that he enunciated.

Elements of Language

For Priscian language consists of sounds that are of four kinds, not all of which are useful for describing language. *Vox articulata* ("an articulated vocal sound") is a sound that is limited or associated with a meaning by a speaker. *Vox inarticulata* is a sound not uttered in order to manifest a meaning. *Vox literata* is a sound that can be written, whether *articulata* or *inarticulata;* and *vox illiterata* is a sound that cannot be written.

A "letter" is the minimal part of a sound that can be written. A "syllable" is a sound that can be written and uttered in one breath with a single accent; it may have as few as one and no more than six letters, for example, *a, ab, ars, Mars, stans, stirps* (the prepositions *a, ab,* "from"; *ars,* "art"; "Mars"; the participle *stans,* "standing"; and the noun *stirps,* "root"). There are as many syllables as there are vowels.

A "word" (*dictio*) is the minimum part of a compound expression and is understood to be a part in terms of the meaning of its whole. Priscian defined it this way in order to prevent the interpretation of a word like *vires* (plural of *vis, viris,* "force") as being analyzable into meaningful parts like *vi* and *res* or *vir* and *es.*

An *oratio* is an acceptable arrangement of words that signifies a complete thought. There are many types of *oratio,* and even a single word in answer to a question is to be considered a perfectly good *oratio,* as when one asks, "What is the greatest good in life?" and another answers, "Honor."

PARTES ORATIONIS   Priscian defined eight "parts of speech," as follows:

1.   The **noun** is a part of speech that assigns to each of its subjects, bodies, or things a common or proper quality.

2.   The **verb** is a part of speech with tenses and moods, but without case, that signifies acting or being acted upon. (Subclasses are given, according to their meanings.)

3.   The **participles** are not explicitly defined, but it is stated that they should come in third place rightfully, since they share case with the noun and voice and tense with the verbs.

4.   The **pronoun** is a part of speech that can substitute for the proper name of anyone and that indicates a definite person. (Priscian declared forms like *quis, qualis, qui,* and *talis* to be nouns, since they are indefinite as to person.)

5.   A **preposition** is an indeclinable part of speech that is put before others, either next to them or forming a composite with them (This would include what we would distinguish as "prepositions" and "prefixes.")

6.   The **adverb** is an indeclinable part of speech whose meaning is added to the verb.

7.   The **interjection** is not explicitly defined, but is distinguished from an adverb, with which the Greeks identified it, by reason of the syntactic independence it shows and because of its emotive meaning.

8.   The **conjunction** is an indeclinable part of speech that links other parts of speech, in company with which it has significance, by clarifying their meaning or relations.

In his further discussion of the various "parts," Priscian was in no doubt as to what criteria he should use: "There is no other way of distinguishing the parts of speech than by attending to the peculiar signification of each." Both his definitions and discussions, however, show that he relies on semantic as well as morphological and syntactic criteria, but in no particular order. For instance, in discussing verbs he took semantic and formal peculiarities into account: "The meaning of verbs, properly speaking, is that of acting and being acted upon. All verbs that have a complete and balanced inflection (*declinationem*) end either in *-o* or *-or*."

He continued:

Those ending in *-o* are of two kinds, active and neutral. The active type always signifies an activity, and the passives are formed from them. Neutral verbs are those that end in *-o* like the actives but from which passives are not formed.

The verbs that end in *-or* are of three kinds: the passive verbs, which are formed directly from the active, which always mean "being acted upon," the common verbs, which signify both "acting" and "being acted upon," but have only *-or* endings, and the deponent verbs, which end in *-or* only, and are called deponent, either because they are used alone or absolutely, or because they "depose" different meanings, and are quite independent, requiring no addition to have meaning.

In his discussion of the nouns, Priscian followed the Stoic formal definition, but the Aristotelian influence is seen in his hesitance about calling the nominative a real "case":

"Case" is the inflection (*declinatio*) of nouns, or of other words with case, which occurs especially at the end of the word. . . . The "nominative" is called the *casus rectus* [*ptōsis orthē*, the "upright case"], either because it falls from the general notion of a name, but like a pen falling from the hand, remains upright; or it is improperly called a "case" since all the others arise from it or because it makes the other cases, by dropping off its own termination. . . .

In another place he repeated this idea:

the nominative is only improperly called a "case" because it makes the other cases . . . but if it is called a "case" because all the nominatives "fall" from the general idea of a name, it must be admitted that all the parts of speech have "case."

Just as the order of the *partes orationis,* or "parts of speech," is supposed to be "natural," so too is the order of cases in noun paradigms:

for the nominative is the first that nature produced and it claims first place . . . the genitive has the second place and has a natural link of origin, since it is born of the nominative and generates the following cases. The dative, which is more appropriate to friends, is third . . . the accusative, which pertains more to enemies, comes next. The Greeks put the vocative last, since it seems inferior to the others in combining only with verbs in the second person, while the others are used with all three. . . . In like manner, the ablative combines with all three. . . .

Priscian claimed that his last two books, on Latin syntax, are based on meaning, but he also employed formal criteria as well. He started with the excellent formal procedure of taking a sample sentence and then examines what the substitution or addition of various "parts" does to it. His sentence is:

> Idem homo lapsus heu hodie cecidit
> [same man fallen alas today has fallen (again)]

This sentence, Priscian said, contains all the parts of speech except the conjunction, which would require the addition of another sentence if it were added. One might note in passing that Priscian did not consider the prepositions, which he listed among the *partes,* and that his study of the cases they govern is incomplete. The pronouns are also omitted.

Priscian was also on solid ground when he stated that he intended to rely on what he has heard from Latin speakers and on what he has read by reputable authors to assist him in deciding what is grammatical. In Book XVII he analyzed the sentence cited above and assigned the proper order of words relative to each other, giving a long treatment of the pronouns, when they are used, and pointing out which cases of the noun can be joined with other cases of the noun, with the typical meanings of such combinations. The inflected *partes* were then examined, especially from the point of view of the grammatical "accidents" they can have in common and how such forms in constructions must agree in such "accidents" as number and gender.

In the last book the moods of the verb are studied (indicative, subjunctive, "optative," and imperative) and four types of constructions are distinguished. The basis for distinguishing construction types is what happens to the personal subjects. Priscian called these constructions (1) intransitive, (2) transitive, (3) reciprocal, and (4) retransitive. The examples he gave are as follows: (1) *percurrit homo excelsus* ("The exalted man ran"), which is intransitive because it is the action of a person not involving other persons; (2) *Aristophanes Aristarchum docuit* ("Aristophanes taught Aristarchus"), which is transitive because one person "acts on" another; (3) *Ajax se interfecit* ("Ajax killed himself"), which is reciprocal because a person "acts on" himself; (4) *Jussit ut tu ad se venias* ("He ordered that you come to him"), which is retransitive because a person is "acting on" another person and this activity "rebounds" upon the actor.

Criticism of Priscian's Grammar

Priscian's grammar can be criticized from a linguistic point of view for many reasons. (1) Although a linguist would be opposed in principle to basing a linguistic description on *a priori* semantic criteria, this is not necessarily the most telling objection. (2) More convincing is the fact that Priscian gave no clear explanation at all of what he understood by "meaning," the concept central to his work by his own proclamation. (3) He used both semantic and formal criteria, but never in any consistent order. (4) As a consequence of this semantic-translational approach, Priscian's description of Latin is factually false, and this can be demonstrated by quoting Priscian himself.

PHONOLOGY   Although the terms Priscian used suggest clear distinction, a little reflection shows that he was confused: his first binary distinction is between articulated and unarticulated sounds; this choice of words suggests the difference between sounds like groans and sighs and language sounds, but his definition of the former shows that they are reflexes of Aristotle's definition of *vox*—"a sound uttered by an animal, associated with some image." This, as we have seen, was Aristotle's explicit statement about meaningful versus meaningless sounds in language. We have no way of distinguishing these on Priscian's definition, since "meaning" in this sense is a consequence of the attention or intention of the speaker. As the next pair of distinctions suggests, a sound that can be written (*vox literata*) can either be meaningful or meaningless as a result of the speaker's intentions. Priscian also failed to specify why it is that some sounds cannot be written. In articulatory phonetics there is no reason, in principle, why any sound cannot be symbolized, as long as we can associate the symbol with the movements required to produce the sound. Notice that his definition of the syllable, though not universally applicable, is nonsemantic, and it is clear (because it is arbitrary) and useful for describing Latin (because it is appropriate). This definition of the syllable still appeals to many people, linguists and nonlinguists alike.

MORPHOLOGY   By denying that the complex form *vires* is analyzable into *vir-* and *-es,* Priscian was guilty of his greatest mistake as a grammarian, since *vir-* and *-es* are clearly distinguishable morphemes in Latin. The reason for Priscian's error was his simplistic notion of "meaning," which he has made the cardinal criterion of grammatical work. This is the simple referential-meaning theory involved in the sound-plus-image idea of Aristotle. The result of this view is to make the study of language a study of vocabulary, principally concerned with terms that have referential meaning: this is profoundly regrettable, since naming vocabulary is the most dispensable feature of any language. By neglecting the study of the bound forms in Latin, and the free forms with no referential, but only grammatical, function, Priscian and grammarians who have followed his lead for centuries ignored those elements that precisely characterize a language as a particular language.

Instead of defining the *partes* in terms of their characteristic morphological construction and syntactic behavior, Priscian relied on a wholly insufficient conception of "meaning," which led to confusion in classifying the verbs, too narrow a definition of adverbs and pronouns, and an inadequate treatment of nominal inflection.

Priscian assumed that the nominative form of the noun is "the first that nature produced," a wholly unverifiable and actually meaningless statement. If the idea is to suggest that at some primitive stage of Latin or any language there was a form not opposable to the other oblique cases, the notion of case itself is evacuated, since each case is what it is entirely through its opposition, morphologically and syntactically, to the other case forms. Because of this lack of formal contrast, the meaning of a "nominative" alone could not possibly be comparable to a "nominative" that must be selected from among a set of six contrasting forms, either semantically or syntactically.

Priscian concluded from this so-called priority that all the other forms are derived from the nominative through the genitive. The nominative is, therefore, the **basic form** in his nominal declensions: this is the worst possible selection for a clear description of Latin morphology. The selection of a basic form is a matter of descriptive clarity and simplicity, not a statement about historical derivation. That form is basic in a paradigm of any kind that is most like the other members of the paradigm and differs most from other paradigms. In the verbal paradigms, for example, Priscian (and traditional grammarians for centuries) put the first person singular as the basic form. Compare how readily the conjugations are distinguishable when the second person is used:

| **First person** | *amo* | *moneo* | *rego* | *audio* |
| **Second person** | *amas* | *mones* | *regis* | *audīs* |

Priscian's preoccupation with final letters, besides preventing him from establishing the inflectional and derivational affixes of the languages, made his directions for forming the various inflected form overcomplex. It also made him inconsistent, since he did not form all the other cases from the nominative or genitive, as he said, but from the form whose *spelling* was most like that of the form to be produced. For example, the following are two forms he discussed, from the traditional fourth and fifth declensions of Latin:

		"Tribe"	"Day"
	Nom.	*tribus*	*dies*
	Gen.	*tribŭs*	*diei*
SINGULAR	Dat.	*tribui*	*diei*
	Acc.	*tribum*	*diem*
	Abl.	*tribŭ*	*diē*
	Voc.	*tribus*	*dies*
	Nom.	*tribus*	*diēs*
	Gen.	*tribuum*	*diērum*
	Dat.	*tribibus*	*diēbus*
PLURAL	Acc.	*tribus*	*diēs*
	Abl.	*tribibus*	*diēbus*
	Voc.	*tribus*	*diēs*

Priscian's directions for arriving at these forms were as follows:

The nominative is *dies,* the genitive and dative are the same, formed from the nominative by dropping the *s* and adding *i;* the accusative is formed from the nominative by changing the *s* into *m;* the vocative is like the nominative; the ablative is formed from the nominative by dropping the *s.* In the plural the nominative, accusative, and vocative are like the nominative singular; the genitive adds *rum* to the ablative singular; the dative and ablative plural are alike, formed from the ablative singular by adding *bus.* . . . The nominative is *tribus;* the genitive is like that; the dative is formed from the genitive by dropping the *s* and adding *i;* the accusative is formed from the nominative by changing the *s* into *m;* the ablative is formed from the genitive by dropping the *s* and lengthening the *u;* the nominative, accusative, and vocative plural are like the genitive singular; the genitive plural is formed from the nominative by dropping the *s* and adding *um;* the dative and ablative are formed from the nominative by changing the *u* to *i* and interpolating *bu.*

This is all quite accurate, but it is a lesson in spelling, not morphology. As has been noted, not all cases are formed from the nominative in his system, despite the claim that this is the "original," or "basic," form. Priscian listed nine forms that are made from the nominative, but took the genitive as the basic form for eleven others, and the dative as basic to eleven more.

His ignorance of morphology also led him to classify the verbs incorrectly. Instead of following the Stoics, who identified active and passive verbs through their syntax (the cases with which they occur), Priscian based his classification on the *frequent,* but *not universal,* meaning of verbs ending in *-o* and *-or.*

Since he based his classification on meaning, Priscian was also misled in distinguishing units of verbal morphology. For example, in discussing tense in the verbs (the Latin is *tempus,* which we translate either as "time" or "tense") he said:

Since we have now dealt with the various meanings of the verbs . . . we must now say something about tense. Tense is an accident of the verb and is apt to signify different kinds of acts. It is usually shown either in the first or last letters of the inflection *(declinatio)*, from which we also recognize person and number: person and number, however, are indicated by the final letters, but tense both by the first and last. . . .

There are, therefore, three tenses: present, past, and future. The past is divided into three: the past incomplete [*imperfectus*], the past complete [*perfectus*], and the past more than complete [*plusquamperfectus*]. . . . Now the Greeks divided the future into two words, a sort of indefinite future like *tupsomai* ["I shall strike"] and a kind of subsequent future like *tetupsomai* ["I shall have struck"]. But the Romans considered the nature of the future better, seeing it to be the most uncertain, and so used only one expression.

This is contrary to the facts: Latin has two morphological constructions dealing with the future, as in *amabo, amavero* ("I shall love," "I shall have loved"), as well as a syntactic construction, *amaturus sum* ("I am about to love"). Priscian noted that Greek has "a past perfect subjunctive, which can have the force of a past imperative, for example, *amatus sit* ["let him be beloved"]." He continued, "That a *construction* like this has the force of a past tense is shown by the past perfect subjunctive." This distinction between morphological and syntactic constructions (for him, only the syntactic were "constructions") can now be compared with another factual error involving that distinction. Greek had morphological constructions in the verb system, identifiable as:

		Indicative	Subjunctive	Optative	Imperative
GREEK	1.	*luō*	*luō*	*luoimi*	
	2.	*lueis*	*luēs*	*luois*	*lue*
LATIN	1.	*amo*	*amen*		
	2.	*amas*	*ames*		*amā*

Priscian discussed the indicative, subjunctive, and optative in Latin, giving as examples of the optative sentences such as:

Utinam Romae	*Filius*	*meus*	*legisset*	*autores,*
would in Rome	son	my	had studied	authors that
propter	*quos*	*ibi*	*nunc*	*moratur*
because of	whom	there	now	is staying

(Would that my son had studied those authors, for whose sake he is staying in Rome)

Utinam	*profectus*	*esset*	*Roman*	*ante*	*XX*	*dies*
would that	set out	had	to Rome	ago	20	days

(I wish he had left for Rome 20 days ago)

It is evident that Latin does not have a subjunctive form opposable to an optative. Greek does. In a sentence like

Utinam	*amicus*	*noster*	*devenias*
"would"	friend	our	you would become

(I wish you would be our friend)

Priscian would have called the form *utinam . . . devenias* an optative. This is sensible only because, if the sentence were translated into Greek, one would have to use the form *genoio,* and not the formally distinct indicative or subjunctive:

eithe	*su*	*hēmin*	*philos*	*genoio*
would that	you	to us	friend	would become

It is obvious that where Greek expresses the "optative" with a morphological construction (for example, *gen* + *oio*) of bound forms, Latin renders the same meaning by a syntactic construction consisting of two free, complex forms, *utinam* + *devenias.* On the basis of translation meaning, English and any language that can express a wish has an optative mood, as well as an indefinite number of other moods and cases which can express "important" meaning differences.

A comparison of some Greek and Latin forms would have shown the structures of the two languages much better than comparing meanings; for example,

Tense Distinctions

	Pres.	Impf.	Aorist	Pr.Pf.	Plupf.	Fu. Pf.Act.	Fu.Pf.Ps.
GREEK	*luo*	*eluon*	*elusa*	*leluka*	*eleluke*		*lelusomai*
LATIN	*amo*	*amabam*	*(amavi)*		*amaveram*	*amavero*	

Voice Distinctions

GREEK	Active	Middle	Passive
LATIN	Active		(Passive)

Number Distinctions

GREEK	Singular	Dual	Plural
LATIN	Singular		(Plural)

Mood Distinctions

	Indic.	Subj.	Optative	Imper.
GREEK	*luō*	*luō*	*luoimi*	
	lueis	*luēis*	*luois*	
LATIN	*amo*	{ *amem*		
		{ *ames*	} *ama*	

Comparisons of this sort, based initially on formal differences and similarities, would have infallibly shown the proper meaning distinctions required. For this reason linguists reject meaning-based descriptions as an initial step, not because they are not interested in meanings but precisely because they are. The proper time for such a discussion, however, is *after* an accurate formal description has been completed. The strength of this approach is that it is much easier to make someone see what you see than to make him think what you think. A conceivable drawback would be the erroneous impression that one is not required to think in making a formal description.

It is unfortunate that the Latin and Greek languages are structurally so similar, since their differences are obscured. The Greeks had no models for their grammatical description, and it is not surprising that their grammatical work was basically formal in approach. This is not to suggest that Priscian's work is without merit or use: it is still a valuable and accurate source of information about Latin, chiefly because he did not follow his own theoretical recommendations exclusively.

Review Questions

For the authors discussed here, and for the rest of the authors considered in their work, the student should be prepared to answer the following six questions:

1. What is the purpose of the study?
2. How many linguistic units are defined in the study?
3. On what criteria are these units established? (For example, various kinds of semantic and formal criteria.)
4. How many systems or levels of analysis are recognized in the study?
5. Are the units and systems discussed apt for the purpose of the study?
6. Are the units and systems useful for linguistic study because of their universality and because they can be established formally? Explain.

The following questions concern the topics discussed in Chapter 4:

1. Explain the *Physis-Nomos* controversy.
2. Can we translate *onoma* and *rhēma* as "noun" and "verb"? Explain.
3. Illustrate and explain the technique of Plato's division with an original example.
4. Compare the work of Plato, Aristotle, and the Stoics and point out the reasons for their advances over one another.
5. Explain the greater precision of the Stoic use of *ptōsis* compared to the use of this term in Aristotle's work.
6. Define "analogy" and explain the anomaly-analogy dispute.
7. Show the connection between the notions of analogy and level of analysis.

8. Compare Varro's use of *declinatio* and Aristotle's use of *ptōsis*.
9. What grammatical innovation did Quintillian suggest? Criticize it.
10. What were the contributions of Remmius Palaemon and Donatus?

Suggested Readings

Arens, H., *Sprachwissenschaft* (Munich, 1955).
Bochenski, I. M., *Ancient Formal Logic* (Amsterdam, 1951).
Robins, R. H., *Ancient and Medieval Grammatical Theory in Europe* (London, 1951).
————, *Dionysius Thrax and the Western Grammatical Tradition*, Transactions of the Philological Society (London, 1957).

5

Traditional Grammar

The doctrine we have been referring to as "traditional grammar" or "school grammar" in Europe and America has a mixed background. The basic terminology for discussing language is that first developed by the Greeks, adopted by the Romans, and passed on to us through translation in various languages. During this passage of time the application of grammatical terms has changed so much that confusion can be introduced into the processes of describing and explaining language.

Besides deriving its vocabulary for the discussion of the more or less formal aspects of language from older work, traditional grammars have also drawn on the semantic theories of the ancients as well as the medievals. Of course, there is no single semantic theory that has been agreed upon in ancient, medieval, or modern times, but implicit in the method of distinguishing among the parts of language is a basically Aristotelian sketch of human cognitive and expressive processes. Despite the comparatively uniform use of the grammatical terms, however, there has always been considerable dispute about the problems involved in applying them.

In this section we will follow the development of some of these fundamental ideas and see that it was the medievals who developed a more sophisticated semantic theory, one implicitly based on the recognition of pervasive syntactic relations in language. Their work, however, did not result in a more precise way of discussing the formal aspects of language. It was not until the nineteenth century that European scholars were in a position to give a confident morphological analysis of either their own or the classical languages.

Besides deriving from the work of Greek and Roman scholars and the medieval elaboration of their ideas, traditional school grammar owes its development to another source. Two important tools of the prescriptive grammarian were the first dictionaries and grammars that found general acceptance in eighteenth-century England. These works were composed during a period when the precise relation of English to its older stages, and to the classical languages, was dimly perceived. It was only at the end of the nineteenth century that the historical development of and relations among these various languages could be accurately described, although "etymology" had long been considered a means of determining the correct forms in the current language.

MEDIEVAL LINGUISTIC STUDY

The world of Thrax, Dyscolus, and Varro was a comparatively orderly one, which favored the flow of information and the development of the scholarly ideas of one's predecessors. This continuity was broken with the fall of the Roman Empire, which resulted in a period of political and intellectual chaos. Libraries were destroyed and education was interrupted. There was a brief revival of learning in Europe during the Carolingian renaissance of the ninth century, but it lost its impetus with the death of Charlemagne. Another intellectual revival gathered momentum in the eleventh and twelfth centuries when works of Aristotle, which had been lost to the West, were translated from Arabic versions circulated by the Moors in Spain and southern Italy. These works extended European knowledge of Aristotelian logic, and enthusiasm for the "new logic" permeated all fields of study in the later medieval period, leading to a new way of discussing language, called the "logicization of grammar."

Until this new way of handling language problems became established, all students were introduced to grammar through the study of the grammars of Priscian and Donatus. Although Priscian's work was the more extensive in its discussions and citation of examples, both grammars had substantially the same approach: the pupil was to learn the proper forms and the rules for their correct combinations according to the examples of classical Latin. These rules were incorporated for memorization in simpler grammars for beginning students, such as the mnemonic verse grammar of Alexander of Villadei and others. The acquisition of Latin through these grammars was for a long time the mark of an educated man, and the study of the classical authors provided an important link in the continuity of Western civilization. The influence of this same tradition is seen, too, in the first grammar of Latin for English students written by Aelfric in the year 1000.

Boethius

The greatest single influence in the area of education in western Europe during the medieval period was Boethius, a contemporary of Priscian. He was born in 470, and, having studied in Rome and Athens, conceived the idea of translating the great monuments of Greek thought for the Latin world. The first of his translations was a commentary by Victorinus (d. 363) on Porphyry's *Isagoge,* or "Introduction" to the *Categories* of Aristotle. He then made his own translation of the work and appended another commentary. He next translated *On Interpretation,* which became known by its Latin title, *De Interpretatione.* To this work he appended two commentaries, one for beginners and another for more advanced students. Besides other commentaries, he composed original works on logic, theology, philosophy, astronomy, mathematics, music, and geometry. Because of these works, and his outline of what education should entail, Boethius was known as the "schoolmaster of the West." His plan for a liberal education consisted of two parts, known through the terms he invented for them, the *Trivium* and the *Quadrivium.* The *Quadrivium* consisted of the study of arithmetic, geometry, astronomy, and music, and the *Trivium* dealt with the three "expressions of knowledge," grammar, logic, and rhetoric. Boethius' own works formed the basis of instruction in these fields.

It was Boethius who introduced the problem of universals to medieval Europe, and centuries were to be spent in disputing it. From the point of view of linguistics, the problem concerns the nature of the meaning to be assigned to common or universal terms, such as "man," "good," "bad," "mortal," and so on. The problem arises naturally enough in a logic of predicates such as that inherited from Aristotle, since such terms would be the variables in the typical deductive syllogism, whose study so captured the imagination of that era. The history of the disputes that arose about universals can be found in the standard histories of philosophy, but it is sufficient to note here that medieval grammar and logic were thought to be the keys to resolving them. We can assume that the basic positions discussed in the *Physis-Nomos* and anomaly-analogy disputes recurred in a more sophisticated form and that the difference between Stoic and Aristotelian logic was relevant to understanding the solutions proposed. From a linguistic point of view this difference can be characterized partially as a difference between a position that discusses words in isolation and one that studies words in sentences.

Theories of meaning and truth were, therefore, intimately related, so that neither grammarians nor logicians nor philosophers were likely to make satisfactory suggestions until their attention was shifted from the abstract meanings of isolated words, as dealt with in the *Categories* and in the definitions of the *Parts of Speech,* to concrete expressions in actual use. This shift required, among other things, a more developed psychological theory, one that would take into account the speaker as a thinking subject. In the meantime it was to the impersonal study of logic that appeal was made for initial steps in solving the problems. Logic became the prestige study of the day, the medieval's most precise and respected intellectual tool. It held the same position in the intellectual world then that science holds now: serious study today must be "scientific"—then it had to be "logical."

Peter Helias

The most respected grammar of the medieval period was that of Priscian. He based his grammatical descriptions on the writing and speech of the best models available to him. In the twelfth century a new method of explaining the regularities of Latin was introduced, beginning with Peter Helias' commentary on Priscian's grammar. The time was favorable for change. Both Latin pronunciation and usage differed from the classic models, since in the universities, which were open to students from many countries, Latin was a living language for international communication. The new pronunciation and grammar were preferred, in spite of the lack of correspondence with classical norms. Instead of basing their rules for correct usage on the ancients, the medievals under the influence of the logical approach to all problems, began to appeal to what they considered the inherent logic of their language. For this reason the period was called that of the "logicization of grammar."

One of the chief contributors to this trend was Peter Helias. About all that is known of him personally is that he taught at the University of Paris about the middle of the twelfth century. In his commentary on Priscian he frequently substituted the logical terminology of Aristotle for the more grammatical terms of Priscian, and, because of the point of view he assumed, furthered the search for logical justification of current Latin usage. This commentary soon became the authoritative guide to the study of Priscian and became required subject matter in Paris by the thirteenth century. Helias' work also gave impetus to the development of philosophic grammars in the thirteenth and fourteenth centuries. Today these grammars are called general grammars.

It will be useful here to distinguish at least three possible types of "grammars," recalling the various approaches of language study. One could be a purely descriptive grammar of the forms speakers use and the combinations in which they are actually found, with or without semantic classifications. Another could be the type with which we are most familiar, a set of rules for the proper use of forms and prohibitions concerning forms or combinations to be avoided, with or without justification of the rules.

A general grammar of the medieval type, also called a speculative grammar, is harder to define. This type of grammar appears to prescind from features peculiar to an individual language and deals with features presumably found in any language. In the work of the Modistae of the thirteenth and fourteenth centuries such grammars discussed the general features of the things with which language deals, as well as the way these features are expressed in Latin. These grammars laid down rules for talking about the nature of things as an end in itself and not as a means of examining the arbitrary linguistic system through which things are discussed. While this view may recall the *Cratylus,* the discussions differ greatly in their range and subtlety.

Linguists have rejected the *a priori* approach of these medieval grammars because they were based almost exclusively on problems peculiar to the Latin language and because of the Aristotelian descriptive frame in which they were cast. But recently there has been a revival of interest in the universal features of language, although this work is based on a great deal more experience with related and unrelated languages and proceeds in a more formal and less *a priori* fashion.

Some quotations from Helias' work will show how his commentary encouraged the use of logical norms for deciding on the correctness of grammatical forms and constructions, although many of the comments he made are obviously inductive rather than logically deductive. In general, Helias accepted the basic definitions of Priscian and then added his own comments, usually based on ideas from Aristotle's logic.

He defined "grammar" as

the science that shows us how to write and speak correctly. . . . It is the task of this art to order the combination of letters into syllables, syllables into words, and words into sentences . . . avoiding solecisms and barbarisms.

It is significant to note that Helias considered grammar both an art and a science. As these terms were used in his day, this suggests that grammar has two characteristics: since it is an art, its most fundamental principles and assumptions will be the consequence of human choice and not impersonal necessity, as in the natural sciences. Since grammar is a science, it will have an exact procedure, for which rules can be formulated, so that one can know when the rules have been applied or when they have been violated. Helias also recognized that there are as many grammars as there are languages:

The types of any art are the quality that the artisan assigns to his material through his art. . . . There are, therefore, many types of this art, as there are many kinds of languages in which grammatical art is practiced, and of which it is composed.

Although his definition of grammar appears to call for a consideration of phonology (the ordering of letters into syllables), Helias did not delay over such an examination. He did, however, discuss word formation and constructions. After giving a reasonable view of what "case" ought to mean, he lapsed into a pseudological explanation of why there are six cases in Latin:

Case is the property of a word being inflected or derived in one way or another [Latin, *proprietas cadendi in aliud vel ab alio*] because of the different ways of speaking about the same thing. And "to be inflected or derived" here means to become a different word ["word," *vocem,* which also means "voice" and, therefore, "sound"] . . . the cause of different cases being invented is the different ways of talking about things . . . six were invented, nor are more required.

The Latins used a single word, *oratio,* for our expressions "phrase," "clause," and "sentence," all of which are constructions. This expression will, therefore, be left untranslated in the following passage in order to illustrate the need for precise technical terminology:

The ancients in discussing *oratio* said that some words were called an *oratio* because of their meaning, not because of their quantity as in *lego* and such like. [Note that Latin *lego* is typically the head of an endocentric construction, with a noun as its expansion, while it must be translated into English as an exocentric construction, "I read."] Others said that an *oratio* was so-called both because of its meaning and its quantity, such as those which consist of two words joined together, as in *homo currit* [the man runs], and this sort of *oratio* was called constructed. To this they added that not all constructions of words could be called an *oratio,* but only those which meant some sort of inherence, that is, conjunction, since there is indeed a conjunction of words in an expression like *in domo* ["in the house"], but not a conjunction of two things, so it is not an *oratio.* On the other hand, an expression like *homo albus* ["white man"], although it is an imperfect *oratio,* still means some sort of conjunction of substance and accident, and so should be called an *oratio.*

Both of these passages reflect the dependence of Helias' views on Aristotelian ideas. Aristotle's study of language began with the principle that there is one aspect in which all languages are alike, despite the fact that there are many languages and that each one is conventional. This basic similarity was to be found in the things men talked about, and perhaps in the way men experienced the things they talked about. In the *De Interpretatione* Aristotle said:

But the mental affections themselves, of which these words are primarily signs, are the same for the whole of mankind, as are also the objects of which those affections are representations. . . .

This assumption has been one that traditional grammars have accepted without examination. Helias' observations about the Latin cases should point out one of its defects. He thought, apparently as a consequence of the ideas in the paragraph just quoted from the *De Interpretatione*, that there are six and only six ways of talking about "the same thing." This is based on the fact that the same root morpheme, with the affixed inflectional morphemes for the nominative, genitive, dative, accusative, ablative, and vocative cases, is frequent in Latin. Greek, of course, has only five cases, if the vocative is included among them, which not all grammarians did. If we take Helias' formal definition of "case" (there are as many cases as there are different inflectional endings) as correct, then English nouns have only two cases at the maximum (for example, "child," "child's"). The second passage also shows a trend of thought that has recommended itself to traditional grammars in their definition of a sentence as the expression of a complete thought. The aim of this sort of definition is fairly clear: the closer one approaches a declarative sentence, the logical "proposition," the nearer one gets to a complete thought. This view is also seen in the definition of the parts of speech. For example, Priscian had defined the verb formally in terms of tense and mood inflections, and semantically on the basis of activity or passivity. Helias added to Aristotle's logical idea that the verb is always a predicate:

In every complete sentence, something is said about something else. The noun was therefore invented to distinguish what one was talking about, and the verb to distinguish what was said of another, especially with respect to activity and passivity. . . .

Involved in this idea of the proposition or declarative sentence being the best illustration of a complete sentence is a ranking of the parts of speech reminiscent of Priscian:

The noun is the first and most noble part of speech, but the pronoun takes its case from the noun and therefore should have its case in the most noble part. But the most noble part of a word, since the meaning is most to be discerned from the ending, is the last part. For the mind generally understands nothing when we hear language until we get to the end of the word. . . .

Since this view is a value judgment, it would be difficult to refute. It is evident, however, that Helias would have difficulty in reconciling his view with the simplistic referential-meaning position of Aristotle in the *De Interpretatione*, since the referential or lexical part of Latin forms is most often found in the first, and not the last, part of a word. This view also goes counter to the structural idea of redundancy in language, according to which more clues to the semantic and grammatical relations of longer utterances are given than are required. Many of the Latin terminations are features of concord, which are entirely predictable in terms of preceding forms; others show features of government that are predictable according to the forms of succeeding words.

Petrus Hispanus

As the work of Helias indicates, little progress was made in the twelfth century in the formal analysis of language, with the exception of the breaking up of "substantival" and "adjectival" nouns into the more familiar classification of nouns and adjectives. What the logicians added, however, was a more refined way of discussing the semantic aspects of language. Grammarians before this period, following Aristotle and the Stoics, gave positive class meanings to the parts of speech in terms of Aristotle's *Categories:* the nouns meant "substance" or "quality," the verbs meant "action" or "passivity," and so on. With the development of further logical studies there came a subtle but important shift in emphasis, which can be accounted for in terms of linguistic form. Instead of discussing *what* a part means, the logicians began to discuss *how* a part signifies something. This shift was a consequence of two developments: a more refined psychological theory and a more detailed method of studying how expressions have meaning when they are constructions with the other expressions of the language.

In the logical work of Petrus Hispanus, the term "signification," like our vague term "meaning," is split up into several distinguishable aspects. Instead of one term Hispanus used three—"signification," "supposition," and "appellation." On the basis of these designations he discussed the properties of terms, a section of his logical work that was much imitated and extended by others.

Petrus Hispanus was born in the early decades of the thirteenth century, studied in Paris, where Albertus Magnus was his professor for Aristotelian physics and metaphysics, and became one of the leading authorities of his time on medicine and logic. He became Archbishop of Braga in 1273 and was elected Pope in September 1276. His reign as John XXI was a brief one. A scholar to the end, he had a special building erected where he might pursue his studies in peace, but it fell in on him in May 1277, and neither his own nor others' medical skill was enough to save him: he died on May 20, a week later. His *Summulae Logicales,* a handbook of dialectics, went through over 160 editions and was used in many universities throughout Europe, influencing the work of Duns Scotus, Ockham, and many others. In it we find an obvious dependence upon the Aristotelian views, as well as advances over that position.

The first advance was an explication of factors in the Aristotelian psychology that one could say are consonant with, but not expressly developed in, the writings of Aristotle. The diagram outlines the kind of acts that were distinguished by the speculative psychologists of Hispanus' day. This sort of psychology is called "faculty psychology" and is largely rejected in modern times, because it is felt that such a scheme splits up human cognitive activities into water-tight compartments. This is by no means a necessary consequence of the view, but is an imaginative trap. Sensation, memory or imagination, intellection, judgment, and reasoning are attributed to various faculties in this sketch, but need not correspond to separate physical parts of the knower. The advocates of this view pointed out that such acts are distinguishable because a man need not always be actively sensing, imagining, understanding, judging, or reasoning about something. It was the ancient and medieval understanding that it is not the eye that sees but the man who sees because he has eyes, and so of the other "faculties."

The order in which the acts or faculties are listed is logical and not a consequence of observation of individual cases, since any of these activities could precede, follow, or be concomitant with any of the others in the mature individual. Figure 4 would be interpreted in the following way: a man comes into contact with objects first perceived by

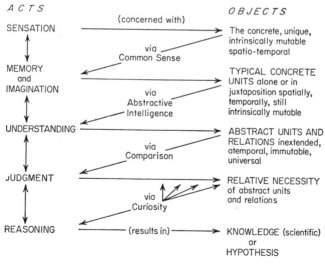

Fig. 4.

the usual senses (sight, touch, smell, hearing, taste) and tends to classify them through an internal sensory faculty, the "common sense," so called since it correlates the findings of the various senses and distinguishes their objects. Such a classification results in typical images or memory traces of past experience, from which basic, necessary factors of similarity are abstracted by the understanding, a faculty that was taken to be immaterial, and, therefore, not restricted to considerations of extension or limitation in time. These abstract classifications were the material from which judgments were formed, and, in view of their genetic history, were considered neither true nor false; judgments involving them could be declared true or false, even though they might be uninteresting. Since we have the experience of often being able to verify the judgments we have made, and since we also have the experience of knowing we were wrong in the past, curiosity impels the thinking man to inquire about the reasons for both successes and failures. The result of such reasoning is the construction of a scheme of things that would give a satisfactory account of why men can attain or fail to attain verified knowledge. In cases where the thinker was satisfied that his information is solidly based and could be proved, one spoke of scientific knowledge. For the medievals, as for the ancients, such knowledge was always deductive, though genetically it was based on induction. In the event that such certainty could not be obtained, a hypothesis was formed, with the hope that later information could prove it as solid as established scientific knowledge.

For Hispanus language is the communication of all of these stages of knowledge. It was a commonplace of that period that the same linguistic items could express an insight at any of the levels mentioned, that of imagery, understanding, judgment, or reasoning.

In the *Summulae* Hispanus began by defining his discipline as the "art of arts and the science of sciences," since it is the one discipline that can discuss and justify the foundations of all others. Knowledge was sought in the medieval scheme of things through oral disputation, thus indicating to him where to begin his account of meaningful language as used in dialectics. He then reproduced the basic ideas of Priscian (and, therefore, of the Stoics), but without the grammatical detail. Sound is "what we hear," but noise is not vocal sound, since the latter is produced only by the vocal apparatus of animals. These vocal sounds can sometimes be written, but not all are meaningful. Some meaningful vocal sounds are such by nature, others only through convention. The naturally meaningful sounds are those such as sighs and groans, which have the same meaning in all languages, while conventionally meaningful sounds, like the word *homo,* can mean only what the one who invented it intends. A vocal sound without a meaning is one that represents nothing to anyone who hears it.

Conventionally meaningful expressions are either simple (the *nomen* and *verbum*) or complex (the *oratio*). The *nomen* and *verbum* are given Aristotelian definitions:

The *noun* is a significant sound, significant by convention, none of whose parts signify anything separately, finite, and in the nominative case.

The *verb* is a vocal sound that has meaning by convention, no part of which has meaning separately, with tense. . . .

Hispanus was quite aware that these are logical, and not grammatical, definitions: "It should be noted that the logician sets up only two parts of a sentence, that is, noun and verb; but he calls the others syncategorematic expressions." The *oratio* is

a conventionally meaningful expression whose parts have meaning separately . . . a perfect *oratio* gives rise to a complete thought in the mind of the hearer, but the imperfect does not, for example, "man runs," "white man."

The perfect *oratio,* or sentence, is then divided into the declarative, imperative, optative (for example, "I wish I were a good cleric": *utinam bonus clericus essem*) and subjunctive (for example, "If you come to me, I will give you a horse": *si veneris ad me, tibi dabo equum*). Of these only the declarative is called a proposition, a sentence that "signifies a true or false judgment . . . the affirmation or negation of something about some other thing."

Hispanus defined a **simple term** as one that signifies a substance, quality, quantity, or one of the other categories of Aristotle. A **complex term** is an expression like *homo currit* ("a man is running"), while *homo* or *currit* alone are said to be simple. A **term** is defined as "a vocal sound signifying a singular or a universal, such as 'man' or 'Socrates' . . . that into which a proposition is analyzed, viz., subject and predicate."

His distinction between **categorematic** and **syncategorematic** terms is, therefore, clear: any term that can stand as the subject or predicate is called categorematic (which appeals to the Stoic use of *kategorema* for the finite forms of the verbs, which were typically predicates). All the other expressions, especially those that are not nouns and verbs, are usually syncategorematic. This is the same distinction Aristotle drew among the *onoma, rhēma,* and *syndesmoi,* although it can now be made with more grammatical insight. For example, an expression like *solus* ("only") could be either categorematic or syncategorematic, depending on the construction. In a sentence like *Petrus est solus* ("Peter is alone") it is categorematic; in a sentence like *Petrus solus scribit* ("Peter alone is writing") it is syncategorematic. In terms of the psychological views of the time, categorematic terms were image words and all words in parallel distribution with image words. They were the typical nouns and nominals, both of which could stand as subjects and predicates. "Subject" was an analogical term, the **prime analogate,** or clearest example, of which was a noun to which a sensory image corresponded, for example, "apple," "house," and the like. A word like "democracy" or "honesty" was considered categorematic, not because a sensory image was associated with it but because it could stand as the grammatical subject and have the same sort of relation to other grammatical expressions as the image words. All subjects or predicates were, therefore, "things," since "thing" is itself an analogical term. This is what is meant in the traditional definition of "noun" as "the name of a person, place, or thing," or "something conceived as a thing."

MEANING   The general term that Hispanus used which corresponds to our vague expression "meaning" is *significatio,* defined as "the representation of a thing through a conventional vocal sound." Of course, this is a paraphrase of Aristotle's definition of "voice," but because of the more developed psychological theories of Hispanus' day, the "representation" was not restricted to that of sensitive imagery. The "things" that could be represented were any of the products in the various stages of knowledge discussed earier in this chapter.

Hispanus also distinguished between **principal signification** and **consignification.** The basis for the distinction is the difference between the meanings signaled by roots and those signaled by the affixes that could be in construction with the roots. Of course, Hispanus was no more able to make an accurate distinction between roots and affixes than the other grammarians of his day, but his distinction of meaning types obviously corresponds to the root *am-* and the affixes *-o, -ans, -ator, -or,* and *-abilis* in the stems *amo* ("I love"), *amans* ("loving"), *amator* ("a lover"), and *amabilis* ("lovable"). All of these expressions can be said to have the principal signification of "love" in very general terms, plus the added signification of the affixes. For example, among the consignifications of *amo* would be "first person," "singular," "active," and "present": the consignifications were the grammatical accidents or the relations the form had.

Hispanus also distinguished between **substantival** and **adjectival** signification. The first term represents the meaning of nouns and nominals and the second the meaning of what we would call "adjectives" (capable of comparison, though formally similar to the nouns in declension) as well as "verbs." These definitions are based on the fact that nouns are said to "stand for" (*supponunt*) what they mean, while adjectivals "link" (*copulant*) their meaning to a substantival. One of the most important distinctions in Hispanus' treatment of meaning is relevant here: signification, as opposed to supposition. Hispanus' explanation of this elusive distinction is as follows:

Supposition is the acceptance of a substantive term for something. But supposition and signification are different, since signification is effected by the imposition of a vocal sound to signify a thing, while supposition is the acceptance of a term that already has meaning for some thing, as when we say "man runs," the term "man" stands for Socrates or Plato and so on for others. Therefore signification is prior to supposition and they are not the same thing, since signification is the property of words, but supposition is the property of a term that consists of a vocal sound and a particular signification. Again, signification is a relation of a sign to the thing for which it is the sign, but supposition is a relation not between a sign and what it signifies but between a substitute and the thing for which it substitutes [*supponentis ad suppositum*].

The relation between signification and supposition has been discussed by others using various sets of terms, for example:

signification	:	supposition
meaning	:	thing(s) meant
intension	:	extension
denotation	:	connotation
concept	:	instances

Confusion about the difference leads to the frequent fallacy of word magic, that is, taking words to be the same as the thing they name. The distinction that Hispanus made, however, depends on a kind of "dualism," in which the concept of the intellect, usually expressed in a definition or a description of the essential characteristics of the thing named, is taken to be of a different nature than either the term or the things for which the term can be used. Even though modern linguists do not care to become embroiled in the psychological disputes that this approach entails, they recognize that what Hispanus called the signification is some persistent and recurrent factor in the situations in which a particular expression is used. The supposition would be the number of situations in which the expression is used.

TYPES OF SUPPOSITION   After distinguishing the two basic types of meaningful expressions in the kind of language he examined (that is, categorematic and syncategorematic), Hispanus reviewed some facets of "meaning modification" for the categorematic terms. He distinguished first between **formal** and **material** supposition. This distinction is readily appreciated by comparing the use of *John* in the two sentences "John is my friend" and "*John* is a noun." In the first example *John* represents formal, or personal, supposition, since the expression is interpreted for the object it was intended to designate. In the second example *John* is taken in material supposition, that is, as a name not for a nonlinguistic object but for itself.

Modern logicians and linguists discuss this distinction in terms of **object language** and **metalanguage**. Developed natural languages contain sufficient categorematic and syncategorematic expressions to describe their own logical or grammatical structure. Such descriptive expressions constitute a metalanguage, a language about language, and the rest of the same language is called the object language with respect to it.

So far in our examination of Hispanus he has discussed supposition in very general terms, as applicable to terms in isolation. When he discussed the same terms in constructions, he spoke of the **amplification** or **restriction** of a term's supposition, that is, of an increase or decrease in the number of things for which the term can stand.

He gave as an example *homo musicus currit,* which must be rather barbarously rendered in English as "The musical man runs" in order to preserve the point of his expression. In such a construction Hispanus pointed out that the term *homo* is now restricted to substitute only for "musical men" because of its construction with *musicus.* This is an example of restriction of supposition.

As an example of amplification he cited *homo potest esse Antichristus* ("a man can be antichrist") and said that the term *homo* in this instance can now apply to all possible men, not merely to existent musical men in the present, as would be the case in *homo musicus currit,* because of its construction with the modal *potest* ("can").

More interestingly, in the section on restrictions Hispanus showed that terms in construction mutually restrict each other. For example, in an expression like *homo musicus,* the term *homo* no longer substitutes for "men who are not musical," and the term *musicus* is not interpretable for anything but "men." This insight approaches the structural idea that elements in a language mutually condition and mutually define each other, but it points out a weakness in the traditional notion of "modification," a process term that has almost invariably been explained as a one-way, and not a mutual, relation. As structural work has shown, the idea that elements in a construction mutually modify or restrict each other is true enough as far as it goes, but it does not go far enough; one must add that the members *present* are also "modified" by the members *absent.* Both formally and semantically the function of any linguistic item is determined by the items that contrast with it in a particular environment. The presence of an item in that environment often is the consequence of a choice among the other items in parallel distribution with it, and this choice is part of the meaning.

This discussion of Hispanus' views on meaning will be completed by pointing out another distinction he made, that among signification, supposition, and appellation. **Appellation** is "the interpretation of a term for an *existent* object," and this definition distinguishes it from sup-position and signification alike, since the latter are indifferently used of things existent or nonexistent. In some cases the signification, sup-position, and appellation of a term (for example, a living person's name) coincide; in other cases they do not (for example, when a dead or mythical person is mentioned). Usually the three terms mean different things, as in an expression like *homo currit*. The signification of *homo* is "man" (in general) or "rational animal." Because it is in a construction with *currit,* the supposition of *homo,* which can include all men, is re-stricted to a single man, now actually running in the present. Its ap-pellation can be only this single, actually existent man.

It should be noted that it is the supposition and not the signification which can be amplified or restricted. This is a consequence of Hispanus' dualistic explanation of meaning, which distinguishes a conceptual con-tent (that is, signification) and individual instances to which the concept applies (that is, supposition). The signification of a term consists of the basic, necessary factors abstracted by the understanding from many in-dividual instances (for example, the "rationality" and "animality" found in many instances of "man"). The relation of signification as he explains it, therefore, is one between a term and a concept, and this concept is the *immediate* meaning of the term; the relation of supposition is one be-tween a term and the things to which the concept may apply, hence the *mediate* meaning of the term is all those things, via the concept.

Similarly, it is the consignification and not the signification that can be amplified or restricted. For example, among the consignifications of a term like *amabilis* ("lovable"), would be "any person," "singular," and "masculine or feminine." In construction with terms like *Petrus est amabilis,* its consignification would be restricted to "third person" and "masculine."

Hispanus' studies were undertaken for a limited goal, which con-cerned the formalization of Latin for the purposes of logic, and especially for dialectic. As a result he studied only a limited number of the total constructions of the language. But because of the nature of his work he came to show very clearly that the parts of speech could not be studied profitably in isolation but only in constructions in which they actually occurred. He also showed, in his examination of sophisms, that con-structions with identical grammatical relations could be interpreted in more than one way, so that neither the pretended lexical definitions of the parts of speech ("a noun is the name of a person, place, or thing") nor the mere grammatical discussions of the functions each part typically assumed (the so-called modes of meaning) could solve problems of am-biguity.

This thinking is shown in the final treatise of the *Summulae Logicales, On Exponibles.* The following is an abbreviated version of only one of the many examples and rules he gave:

An exponible proposition is one whose meaning is obscure and requires an exposition because of some syncategorematic expression implicitly or explicitly contained in it, or contained in some word, as in the following: "Man only is animal." . . . On account of these syncategorematic expressions, the proposition becomes obscure, and requires exposition, and so they are said to make a proposition exponible. . . . Consequently we must investigate them in turn and we will first investigate exclusive signs.

Exclusive signs are those that, in virtue of their consignification, introduce exclusion and so render a proposition exclusive, as do such words as "alone," "single," "only," "merely," "precisely," and so on . . . we now offer rules respecting them.

The first rule is that an exclusive proposition without negation is expounded through an affirmative copulative proposition whose first part is that to which the exclusive sign was prefixed, and the second part of which is a negative proposition denying the predicate of all others apart from the subject; thus "Only man is rational" is equivalent to "Man is rational and nothing other than man is rational."

Without concerning ourselves with this particular example, it can be seen that Hispanus was affirming that some sentences can be understood only when they are related, in a systematic fashion, to other sentences, and sometimes to several sentences:

For example: "No animal except man is rational" is expounded thus: "No animal other than man is rational and man is an animal, and every man is rational" [According to the fourth rule, which says:] "a negative exceptive universal proposition is expounded copulatively by three exponents, in the first of which the predicate is denied of the subject taken with 'other than'; the second is an affirmative proposition in which the term from which an exception is made is asserted of the term which is excepted; in the third, the predicate is affirmed universally of the excepted term."

Although they are basically on a semantic plane, the rules for the formal correspondence of the exponible sentence and its expositions are clearly given. This insight represents an understanding of the term "linguistic system" as found in modern transformational grammars.

The workers who followed Hispanus were called the Modistae, and they exploited only a part of his insights, namely, those concerned with the modes of meaning attached to the typical syntactic functions filled by the morphologically defined parts of speech. Although they did not use this terminology, they tried to distinguish between nouns and nominals, verbs and verbals, and so on. They discussed which terms were always categorematic or syncategorematic and which were sometimes one or the other. They sought to list the kinds of meaning (modes of meaning) that could be expected when a verb (in our terms, morphologically defined), for example, filled the nominal function. Not only did they list these different modes of meaning, which, as mature speakers of the language, they were quite capable of doing, but they tried to explain them as well. This involved them in exploring the relations among the way words have meaning (modes of signification), the way concepts have meaning (modes of understanding), and the way things exist (modes of being). The explanations they developed were not universally accepted, but the kinds of questions they posed influenced Western understanding of language for a considerable period.

THE MODISTAE

Because they concerned themselves with these "modes" of being, understanding, and signifying, those who wrote the speculative grammars, which were entitled "On the Modes of Signification," were called Modistae. They flourished in the late thirteenth and fourteenth centuries at the height of the scholastic period. What they had in common was not, as is often thought, a coherent and agreed-on philosophy but a common logical and dialectic method. Just as there was no single philosophy that could be called "scholastic" as far as content was concerned, there was no common doctrine concerning how the various modes are related. The manner in which the modes are related were seen to depend on the particular kind of ontology (what there is to know), psychology (how we know what we know), and semantics (how we signify what we know) that was held. The Modistae were in agreement about two things: (1) the basic kinds of modes there are and (2) how these modes are principally expressed. The different sorts of modes were expressed in terms of Aristotle's categories, and there were only ten of them: the typical expressions of these modes were to be sought in the Latin language, as analyzed by Priscian.

To help understand what the Modistae were trying to do, it will be useful to show their position in the two main controversies concerning the nature of language. They were firmly on the side of convention in the *Physis-Nomos* dispute, since they did not believe that there is any natural connection between the shape of words and the things words stand for or are connected with. They also took the analogy side in the anomaly-analogy controversy, since they believed that both the universe and grammatical constructions are subject to laws. That is, they believed that both language and the world about them are systematic, in the sense that both consist of a finite number of units that can combine correctly only according to a finite number of laws. It is only these laws that make it possible to obtain knowledge, as far as natural entities are concerned, and to write a grammar, as far as conventional language is concerned. If the Modistae could show a link between the natural laws of the universe and the conventional laws of language, they believed that they could, to that extent, "explain" linguistic usage. Mediating between these two systems was a third, which was concerned with the ways in which we can understand things.

The treatises called "On the Modes of Signification" were often divided into three parts: the first defined and examined the notion of the various modes; the second considered what modes are characteristic of the various parts of speech; and the third dealt with constructions, in terms of their congruity, or bare grammatical correctness, and their perfection, which took into consideration sources of ambiguity on the part of the listener. The speaker presumably would express himself un-ambiguously when he produced a grammatical construction. We can examine the sort of information these three sections provided.

Since the modes are expressed in terms of Aristotle's categories, it will be useful to list them here again:

1. Substance		SUBSTANCE
vs.	*or*	vs.
2. Quantity		
3. Quality		
4. Relation		
5. Place		
6. Time		ACCIDENTS
7. Position		
8. Circumstance		
9. Activity		
10. Passivity		

Listing them in this way brings out the relation between substance and all the rest of the categories. The terms listed here are correlative; that is, substance is what is not an accident, and accidents are what are not substantial; substance is presupposed by accidents, but substance does not (logically) presuppose accidents. Unless there were a substance, a thing, there could not be accidents or properties of a thing, since accidents are, by definition, properties that a thing may or may not have. The *modi essendi,* or modes of being, are, therefore, basically substantial and accidental, and the latter can be divided into the kinds of items listed from 2 to 10. The Modistae make the point that substantiality and accidentality are modes of things and not properties of acts of understanding or signifying.

Turning to the *modi intelligendi,* the ways in which we can know things, the Modistae distinguished active and passive modes of understanding. This distinction was necessary because the expression *intelligendi* in Latin is the sole form of the gerund or gerundive and can be indifferently active or passive. The passive modes of understanding were taken to be properties of things, the capability of a thing being understood in a certain manner. The active modes of understanding were the capacities of the mind or intellect to understand a thing in a particular way. That is, the Modistae considered that since things in the objective order were related to each other substantially or accidentally, they could be understood in those two ways, since this was part of their intelligibility. When, as a matter of fact, the intellect conceived something as a substance or an accident, this was an active mode of understanding, a particular way of conceiving of something.

Correspondingly, in discussing the *modi significandi,* the Modistae distinguished active and passive modes of signifying. The passive modes were properties of things, and the active modes, properties of linguistic expressions, for the same reasons that led to the distinction between active and passive modes of understanding. Table 2 may be helpful in illustrating some of the distinctions that the Modistae made. The fundamental distinction between material and formal (*materialiter* and *formaliter*) draws attention to differences previously discussed in terms of composition versus distribution or function. For example, *materially,* a man is of a certain age, height, weight, national origin, and many other things; *formally,* we could consider him only as a lawyer or taxpayer or taxi driver, and so on.

In Table 2 the Latin terms are given in boldface type, with their English equivalents below.

The point of the distinctions made by the Modistae lies in the fact

Table 2: Some Distinctions Made by the Modistae

	Materialiter	*Formaliter*
	In itself, in its entire concreteness	Functionally, formally, from a particular point of view
Modus essendi	*Proprietas rei*	*Ratio essentiae*
A particular way of existing	A property of a thing, some constituent of its essence	Considered as how a thing is, what kind of thing it is, and not just that it is

Table 2: Some Distinctions Made by the Modistae (*cont.*)

Modus intelligendi activus	*Proprietas intellectus*	*Ratio intelligendi*
A way of actually understanding something	Possessed as an act of the intellect	The function of understanding vs. the function of reasoning or being understood
Modus intelligendi passivus	*Proprietas rei*	*Ratio intelligendi*
A particular way of being understood	A fact or property of a thing that makes it possible to be understood in this way	The function of being understood vs. understanding or existing in a certain way
Modus significandi activus	*Proprietas vocis*	*Ratio significandi*
A particular way of being a sign or particular meaning	Property of a vocal sound to be meaningful, and meaningful determinately	The function of being significant vs. being pronounceable or writable or audible
Modus significandi passivus	*Proprietas rei*	*Ratio significandi*
A particular way of being signified	Property of a thing to be signified in a certain way	This same property, considered precisely as being signified vs. existing, being understood

that words are signs, and, therefore, have active modes of signification, whereas things are not signs but are, rather, signified, and hence, have passive modes of signification. Similarly, things are understandable and thus have passive modes of understanding; but since not all things understand, they need not have active modes of understanding.

As a concrete illustration we can take two items that the Modistae considered to be related as substance and accident: a man and his height. They considered man a substance because he is not related to anything else in the same way as his height is related to him. In this view height is in a substance as in a subject and cannot exist independently, but only as an accidental property of some substance. There is no such independent thing as height in a manner comparable to a tall man, for the man would be a man whether tall or short. From this point of view, then, a man exists in the substantial mode, and his height is in the accidental mode. Men and height being what they are (*modi essendi*), they can be understood as outlined above (have passive modes of understanding). People do generally think about men and their height in this way (active modes of understanding) even though they may not use this terminology.

Further, since men and their height are understood in this fashion, they can be signified as so related (passive modes of signifying); when we express this relation, we use those words that have the active modes of signifying men as subjects and their height as properties of such subjects.

The Modistae then discussed the most basic or general modes of the various parts of speech. With the logicians they distinguished categorematic and syncategorematic terms. They drew a distinction between the principal signification (the lexical meaning of the root) and the accidental signification (also called "consignification," that signaled by the "grammatical accidents" such as gender, number, case, and so on). For the example discussed above, they would find the expression *homo altus* satisfactory, since it is a construction of *nomen substantivum* (noun) and a *nomen adjectivum* (adjective). The general mode of signification for nouns was *per modum entis* or *per modum per se stantis*, that is, "in the mode of an entity," or "something that exists independently." The general mode of the adjectives was *per modum adjacentis*, "in the mode of something that has to inhere in another." The general mode for pronouns was *per modum substantiae*, "in the mode of substantiality," but in an unspecified way, since the pronouns could refer to various kinds of nouns, any of which might be substantial, but could differ among themselves. Besides the general modes of signification, the Modistae, as their work progressed, distinguished "special," and then "very special," modes to take care of examples that did not readily fall into the basic classification. Since these classifications were evidently drawn from the grammatical analysis of Priscian, they therefore share the weakness of that analysis, particularly in the realm of syntax. But the Modistae thought that by using this method they could show that there was a conformity among the modes of signifying, understanding, and being.

Notice that here, for the first time, the question of truth is explicitly raised, that is, the conformity of linguistic expression to thought (moral truth, as opposed to lying) and the conformity of thought to things (ontological truth, or objective knowledge). Although the Modistae were not agreed on the problems involved, it is precisely on this point that later Scholastics attacked them and later thinkers ridiculed them.

At first glance it would appear that this ridicule was justified, since the system of the Modistae seems to equate the structure of the world of things with that of the human mind, and both of these with the structure of the Latin language they used. It seems not unreasonable to assume, too, that some of the Modistae actually believed just that. Such a view, however, is neither justified by their system, nor coherent with their positions on the *Physis-Nomos* and anomaly-analogy controversies. Neither is it a necessary consequence of the Aristotelian notions employed, according to the prevalent understanding of that period.

After listing the categories, Aristotle had pointed out that the terms in which they were expressed, since they were terms in isolation, were neither true nor false, since truth and falsity in his system were found only in "conjunction" of terms, in propositions. As obvious as this may seem, it may be worthwhile to make explicit what seems to be implicit in this position.

1. The ten categories represent one of an indefinite number of ways in which the data of experience can be divided into descriptive sets. Others have proposed longer or shorter sets of categories and have shown how Aristotle's ten categories sometimes overlap.

2. These categories are not in a one-to-one relation with either the parts of speech or the basic, obligatory constructions of either Greek or Latin.

3. Because Latin and Greek have a particular set of parts of speech and obligatory constructions, these languages are two of an indefinite number of ways in which the data of experience can be divided into descriptive sets. In this connection languages resemble the categories, but are more complex sets of descriptive expressions than the categories.

4. Other languages have neither the same number nor the same kind of parts of speech and obligatory constructions as Latin and Greek.

5. Nonetheless, it is possible to make statements that are true (not lies) or false (lies) in any language.

6. It is also possible to make statements that are true (objective, verifiable knowledge) or false (refutable, misrepresentations) in any language.

7. Because their structures differ, not all languages are required to make the same kinds of observations about the data of experience.

8. Since the physical and psychological endowment of human beings appears to be about equal, most observations could probably be made in any language: easily in some, laboriously in others.

Most of these points escaped the Modistae and the rest of the medievals; they were not well enough acquainted with languages other than Latin or Greek. It is understandable, then, that later attacks were based mainly on differences of opinion about ontological and psychological problems.

The work of the Modistae had advantages as well as disadvantages. Some of the weak points are obvious: they were tempted to conclude that there was some kind of mechanical connection among the properties of things, the way things are conceived, and the way they are expressed. As inconsistent as this thinking was, it would return the study of language almost to the plane of the *Cratylus*. Again, the Modistae, following the logical tradition, were mainly concerned with examining declarative sentences, in a way that required more deliberate attention than most people are capable of. Finally, the real difficulty was that the kind of "grammar" they examined was semantic, not formal. Roger Bacon, who wrote one of the first speculative grammars, thought that grammar is substantially the same in all languages and that differences are only accidental. He concluded that "a person knowing grammar in one language knows the grammar of all languages, except for accidental differences." Since the Modistae were studying a "grammar of meanings," Bacon's statement is really an affirmation that the languages he studied (he had written a grammar of Greek and Hebrew) could—or did—express the same sorts of content in similar ways.

However, there were some positive results yielded by the method of the Modistae as well as the negative ones cited by later critics. Since the grammar of the Modistae was based on meanings, it did rigorously show the relations among (1) a language like Latin as used in the medieval universities; (2) the world as the medievals described it to themselves; and (3) the language used by people of common educational background. Their work reminds us forcibly that much of grammar, and linguistics, consists of a particular way of talking about language, however it is defined. Those who share the same experience can talk to each other readily. Those with divergent interests and problems communicate less well, since they lack a common language. As a matter of historical fact, the work of the dialecticians and the Modistae resulted in a more rigorous criticism of texts in all the faculties of the universities, since the common method of instruction in all of them (arts, medicine, law, philosophy, and theology) was the reading of a text followed by an analytic commentary on it. Because of the rigor of their method and their insistence on clear definitions, the work of the Modistae was easy to refute. Later critics of their work learned a good deal, not so much from their positive doctrine as from their clear formulation of the kinds of problems that had interested them.

ETYMOLOGY

One way in which the meaning of an expression was assigned by the medievals—a method still often used today—was to consider its etymology. There was little accurate information about the history and development of languages at that time, although Latin and Greek texts from various periods were available for comparison. It was simply a known fact that language did change, and, in particular, that the medieval form of Latin was not that of the classic period. The medievals were also well aware of the existence of many other languages, but few were interested in learning languages other than those in which the Scriptures had been written or into which they had been translated. It should be clear, then, that the definition the medievals gave "etymology" was not what we would expect to find in a modern dictionary.

The most authoritative source for medieval etymology was the twenty-volume *Etymologies* of Saint Isidore of Seville (d. 636). The work deals with varied subjects, including grammar, rhetoric, dialectic, mathematics, medicine, law, ecclesiastical matters, geographical and political topics, mineralogy, farming, warfare, shipbuilding, housekeeping, and many others. Some of the summary accounts of the liberal arts are still useful, but the majority of the chapters, though amusing as a Sunday supplement, are rarely as reliable.

Isidore described etymology as follows:

Etymology is the origin of words, whence the meaning of a noun or verb is gathered by interpretation. . . . A knowledge of this is often necessary for interpretation, since when we see where a name comes from, we more quickly understand its meaning. The study of any subject is easier when the etymology of the terms used in it is understood. Not all names were imposed according to the nature of things, just as we are accustomed to name our slaves and possessions as the mood moves us.

That is why many etymologies can no longer be found, since some of the words no longer have the qualities they originally had, but, according to the whim of men, have become other words.

But the etymology of words is assigned (1) from a cause like *reges* from *regendo* ["rulers" from "ruling"], (2) from origin, like *homo* from *humo* ["man" from "the slime of the earth"], (3) from contraries, like *lutum* from *lavando* ["dirt" from "washing"] since *lutum* is not clean, or *lucus* ("grove") from *lucendo* ("shining") since deep shade gives little light [*parum luceat*].

Some etymologies are also made (4) from the derivation of a name, like *prudens* from *prudentia* ["prudent" from "prudence"] and some from (5) vocal sounds, like *graculus* ["jackdaw"] from *garullitate* ["noisy chattering"], and some (6) from a Greek source, but declined in a Latin fashion, like *silva* and *domus*. Some are derived (8) from the names of places, cities, and rivers, and many (9) from the languages of different nations, so that their origin can hardly be known, for there are very many foreign names that are not intelligible, both in Latin and in Greek.

Further quotations from Isidore's work will indicate the kind of information it contains. We can also see how little "folk etymology" has progressed over the centuries:

DIFFERENT LANGUAGES

The different languages are a result of the Tower of Babel, and before that, there was a single language, Hebrew, both spoken and written by the Prophets and Patriarchs. . . . The three sacred languages are Latin, Greek, and Hebrew . . . and because of the obscurity of the Scriptures, they are useful, since one can compare the rendering in one with that in another. . . .

Greek is considered the clearest of all languages, since it is more sonorous than Latin and all other languages, and its varieties can be divided into five: the first is called *koinē* or *mista* (common or mixed), which all use; the second is Attic or Athenian, which all the Greek writers used. The third is Doric, which the Egyptians (Alexandrians?) have, and the fourth is Ionic, the fifth Aeolic, which the Aeolians use, and in which one can note certain differences in the observance of the Greek language, for their usage is divergent.

Some have said that there are four Latin languages, the Original, the Latin, the Roman, and the Mixed [*Prisca, Latina, Romana, Mista*]. The Original was what the ancient inhabitants of Italy used, under Janus and Saturn, and it is found to be irregular. . . . The Roman language began after the people of Rome demanded kings; Latin was spoken under Latinus and the kings of Tuscany by the rest of the people in Latium. Roman was the language in which the poets Naevius, Plautus, Ennius, and Virgil wrote, and the orators like Gracchus, Cato, and Cicero. The Mixed or Common language arose after the fall of the Empire and spread with the customs and men descending upon Rome, corrupting the integrity of words by solecisms and barbarisms.

All the Oriental nations jam tongue and words together in the throat, like the Hebrews and Syrians. All the Mediterranean peoples push their enunciation forward to the palate, like the Greeks and the Asians. All the Occidentals break their words on the teeth, like the Italians and Spaniards. . . .

But the language of each and every man, whether Greek or Latin or other nation, can be learned either by listening to it or by studying with an instructor. Even though the knowledge of all languages is a difficult task for a single person, no one is so idle that he would be ignorant of his own language when he lives among his own people. For what else could be thought of such a man, than that he is worse than the brute animals? They at least manifest themselves with the noise of the voices they have, and he would be worse than they, who lacked knowledge of his own tongue.

DIFFERENT NATIONS

The Germans are so-called because of their immense bodies (*GerMANIae: imMANIa corpora*). . . . The Saxon nation, on the shores of the Ocean and in impassable swamps, are famed for their valor and agility, and thus they are so called because they are a hardy and powerful race of men and excel the other pirates. [*Saxonum* probably recalls *saxa*, rocks.] The Franks, some think, are so called from one of their leaders, but others believe that the name comes from their wild customs and natural ferocity. . . . It is suspected that the Britons are so called in Latin because they are brutes [*Britones: bruti*], and a race dwelling as it were outside the earth. Virgil has this to say of them, that "they are cut off from the whole world." . . .

GRAMMAR

The basic elements of the grammatical art are the Letters, which are common both to writers and calculators. Letters were discovered in order to remember things . . . letters are so called because they provide a journey to the reader, or because they are repeated in reading. [In Latin: *litterae autem dicuntur quasi legiterae quod in lectione iterentur.* . . . . In Latin "journey" is *iter;* the word *iterentur* here means "they are repeated."]

The Latin and Greek letters seem to be derived from the Hebrew, for among them the first letter is called *Aleph,* so that, because of the similar pronunciation, the Greeks have *Alpha* and the Latins *A.* But the Hebrews have 22 characters, the Greeks 24, and the Latins 23. . . .

Grammar is the science of correct speaking, the origin and basis of the liberal arts. It is also an art, following rules and regulations. . . .

Aristotle first set up two parts of speech, the noun and verb. Then Donatus defined eight, but all of them revert to the two principal ones, that is, to the noun and verb, which signify person and act. The rest are appendixes and take their origin from them. For the pronoun derives from the noun, whose function it fulfills . . . the adverb derives from the noun, like *doctus, docte;* the participle is from the noun and verb, as in *lego, legens,* but the conjunction, preposition, and interjection are a mixture of all of them.

A noun is a kind of notification (*nomen, notamen*) . . . the pronoun is so called because it takes the place of a noun . . . the verb is so called because it makes the air reverberate . . . and the adverb is something that happens to a verb . . . the participle is so called because it shares the parts of the noun and the verb (*PARTICIPium PARTes CAPIat* . . .) the conjunction, because it joins thoughts, the preposition, because it is preposed to the noun and verb, and the interjection, because it is interjected into the sentence.

It is signicant that Isidore himself did not attach historical significance to any of his etymologies, except those that were derived from known place names or forms thought to be Greek borrowings. When the origin of an expression is unknown, as is usually the case, it is supplied, as Isidore put it, by "interpretation." This method appears to be the substitution of a more familiar expression for the less familiar, since the purpose is to assist the memory of students in learning the vocabulary of a particular discipline. Sometimes these "equivalents" are more or less convertible through translation, as in the familiar case of "philosopher" = "lover of wisdom," but in the more memorable cases of medieval etymology, they are not: for example, *lapis* ("stone") is said to have as its *etymon,* or "original form," *LAedens PEdem,* more easily seen when the word is in the accusative, *lapidem.* Better still is the etymology of cadaver ("corpse"), from *CAro DAta VERmibus* ("flesh given to the worms").

As fanciful as such etymologies were, they were quoted faithfully for centuries, and for some scholars provided a basis for argumentation. The level is obviously not higher than that attained in the *Cratylus,* but scholars would not be able to do much better until much more rigorous methods for comparing languages were developed in the nineteenth century.

PRESCRIPTIVE GRAMMAR

When discussing traditional grammar in America or England we are referring to two main sets of data: the general and speculative views about the nature of language, which we have seen develop from the Greek period, and the work of a number of English grammarians in the eighteenth century who subscribed to these views. It will be useful to inquire about the kind of information they had about language and the work that had been done before the definitive character was given to English grammar in the eighteenth century.

Exploration and the expansion of trade had brought about an increased awareness of the great variety in languages, and tentative comparisons of English and other languages were made. Scholars were uniformly convinced of the basic nature of language as explained by Aristotle: it was conventional, a sign of thoughts and ideas. Writing was a respresentation of sounds, and both writing and sounds varied from one nation to another, but the things people talked about were substantially the same. These ideas were expressed by Roger Bacon (1214–1294), the author of Greek and Hebrew grammars. The fact that languages change was also appreciated fully, and this change was generally considered a kind of inevitable corruption. The author of an anonymous dictionary of the seventeenth century put it this way:

The Confusion of Languages at Babel (for before it, all the World spoke the same Dialect, supposed to be Hebrew) gave Rise to all the several Languages in the Universe; of which the primitive Language of this Nation was one; and had it not been corrupted, perhaps as good and intelligible as the best . . . altered in a thousand or two thousand Years by Conquests, Invasions, Transmigration of the Government; so that . . . it is brought to what we now find it, even a Composition of most, if not all the Languages of Europe, especially Belgick or Low-Dutch, Saxon, Teutonick or High-Dutch, Cambro-British or Welsh, French, Spanish, Italian and Latin; and now and then of the Old and Modern Danish and Ancient High-Dutch; also of Greek, Hebrew, Arabick, Chaldee, Syriack and Turckick.

[Preface, *Gazophylacium Anglicanum,* 1689]

But the persuasion that foreign borrowings necessarily entailed corruption of the language was not universal:

Whereas our tongue is mixed, it is no disgrace, when as all the tongues of Europe do participate interchangeably the one of the other, and in the learned tongues, there hath beene like borrowing one from another. . . . It is false . . . that our tongue is the most mixt and corrupt of all other. For if it may please any but to compare the Lords' Prayer in other languages, he shall

find as few Latine and borrowed forraine words in ours as in any other whatsoever. . . .

[William Camden (1551–1623), *Remaines
Concerning Britaine*]

Variety in the vocabulary and usage in the different parts of England
were also a source of confusion. The printer Caxton related that a
merchant from Sheffield was mistaken for a Frenchman when he asked for
"eggs" instead of "eyren" near London (Prologue to the *Eneydos*, 1490.)
Another observer, Richard Verstegan of Rowlands, saw that this was a
natural development of the language and not the result of borrowing:

we see that in the seueral parts of England it self both the names of things,
and pronountiations of woords are somewhat different, and that among the
countrey people that neuer borrow woords out of the Latin or French, and of
this different pronountiation one example in steed of many shall suffise, as this:
for pronouncing according as one would say at London I would eat more
cheese yf I had it the northern man saith, Ay sud eat mare cheese gin ay hadet
and the westerne man saith: Chud eat more cheese and chad it. . . . These
differēces in one same language do commōly grow among the common people
& sometimes vpon the parants imitating the il pronountiation of their yong
children, and of il pronountiation lastly ensuyeth il wryting. . . .

[*A Restitution of Decayed Intelligence*, 1605]

As a consequence of these difficulties in understanding, there was a
lively demand for dictionaries. The first of these, published in England,
was Robert Cawdrey's *Table Alphabeticall*, which appeared in 1604.
The title page of this work set the scope, audience, and arrangement of
a long line of successors:

A

Table Alphabeticall, con-
teyning and teaching the true
writing, and understanding of hard
usuall English Wordes, borrowed from
the Hebrew, Greeke, Latine
or French, etc.

with the interpretation thereof by
plaine English words, gathered for the benefit &
helpe of Ladies, Gentlewomen, or any other
unskilfull persons

Whereby they may the more easilie
and better understand many hard English
wordes, which they shall heare or read in
Scriptures, Sermons, or elsewhere, and also
be made able to use the same aptly
themselves.

The ladies, in particular, seemed to have been considered in need of such helps, since they were often classed with "young Schollers, Clarkes, Merchants, as also Strangers of any Nation" (Henry Cockeram's *The English Dictionaries*, 1623). Thomas Blount intended his *Glossographie* (1656) for "the more knowing women and less-knowing men." Later works professed to be dedicated to a more general public, "as well for the Entertainment of the Curious, as the Information of the Ignorant" (Nathan Bailey's *Universal Etymological English Dictionary*, 1721). When less grand goals were aimed at, as in Dyche and Pardon's *New General English Dictionary* (1735), the book was thought worthy

for the Information of the Unlearned, and particularly recommended to those Boarding-Schools where English only is taught, as is the case commonly among the Ladies [who could expect not only to learn to spell, but also to write] . . . coherently and correctly, the Want whereof is universally complained of among the Fair Sex.

These early dictionaries showed an uncertain wavering between the ordinary problems encountered by schoolmasters with their pupils and the need of synonyms for the "hard words," derived from classical Latin and Greek sources, liberally sprinkled through contemporary writings to "give an air of elegance." Some such dictionaries seemed to vie with each other in classical terms of ever greater obscurity, so that one lexicographer accused another of introducing

An innumerable multitude of Greek, Latin, French, Italian, Spanish, British, Saxon and Old English Words . . . without changing their Original Terminations, and which are never used in English; with others . . . never us'd or understood any where else.

[Preface to J.K.'s *A New English Dictionary*, 1702]

The lexicographer was also tempted to become an encyclopedist, reminding one of the *Etymologies* of Isidore of Seville. One of the earliest dictionaries promises to give full information on

God and Goddesses, Men and Women, Boyes and Maids, Giants and Devils, Birds and Beasts, Monsters and Serpents, Wells and Rivers, Herbs, Stones, Trees, Dogs, Fishes, and the like

[Part III of Henry Cockeram's *English Dictionarie*, 1650]

In this work we read:

Crocodile, a Beast hatched of an Eg, yet some of them grow to a great bignesse, as ten, twentie, or thirthy foot in length, it hath cruell teeth, and a scaly back, with very sharp claws on his feet; if it see a man afraid of him, it will eagerly pursue him, but on the contrary, if he be assaulted, he will shun him. Having eaten the body of a man, it will weep over the head, but in fine eat the head also; thence came the Proverb, She shed Crocodile tears, viz. fained tears.

Dictionaries included treatises on classical literature, mythology and biography, gradually turning to the inclusion of ordinary, as well as learned, words and the explanation of the newest terms in current science, particularly Newtonian mathematics. At first the "ordinary words" were given synonyms, at best, and at worst:

ABOUT, as about Noon
To sit ABROOD upon eggs, as a bird does
to ACCENT words
AKE, as, my head akes
              . . .
An ELEPHANT, a beast
A GOAT, a beast. . . .

[J.K.'s *A New English Dictionary*, 1702]

A revised edition of this work (1713) had considerably improved definitions:

A GAD, a measure of 9 or 10 feet, a small bar of steel
A GALLOP, the swiftest pace of a horse. . . .

Another attempt to help the reader understand the meaning of "hard words" was to assign their etymology. The first to do this was Thomas Blount in his *Glossographia*, modeled on the work of Latin-English dictionaries. Some of his "etymologies," as well as later ones are a bit far-fetched:

SHREW, a kind of Field-Mouse, which if he go over a beasts back will make him lame in the Chine; and if he bite, the beast swells to the heart and dyes. . . . From hence came our English phrase, *I beshrew thee,* when we wish ill; and we call a curst woman, a Shrew.

[Blount, *Glossographia*, 1656]

A JADE or tired horse, from the AS. *Eode, he went;* [that is] he went once, but can go no more; as we say in Latin *vixit* for *mortuus est.* Or from the Lat. *Cadere,* to fall down: Or from the AS. *Gaad,* a goad, or spur; [that is] an horse that will not go without the spur.

[*Gazophylacium Anglicanum*, 1689]

An earlier method, not followed by subsequent dictionaries, was to arrange words in natural meaning groups, such as *ship, shipwright, keel, prow,* and so on (John Withals' *A Shorte Dictionairie for Yonge Begynners, in the Study of Latin,* 1553). As the title of Cawdrey's work suggests, later works were alphabetically arranged, though sometimes divided into topical sections.

Some scholars, for example, Blount in his *Glossographia,* 1656, tried to convey the meaning of an expression by showing its use in the writings of current authors. This practice was not followed with any degree of consistency until the appearance of the work of Benjamin Martin (*Lingua Brittanica Reformata,* 1749) and Samuel Johnson (*A Dictionary of the English Language,* 1755).

The task of these early dictionaries was not merely to give the meaning of difficult and ordinary words but also to stabilize spelling. The selections given above indicate that English habits of spelling were hardly fixed. There were two principal attempts to bring some regularity into English spelling—a statement of preferences by various authors and reform movements led by those who had prestige and influence. In his *Familiar Letters* (c. 1645) James Howell (d. 1666) explained that he would omit the final *e* in words like *done, some, come* because foreigners are deceived into pronouncing the endings as "disillables"; he also preferred the Latin to the French spelling of Latin derivatives, *Physic* to *Physique,* and *Afric* to *Afrique,* which also served as a warning that he would omit the "Dutch K" in *physick* and *Africk.* Also recommended were the Latin forms *honor, favor,* and *labor* instead of *honour, favour,* and *labour; war* and *star* for *warre* and *starre; pity* and *piety* for *pitie* and *pietie.* Christopher Cooper, in his *Grammatica Linguae Anglicanae,* allowed a choice between *Apricock* and *abricot, balet* and *balad, bankrupt* and *bankrout, clot* and *clod, licorice* and *liquorish, vat* and *fat, yelk* and *yolk* (1685). Thomas Dyche (*A Guide to the English Tongue,* 1710) agreed with Howell on the spelling of *honor, humor,* "because, when the Word increases, it drops, as *humour, humorist, humorsom.* . . ."

Despite the efforts of authors, pedagogs, and specialists, however, the task of the dictionaries seemed in vain, since many had tried, but none had succeeded, in reforming the orthographic habits of the English:

several persons have taken much pains about the Orthography. . . . Sir Thomas Smith, Secretary to Queen Elisabeth . . . after him, this subject was in another Discourse prosecuted by one of the Heralds who calls himself Chester . . . followed by one Wade . . . Bullaker endeavored to add to, and alter divers things . . . succeeded in the same attempt by Alexander Gill. . . . Yet so invincible is Custom, that we still retain the same errors and incongruities in writing which our Forefathers taught us.

[John Wilkins (1614–1672), *An Essay Towards a Real Character and a Philosophical Language,* 1668]

Linked to the problem of correct spelling, of course, was that of correct pronunciation, which, during this period, was termed "orthoepy." One reason for the difficulty was a lack of phonetic sophistication. As early as the mid-seventeenth century instructions were given in an English grammar concerning the production of sounds, but of a quite elementary sort:

If the breath, expelled through the throat to the lips, is intercepted by the closed lips, the letter P is formed . . . if it does not reach the lips, but is intercepted in the palatal region (the tip of the tongue being moved to the front of the palate, or, which is the same thing, to the roots of the upper teeth), the consonant T is formed. . . .

[John Wallis, *Grammatica Linguae Anglicanae*, 1653]

The dictionary practice of indicating the accent on words was introduced by Thomas Dyche (1723) and continued by Thomas Bailey in a revision of his *Universal Etymological Dictionary* in 1727. By the beginning of the nineteenth century tentative descriptions of the "organick formation of the vowels" were given in the dictionaries, for example, in John Walker's *Critical Pronouncing Dictionary*, which included rules for the "native of Scotland, Ireland and London, for avoiding their respective peculiarities." Walker recognized three degrees of stress in English, but was wholly inept in his description of the vowels. In describing the consonants he said that the difference between voiced and voiceless sounds was "a nice distinction," and thought the whole question of a physical description of the production of sounds "rather curious than useful."

Even more hotly disputed than differences of vocabulary or pronunciation were problems of grammar. No better proof could be offered that the norm of "correctness" in language was sheerly a matter of prestige than to quote some of the positions and counterpositions taken during the eighteenth century concerning the nature of grammar in general and the state of English grammar in particular. No one questioned that language was conventional, that usage or custom was the ultimate arbiter of correctness. Yet, in expressing their annoyance at the grammatical habits of other authors, leading figures of this period spoke of reforming and fixing the language in such a way as to suggest that there was a viable universal grammar, from which the rules for contemporary English usage could be deduced.

It was not that there was a dearth of English grammars. Since medieval times there had been grammatical studies for schoolboys, and summaries, or "compendious grammars," were added to the dictionaries after Dyche and Pardon's *New General English Dictionary* (1735). More or less extended grammatical works on English were published by Bullakar (1586), Wallis (1653), Wilkins (1668), Cooper (1685), and Harris (1751).

What was chiefly lacking was a grammatical work by an author whose prestige and reasoned approach could motivate others to accept him as the final arbiter. Another factor that inspired the English to standardize spelling and grammatical usage was the example of the French and Italians, both of whom had established academies for the regularization and codification of their languages. The English envied the success of the Italian Academia della Crusca (1582) and the French Académie, founded by Cardinal Richelieu in 1635. Both of these bodies had published authoritative works on what was acceptable and what was not in vocabulary, pronunciation, and grammatical construction.

In 1694 the *Dictionnaire de L'Académie Française* was completed. In 1698 Daniel Defoe proposed a society similar to the French Académie,

to encourage polite learning, to polish and refine the English tongue, and to advance the so much neglected faculty of correct language, to establish the purity and propriety of style, and to purge it from all the irregular additions that ignorance and affectation have introduced, and all those innovations in speech, if I may call them such, which some dogmatic writers have the confidence to foster upon their native language, as if their authority were sufficient to make their own fancy legitimate. . . .

> [*The Earlier Life and the Chief Earlier Works of Daniel Defoe,*
> H. Morley, ed., London, 1889, pp. 125–126]

Dryden too felt that there was need for some standard of correctness, such as the French and Italian academies:

How barbarously we yet write and speak, your lordship knows, and I am sensible in my own English. For I am often put to a stand, in considering whether I write the idiom of the tongue or false grammar. . . . I am desirous, if it were possible, that we might all write with the same certainty of words, and purity of phrase, to which the Italians first arrived, and after them the French; at least that we might advance so far, as our tongue is capable of such a standard.

> [Dedication of "Troilus and Cressida" to the Earl of Sunderland]

The formation of such a society was long discussed and debated, but never successfully founded, although several members of the Royal Society were appointed to function as such a body. As a result many authors lamented the lack of a standard. Thomas Stackhouse, in 1731, wrote, "We write by guess, more than by any stated rule, and form every man his own diction, either according to his humor and caprice or in pursuance of a blind and servile imitation." And William Warburton, in 1747, complained that the English tongue

is yet destitute of a Test or Standard to apply to, in cases of doubt or difficulty . . . for we have neither Grammar nor Dictionary, neither Charts nor Compass, to guide us through this wide sea of words.

Besides their uncertainty about what was and what was not "grammatical," many people were convinced that English had to be refined as well as standardized. What was the source of this refinement? For the most part, it was the language of some previous author or period, the "good old days" to which they looked as an ideal, an ideal to which subsequent writers had been false. The views of this period, however, varied considerably from author to author. Dryden felt that the "purity of the English tongue" began with Chaucer, and he doubted that it had been going downhill as much as others suspected. Swift's opinion was that English had begun to be a refined tongue with the beginning of Elizabeth's reign and had ceased to be so "with the great rebellion in '42":

From the civil war to the present time, I am apt to doubt whether the corruptions of our language have not at least equalled the refinements in it, and these corruptions very few of the best authors have wholly escaped.

[*Proposal for Correcting and Ascertaining the English Tongue*, 1712]

Samuel Johnson seems to have agreed with this position, and in his *Dictionary* he said: "I have studiously endeavored to collect examples from the writers before the Restoration, whose works I regard as the wells of English undefiled, as the pure source of genuine diction."

Writers of a later date, for example, Priestley, Sheridan, and the American Noah Webster, looked back on the period of the Restoration, or that of Swift, as the golden age of English.

It is a useful oversimplification to divide the men of this period who were concerned about the state of English and what should be done about it into conservative and liberal camps. The conservatives were typically concerned with arresting linguistic change and restoring past glories to the tongue, since they would then be in more secure and familiar surroundings. The liberals were more able to admit the presence of innovations and willing to let such novelties stand their own test of popularity and time. The conservatives, for peace of mind or peace in the coffee house, were willing to put their trust in the authority of a single pundit; the liberals preferred the slower verdict of a more diffuse kind of approbation, the acceptance of respected writers.

The following passage would seem to classify Lord Chesterfield among the conservatives, if only tongue-in-cheek:

It must be owned that our language is at present in a state of anarchy; and hitherto, perhaps, it may not have been the worse for it. . . . The time for discrimination seems to be now come. Toleration, adoption and naturalization have run their lengths. Good order and authority are now necessary. But where shall we find them, and at the same time, the obedience due them? We must have recourse to the old Roman expedient in times of confusion, and chuse a dictator. Upon this principle, I give my vote for Mr. Johnson to fill that great and arduous post. And I hereby declare that I make a total surrender of all my rights and privileges to the said Mr. Johnson during the period of his dictatorship . . . and hold him infallible while in the chair; but no longer.

["The World," 28 November, 1754]

One reason that the conservatives were desirous of "ascertaining" the language was that they feared their works would be as unintelligible to an audience in 300 years as Chaucer's works were to them. When he

published his celebrated plan for the *Dictionary* in 1747 Johnson seemed
to think that he could avert such a tragedy. He proposed to produce
"a dictionary by which the pronunciation of our language may be fixed
and its attainment facilitated; by which its purity may be preserved, its
use ascertained, and its duration lengthened."

When he had completed the work in 1755, however, Johnson saw
that this was a forlorn hope:

When we see old men die at a certain time, one after the other, century after
century, we laugh at the elixir which promises to prolong life to a thousand
years, and with equal justice may the lexicographer be derided, who, being
able to produce no sample of a nation that has preserved their words and
phrases from mutability, shall imagine that his dictionary can embalm the
language, and secure it from corruption and decay. . . .

He pointed out that "sounds are too volatile for legal restraints"
and that the "French language has visibly changed under the inspection
of the Academy." After the publication of Johnson's *Dictionary*, and
the *Grammar* of Bishop Lowth, there was less demand for an English
academy, possibly because a substitute had been found in these twins of
prescriptive grammar. Both Johnson and Lowth saw very clearly that
language is what custom has made it, and no individual can legislate
linguistic reality out of existence. Yet both of them, secure in the sound-
ness of their judgment, felt justified in prescribing some expressions and
proscribing others.

Taking up Swift's accusation that the writing of England's best
authors is ungrammatical, Lowth distinguished between the idea that
English is "in its nature irregular and capricious, not hitherto subject,
nor easily reducible to a System of rules" and that which held that the
usage of the "politest part of the nation . . . our most approved authors,
often offends against every part of Grammar." He believed that English
has simple rules and that the best authors violated them. He felt that
the reason for these offenses is not that English is complex, but that,
unlike the ancient languages, it has few formal distinctions:

Its Substantives have but one variation of Case; nor have they any distinction
of Gender, beside that which nature hath made. Its adjectives admit of no
change at all, except that which expresses the degrees of comparison. All the
possible variations of the original form of the Verb are not above six or
seven; whereas in many Languages they amount to some hundreds; and almost
the whole business of Modes, Times and Voices, is managed with great ease
by the assistance of eight or nine commodious little Verbs, called from their
use, Auxiliaries. . . . The Truth is, Grammar is very much neglected among
us. . . . Yet the want of it will not be effectually supplied by any other
advantages whatsoever. . . .

[Preface, *A Short Introduction to English Grammar; with Critical Notes,* 1762]

The reason for the need of a grammar is not far to seek: the best English authors have had the advantage of each others' company, but they still write ungrammatical English. Bishop Lowth seemed to be convinced that there is a universal grammar, but that it cannot be taught abstractly. Thus he felt it best to start the young student with the grammar of our native language, and "when he has a competent knowledge of the main principles of Grammar in general, exemplified in his own language, he will then apply himself with great advantage to the study of another."

Lowth's position represented an advance over the idea that in studying Latin one first learned "grammar" pure and simple. Yet Bacon's view that "grammar" is somehow substantially the same in all languages, with the differences merely accidental, persisted. This idea would be true of a "grammar of meanings" if the meanings were shared consistently by the cultures of several language groups, but certainly it does not apply to the formal grammatical properties of two languages as different as Latin and English. If we granted that students were taught to look first for examples of formal contrasts rather than for expressions of predetermined meanings, we could agree with Lowth's opinion that

if children were first taught the common principles of Grammar, by some short system of English Grammar, which, happily by its simplicity and facility is perhaps better fitted than that of any other language for such a purpose, they would have some notion of what they were going about, when they should enter upon Latin Grammar. . . .

[Preface to *A Short Introduction*]

Lowth made an excellent formal observation about the modes of the verb: "there are no more Modes in any language than there are forms of the Verb appropriated to the denoting of such different manners of representation." Unfortunately, he went on to show that there is a subjunctive in English, which confuses the morphological distinctions in the verb with the syntactic constructions that would translate the various uses of the subjunctive in Latin. He took up the rule of *shall* and *will* found in John Wallis' *Grammatica Linguae Anglicanae* (1653), "*shall* is the simple future in the first person, where *will* promises or threatens; in the 2nd and 3rd persons, *shall* promises or threatens, *will* is the simple future," but added that the reverse is true in questions (*A Short Introduction*).

The form of the past participles gave Lowth some concern, and he allowed *beaten* as an alternative to *beat, bursten* to *burst, hoven* as the past participle of *heave, strucken* and *striken,* and *-en* forms for *sit, lie* (*lien*), *bake, fold, wash,* and *wreathe,* considering these the "regular" formations. But some forms have the sanction of custom, and, although barbarous, must be admitted, for example, *I have wrote, I have drank.* Citing a passage of Milton, Lowth called for the nominative form in phrases where *when, while, after,* and so on are omitted:

> God from the mount of Sinai, whose gray top
> Shall tremble, *He* descending. . . .

Dr. Bentley, a contemporary of Lowth, suggested *Him descending,* since it is equivalent to an ablative absolute in Latin, or perhaps *his,* because it could be a genitive absolute in Greek.

In his desire to reduce the grammar to rules, Lowth declared ungrammatical many expressions that were in common use among the best writers of his day; for instance:

It has been rightly observed, that the Verb *had* in the common phrase *I had rather,* is not properly used . . . it seems to have arisen from a mere mistake, in resolving the familiar and ambiguous abbreviation *I'd rather* into *I had rather* instead of *I would rather,* which latter is the regular, analogous and proper expression.

Other expressions outlawed by Lowth have had lasting influence, and today some of them are now regarded as being as inherently logical because they are our present regularities, although they are actually in use as a result of one man's preference.

For example, reputable authors of Lowth's day commonly used *you was,* which Lowth rejected for *you were;* they also had *He is taller than I* and *He is taller than me* as free variants. Lowth formulated the rule now taught, that the form of the pronoun depends on the construction that follows, for example, *He is taller than I* (*am*), which makes *than* a conjunction and *like* a preposition. Double negatives were often used, as in *He doesn't have none,* but appeared barbarous to Lowth, who formulated the rule that two negatives make an affirmative.

There were other writers who took up linguistic problems, but none enjoyed the prestige and influence of Lowth. Lowth's *A Short Introduction* went through many editions, and its influence was seen in the widely used grammar of Lindley Murray, which was modeled on Lowth's work. Other grammars were presented as "introductions" to Lowth's work.

After the publication of Johnson's *Dictionary* and Lowth's *Grammar* there was still lively discussion about the fundamental principles involved in correct usage. One of the better-developed accounts is found in sections of George Campbell's *Philosophy of Rhetoric* (1776). Campbell pointed out that while the logician may, in some sense, be dealing with universals to be found in any culture, "the art of the Grammarian is always particular and local." The term "universal grammar" is, therefore, a misleading expression, since there is no universal language. Each particular language is purely a "species of fashion" and that fashion is the sole authority for the rules the grammarian reports. It makes no difference whatever what source these fashions have, according to Campbell, since "they no sooner obtain and become general than they are laws of the language, and the grammarians' only business is to note, collect and methodize them."

Of course, Lowth would have said that this was all he was doing—that is, discovering the analogies of the language and ironing out jarring exceptions to the prevailing regularities. Campbell thought this illegitimate:

> Every single anomaly, then, though departing from the rule assigned to other words of the same class, and on that account called an exception, stands on the same basis on which the rules of the tongue are founded, custom having prescribed for it a separate rule.

This being the case, Campbell agreed with Lowth's basic answer to Swift's complaint that "in many instances, our language offends against every part of grammar," since this statement seemed to presuppose some abstract grammar to which all the particular grammars of different languages are supposed to conform. Once it is admitted that "grammar is from general use," it is absurd "to accuse the language, which is purely what is conformable to general use in writing and speaking, as offending against general use."

If what Swift meant is that English has no rules, then he put his point poorly, since, according to Campbell, "where there is no law, there is no transgression." Campbell was persuaded that not only English but "the most uncultivated language on earth" is under the influence of grammar.

"Usage" as Campbell employed the term requires some explanation. In his view it is not just any kind or anyone's usage that makes an expression correct. Campbell suggested that usage must be (1) reputable, (2) national, and (3) contemporary. Usage must be "reputable," since he believed that 99 percent of his contemporaries spoke and wrote poorly as a result of their lack of education and contact with suitable models. Yet he said there is a norm for good language, since the latter has won "the approbation of those who have not attained it." This is the style of the more celebrated—not necessarily the best—authors, a qualification that is difficult to determine. The majority of these writers use the norm, Campbell pointed out, and it is national as opposed to provincial or foreign. These models must also be more or less contemporary authors, and he decided that it was prudent not to cite living authors, since their fame was not assured. But Campbell avoided reliance on works written before the Revolution as well, with the exception of the vernacular version of the Bible, which has continued to be universally used and approved.

Some criterion must be used for determining who these "present" authors are, Campbell said, since there has been disagreement about how far back we should look for authorities. No one would cite Hooker or Raleigh, though they are justly famed, he believed, and he found Lowth inconsistent in approving the revival of participial forms "which would have been rejected by all good writers, of every denomination, for more than a hundred and fifty years." This reference suggests Middleton's "restoration" of the "true participle *sitten*." On such premises Campbell could not see why Middleton did not "restore" the "true participles" *pight* for *pitched, raught* for *reached, blent* for *blended,* and *shright* for *shrieked,* or why Lowth himself did not revive *hitten, casten, letten, putten, setten, shutten, slitten, founden,* or *grounden,* or why anyone, for that matter, could not revive any form from any period he happened to fancy. Since he required contemporary usage as the norm, he also rejected an appeal to etymology. He therefore found Johnson, who acknowledged the "absolute domination of custom over language," inconsistent in rejecting a word "though common and used by the best writers" as barbarous on etymological grounds. This is not to say that we must approve every innovation, Campbell continued, but we can grant to the contemporary popular figures in the Commons their right to coin words, since "the people, always fickle, will drop them as soon as they picked them up . . . such words are the insects of a season at most."

Because even contemporary, national, and reputable usage is not uniform, Campbell proposed some canons to use in doubtful cases: (1) when two forms are competing we should choose the one that is unambiguous in meaning; (2) in doubtful cases we should appeal to the analogies of the language; (3) when equal in other respects the form most pleasant to the ear should be used; (4) if no other norm applies choose the simplest expression; (5) when none of the rules are applicable choose the form that most conforms to previous use.

In the case of adverbs, on the basis of canon (1), Campbell preferred to use *extempore* instead of *extemporary, scarcely* instead of *scarce,* and *exceedingly* instead of *exceeding.* Canon (2) led him to prefer *contemporary* to *cotemporary.* Canon (3) accounts for the ceding of *delicateness* to *delicacy,* and the statement that "*authenticity* will soon take the place of *authenticalness.*" On the basis of canon (4) he preferred *admit* to *admit of, accept* to *accept of,* and so on. Canon (5) led him to prefer *ye* to *you* in the singular and *jail* and *jailer* to *gaol* and *gaolor.*

Custom, however, is always subject to criticism, and Campbell agreed with Swift, who said, "there are many gross improprieties, which, though authorized by practice, ought to be discarded." Campbell believed that we should be legitimately concerned to ban the harsh and unharmonious words (for example, *barefacedness*), forms difficult to pronounce (for example, *CHRONiclers, reMEMbrancer*), words in which too many syllables follow the stressed syllable (for example, *PRImarily, SUMarily VINdicative*), and forms in which similar short, unaccented syllables are repeated (for example, *HOLily, SILily*).

In addition, he proposed the "dismission" of (1) words that clearly offend against both the etymology and analogy of the language, such as the use of *unravel* to mean *disorder, untangle;* (2) words that are obsolete, or used only in particular phrases, for example, "I had as *lief* go myself," "He made them yield by *dint* of arms," "He is not a *whit* better," "The case you mention is a *moot* point," "The question was debated *pro* and *con*"; and, finally, expressions that contain solecisms or have a different meaning than they seem to have, including "a number of vile, but common phrases, sometimes to be found in good authors, like . . . *currying favor, dancing attendance.*"

Lack of an established etymology is no argument against acceptance, Campbell said, and he noted that Johnson was inconsistent in rejecting *punch* ("a certain mixed liquor well known") and accepting *sherbet* because of its Arabic derivation. For all we know, *sherbet* is cant Arabic, and the Arabs might take up *punch,* which we would then have to accept as respectable. "This, I own, appears very capricious," Campbell concluded. We need not accept words known to be of low origin, "which may be said to proclaim their vile and despicable origin," such as *dumbfound, bamboozle, topsy-turvy, pellmell, helter-skelter, hurlyburly.* Barbarisms were also to be avoided, such as the obsolete words *cleped, uneath, whilom, behest, fantasy, tribulation, peradventure, selfsame, anon.* He recommended shunning unsuitable new words, for example, *verbiage;* remodeled forms of good words, for example, *analyze;* and innovations like *rep* for *reputation, incog* for *incognito,* and *extra* for *extraordinary.* Of the last category the only word that has "gained public suffrage" is *mob* for *mobile.*

Linguists have been unjustly accused of approving any form as long as it is used by someone; however, it is not the role of a linguist, as such, to approve or disapprove. Campbell's description of the grammarian's task gives a fairer account of what the linguist does—he "notes, collects and methodizes" the data he actually finds. There is clearly a need in any society for a group whose task it is to point out the *prestige* forms and expressions in that society. But such work should be the consequence of an actual survey and not the reflection of individual preference. Because of the limitations of travel and methods of gathering information, Lowth and Johnson were not in the favorable position we are in today. It is interesting to examine some of their proscriptions in the light of how educated people in the United States today speak. Representative samples of present-day speech can be found in Margaret M. Bryant's *Current American Usage*. Compiled from thousands of books and articles, the selections in this book are catalogued according to three styles: formal, informal, and colloquial style as used by speakers of Type I (little formal education, reading, or social contacts), Type II (secondary education and some reading), and Type III (college or beyond, wide reading and social contacts). Usages

prevalent among persons of Type III are unquestionably standard English; usages more common among persons of Type II than among those of Type III are questionable. Forms not employed by persons of Type III are not standard English. Universal use of a form by persons of Type I does not necessarily mark it as either acceptable or undesirable.[1]

In this survey we find that Lowth's proscription of *I had rather* in favor of *I would rather,* though still the letter of the law, goes unobserved, since the two expressions are in free variation for speakers of Type III. Lowth preferred *different from* to *different to,* and so do modern American speakers of Type III. The eighteenth-century grammarians had legislated that *between* was to be used only with pairs and *among* when larger numbers are involved. Eighty percent of the time this rule is observed, but one finds "An agreement between three people," "between us lawyers," "between meals, songs," and "a number between one and ten." Wallis in 1655, Ward in 1765, and Lowth in 1776 set up the restrictions for *shall* and *will.* The facts show that in current English, and possibly in all stages of English since the seventeenth century, *shall* and *will* are used indiscriminately for all grammatical persons. The distinction among simple futurity, threats, and promises is most often expressed by stress differences or the addition of words like *certainly, surely,* or *indeed.*

The result of this grammatical work was to settle many disputed points among speakers of English during an unsettled period. Despite the fact that some individual items were simply reflections of the author's own usage, those who were so inclined could imitate them with the guarantee that their manner of speaking was "according to the book." Many personal preferences of these grammarians have come into official usage, for example, the distinction of former free variants, the past tense and the past participles like *wrote, written* and *took, taken.* These are simply facts of the language with which the linguist has no quarrel.

[1] Margaret M. Bryant, *Current American Usage* (New York: Funk & Wagnalls, 1962).

He would object, however, to the notion that such distinctions are "correct" or "incorrect" as a consequence of anything other than the *de facto* usage of the prestige group: the norm of correctness is social and conventional and not logical, etymological, mathematical, or metaphysical. Proclamation of grammatical rules in this sense, then, will always be a matter of rhetoric, in which one of the best arguments is the loudest voice. We will conform to the usage of those whose ridicule of departures from it causes the greatest discomfort.

One of the difficulties teachers of grammar have with the very young or the very ignorant is that both groups seem content to identify themselves with their dialectal out-group rather than with the prestigious in-group. Some teachers feel that linguistics encourages these attitudes of laudable self-confidence and disdain for the inconsequential approval of others, as reflected, perhaps, in Hall's *Leave Your Language Alone.*[2] But the advice to "leave your language alone" is on exactly the same plane as "change your language" and is subject to the same conditions for success. The conflicting views about how language and the world are connected, as discussed by the ancient Greeks, are still with us, in more elaborate, but often no less confused, ways.

TRADITIONAL GRAMMAR VERSUS LINGUISTICS

We can briefly compare the positions of the traditional grammarians and the linguists in the following outline. By traditional grammar is meant the basically Aristotelian orientation toward the nature of language as exemplified in the work of the ancient Greeks and Romans, the speculative work of the medievals, and the prescriptive approach of eighteenth-century grammarians. By linguistics is meant the empirical, structural approach to language as represented principally by American linguistics during the period of the early 1940s to mid-1950s, since this is the work best known to those of the traditional approach. Since the comparison focuses on the extremes of both groups, it is probably fair to no single worker.

Differences between Structural and Traditional Grammar

The cardinal differences between the classifications and rules of traditional and modern structural grammars are those that distinguish empirical sciences and humanistic studies.

[2] Robert A. Hall, *Leave Your Language Alone* (2d ed.; New York: Doubleday, 1950). Revised edition, 1960, titled *Linguistics and Your Language.*

1. By defining classes and assigning rules for language based on meaning, traditional grammar proceeds *subjectively,* explaining how important features of language can be related to *me.*

    a. By defining classes and assigning rules in language based on a structural analysis of the phonology, morphology, and syntax of a language, structural linguistics proceeds *objectively,* showing how important features of a language are related to each other.

2. Traditional grammars appear to assign the reason *why* certain grammatical features of a language occur, and how they must behave.

    b. Formal, structural grammars merely state the observable facts of language without attempting an explanation for nonlinguistic correspondences. Insofar as "explanation" is given, it consists in the correspondence between facts of language and an empirical, general linguistic theory.

3. Traditional grammar confuses levels of analysis that can be easily distinguished by using expressions such as "understood as," or "used in place of" to describe the overlap in the class membership of morphologically defined classes. In a sentence like "Walking is healthful," *walking* is often said to be "considered as" a noun or "taking the place of" a noun. Other words are said to be "understood" in expressions like *Good! Dog* is described as a noun "used in place of an adjective" in an expression like *dog house.*

    c. Structural grammars distinguish various levels of analysis, for example, morphological (at which level "nouns," "verbs," and so on can be defined for English) and syntactic (at which level morphological "nouns" may have the same distribution as morphologically defined "adjectives"). Since interjections are used universally without the need of other accompaniments in languages, speaking of other forms "understood" is as unnecessary as it is undemonstrable.

4. The fact that traditional grammar is generally understood is due to its cultural history, which links it to a fundamentally Aristotelian psychological theory of a dualistic type, with the semantic doctrines of the medievals and the individual preferences of eighteenth-century authors, although many teachers of school grammar may be unaware of this justification.

    d. As much as possible structural linguistics has prescinded from disputed psychological, logical, or metaphysical systems. The facts recorded in such an empirical description may be interpreted according to any of the other systems.

5. Because the Greek investigation of language started with logic, traditional grammar has unthinkingly taken the declarative sentence

as "basic." The "parts of speech" are defined, therefore, according to their function in that sentence type alone. Other sentence types are "explained" as deviant forms of the declarative sentence, from which they are often said to be derived by a conscious psychological process.

e. Structural linguistics has studied all utterances on the same terms, and states the distinguishable behavior of formally different types. The declarative sentence is taken as basic on the norm of frequency and descriptive convenience. Although this kind of investigation may give support to the traditional view, it will do so first through proven descriptive convenience and not *a priori* psychological assumptions.

6. Traditional grammarians accuse the structuralists of giving no explanation of language; of naïvely assuming that mere description will provide its own interpretation; of criticizing, but not producing, grammars; of dehumanizing language study by equating it with any formal signal system; of failing to distinguish the strictly human from the general animal use of language; of so stressing the differences between languages as to obscure the preponderance of similarities that are more impressive on comparison.

f. Structuralists accuse traditional grammarians of giving pseudo-explanations of carefully selected, inadequately described utterances manufactured to fit their rules; of too readily declaring sentences that do not fit the rules "idioms," "exceptions," or "ungrammatical"; of assuming that *a priori* views of language can substitute for accurate description; of producing endless grammars without examining their methodological presuppositions; of applying a mixture of semantic, morphological, and syntactic criteria in no fixed order; of starting with *meaning* instead of the differential signals of meaning common to any human language; of failing to see that stressing the similarities in what all languages *can* say results in missing the unique expressive elements a language *must* employ.

These positions and counterpositions are intended to portray the linguist and the traditional grammarian at their worst, in the eyes of the other. They cannot be thought, therefore, to fairly characterize individuals in either field. The problem that most separates the two concerns the role of *meaning* in the analysis of language. The following summary may indicate why the structural linguist chooses to view meaning as a basically differential function in the initial stages of linguistic analysis.

1. Since the association of meaning and form is arbitrary, it is a poor starting point for examining a new language, which is presumably a unique system, as all languages are assumed to be. It is most likely

that a given linguistic structure can have more than one meaning and that any meaning can be signaled by more than one structure.

2. If a semantic basis, such as the traditional "parts of speech" and their accidents, is used, we will impose a content structure familiar to us because of some 2000 years of cultural unity. This would result in "translating" the language we describe into Latin or Greek and would not reveal what this language *must* say in a minimally grammatical expression, but what it *may* say, corresponding to the minimal grammatical requirements of Latin and Greek.

3. Because of its logical origin, traditional grammar tends to deal with all sentences and their parts as though they had the same referential function they serve in deliberately constructed propositions. This method is inadequate for the full description of any language, ancient or modern.

The linguist concludes, therefore, that questions of grammatical correctness can be settled only by data intrinsic to each language and not by rules derived from Latin and Greek. While literary or logical models have their own excellence, utterances of other types must be judged on their own uses and merits and not as though they were distortions of a logical proposition or literary declarative sentence. Such sentences depart from the norms for these other two not because of ignorance or carelessness but because of the exigencies of style. We should avoid the grammatical terminology required for the description of the classical languages unless the nature of the language under description justifies its use. A good example of this is the use of the term "case" in the description of the English language.

If we compare a Latin sentence like *Sceptrum dedit regi* to its English equivalent, (a) "He gave the scepter to the king" or (b) "He has given the scepter to the king," we can see that it is impossible to use the same number and the same type of grammatical categories to describe the two. There is an obvious difference in the number of words used; there is an alternative translation in English that cannot be selected on the basis of the form of the Latin sentence alone. The pronouns are grammatically required in English, but would not be required in Latin; English has an article, Latin does not; the Latin consists of three complex forms, the English of (a) six simple forms and one complex or (b) seven simple forms and one complex; the word order in Latin is stylistically preferred, but grammatically, any of the forms used could appear in any of the three possible positions; the word order in English is required to distinguish the subject the object, and so on.

Some traditional grammarians would say that "king" in both of the English equivalents is in the dative case. The ultimate reason is that, were the English translated into Latin again, only *regi* would be the grammatically correct form, and *regi* is morphologically and syntactically different in Latin from *rex* (nominative), *regis* (genitive), *regem* (accusative), and *rege* (ablative). The fact that the same meaning can be expressed in both languages leads the grammarian to discuss the similarity in vocabulary, which developed as a consequence of Greek and Latin grammar and not English-Latin or English-Greek translations. The similarity of meaning obscures the difference in the formal structure of the languages involved, since both Latin and Greek would use a morphological construction (consisting of two bound forms) where English must use a syntactic construction (consisting of three free forms). It is, of course, important and convenient that English can express the same meanings as those required by the grammar of the classical languages. But this does not justify obscuring the grammatical requirements of English by discussing facts of English form in the vocabulary designed to codify Greek and Latin form.

Strengths and Weaknesses of the Two Approaches

TRADITIONAL GRAMMAR

Strengths
1. It is the most widespread, influential, and best-understood method of discussing Indo-European languages in the Western world.
2. It is fairly well understood and consistently applied by most of those who teach it and have studied it. Many grammars of many languages are available.
3. It is humanistic in origin and, therefore, an answer, however inadequate, to the kind of problems it raises.
4. It distinguishes rational, emotional, automatic, and purely conventional types of discourse in theory, if not in grammatical practice.
5. It gives a fairly thorough and consistent analysis of the declarative sentence, the most frequently used type in written and spoken discourse.
6. It contains a theory of reference by which the meaning of declarative sentences can be explained and to which other uses may be reduced.
7. It is the vehicle by means of which ordinary students and scholars have mastered many languages successfully for centuries.

Weaknesses
1. It is normative, basing its rules frequently on illogical grounds; it is internally inconsistent and externally inadequate as a description of actual language in use.

2. It suggests that usages which are not amenable to its rules are "ungrammatical" in some imputable sense.

3. It is based mainly on European languages; the categories developed for these are inadequate for all uses of European languages, and certainly inadequate for non-European languages.

4. While giving a reasonable account of Latin and Greek, its hazy distinction of morphology and syntax results in an inadequate notion of "modification" and of the criteria for "parts of speech." It is, therefore, a poor model for the grammars of languages that differ from Latin and Greek.

5. It does not adequately distinguish (a) lexical, morphological, and syntactic meanings; (b) the difference between grammatically minimal and stylistically permissible constructions; and (c) particular and universal features of languages.

STRUCTURAL GRAMMAR

Strengths

1. It is empirical; it makes exactness a methodological requirement and insists that all definitions be publicly verifiable or refutable.

2. It examines all languages, in terms of their phonological and grammatical systems, which can be determined by empirical methods.

3. Because its description is structural, the uniqueness of each language is recognized and done justice; but it also facilitates comparison, since the method also reveals what languages have in common.

4. It describes the minimum, required contrasts that underlie any construction or conceivable use of a language and not just those discoverable in some particular use.

Weaknesses

1. For many linguists only the description of language and not its explanation has been the goal of their discipline. However, this situation has changed in recent years.

2. It prescinds from psychological factors that are important to all speakers.

3. It has produced almost no complete grammars comparable to the exhaustive treatments by traditional methods, concentrating on critical studies of how grammars should be written, partial sketches of exotic languages, and partial structural analysis of familiar languages.

4. Some linguists have examined all forms of discourse on the same level, whether it be fully rational and considered or wholly indeliberate speech.

5. Since many linguists do not discuss meaning in the description

of languages, it is difficult to attach importance to their statements that meaning has been avoided in a particular description.

6. In the situational description of meaning the assumption that the "relevant" linguistic facts can be correlated with the "relevant" non-linguistic items in a completely objective manner has concealed many nonlinguistic assumptions.

It must be repeated that this list of strengths and weaknesses by no means applies to the work of individual linguists, since the items are stated in extreme fashion. The strengths are those claimed by one group for itself, and the weaknesses are those pointed out by representatives of the opposing view.

Reconciliation of Traditional and Structural Grammar

To the extent that both traditional and structural grammars are descriptive disciplines, there is no reason why each could not profit from the experience of the other. It may be worthwhile, therefore, to point out a few of the basic points in each area that could be mutually profitable.

Since the mid-1950s many linguists have been dissatisfied with the conception of linguistics as a mere taxonomic or descriptive discipline. It has been proposed that a satisfactory general linguistic theory must provide the basis for an explanation as well as an accurate description of language. Such a proposal, if adopted, would require the inclusion of meaning considerations in the descriptive and explanatory mechanism. Traditional grammar has shed some light on the matter of meaning in language which may be useful to our structural examination.

Basic to the ancient and medieval treatment of language is the use of Aristotle's *Categories*. It has been pointed out that the entire set of the ten categories can be considered as an apposition between two terms, "substance" and "accident." The grammatical notions of noun, pronoun, and subject all derived from the notion of substance, and that of the verb, adjective, and predicate from the notion of accident. "Substance" and "accident" were defined by means of the same kind of implicit method the structural linguist uses to define units in a language. That is, "substance" was "defined" as what is not an accident, and "accident" as what presupposed substance. The "definitions" can, therefore, be considered distributional or functional in the sense that the two terms are identified through their oppositions to each other and not according to the positive features they have. As a consequence both the notions of substance and accident are analogical (systematically equivocal) and not univocal: their instances need not have a single, positive, additive definition through parts that is appropriate regardless of their environment (that is, a univocal definition remains unchanged in each use). The notions of substance and accident have a contrastive, systematically varying definition in terms of parts, according to the level of analysis on which they are discussed or according to the environment in which they are found (that is, the definitions are analogical, systematically varying according to the universe of discourse). It is on similar grounds that we have distinguished nouns and nominals.

The traditional grammarians did not take the foregoing distinctions into sufficient consideration when they substituted obvious examples of substance to define "noun" instead of retaining the implicitly defined notion, since *persons* and *things* presumably are entities that can be given explicit definitions. It is on this basis that many linguists have criticized the traditional definitions of "the noun," pointing out that we could not use the traditional definition of "name of a person, place, or thing" to identify *electricity* or *fire* as nouns, since, according to the physicist, these are activities and not things.

This criticism really misses the point, however, since the original definitions had to do primarily with ways of describing or conceiving things and not with how they actually exist. In this tradition it has always been clear that descriptive categories or words in isolation are not subject to verification or refutation. They are either useful or not useful for handling a particular problem, and their value is discovered by verifying or refuting the propositions in which they occur.

In an important way, then, structural work on language has exploited more consistently than the traditional one of the fundamental insights that underlies traditional grammar. The technique of substituting examples for the terms in a relation of opposition instead of looking for such oppositions has resulted in the development of a particular set of meaning types in traditional grammars that are linked to the way a particular culture conceives of things. While universal principles may underlie this process of conceptualization, the instances have been more stressed than the principles, and recent sociological and anthropological work has shown that this method is neither the best or the only way of describing cultural entities. The structural approach employed in linguistics and other sciences can free us from a particularized cultural bias and can lead to a higher point of view from which we can more efficiently organize the similarities and differences found in languages and the cultures that use them.

The fact that structural linguists, who have largely been trained in traditional grammar, so readily abandon traditional descriptive methods should interest those who are not acquainted with all of the developments in linguistics. Adherence to the structural point of view does not entail a rejection of the traditional values, but a preference for a more revealing and exact description, and eventual explanation, of linguistic facts. Since it is a descriptive discipline, linguistics does not, because it cannot, prove or undermine any philosophic position. The rejection of "mentalism," by Bloomfield and his successors, is the rejection of a grammatical method and not necessarily of a philosophic commitment. The most recent developments in linguistics have largely returned to the traditional goals of grammatical work, but with the rigor of the formal, structural methods developed by many linguists over a period of many years. It now appears to be more than wishful thinking to hope that the best of both approaches can be combined for a more exact and productive understanding of language and languages.

Review Questions

1. What innovations in language study were made in the eleventh century?
2. What is meant by the "logicization of grammar"?
3. Distinguish three kinds of grammars and state their likely goals and justification.
4. Explain the importance of Peter Helias and Petrus Hispanus in the logicization of grammar.
5. Explain Hispanus' treatment of meaning and the role he gave to signification, supposition, appellation, and consignification. Which of these are affected by extension and restriction?
6. Explain the "modes" studied by the Modistae.
7. Contrast etymology as practiced by Isidore of Seville with modern practice.
8. Sketch the development of English dictionaries up to Johnson's.
9. Explain the attitude of the eighteenth-century grammarians and its justification.
10. Explain Campbell's notion of "use."
11. Compare traditional and structural grammars.
12. Sketch the traditional relation of substance and accidents to the grammatical notion of noun and verb, subject and predicate.
13. What is the most basic similarity between structural and traditional grammatical methods?

Suggested Readings

Arens, H., Sprachwissenschaft (Munich, 1955).
Baugh, A. C., A History of the English Language, 2d ed. (New York, 1957).
Bochenski, I. M., Summulae Logicales Petri Hispani (Rome, 1947).
Boehner, P., Medieval Logic (Manchester, England, 1952).

Bursill-Hall, G., "Medieval Grammatical Theories," *Canadian Journal of Linguistics*, 9 (1963), 1.

Moody, E. A., *Truth and Consequence in Medieval Logic* (Amsterdam, 1953).

Robins, R. H., *Ancient and Medieval Grammatical Theory in Europe* (London, 1951).

Starnes, D. T., and G. E. Noyes, *The English Dictionary from Cawdrey to Johnson* (Chapel Hill, N. C., 1946).

Thomas of Erfurt, *De Modis Significandi seu Grammatica Speculativa*, ed. F. M. Fernández García (Quarrachi, 1902).

Thurot, C., *Extraits de divers manuscrits latins pour servir à l'histoire des doctrines grammaticales au moyen âge* (Paris, 1869).

Tucker, S., ed., *English Examined: Two Centuries of Comment on the Mother-Tongue* (Cambridge, 1961).

6

The Nineteenth Century
Historical and Comparative Linguistics

One theme of language study that the twentieth century has in common with the period up to the nineteenth century is the so-called synchronic point of view, according to which languages are described without reference to their history. From the ancient to the medieval period, of course, the absence of historical analysis was chiefly due to an ignorance of linguistic history. The motivation for pursuing the etymology of expressions, and what was understood by the term, will serve to differentiate the kinds of investigations undertaken in former eras from the historical inquiries of the nineteenth century.

The term "etymology" was coined by the Stoics. They were convinced that language was, or should be, regularly related to its content, but that the state of the Greek language at the time of their investigations was such that complete regularity could not be established. They concluded, therefore, that the language of their time had undergone a process of corruption and that the true, regular relation between language and the universe could be seen only when the original forms—the *etyma*—of current expressions had been restored. The source of this irregularity, according to Varro, was human choice; the source of regularity was the nature of language and of the world. There was, therefore, the conviction that language should be understood in terms of some set of regularities, from which language in its current state had deviated.

In the Judeo-Christian tradition the same conviction was based on the Biblical account of the Tower of Babel. It was held that all men once spoke the same language—traditionally thought to be Hebrew—and that at a certain time this linguistic unity was broken up into the many languages of the world. This view resembles that of the Stoics and some analogists, who believed that language is, in some sense, regular, but that current languages, and current forms within languages, show deviations, which are mostly corruptions, from that unity.

The *Etymologies* of Isidore of Seville follows the same line of thought. He stated that the original language was Hebrew and that the multiplicity of languages in his day was a consequence of the "confusion of tongues" at the Tower of Babel. He saw that there were variant forms of Latin and Greek and held that the Latin of his day showed the corrupting influence of the barbarian conquerors of Rome. Etymology is, according to him, a study without a unifying principle, since it is partially historical (the derivation of some Latin forms can be traced to Greek, others to Latin place names) and partially mnemonic (unfamiliar expressions are "explained" by "interpretation" through causes, opposites, and so on). The medievals advanced little beyond Isidore's views, although they were in a position to know more languages. The "regularity" of languages was not formally discussed at this time. It was presupposed that there was a semantic unity behind all languages, an idea based on Aristotle's notion that the concepts words express are the same for all men, and so are the things of which concepts are formed. In this sense "grammar" is the same, substantially, for all languages, since it concerns possible meaning arrangements.

Europeans became acquainted with many more languages after the period of exploration and colonization, but the same opinions about the relation of languages were held. For the curious, word lists were compiled, and an effort was made to show how languages were related. For example, Julius Caesar Scaliger (1484–1558) compared Latin and Greek, and his son Joseph Justus Scaliger (1540–1609) tried to classify all the languages of Europe according to a limited number of "matrices," which indicated the closer relation of some than others. He was of the opinion that English would ultimately be traced to Persian.

Etienne Guichard compiled an *Etymological Harmony of Languages* in 1606, which treated Hebrew, Chaldaic, Syrian, Greek, Latin, French, Italian, Spanish, German, Flemish, and English. In this work he tried to show that all languages can be traced to Hebrew. His method is interesting, since it shows one of the fundamental confusions that dominated the work of the ancients and medievals, who knew the difference between letters and sounds, but did not insist on technical terms to distinguish them. Guichard appears to have assumed that since all of these languages can be represented in alphabets, one has to do with a limited number of items, and the task of the etymologist is to "unscramble" the alphabetical confusion that began at the Tower of Babel:

As for the derivation of words by the addition, subtraction, transposition, and inversion of letters, it is certain that this can and must be done in this way, if one wants to find etymologies. This is not difficult to believe, if we recall that the Hebrews wrote from right to left, and the Greeks and others from left to right.

According to this method, Guichard would take the Hebrew *dabar* and show by omission and transposition that it was the same as *worde* in English, *wort* in German, and, perhaps, *fari* and *verbum* in Latin, all expressions having to do with "word" or "speaking." The same expression also meant "spoil," so with a bit of transposition, omission, and substitution, it is not difficult to see, according to Guichard, that the Greek *pertho* and the Latin *perdo*, as well as the German *derben*, come from the inverted version *barad*. As can be seen, Guichard was not without an elementary appreciation of the similar points of articulation, despite the other phonetic differences that would distinguish the sounds represented by these letters. One of the founders of the historical study of language in the nineteenth century, Rasmus Rask, remarked that the etymologists of the sixteenth and seventeenth centuries had "proved" to everyone's satisfaction that all languages derive from Hebrew and that "it is not surprising that it worked so well, since all were so convinced of it" before the "demonstration." Leibniz (1646–1716) showed this derivation to be impossible, and Voltaire expressed the skepticism of later critics in his characterization of etymology as the science in which "the vowels count for little, and the consonants for nothing."

In the seventeenth and eighteenth centuries encyclopedic collections of information were made on all possible topics, including languages. Leibniz was interested in collecting word lists and grammatical sketches of various languages and was in correspondence with the Jesuit missionaries in China and with other interested people around the world. Catherine the Great of Russia prepared a list of words and had officials in all the countries where she was represented obtain the local equivalents. The results of this survey were published and edited by Simon Pallas (1744–1811), but the work was hastily done and full of errors in phonetic rendition. An edition of the lists, entitled *Linguarum Totius Orbis Vocabularia Comparativa*, was brought out between 1768 and 1787, with information from 200 languages and dialects of Asia and 51 European countries. It was issued again in 1791 in four volumes, containing material on 272 languages, with the addition of some African and American expressions.

A Spanish Jesuit, Lorenzo Hervas y Panduro, compiled a 21-volume encyclopedia called *Idea dell Universo,* with the intention of showing that human beings are fundamentally the same in all parts of the world. The seventeenth volume contained a "Catalogue of known languages with a statement of their affinity and diversity" (1794). A six-volume augmented version of this work was later published in Spanish in Madrid in 1800–1804. In this work he dealt with over 300 Asian, European, and American languages, in which he had compiled grammars and word lists. In deciding on the affinity of languages he held that similarity of grammatical structure and not lexical resemblance is the determining factor. He is supposed to have himself written 40 of the grammars of the American languages presented in his work.

The last, and probably the greatest, of these collections of word correspondences was the four-volume *Mithradates, oder Allgemeine Sprachenkunde mit dem Vater Unser als Sprachprobe in Beynahe 500 Sprachen und Mundarten* by Johann Christoff Adelung, published in Berlin between 1806 and 1817. This work compared not just isolated words but versions of the Lord's Prayer in many of the 500 languages dealt with. Unfortunately, the text was marred by many mistakes and poor editing; and the choice of a prayer as a standard for comparing languages was hardly apt to show the correspondences among living languages.

Another work based on an *a priori* assumption was that of John Horne Tooke (1736–1812), *Epea Pteroenta,* or *Diversions in Purley.* The author assumed that words in all languages had developed from single, unanalyzable sounds and that no word by itself is a predication. For example, when we find a word like the Latin *ibo,* "I will go," we must assume that we have to do with three words, not one. Tooke, therefore, analyzed it into *I* (the presumed verbal root of the Latin *ire,* "go"), *B* (from the *bo, bou,* or *boul* of Greek *boulomai,* "I want" or "I will"), and *O* (from the Latin *ego,* "I"). He did not say why Latin words should be composed from Greek and Latin roots or why the Latin had to be broken down according to the requirements of English syntax, which uses three words where the Latin and Greek use one, or how the Latin *ibo* is related to the Greek equivalent *eimi.*

Part of the merit of these works was that they rested on a rather clear basic theory about the nature of language and, therefore, how languages should be compared. The clarity of their presentation enabled others to criticize their views and to bring to light the kind of scholarship that could handle the same data more satisfactorily. For example, in a review of Pallas' work Christian Jakob Kraus (1753–1807) had some sensible remarks to make:

There is a twofold goal which all philosophical investigation of language comparison must presuppose: the languages first of all in themselves, as methods, representations of the soul through the sounds of the mouth, are at the same time portraits of the thought system of the speakers, and through their speaking, they show the content and relations of their concepts, as well as their logical progression in conceiving and expressing them. . . .

By "philosophic" Kraus meant what we would now call "scientific." His "modern" insight was his willingness to consider each language an autonomous system, without presupposing that its unity or regularity is imposed from without, either by Hebrew or Latin or by some universal sort of grammar. He continued his critique by pointing out that, since each language is a unique system, word-to-word correspondence is not to be expected. For that reason the study of word meanings in isolation is a deceptive waste of time, since each word must be set into the grammatical structure of each language. On the positive side he suggested that language comparison should begin by setting up a phonetic rendering of the letters, without the supposition that there is a "normal" way of pronouncing them; then the grammatical structure of both languages should be explained, and on that basis, a translation or semantic correspondence between the two could be established.

Kraus's views are doubly remarkable considering the amount of information about languages that Europeans had available to them at that time and the examples from which he had to draw in order to make his comparisons. At that point Europe was on the threshold of the single discovery that was to revolutionize language description as well as thinking concerning how languages are related. This was the "discovery" of Sanskrit and its marvelously articulated description in the work of the Indian grammarians, the most notable of whom was Panini, whose grammar was written in about the fourth or third century B.C.

A typical report on the implications that this discovery held for philology was Sir William Jones's "Asiatick Researches," which appeared in 1786 in the *Journal* of the Asiatick Society he founded in Bombay:

The Sanskrit language, whatever be its antiquity, is of a wonderful structure, more perfect than the Greek, more copious than the Latin, and more exquisitely refined than either, yet bearing to both of them a stronger affinity, both in the roots of verbs and in the forms of grammar, than could possibly be produced by accident; so strong, indeed, that no philologer could examine all three, without believing that they have sprung from some common source, which, perhaps, no longer exists; there is similar reason, though not quite so formidable, for believing that both the Gothick and the Keltick, though blended with a very different idiom, had the same origin with Sanskrit; and Old Persian might be added to the same family; if this were the place for discussing any question concerning Persian antiquities. . . .

The information derived from an examination of Sanskrit served to stimulate "philologers" of many different persuasions, since it corresponded to the oldest and newest views concerning the affinity of languages. For example, it confirmed the opinion of those who thought that grammar was "substantially the same and accidentally different," and it fitted the notion that the development of language over time had been a process of progressive corruption, since Latin had long been held to be a kind of corrupt Greek—and here was Sanskrit, more perfect than Greek. The study of Sanskrit also gave strength to the assumption of the comparative method, that languages which are clearly related in their grammatical structure must be related genetically and not accidentally, and it suggested the possibility of the discovery, or at least the reconstruction, of the *Ursprache*, the original, oldest language, from which all languages were descended. Finally, the discovery of Sanskrit suggested that a study could be made of Eastern and Western languages which would show their familial relations.

As has been noted, students of language had become increasingly aware that similarity of grammatical structure rather than word correspondences is the more important consideration for establishing relations between languages. This was the conviction of Panduro and Kraus, and it laid the foundation for the scientific study of language development in the nineteenth century. What was required for more rapid progress in language analysis was some system for explaining the differences among languages in a regular way. The problem presented no challenge when words in one language were obvious transliterations of words from another language. The method of Guichard was based on pure semantic resemblances, in which the form was twisted and distorted in order to show formal correspondence.

One of the first to propose a system to account for the regular correspondences of differences in forms among languages was Rasmus Rask, a Danish scholar who published a prize essay, "An investigation into the Origin of the Old Nordic or Icelandic Language" (1818). He pointed out that experience had showed lexical correspondence to be an unreliable index of the common origin or relation of languages. Such correspondences could be due to either borrowing or pure chance. Inflections and derivational processes within a language, however, are rarely borrowed, he said, so that the surest way to compare languages is to attend to (1) the roots of the languages and (2) the sound correspondences among the roots of the languages. He anticipated formulations of the so-called Grimm's law, which will be discussed later in this section.

Rask and Grimm were not the first to deal with regular correspondences among the sounds of related languages, but they were the first to do so systematically. Others had already noted some obvious parallels, for example, John Wallis in his historical account of the development of the English language, *Grammatica Linguae Anglicanae*, published in 1653. In his Preface he noted that

Wales and Gaul have a name in common, for there is a very frequent interchange of G and W:

guerre	garant	gard	gardien	garderobe	guise
warre	warrant	ward	warden	wardrobe	wise
guile	gage	guichet	guimblet	guerdon	Guillaume
wile	wager	wicket	wimble	reward	William
gaigner	gaster	guetter			
to win	waste	wait.			

Rask's work remained largely unknown, since it was first written in Danish and a later partial translation of it into German was poor. An important start in the study of historical linguistics was made at the University of Paris, which was among the first schools to offer courses in Sanskrit. It was there that pioneering German scholars like Friedrich and Welhelm von Schlegel and Franz Bopp first became acquainted with it. The Germans then took this discipline to their own universities, where the study of Indo-European languages became almost a German monopoly. Friedrich von Schlegel wrote one of the earliest works that aroused European interest, *Über die Sprache und Weisheit der Inder* (1808). Although his sketch of the grammar of the language was imperfect compared to later works, his translations of Indian poetry attracted wide attention. His brother Wilhelm published more solid information about the grammatical aspects of Sanskrit and held a professorship in that field at Bonn from 1818 until his death in 1845. Franz Bopp was a contemporary of the older von Schlegel, and his first publication on Sanskrit, in 1816 compared the conjugational systems of Sanskrit, Greek, Latin, Persian, and German. Although it was not skillfully handled, the publication exemplified the basic insight of Kraus, Rask, and others that the grammatical structure of languages was essential to linguistic comparison. One difficulty that limited Bopp, and especially Grimm, was an inferior understanding of articulatory phonetics.

As is often the case, it was not that the study of phonetics had been neglected, but the findings of these studies had been largely ignored. The Dane Jakob Aarus (1538–1586) had already published respectable work on phonetics, and Wolfgang von Kempeln had studied articulations so thoroughly that he proposed a design for a talking machine in his *Mechanizmus der menschlichen Sprache nebst der Beschreibung einer sprechender Maschine*, published in 1791.

On the other hand, it was perhaps a lucky accident that the first students of linguistic relation were so much in the dark about the kinds of sounds the letters of familiar alphabets could represent. As it was, they worked with a very limited inventory of letters, whose correspondences they sought. If, instead of a single letter, they had tried to deal with three or five or more components, they might not have discovered as quickly as they did some of the more obvious rules of correspondence. For example, a set like

Sanskrit	Greek	Latin
asmi	*eimi*	*sum*
asi	*ei*	*es*
asti	*esti*	*est*

suggested a possible regularity to investigators between the *a* sound of Sanskrit and the *e* sound of Greek and Latin. Another factor that encouraged them was that these verbal forms were comparatively "irregular" in all of these languages. Such correspondences were much more suggestive than, say, the first-person correspondences between Greek and Latin verbs like *ago*, "drive" or "lead," since the *o* termination was the regular one in both languages. The forms for the verbs *to be* were consequences of the grammatical structure of the languages studied, unlike "culture words" that could be readily borrowed, for example, the current English expressions *coffee, tea, cocoa, ketchup,* which we have borrowed from other languages, or words like *automobile, telephone, telegraph,* which we have exported to many languages.

Given consistent correspondences such as those illustrated so briefly in the forms for *to be* (very many others could be listed), several possibilities about how the languages in which they occur are related may seem plausible: (1) each of the languages is derived in turn from the other, which accounts for the resemblance; (2) each is derived from another common language; (3) each has developed, independently, in the same way. The last possibility, that of convergence, cannot be ruled out, but there are other, nonlinguistic, reasons for preferring the second hypothesis in some cases and the first in others. The Romance languages, for instance, derive from Latin, and we have documents through which this development can be traced, linguistically, geographically, and politically. For a while, some people thought that Sanskrit itself was the *Ursprache,* or original language, that had given rise to all others, but this opinion was soon seen to be untenable. The fundamental assumption of linguists after the midnineteenth century, then, was that the languages we have mentioned, along with other European languages, were derived from another original, or proto-, language, which no longer exists. Reconstructing that language became the aim of the philologists. This may seem to have been a rather bold, if not hopeless, task, since it was assumed that this proto-language no longer existed, and there was thus no way of checking the accuracy of such a reconstruction. But if we see what is implied in the development of the comparative method, by which the sound correspondences among related languages are established, and through which the grammatical parallels can also be stated, it can be seen how we are to interpret this. Once these correspondences have been stated, we can say what the languages examined have in common. Historically they have their origin in common. The statement of the correspondences, then, leads to the reconstruction of the original form.

This reconstruction was to be accomplished through the establishment of the way in which the spelling of words in earlier forms could be transformed according to definite rules into the spelling of words in later attested stages of languages. The earlier language states, for example, Sanskrit, Greek, and Latin, were called "Indo-European" as opposed to later "Germanic" languages. The term "Indo-European" came to be used to refer to the entire family of languages that are considered interrelated because of their presumed development from the proto-Indo-European language. The abbreviations for these language groups are, respectively, IE and PIE. From approximately 1820 through the 1870s scholars progressed from the notion of sound shifts between these language stages to sound laws that accounted for changes. The significance of the sound laws and the conclusions that were drawn from them about linguistics as a science can be understood best by tracing the development of how these sound changes were studied and explained by Grimm as well as by the later grammarians of the 1870s, who were called the "neogrammarians," or *Junggrammatiker*.

Jakob Grimm (1785–1863) published his first edition of the *Deutsche Grammatik* in 1818. This work was not, as its title may suggest, a grammar of German alone, but a sketch of the grammatical structures of the older and modern forms of Germanic languages. In the second edition of 1822 Grimm set out clearly the sound correspondences he had noted between Sanskrit, Greek, and Latin (IE) and the Germanic languages. These *Lautverschiebungen,* or "sound shifts," as he called them, came to be known as Grimm's law. They are illustrated in sets like those in Table 3, although very many more were required to establish the relations as predictable.

The relations seen here were presented schematically as

where the letter *T* stood for *tenuis, A* for *aspirate,* and *M* for *media.* In this division we can see the same distinctions made by Dionysius Thrax,

Table 3

	Sanskrit	Greek	Latin	Germanic	
				Gothic	English
1.	p	*pous*	*pes*		
		podos (gen.)	*pedis*	*fotus*	foot
	t	*treis*	*tres*	*threis*	three
	k	*kardia*	*cor*	*hairto*	heart
2.	b	*turbē*	*turba*	*thaurp*	thorp
	d	*dakru*	*lacruma* (*dacruma*)	*tagr*	tear
	g	*agros*	*ager* *agri* (gen.)	*akrs*	acre
3.	bh	*pherō*	*fero*	*baira*	bear
	dh	. . *tithēmi*	*facio*		do
	gh	*chen*	*anser*	*gans* (German)	goose

and as was noted before, the contrasts are sometimes better expressed as
follows:

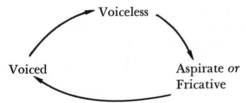

Some of the consistent relations foreseen by Grimm's law can be illustrated in the following set of forms:

(a) Greek   *phrater*   =   brother   (aspirate becomes voiced)
(b) Latin   *duo*   =   two   (voiced becomes voiceless)
(c) Latin   *tres*   =   three   (voiceless becomes fricative)

Exceptions to Grimm's law were not hard to find; for example, the
regular appearance of voiceless stops after Germanic fricatives, in forms
where the classical languages had also shown voiceless stops. These stops
should have followed the (c) pattern:

Latin	Gothic	
captus	*hafts*	(married)
spuo	*speiwan*	(spit)
est	*ist*	(is)
noctis	*nahts*	(night[s])

The discovery of the factor that regularizes the correspondences contains an implicit criticism of Grimm's basic method of comparing sounds without sufficient attention to their environments, since the voiceless stops in Germanic are predictable in such pairs as these because of the preceding Germanic voiceless fricatives.

By taking further environmental factors into consideration Hermann Grassmann was able to solve other apparent exceptions to Grimm's law. The phonology of Sanskrit and Greek did not permit successive syllables to begin with aspirates. This can be illustrated in the Greek verbal system, where the general formation of perfect tenses requires the reduplication of the verbal root, as in *luo* ("I loose") and *leluka* ("I have loosed"). But according to this phonological restriction, the perfect of *thelō* ("I wish"), which contains an aspirate, will be *tetheléka* ("I have wished"). Grassmann showed that, on the assumption that the proto-language was "irregular" by allowing successions of aspirates, the correspondences in Germanic could be considered "regular" instances of Grimm's law with respect to PIE. The significant advance here was that the environment was considered to involve more than the immediate consonant clusters, thus requiring examination of successive syllables within the word.

In 1875 Carl Verner was able to dispose of the irregular status of other exceptions to Grimm's law by showing that another conditioning factor which had to be considered was the place of the accent in IE languages. When this element had been included all of the factors pertinent to the phonological word had been taken into consideration—not only correspondences between single sounds but also sounds in clusters, sounds in successive syllables, and sounds in relation to accentual features of the word. By identifying sounds as units in a system of systems the systematic nature of the sound correspondences was more clearly shown.

When Grimm proposed the correspondences that others called his "law," he had stated that "the sound-shifts succeed in the main, but work out completely only in individual sounds, while others remain unchanged." That is, he thought that the correspondences he had noted were frequent, but not without exceptions, since he too had seen the cases that later workers had succeeded in regularizing. There were good reasons for Grimm's modesty, and reasons as well for his need of it. For one thing, Grimm was convinced that "we speak from the letters"; he did not deny what everyone in the West had held since antiquity, that letters stand for sounds and that the two are not the same thing. But he did not think he had need of investigating the phonetic nature of the sounds represented by the letters in great detail. He held that there are as many sounds as there are letters, so that in a German word like *Schaf* ("sheep"), for example, he would say that there are five sounds, since the word is spelled with five letters, whereas we would analyze it into three phonemes, /šaf/.

Despite this weakness, however, the prodigious diligence and patient gathering of examples that resulted in his basic formulation of the notion of sound shifts must be acknowledged. It laid the basis for further progress when additional conditioning factors were taken into account and when phonetic information, which was being rapidly developed all during this period, became more accurate and available to scholars in the field. All of these factors gave confidence to linguists that they could discover the basic patterns of correspondence, and a more sophisticated approach to their problems, which included consideration of more environmental factors than those within single words, was developed under the name "analogy."

In earlier chapters the preference of the linguist for a formal consideration of language was stressed, and the observation of functional relations, viewed as observed covariation, was noted. These functional relations are another expression of analogy. For we can state that there is a functional relation between 2 and 4, if the value of one is doubled when the value of the other is doubled, or we can state the same facts as $\frac{2}{4} = \frac{4}{8}$. In the materials that Grimm considered the correlations were so elementary that such a formulation was not worth the trouble: $IE/$ $voiced = Germanic/voiceless$ is not much more revealing than Grimm's formulation, since the principle of similarity behind the analogy is so evident. In the environment of formally and semantically similar expressions, correspondences such as those illustrated in the tables earlier in this section were observed. When, however, additional environmental criteria were required for the establishment of sound-shift regularities, a larger number of variables entered into the functional relations. It was then that the German scholars took up an idea attributed to the American Sanskrit scholar W. D. Whitney. In his *Language and the Study of Language* (1867) Whitney had used the term "false analogy" to explain the use of "bringed" and "fighted" by children, on the false analogy of *love, loved,* the "regular" formation. The notion, first in the sense of false analogy and then simply as analogy, was used by W. Scherer in his *Zur Geschichte der Deutschen Sprache* (1868) and then by Leskien, Osthoff, and Brugmann in various works. For example, one of the regular sound laws that Grimm had noted was the change of the early Latin *s* in intervocalic position to *r* in later Latin. When *s* was in final position, as in *servus, genus, civitas, urbis, amas,* after a vowel, we find no change in the later forms. But there were some forms in which later Latin showed an *r* instead of the expected *s,* such as *melior* ("better") instead of *melios; arbor* ('tree") instead of *arbos;* and *honor*

("honor") instead of *honos.* The assumption was then made that there must have been three stages in which this pattern developed:

1. The first period, when the regular declension of such forms was

melios	*arbos*	*honos*
meliosis	*arbosis*	*honosis*
meliosi	*arbosi*	*honosi*
etc.		

2. Then a period when the inflection was

melios	*arbos*	*honos*
melioris	*arboris*	*honoris*
meliori	*arbori*	*honori*
etc.		

which is the consequence of the regular "rhotacism," or changing of intervocalic *s* to *r.*

3. Then a period when the accepted forms were

melios OR	*melior*	*arbos* OR	*arbor*
	melioris		*arboris*
	meliori		*arbori*
	etc.		

During this period *arbos* and *arbor* were most likely free variants, but after a while the *arbos, melios, honos* forms seemed to be obsolete and so dropped out of prose usage.

This change was explained through analogy, by pointing out that there were, contemporaneous with the forms in *-os,* a great number of similarly declined forms in *-or,* such as *orator, oratoris* ("orator") and *soror, sororis* ("sister"), so that the analogy was expressible as

$$\left.\begin{array}{l} oratoris \\ oratori \\ oratorem \\ oratore \end{array}\right\} \; orator \;\; = \;\; \left.\begin{array}{l} honoris \\ honori \\ honorem \\ honore \end{array}\right\} \; X \quad \begin{array}{l} \text{(that is,} \\ honor, \\ \text{rather than} \\ honos) \end{array}$$

As has been noted before, analogy can either be considered as a static relation (for example, "double") or as a process (multiplication). The nineteenth-century linguists considered analogy as a process and thought that with this and the process of sound change they had discovered the secret of life for languages. Language was considered to be a kind of organism, which had its own laws of life, growth, and decline. One force that caused language to change was an impersonal, inexorable sound law. Sound laws as such were said to be wholly without exceptions. Any apparent exception was considered to be the operation of another law as yet unobserved or the result of analogy. When any sound change was unexplained, therefore, the linguist was to look harder and longer in the confident expectation that he would discover the cause at work. Analogy, however, was held by some to be a separate, conscious force that could arrest the normal workings of the impersonal sound laws.

This conflict was focused on the pronouncements of the *Junggramatiker*, the most noted of whom were Brugmann and Leskien. The success of Grassmann and Verner in clearing up exceptions to Grimm's law gave these scholars confidence that they could develop a science of language, much like the prestige sciences of their day. Newtonian physics gave them a model of a closed system in which there could be no exceptions. Darwinian biology offered a model of organisms developing according to inexorable laws of change. The conviction grew among linguists that their study should rank among the natural sciences, and that this science was necessarily historical. This was the opinion of the *Junggrammatiker*, and support for the view was expressed in the words of Darwin, "If we know not how a thing became, we know it not."

Those linguists who dissented from this view pointed out that the operation of analogy in sound change introduces an element of unpredictability, and this alone serves to eliminate linguistic study from the ranks of "science," if it is granted that one of the first requirements for a scientific study is the prediction of future events. These scholars objected to the quasi-biological image of language that considered analogy as a kind of "organic" reaction against threatened disruptions of the linguistic system.

Whatever the theoretical quarrels that divided scholars of this period, there were tremendous advances in information gained and in refinement of descriptive technique. These included (1) the investigation and systematic comparison of many languages, including Sanskrit, Latin, Greek, Persian, and Germanic verbal systems (Bopp, 1816); the discovery of relations among Germanic languages (Rask and Grimm, 1818, 1819); the etymological study of IE languages (Pott, 1833–1836); comparative work in the grammar of IE languages (Schleicher, 1861; Brugmann and Delbrück, 1866–?); the description of Celtic (Zeuss, 1853), Romance languages (Diez, 1836–1844), and Slavic (von Miklosich, 1852–1874); and (2) the development of accurate systems of articulatory description of sounds (Sweet, 1877; Ellis, 1869–1889; Sievers, 1888; and Jespersen 1904), as well as the discovery of physical and physiological information concerning the properties of sound (von Helmholtz, 1862) and instrumental methods of recording and describing sounds (Rousselot, 1891–1908).

The results of this work enabled scholars to propose various methods to distinguish language families as well as to explain the relations among languages within families. These methods are discussed in greater detail in Chapters 8 and 9 on Sapir and Bloomfield.

From this brief survey of the accomplishments of the nineteenth century it can be appreciated that great strides were made toward the structural point of view in the description and comparison of languages. The conditions under which progress was chiefly made can be seen in the explicit affirmation of the importance of analogy in language, since this process involves the assumption of an important resemblance among terms that differ. A voiced sound is phonetically different from a voiceless one, but the work of Grimm showed that this difference can be reduced to a significant unity by assuming a different point of view. He was able to show that in this case we do not have to do merely with two synchronic differences but with a unity through historical change. The ability of later scholars to give more and more accurate descriptions of the elements involved in these relations provided additional evidence of the systematic nature of languages and a model for describing the systems of systems in a language.

Review Questions

1. Explain and criticize the work in etymology up to the nineteenth century.
2. Compare the attitudes of C. J. Kraus and Sir William Jones concerning the relations among languages.
3. Explain the importance of phonetics in historical language study and Grimm's attitude toward the subject.
4. Explain the presuppositions of historical and comparative linguistics with respect to the languages they study.
5. Explain what is meant by "sound laws." What was Grimm's conception of his law?
6. Criticize Grimm's basic phonetic terms, *tenuis, media,* and *aspirata*.
7. Explain why Grassmann and Verner could progress beyond Grimm's formulation of sound correspondences.
8. Explain the notion of analogy and how it was conceived by the nineteenth-century linguists. Compare this to Campbell's ideas (Chapter 5).
9. Explain the role of analogy in sorting out the apparent irregularities of sound change in the development of *arbor, arboris* from *arbos, arbosis*.
10. Compare the notions of analogy and grammatical structure.

Suggested Readings

Arens, H., *Sprachwissenschaft* (Munich, 1955).
Bloomfield, L., *Language* (New York, 1933).
Hoenigswald, H., *Language Change and Linguistic Reconstruction* (Chicago, 1960).
Jespersen, O., *Language, Its Nature, Development, and Origin* (London, 1922).

Lehmann, W. P., *Historical Linguistics: An Introduction* (New York, 1962).
Meillet, A., *Linguistique historique et linguistique générale* (Paris, 1921).
———, *La méthode comparative en linguistique historique* (Oslo, 1925).
Pedersen, H., *The Discovery of Language* (Bloomington, Ind., 1962).
Sapir, E., *Language: An Introduction to the Study of Speech* (New York, 1921).
Waterman, J., *Perspectives in Linguistics* (Chicago, 1963).

7

Ferdinand de Saussure

The study of language in any period of history has always reflected the predominant interests of the time. At one time or another rhetoric, logic, literature, psychology, philosophy, physics, and biology have stood as goals or models for the study of language. In some instances methods of other disciplines have been adapted to linguistic purposes.

During his studies Ferdinand de Saussure had become dissatisfied with the idea that the sole method of studying language scientifically is from a historical point of view. But he did not see how a study that does not take the historical development of language into consideration could be made accurate until he became acquainted with the work of Émile Durkheim (1858–1917) in sociology. It will be helpful to examine some of Durkheim's basic ideas and to see how they can be applied in making the study of language a "science" without requiring an appeal to history.

DURKHEIM'S "RULES OF THE SOCIOLOGICAL METHOD"

Durkheim's little book *Rules of the Sociological Method* is still considered a classic in the field of sociology, even though its principles and findings have been challenged. What makes the work important is that it was among the first to raise the possibility of making sociology a social science that would be distinct from anthropology and psychology. In order to outline what such a science would encompass Durkheim attempted to define social facts as "things," comparable to the "things" studied by the physical sciences. It was this idea that led de Saussure to see a new way of examining language, a method that utilizes scientific study without requiring historical inquiry.

Durkheim defined a "social fact" as

any kind of action, whether of a set nature or not, capable of exercising *external constraint* over the individual. . . . [Its chief property was that of] being general throughout the extent of a given society.[1]

In this view social facts are, therefore, radically distinct from individual psychological acts, since they are of a general nature and exercise constraint over the individual. This position resulted in postulating the existence of a collective consciousness distinct from the totality of individual consciousness. Durkheim felt that this was justified on the analogy of life, which he did not think explainable in terms of the addition of the factors that compose an organism.

One of the most general criticisms of Durkheim's position was that he had needlessly made things out of social facts. He therefore felt obliged to defend himself against this charge of "needless reification" in the Preface to the second edition of the *Rules*. He claimed that the source of his critics' dissatisfaction with his calling social facts "things" was their naïve understanding of what a thing is. For him a thing is different from an idea in the same way that sensation is different from intellection. A thing includes all objects of knowledge that cannot be conceived without data from experience, observation, and experiment; it is not the consequence of purely internal mental activity. Thus when Durkheim dealt with objects of knowledge as things he did not consider this view to

place them [things] in a certain order of reality, but to assume a certain mental attitude toward them, on the principle that when we approach their study, we are absolutely ignorant of their nature. . . .

He added that, since this definition of "social fact" is placed at the beginning of his investigation,

it cannot possibly aim at a statement concerned with the essence of reality; this must be obtained later. The sole function of the definition is to establish contact with other things . . . it does not explain things thereby; it furnishes a basis for later explanations.

Continuing his attack on the critics Durkheim showed some of the consequences of considering social facts as nothing more than our personal constructs. All we would have to do, since we are their originators,

[1] Émile Durkheim, *Rules of the Sociological Method*, 8th ed., trans. Sarah A. Solovay and John H. Mueller, ed. George E. G. Catlin. Copyright 1938 by The Free Press of Glencoe and reprinted with their permission. All quotations from *Rules of the Sociological Method* appearing in this chapter are from this edition.

is examine what we attribute to them and how they cohere logically. But in the case of social phenomena, this is hardly promising:

We must remember that the greater part of our social institutions were bequeathed to us by former generations. We ourselves took no part in their formation. Even when we have collaborated in their genesis, we can only with difficulty obtain even a confused and inexact insight into the true nature of our action and the causes which determined it. . . . the important thing to know is not the way in which a certain thinker individually conceives a certain institution, but the group's conception of it; this conception alone is socially significant.

What is meant by the "external constraint" that these social facts exercise? We are not always aware of this

social constraint which is one of the tests for a truly social fact . . . when I fully conform and assent to them [social facts], the constraint is felt only slightly, if at all, and is therefore unnecessary. . . . I am not obliged to speak French to my fellow-countrymen, nor use the legal currency, but I cannot possibly do otherwise. . . . It becomes immediately evident that all education is a continuous effort to impose on the child ways of seeing, feeling and acting which he could not have arrived at spontaneously . . . if the constraint in time ceases to be felt, it is because it gradually gives rise to habits and internal tendencies which make the constraint unnecessary.

The application of these ideas to language study is obvious. Language can be considered a "thing" separate from our use of it as individuals, because it is inherited entire from the other speakers who teach it to us and is not our product. Language is a social fact, since it is general throughout a community and exercises a constraint on the speakers. This constraint is peculiar, since (1) it consists in our lack of any alternatives, if we wish to communicate through it, and (2) it is imposed on us by education, but when we master it, we are aware of no constraint. We are not committed to saying what kind of a thing language is. We define it this way at the beginning of our study because we want to know what it is and because the formulation is presumed useful to relate it to other things.

Language, or a social fact, is also independent of historical development:

If more recent societies were merely a continuation of their predecessors, each would be a more advanced duplication of the preceding . . . but a group which succeeds another is not simply a prolongation of the latter . . . it is qualitatively different from it, having gained some properties and lost others. It consists of a new individuality . . . the peculiarity of social constraint is that it is due, not to the rigidity of certain molecular arrangements, but to the *prestige* with which certain representations are invested.

Language, like social facts, will also be studied best when a minimum of attention is paid to the individual speaker's performance:

We may lay it down as a principle that social facts lend themselves more readily to objective representation the proportion that their separation from the individual facts expressing them is more complete. . . .

When we examine some of de Saussure's distinctive contributions to the structural approach to language we can appreciate how much these ideas of Durkheim's influenced him. It should not be thought, however, that de Saussure merely translated Durkheim's sociological ideas into linguistic terms; rather, the work of Durkheim provided a model and stimulus for him in the study of language.

FERDINAND DE SAUSSURE

Although de Saussure's fame rests principally on his work in synchronic, structural linguistics, the basis of his reputation in the learned world for a long time was based on his brilliant work in historical linguistics. He was born of a French refugee family in Switzerland, November 17, 1857, and took his elementary and secondary studies in Geneva. At the age of 18 he began his university studies in Leipzig as a student of G. Curtius. Among his fellow-students were the future *Junggrammatiker* Leskien and Brugmann. These men were already attracting attention by the quality of their work, and in 1879, at the age of 22, de Saussure proved himself their equal in his memorable *Mémoire sur le Système primitif des voyelles dans les langues indo-européennes.* This work established his name immediately as one of the leading authorities of the day.

His studies completed, he went to the University of Paris and took an active part in the *Société Linguistique.* From 1881 until 1889, beginning when he was 24, he lectured on comparative grammar in place of Bréal. His pupils were greatly taken both by his manner and by the material he taught. After 1891 he lectured at the University of Geneva, first on comparative grammar and then on general linguistics. When he died in 1913 his renowned *Cours de Linguistique Générale* had not yet been published. The book was assembled by some of his students by comparing their notes and some of the lecture outlines of the author.

In the *Cours de Linguistique Générale* we find that de Saussure had crystallized his objections to the *Junggrammatiker* notion that restricted the scientific investigation of language to its historical aspects. In effect he proposed that an entirely different kind of study is the sole scientific approach to language. It can be said that he set himself three goals: (1) to make the synchronic study of language scientific; (2) to show that linguistic facts exist; and (3) to establish the methods for identifying and dealing with linguistic facts.

Some of his main contributions to linguistics can be summarized by examining the terms he either coined or to which he gave a characteristic stamp: (1) the distinctions among *la langue, la parole,* and *le langage;* (2) the distinction between diachronic and synchronic language study; (3) his definition of the "linguistic sign"; (4) the distinction between associative and syntagmatic relations in language; (5) the notion of content, as opposed to linguistic signification and value; and (6) his description of the concrete and abstract units of language.

La Langue, La Parole, Le Langage

In Chapter 1 of this book it was suggested that there are many sets of data to which the term "language" can be applied. These include (1) linguistic forms, (2) relations among linguistic forms, (3) meanings of linguistic forms, (4) relations among meanings, and (5) relations between linguistic forms and meanings. In French there are three expressions referring to language that de Saussure used to call attention to distinct aspects of language that he considered important.

His reason for making these distinctions was that he wanted to define language in such a way that it could be considered a thing, an object that could be studied scientifically. One of the properties he required of this object was that it be investigable without reference to its historical development. He proceeded, therefore, according to the principles of Durkheim, who said that we have social facts that can be studied scientifically when we "consider them from an aspect that is independent of their individual manifestations."

The term de Saussure used to refer to the individual manifestations of language is *la parole,* "speaking." Similar to Durkheim's individual psychological factors, "speaking," according to de Saussure, includes the following properties:

it is the sum of what people say, including individual constructions that are the consequence of a speaker's choice, acts of articulation that are equally matters of free choice, required to produce these constructions.[2]

Defined in this way, "speaking" is not a social fact, since it is a conscious and fully individual product, whereas a social fact should be general throughout a community, exercising constraint rather than allowing free choice. If we added together all the acts of speaking in a community, however, we would have both many acts of speaking (*la parole*) and the realization of the grammatical constraints of a language, assuming that all the speakers use the language grammatically. The sum of *la parole* and the rules of language de Saussure called *le langage*. While *le langage* has both the generality and the requirement of constraint, as found in grammatical rules, it is not a social fact, pure and simple, since it includes the individual factors attributable to the individual speakers. There will always be an element of the voluntary, and, therefore, the unpredictable, when individual speakers and their performances are included. *Le langage,* therefore, does not have a principle of unity within it that enables us to study it scientifically.

If we could subtract the individual elements from *le langage* we could eliminate the unpredictable. This will give us a definition of language that fits the notion of a social fact. One definition that de Saussure gave of *la langue* is "*le langage* minus *la parole*." *La langue* is the set of passively acquired habits we have been taught by our speech community, in terms of which we understand other speakers and produce combinations other speakers of our community understand. When we hear *la parole* of another community we perceive the noises made, but not the social fact of language. We cannot connect the sounds produced and the social facts with which the other speech community associates the sounds. When we hear *la parole* within our own community we perceive the sounds as associated with social facts, according to a set of rules. These rules, which can be called the convention, or grammar, of the language are habits that education has imposed upon us. They have the property of being general throughout the community (that is why all the speakers can understand each other) and they exercise constraint on the individual speakers (we are not given alternative ways of linking sounds with social factors for successful communication). Mature speakers of a language, of course, are not aware of any constraints. Children, however, are often puzzled about why they must use one form instead of another.

When we consider the properties found in these three aspects of language we can see that de Saussure, in defining *la langue,* studied language "independent of its individual manifestation." Because it is individual, active, and voluntary, *la parole* is not a social fact; *le langage* includes both social and individual aspects and is not, therefore, a pure social fact; *la langue* is the social fact, being general throughout a community and exercising constraint over the individual speakers. Like Durkheim's collective consciousness, *la langue* is not found complete and perfect in any individual. *La parole* includes anything a speaker *might* say; *le langage* encompasses anything a speaker *might* say as well as the constraints that prevent him from saying anything ungrammatical;

la langue contains the negative limits on what a speaker *must* say if he is to speak a particular language grammatically. It is concerned more with a manner of speaking than with the matters spoken about. It is, therefore, a kind of code, an algebra, according to de Saussure, "a system of pure values that are determined by nothing except the momentary arrangement of terms."

Viewed in this way *la langue* appears to be an abstraction. De Saussure was well aware of this, but he found it no inconvenience for the scientific study of language. First, he held that "the point of view creates the object" we study. Second, no science can possibly study entities in their concrete reality, since such a study would involve an infinite number of individual properties. In order to make any study scientific we require "a conventional simplification of the data" to be examined. That is, we must abstract from some of the undenied concrete properties of the things a science studies in order to have a precisely definable object.

For a synchronic study of language we abstract from the undeniable fact that language changes. Language can then be studied as though it were a stable system or state, with neither a past nor a future. This view requires some justification, and de Saussure provided it by comparing the properties of *la parole,* as he defined it, and *la langue.*

1. Acts of speaking (*la parole*) are invariably individual, variable, whimsical, and inventive. There is no principle of unity within speech considered in this way, and, therefore, it is not amenable to scientific study.

2. For a scientific study of anything we must have an object that "holds still," since we want to count and measure it; *la parole* consists of an infinite number of individual choices, acts of articulation, and novel combinations. Its description must, therefore, be infinite.

3. *La parole* is not a collective instrument; all its manifestations are individual, heterogeneous, and momentary; it is only the sum of individual acts, expressible in the formula:

$$(1 + 1' + 1'' + 1''' \ldots)$$

4. *La langue,* however, is a collective pattern; it is something common to all the speakers, and, therefore, can be expressed in a different formula:

$$(1 + 1 + 1 + 1 + 1 \ldots) = 1$$

5. *La langue* exists in the form of "a sum of impressions deposited in the brain of each individual," which are "almost like a dictionary of which identical copies have been distributed to each individual . . . it

exists in each individual, yet it is common to all. Nor is it affected by the will of the depositaries."

6. *La langue* is both "a social product of the faculty of language and an ensemble of the necessary conventions adopted by the social body to permit the exercise of that faculty."

7. Since *la langue* is "a deposit of signs which each individual has received" from other speakers of the community, it is essentially a passive thing, as opposed to *la parole,* which is active.

8. *La langue* is a set of conventions that we all receive, ready-made, from previous speakers of the language. It would appear that language changes so slowly that we are justified in studying it as though there were no change.

What is an abstraction from one point of view can be concrete from another. De Saussure concluded that it would be "fanciful . . . to consider *la langue* and *la parole* from the same viewpoint. . . . Taken as a whole, *la parole* cannot be studied, since it is not homogeneous." *La langue,* on the other hand, obviously can and has been studied. We can easily study dead languages and absorb their linguistic organization, without recourse to speech; in fact, language can be studied scientifically only if we dispense with speech. *La langue* is, therefore, concrete from this point of view: it is a set of linguistic signs that bear the stamp of collective approval. Linguistic signs can be reduced to conventional written symbols, whereas it is impossible to provide detailed representations of the continuum of *la parole,* because the pronunciation of even the smallest word involves an infinite number of muscular movements that can be recognized and put into graphic form only with the greatest of difficulty.

In summary, then, de Saussure saw as the sole object of linguistic science that aspect of language which corresponds to a social fact. While this idea may seem to be an abstraction from the physical point of view, language (*la langue*) is not and cannot be a physical fact. It is a social fact, which can be successfully studied when we consider the pattern behind individual utterances. It is the pattern that is stable, both through time and in the consciousness of the speakers. The pattern changes so slowly that we can even afford to abstract from the reality of the change. Successful assimilation of dead languages should be proof enough that speech is not required of us to master *la langue.*

Synchronic versus Diachronic Study of Language

The *Junggrammatiker* had proclaimed that the sole means of studying language scientifically is to examine it historically, that is, **diachronically,** through time. De Saussure flatly contradicted this idea. In this connection he had a good word to say for traditional grammars: they were purely synchronic; that is, they did not confuse contemporary language usage, and the presumed reasons for correct usage, with factors derived from the historical development of a language.

Unfortunately, the other shortcomings of traditional grammar cannot be overcome by this laudable, if lonely, accomplishment. Some insights into the nature of language can be gained only by examining its history, just as there are facts about language that can be illuminated only by assuming a rigorously synchronic viewpoint. The kind of information that we can expect from each of these two approaches can be illustrated by the two kinds of sections we can make of the stem of a plant or the trunk of a tree—a horizontal section across the stem or a vertical section from the bottom to the top.

The kind of data yielded us by a horizontal section are comparable to the type of information that a synchronic study of a language reveals. This kind of cut would show us a particular stage or state of a language (*état de langue*). The face that such a cut would lay open consists of a set of cells, rings, and fibres that can be compared and that are distinguishable from each other because of their place in the surface. Examining the data in this way does not require us to know anything about the previous history of what we see: we can accurately locate, describe, and define each item merely by relating it to all the other items that are found with it. In a similar fashion speakers use the signs of which a language consists. They do not need to know the etymology of a word in order to use it as other speakers use it; they rarely know the process by which the present inflectional system of a language developed from earlier states, nor do they require such information to use the system correctly. Throughout their lifetime the speakers need not be aware of any significant changes in the elements of their language or their historical relations to each other.

When the cut is made from the bottom to the top of the stem or trunk a different kind of picture is revealed: we see lines that have slender beginnings branch out and split, widen along the trunk, or disappear into other fibres as we look higher up the section. It is also obvious that this kind of section does not present us at all with the kind of data the horizontal section gave us: there, the complete set of items extended from the center to the circumference of the trunk. The vertical section can show us only a thin slice, corresponding to the historical development of a single set of units in the synchronic state.

From this analogy it appears that the synchronic study of language has decided advantages, from a practical as well as a scientific point of view, over the historical. The historical approach cannot profitably be used to study the development of any set of linguistic forms unless one has been reliably informed about (1) the systematic relations of these forms in an earlier state of a language and (2) the differences to be found in their systematic relations at a different state of a language. It may be that data from an earlier stage has completely disappeared. For example, a horizontal cut of an "English tree" at the period of Chaucer would reveal the presence of a certain number of nominal inflections; another cut of the "same" tree at the present time would show fewer such inflections. The vertical cut may or may not show nouns at all: the apt or judicious vertical cut could be made only on the basis of information derived from the two horizontal cuts.

Far from being the sole means of studying language scientifically, then, historical linguistics is not even scientific in its approach. That is, it does not and cannot employ the methods and principles of scientific investigation. Both for examining the history of a language and for comparing two related languages, accurate synchronic descriptions of at least two comparable states are indispensable.

The Linguistic Sign

So far we have seen that for de Saussure scientific linguistics must study the patterns that make individual utterances conform to the social restraint imposed by a speech community. We have also seen that, according to de Saussure, diachronic linguistics, far from being the only scientific study of language, can be considered scientific only in a derivative sense, since it presupposes the findings of synchronic linguistics. It is at this point that we must examine de Saussure's definition of the "concrete and integral" object of linguistic science. This object is *la langue,* of course, but not in the all-inclusive sense in which the expression could be understood. Since *la langue* is a "deposit of signs," the "concrete and integral" object of linguistic science is the linguistic sign.

In defining the linguistic sign, de Saussure refined the notion of *la langue* as a "deposit of signs." To some people this definition suggests that language consists of a list of vocabulary items. This view is wholly mistaken, since it suggests that, prior to the development of language there was a set of things waiting to be named; it also introduces a confusion concerning the idea of a name as a vocal, as opposed to a psychic, entity. In de Saussure's view the linguistic sign "unites, not a thing and a name, but a concept and an acoustic image . . . a psychic entity with two sides." This definition is illustrated in the diagram.

De Saussure was at pains to insist that the linguistic sign is a psychic entity, because this relieved him of the responsibility of considering entities of *la parole*. He envisaged that a linguistic study of speech could and should be made, but that linguistics proper is a study of *la langue;* when that study has been completed, the same principles could be applied to *la parole*. There are other reasons for his defining the sign in this way: when he spoke of an "acoustic image" he dealt with a memory or the sound trace that we can hear in our imagination, not an actual, spoken word. Again, this view relieved him for the moment of dealing with the phonetic problems involved. One of the advantages of the sound image is that its components are discrete, whereas the actual sounds we pronounce are not; the acoustic image can be written accurately, the actual sounds cannot. The "sound image" is, de Saussure continued, "nothing more than the sum of a limited number of elements or phonemes, which in turn can be called up only by a corresponding number of written symbols." De Saussure did not go into detail about how he conceived of these sound entities, but it is evident that he was trying to find an analogue of a social fact on the sound plane of language as well: concrete sounds will always have the individual mark of speakers; the sounds that compose the acoustic image, the "phonemes," will be the permissible ranges of sound differences imposed by the phonology of a particular language. Although most orthographies are imperfect, a perfect alphabet would have as many symbols as there are distinctive sound differences in a language.

The other part of the psychic totality called a sign consists of a concept. Again de Saussure did not go into detail about what he meant by a "concept," except to remark that it is "generally more abstract" than the sensory acoustic image, which is "the psychic impression of a sound, the representation of it which our senses give us," as opposed to the actual material sound. Like any other part of *la langue,* concepts are "purely differential," and they are directly dependent upon the sound images with which they are associated. For this reason the sign is said to have "two faces," which cannot be separated. De Saussure called the concept the "*signifié,*" or "thing meant," and the acoustic image the "*signifiant,*" or "signifier," terms that recall the distinctions of the Stoics. None of these items is the sign; rather, the sign is the indissoluble unity of the two sides or faces. These two sides are so intimately related that they can be compared to a piece of paper, since it is impossible to cut one side of the paper without cutting the other. So too in the linguistic sign, an alteration in the acoustic image must make a difference in the concept, and vice versa. This view does not appear to take homonyms into account.

The sign, as defined here, is said to be the concrete and integral object of linguistic science. This definition appears to derive from de Saussure's idea of how to make linguistics a science: we require a conventional simplification of the data. That is, linguists must agree among themselves what the necessary and sufficient object of their discipline will be. Their agreement constitutes the "conventional" simplification; the simplification in this case consists in studying the psychic, not the spoken, aspects of linguistic signs. The sign as de Saussure defined it is, therefore, concrete in this peculiar sense, that nothing has been omitted from the definition which his point of view requires, since it is the point of view that creates the object. That is, the point of view determines what is considered **concrete** (whole, entire) as opposed to **abstract** (partial). For the same reasons the sign is the **integral** object of the science. To study either of the two faces of the sign, that is, the *signifié* or the *signifiant,* in isolation would be to study an abstraction and not a fact of *la langue.*

The term "sign" as de Saussure used it is a quite general expression. It can refer to what others distinguish as sentences, clauses, phrases, words, or morphemes. His use of the term "morpheme," however, is restricted to stand only for inflectional and derivational affixes and not for roots or stems. However, signs are of two basic types, which will account for an important difference in the discussion of the properties of the sign. If a sign cannot be analyzed into constituent signs, it is a **simple sign;** if it consists of two or more meaningful parts, it is called a **syntagme.**

All signs have two central properties: they are **arbitrary** and **linear.** De Saussure's notion of the arbitrariness of signs was the traditional one that no motivation for the phonetic constitution of a sign is to be found in the thing for which it is a sign. However, this is true in a strict sense only of simple signs. In the case of syntagmes (such as, complex or compound words, syntactic constructions) there is **relative motivation:** for example, inflected forms are similarly constructed to signal the same meaning relations; syntactic constructions used in similar situations are similarly constructed. Syntagmes are, therefore, motivated relative to each other.

Because the term "symbol" suggested a measure of motivation to de Saussure, he preferred the word "sign" to describe expressions in language. Onomotapoeia may appear to limit the arbitrariness of signs, but he did not believe that such signs are sufficiently numerous or important in language to invalidate the basic principle.

The linearity of the linguistic sign is seen principally in the *signifiant,* which can be segmented into parts succeeding each other in time. This succession forms what de Saussure called the **chain of speech.** He foresaw that the consequences of this obvious fact are "incalculable" in linguistics, since linearity is the entire basis of linguistic mechanisms and the criterion by which language can be distinguished from other sign systems.

In addition to the two properties just discussed, de Saussure attributed two apparently contradictory properties to signs: they are both **immutable** and **mutable,** but not from the same point of view. The basic reason for the immutability of language signs is the fact that each generation inherits its language and the signs that constitute it, and both the community and the individual are passive in receiving them. This indicates that the "conventional" nature of language is of a peculiar type, and the notion that there is an explicit "contract" about meanings among speakers is quite misguided. De Saussure thought that language in this instance illustrates very well that "a law accepted by the community is a thing that is tolerated, and not a rule to which all give their free assent."

He assigned four reasons for the immutability of linguistic signs, and, therefore, of *la langue:* (1) since signs are arbitrary, any sign is as good as another. Therefore, there is no basis for discussion or preference among the speakers of a language; (2) while people might prefer to change an arbitrary writing system, because the elements are limited in number and could become an object of criticism, the signs of language are infinite, and this infinity deters linguistic change; (3) language is an extremely complex system, of which only a handful of experts are aware. Even these experts have not succeeded in changing languages significantly; (4) language is the only social system that all people use, and this fact helps to account for the conservatism of speakers concerning the alteration of their linguistic habits.

The mutability of linguistic signs—and of language—is an obvious fact of history. But it is really from a different point of view that language is mutable—that is, the viewpoint of history, which brings about shifts in the relation of *signifiant* to *signifié* as a consequence of sound change and analogical shifts. From the viewpoint of the contemporary speaker, all the reasons for language not changing are visible. For the sake of scientific study, as has been shown, the fiction of a stable language is not only defensible but is necessary. But a more objective view of the life of a language would require that we consider the cumulative effects upon the system by the group of people who speak it and the passage of time.

Associative and Syntagmatic Relations

De Saussure's notion of linguistic science as far as we have discussed it opposes the static, unchanging (*la langue,* synchronic linguistics) to the dynamic, developing (*la parole,* diachronic linguistics). The object to be studied as minimally required data is the linguistic sign, which has two principal characteristics: it is arbitrary and linear. It is the latter property that is the basis for the distinction between associative and syntagmatic relations.

These relations serve to distinguish *la langue* and *la parole* in a revealing way and show why de Saussure thought that the consequences of the linearity of language would be incalculable for linguistics. In the chain of speech the various links follow each other in time, but there is no evident reason for one link to follow or precede another. Part of the notion of *la parole* is this possibility of free, unpredictable combinations. But speech within a given community is subject to some limiting restraints, called *la langue.* Even though we may not see by examining the successive units of an utterance why some combinations are permitted and others forbidden, we can determine the rules for the permissible constructions by considering the separate links in an utterance and asking what other links could have appeared in it.

ASSOCIATIVE RELATIONS   Any link in the chain of speech will suggest other language units to us, because the units either resemble or differ from each other in form or meaning. De Saussure illustrated this point by his example of the French expression *enseignement,* which can be equally well exemplified by its English equivalent, "teaching." This word could remind us of others that have a similar form, for example, any word ending in *-ing,* such as *walking, riding;* other compounds of *teach-,* such as *teacher, teaches, taught;* other words with similar meanings but different forms, such as *tutor, mentor;* or words different in both form and meaning, such as *chalk, recess, blackboard.* Associative relations are called relations *in absentia,* since the terms consist of an item present in the utterance and others that are not actually in the utterance.

The term *associative* of de Saussure has not been retained; instead, the term "paradigmatic" has been substituted at the suggestion of the Danish linguist Louis Hjelmslev. One of the difficulties with the notion of associative relations as defined by de Saussure is that every other item in the language either resembles or fails to resemble in form or meaning any given item.

SYNTAGMATIC RELATIONS   Syntagmatic relations, which hold between the successive members of a given chain, are called relations *in praesentia,* since the terms of the relations are actually co-occurent items. For de Saussure a *syntagme* was any combination of discrete, successive units, of which there are at least two, with no limit on the possible number. These segments could be phonemes, syllables, morphemes, words, parts of words, phrases, and so on. As examples of syntagmes English expressions like *reread, against all, human life, God is good, If the weather is nice, we'll go out* illustrate those that de Saussure gives in French. For him the most obvious example of a syntagme is a sentence.

De Saussure saw that it is in terms of the associative (or paradigmatic) and syntagmatic relations that the forms of a language can be accurately described. An example from nonlinguistic spheres that illustrates the importance of this idea is de Saussure's example of the columns on a building. The columns have certain relations to each other and to the rest of the building (syntagmatically, relations among terms simultaneously present) and relations as well to other kinds of columns that might have been used, for example, Doric, Ionic, Corinthian (associative relations between the present columns and those of which they remind us, which could have been present, but are not).

Linguistic Value, Content, and Signification

De Saussure viewed linguistic science as synchronic, and, therefore, static. As a consequence *la langue* is conceived as a stable set of relations among linguistic signs. The relations among signs are of two types, syntagmatic and paradigmatic. The way in which signs can be linguistically described is through these relations, and the result is called a statement of linguistic **value.** This term summarizes one of de Saussure's most basic insights into the organization of language.

The approach to this realization begins with the fact that linguistic signs are important not as phonetic events but as tokens or substitutes for nonlinguistic items. In other words, the notion of meaning in its most undefined sense tells us the most important thing about linguistic signs, and, therefore, about language. Since our basic acquaintance with signs is hearing them, we can learn something here about the functioning of language, since we rarely focus on a person's pronunciation. We attend to the ideas or the things and situations that the speaker's utterance calls to our attention. From this idea de Saussure concluded that linguists are in a peculiar situation compared to workers in other fields. He thought that the zoologist has his units "given" in a way the linguist does not, and that the astronomer has the same advantage over the linguist.

Language has the strange, striking characteristic of not having entities which are perceptible at the outset, and yet of not permitting us to doubt that they exist, and that their functioning constitutes their existence.

In other words, the most important features of signs are not to be sought in the properties characteristic of speech but in their association with nonlinguistic items, through a kind of social convention. This idea led de Saussure to cite the first characteristic of a value—that it concerns the substitution or exchange of one thing for another thing which is of a different nature. Money is an obvious example.

To show how the notion of value applies to language study, de Saussure said that we must discuss, in order, linguistic identities, linguistic realities, and, finally, linguistic values. He then showed that the notion of linguistic value includes and envelops the other two.

LINGUISTIC IDENTITIES   According to de Saussure, when we discuss linguistic **identities** we are saying that the "same" linguistic item recurs. In what sense can we say that a linguistic sign in one utterance is the same as the sign in another? De Saussure considered the French word *pas*. He noted that the word is etymologically related to the Latin *passum*, "step." But diachronic considerations will not solve the problem, he continued, since the question concerns synchronic identities. How could we decide that the *pas* in *Je ne sais pas* and *Ne dites pas cela* are the same? De Saussure replied that the sameness is not to be found in the phonetic similarity, nor even in the meaning. He used an example to illustrate this point. How would we identify the 8:15 train to Geneva from Zurich on successive days? It really makes no difference if the train is pulled at various times by electric, steam, or diesel engines; it does not make any difference what kind of cars make up the train; what makes it the "same" train each time is the fact that (1) it leaves at 8:15 and (2) it goes to Geneva from Zurich. It would not be the "same" train if it left at a different time or from a different place or for a different destination.

He then studied what we are to consider a synchronic **reality**, that is, something we discover *in* a language rather than something we impose *upon* it. He questioned, for instance, whether the traditional distinctions of the "parts of speech" are linguistic realities in this sense—something the structure of the language forces us to recognize or something justifiable by exterior criteria only, which, we use to talk about the language. In the expression *ces gants son bon marché*, can we consider *bon marché* an adjective? From a semantic point of view it seems to have the same function as an adjective, but grammatically it has none of the properties of an adjective, since the expression is invariable and never precedes the noun. Could we say that *marché* is a noun and *bon* an adjective? De Saussure said:

This would explain nothing. We are then dealing with a defective or incomplete classification; the division of words into substantives, verbs, adjectives, and so on, is not an undeniable linguistic reality.

He concluded, therefore, that "to be rid of illusions, we must first be convinced that the concrete entities of language [*la langue*] are not directly accessible."

He then listed the second characteristic of a value. In the game of chess, he inquired, is the chessman really an "element of the game"? Can we speak of a chessman as a reality in the game of chess, if we restrict ourselves to this particular piece, of this particular shape, made of this particular material? Under these conditions we cannot, since

by its material make-up—outside the conditions of the game and its square— it means nothing to the player; it becomes a real, concrete element only when endowed with value and wedded to it.

The "value" of a chessman consists in its relations to the other pieces and in the moves it makes, which are different from those of the other pieces. Its material composition is irrelevant, since if it were lost or broken anything that would fit on the board—a stone or a bottle top— could take its place, and as long as it made the moves characteristic of the piece, it would serve as well as the original. Its definition, its reality, then, is not to be discovered by considering its composition, which tells us what it is, but by studying how it differs from the other pieces, which tells us mostly what it is not. From these considerations de Saussure concluded:

in a word, that is why the notion of value envelops the notions of unit, con- crete entity, and reality. But if there is no fundamental difference among these diverse notions, it follows that the problem can be stated successively in several ways.

A value, therefore, can be exchanged for something of a different nature, of which it is said to be the value (for example, money for bread); and it is also defined through things similar to itself (for example, Ameri- can dollars in comparison to British pounds).

Linguistic values should, therefore, be studied from two points of view, conceptual and material. For de Saussure, thought is "a shapeless and indistinct mass" apart from its "expression in words." It is, therefore, impossible to discover entities, or units of thought, except through lan- guage. It is equally impossible to discover entities of language by study- ing sounds alone. A linguistic identity, or reality, then—language itself— can be "pictured in its totality as a series of contiguous subdivisions marked off on both the indefinite plane of jumbled ideas and the equally vague plane of sounds."

As a consequence, there are no thought units prior to linguistic ex- pression, just as there are no autonomous sound units to which meanings are subsequently given. The articulation of language, that is, the process of forming units, is something that works simultaneously on the conceptual and material (phonic) planes of language, so that *la langue* "works out its units while taking shape between two shapeless masses." De Saussure concluded, therefore, that it is characteristic of linguistics that "it works on the borderland where elements of sound and thought combine: their combination produces a form, not a substance."

This idea explained for him the arbitrariness of signs quite well, since there is no externally imposed system that controls the combinations of forms and meanings. It also explained why linguistic values remain entirely relative, and this in turn explained why the social fact alone can create a linguistic system:

The community is necessary if values that owe their existence solely to usage and general acceptance are to be set up; by himself, the individual is incapable of fixing a single value.

When dealing with the conceptual side of value de Saussure made some observations that led to the use of a convenient trio of terms for dealing with meaning. De Saussure himself did not use these terms as technical definitions in the sense that will be proposed here, but a careful reading of the text where these ideas are discussed will show that they are consistent with his thought on the subject.[3] These three terms are linguistic **signification, value,** and **content.**

"Signification" is defined as "the association of a given sound with a given concept," and, therefore, essentially implies the traditional notion of referential meaning. The linguistic "value" of a term is established by studying the other terms of the linguistic system, to which it is opposable, on both the paradigmatic and syntagmatic axes, since, according to de Saussure, *la langue* is "a system of interdependent terms in which the value of each term results solely from the simultaneous presence of the others." The "content" of a term can be considered the sum of the signification and the value. In the passage cited above de Saussure spoke of signification in positive terms, but of value, which he was trying to distinguish from signification, in predominantly negative or relative terms. The term *contenu* is used as though neutral with respect to the other two. Elsewhere de Saussure stated that signification is the sole positive fact of language, whereas everything else consists of differences. Considering the content of a term, he said:

Its content is truly determined only by the contrast with what exists outside of it. Since it is part of a system, it is endowed not only with a signification but also, and especially, with a value.

From this he concluded that

[3] See pages 158–162 of de Saussure's *Introduction to General Linguistics,* trans. Wade Baskin (New York: The Philosophical Library, Inc., 1959).

the idea of value, as defined, shows that to consider a term simply as the union of a certain sound with a certain concept is grossly misleading. To define it this way we would isolate the term from its system, and this would mean assuming that we can start from the terms and construct the system by adding them together, when, on the contrary, it is from the interdependent whole that one must begin, and through analysis, obtain its elements.

This passage is a telling critique of the methods employed by traditional grammars. The distinctions that derive from it concerning signification, value, and content can be illustrated in de Saussure's discussion of the difference between terms in two different systems, English and French. In comparing the English words "sheep" and "mutton" with their French equivalent, *mouton,* he pointed out that in some circumstances "sheep," "mutton," and *mouton* could clearly have the same signification (association of a given sound with a given concept), since the English "sheep" names the live animal and "mutton" the meal prepared from it, while the French *mouton* indifferently characterizes either. But *mouton* obviously does not have the same value as either "sheep" or "mutton," since it forms part of a system in which all the other members are the names of live animals *or* the meat they provide, while the English "sheep" belongs to a lexical system in which all the other members are the names for live animals and "mutton" is in a set whose other members are food terms. These terms, therefore, do not have the same content (the sum of the positive signification and the negative or relative value: the sum of terms to which a term is opposable), although they can be said to have the same signification in the proper contexts.

De Saussure used the notion of value to examine not only the conceptual but also the material, or phonetic, aspects of language. As the examples using the train and the chessman suggest, all that is required of language units materially is that they be distinguished from the other units of the same kind. Phonetically it does not matter what kinds of sounds a language uses as long as the sounds differ from each other; the same is true of writing, since we can form letters differently according to their position in words. The point can be seen by examining the way the following word is written:

Abracadabra
AbracAdAbr*A*

This example illustrates how de Saussure conceived of the independence of *la langue* from *la parole:* all of the *a*'s in the word are different, but they do not contrast with each other but only with the other letters of the alphabet. De Saussure was so convinced that language is a form and not a substance (that is, something identical with its material composition) that he believed entirely different sounds could be substituted for those in a given language, and we would still have to do with the "same" language, as long as the same number of contrasts is preserved.

La langue is, therefore, a deposit of signs; a sign is the unity that results from the association of an acoustic image with a concept, and this association is the sole positive fact of language. To study either in isolation from the other would be to study an abstraction. But a sign can be identified fully only when its place in the system has been established. This is done accurately because of the linear nature of language, which allows us to specify the syntagmatic and paradigmatic relations into which each sign enters. While this sounds simple enough, de Saussure warned that experience will show that its application is anything but simple. We are apt to confuse fundamentally different aspects of language, he said:

A unit and a grammatical fact would not be confused if linguistic signs were constituted by anything but differences. But la langue being what it is, nothing simple is to be found; always and everywhere we will find the same complex equilibrium of terms that condition each other reciprocally. In other words, la langue is a form and not a substance. One cannot be too convinced of this truth, since all our errors in terminology, all our incorrect ways of naming linguistic facts derives from this supposition which has not been thought through, that there must be a substance in the linguistic phenomena. . . . Linguistics . . . works on the borderland where the elements of two orders are combined: this combination results in a form, not a substance.

This image of linguistic structure that de Saussure originated has had, to use his expression, "incalculable" effects on the work of all structural linguists. While they may not employ his terminology, and while most would reject the dualism inherent in his concept of the sign, all are indebted to him for the basic insights brought out in the Cours. These pages have given only an indication of some of the more important contributions he made to linguistics and cannot serve as a substitute for reading the Cours itself.

Review Questions

1. Explain the importance of Durkheim's work for de Saussure's linguistics.
2. How did Durkheim reply to the accusation that he had "needlessly reified" social facts? What is the relevance of his reply with respect to defining linguistic units?
3. How would Durkheim explain the "constraint" of a social fact such as language?

4. Give an illustration in English of the distinction de Saussure made among *la langue, la parole,* and *le langage.*
5. In what sense did de Saussure consider *la langue* active? passive?
6. In what sense is the history of a language relevant and irrelevant to factors in the language at a given stage?
7. What merits would de Saussure find in traditional grammars? what defects?
8. How is the notion *état de langue* important for synchronic linguistics? for diachronic linguistics?
9. How does de Saussure's acoustic image differ from spoken sounds?
10. How did de Saussure describe (a) a simple sign (b) a syntagme, (c) a morpheme?
11. What are the two cardinal characteristics of signs for de Saussure?
12. Give de Saussure's distinction between syntagmatic and associative relations. What difficulty is there in establishing associative relations?
13. Explain de Saussure's distinction between linguistic realities and identities.
14. Explain the analogy of the chessman as an instance of value and give an original example.
15. Distinguish signification, content, and value.

Suggested Readings

Godel, R., "L'école Saussurienne de Genève," in *Trends in European and American Linguistics, 1930–1960,* edited on the occasion of the Ninth International Congress of Linguists by C. Mohrmann, A. Sommerfelt, and J. Whatmough (Antwerp, 1961).

———, Les *Sources manuscrits du cours de linguistique générale* (Paris, 1957).
Saussure, F. de, *Cours de Linguistique Générale* (Paris, 1915); English ed., *A Course in General Linguistics,* trans. Wade Baskin (New York, 1959).
Wells, R. "De Saussure's System of Linguistics," in *Readings in Linguistics,* ed. M. Joos (Washington, D.C., 1957).

8

Edward Sapir

FRANZ BOAS

De Saussure had obtained a model for his linguistic work from a different, if allied, field. Similarly, the most important influence on Edward Sapir's linguistic career was contact with his fellow-anthropologist and linguist, Franz Boas. Boas was self-taught in linguistics. His first interest in his university years had been the physical sciences, and it was primarily an interest in geography, with its anthropological implications, that took him to Baffinland. There he found, contrary to the current teaching, that it is the cultural tradition of peoples and not their environmental situation which is most influential in forming a society. He also appreciated that any description of a culture made in ignorance of the language and literature of the people would likely be misleading and superficial.

Boas was born in 1858, the same year as Durkheim. Sapir was twenty-six years his junior when they met in New York in 1904. At that time, he was pursuing his master's degree in Germanic studies and felt confident that he understood the subject and the nature of language quite well. After meeting Boas, who had gathered a wealth of information about American Indian languages, Sapir reported that he felt as though he had everything to learn. As a result of the meeting he undertook the description of an American Indian language after Boas' method, using a native informant in his own cultural surroundings. This was a novel experience for Sapir, and a radical departure from the

213

traditional practice of trying to impose the grammatical categories of Indo-European languages upon all other languages.

Boas had worked out his own scheme for the orderly description of languages, and he outlined it in the Introduction to the *Handbook of American Indian Languages*.[1] This work called for three basic divisions in the description: (1) the phonetics of the language; (2) the meaning categories expressed in the language; and (3) the grammatical processes of combination and modification by which these meanings must be expressed.

Phonetics

In discussing phonetics Boas showed that he was approaching by experience the views of de Saussure concerning the systematic nature of language sounds:

The number of sounds which may be produced is unlimited. In our own language, we select only a limited number of all the possible sounds; for instance, some sounds, like *p*, are produced by the closing and sudden opening of the lips; others, like the *t* by bringing the tip of the tongue into contact with the anterior portion of the palate, and producing a closure at that point and by suddenly expelling the air. On the other hand, a sound might be produced by placing the tip of the tongue between the lips, making a closure in that manner, and by expelling the air suddenly. This sound would to our ear partake of the character both of the *t* and *p*, while it would correspond to neither of these. A comparison of well-known European languages, like German, French and English—or even of the various dialects of the same language, like those of Scotch and of the various English dialects—reveals that considerable variation occurs in the same manner of producing sounds, and that each dialect has its characteristic phonetic system, in which each sound is nearly fixed, although subject to some slight modifications which are due to accident or the effects of surrounding sounds. One of the most important facts relating to the phonetics of human speech is that every language has a definite and limited group of sounds, and that the number of these in any particular dialect is never excessively large. . . .

Unlike de Saussure, Boas intended to focus on *la parole*. For him language is only "articulate speech; that is . . . communication by means of groups of sounds produced by the articulating organs." These sounds can be accurately described for any language, he believed, and he thought that reports by some analysts that speakers of primitive languages are sloppy in their pronunciation tells us more about the analyst

[1] Franz Boas, Introduction to the *Handbook of American Indian Languages* (Washington, D.C.: Smithsonian Institution, Bureau of American Ethnology, Government Printing Office, 1911), Bulletin 40. The Introduction was reprinted in 1964 by Georgetown University Press. All quotations from Boas appearing in this chapter are from this source and are reprinted with the permission of the Smithsonian Institution.

than the language analyzed. Boas said that, in fact, we can often determine the nationality of the analyst "from the system selected by him for rendering the sounds," which he will tend to hear in terms of his own language sounds.

Grammatical Categories

Besides having its own peculiar phonetic system, Boas held that each language has its own grammatical system. Of all possible phonetic sequences, each language uses only some, those with which meanings are associated. The selection of meanings is as varied and autonomous as the phonetic individualities:

This implies that the total number of ideas that are expressed by phonetic groups is limited. Since the total range of personal experience which language serves to express is indefinitely varied, and its whole scope must be expressed by a limited number of phonetic groups, it is obvious that an extended classification of experience must underlie all articulate speech.

It is important at this point to emphasize the fact that the group of ideas expressed by specific phonetic groups show material differences in different languages, and do not conform by any means to the same principles of classification. To take again the example of English, we find that the idea of *water* is expressed in a great variety of forms: one term serves to express water as a *liquid;* another one, water in the form of a large expanse *(lake)*; others, water as running in a large body or a small body *(river* and *brook)*; still others express water in the form of *rain, dew, wave* and *foam.* It is perfectly conceivable that this variety of ideas, each of which is expressed by a single term in English, might be expressed in other languages by derivations from the same form. . . . In Dakota, the terms *naxta'ka* (to kick), *vaxta'ka* (to bite), *ic'a'xtaka* (to be near to), *boxta'ka* (to pound) are all derived from the common element *xtaka* (to grip) which holds them together, while we use distinct words to express the various ideas.

From experiences with Indian languages Boas concluded that we cannot impose the form of our language upon other languages, but must look to see what kinds of forms they use and how they express relations among ideas. The kinds of classification we find, he believed, are largely due to the peculiar interests of each culture. In addition, mere translations are useless, since the translation process suggests that the language and the culture consist of isolated items. Languages all show both content forms and relational forms that have no meaning but relate those that do:

If each idea could be expressed by a single phonetic group, languages without form would be possible. But since ideas must be expressed by being reduced to a number of related ideas, the kinds of relations become important elements in articulate speech; and it follows that languages must contain formal elements, and that their number must be the greater, the fewer the elementary phonetic groups that define special ideas. In a language which commands a very large, fixed vocabulary, the number of formal elements may become quite small.

Some of the conclusions Boas drew from these remarks include the idea that "the natural unit of expression is the sentence" and not the word, which "as such is only known by analysis." He believed that this view is supported by the fact that we have difficulty finding a meaningful use for words in isolation, especially "form words." Of course there are exceptions:

A sentence like "He sings beautifully" might elicit the reply "sang"; or a laconically inclined person might even remark, in reply to the statement, "He plays well," "-ed" which his friends might well understand.

He would define a "word" as "a phonetic group, which, because of its permanence of form, clearness of significance, and phonetic independence, is readily separable from the whole sentence." The weakest part of the definition, for Boas, was the phonetic.

European ideas about the difference between lexicon and grammar, he thought, depended to a large extent on the peculiar nature of IE languages, in which there are comparatively few affixes and a large number of roots or stems. It is this imbalance between stem and affix that lays the basis for the lexicon-grammar distinction, in which the "stems" express "subjects and predicates" and the "affixes" handle "relational ideas." In a language in which the affixed and unaffixed members are approximately equal in number, the distinction between the modifier and the modified, as well as the lexicon-grammar boundary, becomes arbitrary, and these elements are best treated as coordinate.

Boas considered the study of the grammatical categories peculiar to each language to be the most important task of the linguist, since European grammarians had tended to assume that the categories of their own languages are universal, while his experience showed this view to be false. He therefore discussed some prevalent grammatical classes in IE languages and showed how they can be dispensed with in other languages.

NOUNS   In most IE languages nouns are classified according to the categories of gender, modified by forms expressing singularity and plurality, and appear in syntactic combinations in various cases. According to Boas, "none of these apparently fundamental aspects of the noun are necessary elements of articulate speech." He pointed out that suppression of gender does not hamper clarity, that it is not the same thing as sex, and that other classifications (or none at all) are possible. For example,

Some of the Siouan languages classify nouns by means of articles, and strict distinctions are made between animate moving and animate at rest, inanimate long, inanimate round, inanimate high and inanimate collective objects. *Number* seems absolutely fundamental to us, yet even English has examples like "The wolf killed the sheep," where singularity-plurality would only be determinable from the context. . . . It is entirely immaterial to the Kwakiutl whether he says "There is a house" or "There are houses." The same form is used for expressing both ideas . . . but . . . the Kwakiutl are very particular in denoting whether the objects spoken of are distributed here or there.

For us case does not seem to be wholly absent, even when we use preposi- tional expressions instead of inflected forms. But it is entirely missing in Chinook, in which expressions that we would transliterate *he her it with cut man woman knife* correspond to the normal English *The man cut the woman with a knife.* Here we find merely a string of nouns in ap- position with a number of pronouns, even though the language does distinguish subject and object pronouns. Even English has expressions that cross over this logical vs. formal boundary, as in *my future wife* or *my late husband,* which are comparable to tense classification in some American Indian languages.

PRONOUNS   The IE classification of pronouns is quite arbitrary, Boas showed, since it does not exhaust the logical possibilities inherent in the notion of person:

Logically, our three persons of the pronouns are based on the concepts of the self and the not-self, the second of which is subdivided, according to the needs of speech, into the two concepts of person addressed and person spoken of. When, therefore, we speak of a first person plural, we mean logically either self and the person addressed, or self and the person or persons spoken of, or, finally, self, person or persons addressed and person or persons spoken of. A true first person plural is impossible, because there can never be more than one self.

American Indian languages vary in the number and nature of selections they make from among these possibilities, and they often add other obligatory classifications besides. For example, Kwakiutl and others add the concept of visibility and invisibility, and Chinook adds present and past:

Perhaps the most exuberant development of the demonstrative idea is found among the Eskimo, where not only the ideas corresponding to the three personal pronouns occur, but also those of position in space in relation to the speaker—which are specified in seven directions; as center, above, below, in front of, behind, right, left—and expressing points of the compass in relation to the position of the speaker. It must be borne in mind that the divisions which are mentioned here are *necessary* parts of the clear expression in the languages mentioned.

VERBS   Boas found the IE verbal categories such as person, number, tense, mood, and voice to be equally arbitrary and "quite unevenly developed in various languages." We find an expression like *The man is sick* neither overly explicit nor particularly detailed, but when we compare it with various languages we find that it could be considered both, for it means *The single definite man is sick at the present time.*

The Eskimo will simply say *single man sick* . . . the grammatical form of his sentences does not *require* the expression of the tense relation. In other cases, temporal ideas may be expressed with much grater nicety than we find in our familiar languages. . . . In Kwakiutl, this sentence would have to be rendered by an expression which would mean, in the vaguest possible form that could be given it, *definite man near him invisible sick near him visible* . . . and idiomatic expression would be much more definite. . . . *That invisible man lies sick on his back on the floor of the absent house.* . . . In Ponca, we might have a form like *the moving single man sick.*

Boas concluded his Introduction by saying that any description of a language should concentrate first on what "according to the morphology of the language *must* be expressed" and not just on what the language *might* say. This is an implicit criticism of the traditional grammarians, who imposed the IE scheme upon other languages. They found "nouns" and all the other parts of speech because the language in question *could* express the same idea. But they did not inform us of what this language, because of its own morphological construction, *had to* differentiate.

This is the same point that de Saussure approached in the distinctions we have labeled "signification," "content," and "value." The mistake of the traditional grammarian was to deal with all languages in terms of signification, the sole positive fact of language, ignoring the difference in content, which is a result of the linguistic value, which in turn is an expression of the structural relations of a term in its system.

These distinctions can also cut across some other misconceptions that have resulted from structural work, even in de Saussure's own writings. One misconception is that languages are incomparable because they are systems of signs in which each term's entire definition is to be sought in its structural relations to the other co-existent terms of the system. The other misconception is seen in the so-called Sapir-Whorf hypothesis, one expression of which is hinted at in the passages quoted from Boas. This view, advanced in 1836 by Wilhelm von Humboldt in his *Über die Verschiedenheit der Menschlichen Sprachen,* suggests that language introduces a principle of relativity, because languages, being unique structures, either help or hinder their speakers in making certain observations or in perceiving certain relations.

The point is that the signification of all the sentences Boas quoted can be the same, namely, *man sick:* the renderings he gave are explications of the differences in content, that is, the sum of the signification (what the term *does* mean) and value (what the term does *not* mean). This can be seen by comparing his two versions of an English sentence: (1) *The man is sick;* (2) *The single definite man is sick at the present time.* Without using the terminology, Boas was showing the paradigmatic and syntagmatic relations into which each member of the original sentence enters. For example, *The* could be replaced by *a;* either *man* or *men* could follow *the,* so the choice of *the man* has the content *The single definite man,* and so on for the other members of the sentence.

While it is important to stress the differences among languages, it should not be done to such an extent as to suggest that they have nothing in common. All of the sentences quoted obviously have the signification of the sentences in common, in the technical sense used above. Since signification is said to be the sole positive fact of language in structural description, it is most likely that it is the one feature of which speakers are positively aware. Only if someone were to make a mistake would most English speakers become conscious of the second version of Boas's sample sentence. While it was assuredly the weakness of traditional grammars to obscure the differences among languages by basing their grammarical description on signification, ignoring value, it would be equally misguided to base a description wholly on value and ignore signification.

Whatever Boas's conception of the influence of language on thought, he did not think that language as such makes abstractions impossible, even though Kwakiutl, for example, does not use abstract terms. He experimented with the Kwakiutl language of Vancouver Island,

in which no abstract term ever occurs without its possessive elements . . . isolating the terms for *love* and *pity,* which ordinarily do not occur without possessive forms, like *his love for him and my pity for you.*

The presence or absence of such terms, he felt, was an indication rather of the interests of the speakers, not their abilities. This was true of numbers as well. In many languages numbers are not needed for practical life, even if the speaker is a shepherd, since he might well know his sheep by name and never need to count them. Boas did not believe that there is a direct relation between language and culture

except in so far as the form of the language will be molded by the state of the culture, but not in so far as a certain state of culture is conditioned by the morphological traits of the language.

Boas was convinced that both in language and in the customs of a tribe we find a kind of "subsequent explanation" of what had an unconscious origin, which seeks to rationalize what is simply there. Table manners are a case in point. Europeans do not put their knives in their mouths at table, and the explanation has been given that this is to avoid injury, but Boas thought that the relatively recent invention of the fork and the centuries-long use of dull knives makes this explanation as dubious as the reason the Omahas offer for their table customs: it is impolite among them not to smack the lips when eating, since this would show displeasure with the meal.

Unlike features of social life, however, people rarely become aware of the grammatical features (Durkheim's "constraints") of their languages, and, therefore, it is easier, in the case of linguistic categories, to follow "the processes which lead to their formation without the misleading and disturbing factors of secondary explanation which are so common in ethnology."

EDWARD SAPIR

After his stimulating encounter with Boas Sapir gave up his work in classical philology and, following the methods developed by Boas, started on the analysis of Takelma, an American Indian language spoken in the Northwest. His own reputation as a master of many languages, both from a theoretical as well as a practical aspect, quickly grew. During his career he published articles on linguistic aspects of the usual European languages, many of the classical languages, Chinese, and Gweabo, an African language. But his principal work was with American Indian languages, and the titles of his articles refer to Kwakiutl, Chinook, Yana, Wishram, Wasco, Ute, Nootka, Nahuatl, Cheyenne, Wiyot, Yurok, Comox, Na-dene, Kutenai, Coahuiltecan, Haidan, Tsimshian, Navaho, and others.

To his contemporaries Sapir was a genius; his interests were not confined to anthropology and linguistics, but ranged over a wide spectrum of scientific and humanistic subjects. Between 1917 and 1931 he published over two hundred poems, composed music, and wrote critical reviews in the arts and other fields. The style of most of his book *Language* attests to his skill, as its content does to his erudition. Interestingly enough, *Language* was the only book he wrote, and it was dictated over a period of two months from a handful of notes. The rest of his writings were published in professional journals and other periodicals.

Sapir's Language

In the Preface to *Language* Sapir made it clear that the book was not to be a technical introduction to the description of languages, but, he hoped, a way of communicating some new insights into the nature of language for the general reader. He said that although he mentioned psychological factors involved in language use, he had not intended to go very deeply into the psychological bases. Most of what he said in this vein can be understood in terms of the traditional views of psychological processes discussed in Chapter 5 of the present book.

LANGUAGE DEFINED   The introductory chapter of *Language* contains a definition of language that at first seems to be nothing more than a summary of the traditional view: "Language is a purely human and non-instinctive method of communicating ideas, emotions and desires by means of a system of voluntarily produced symbols."[2]

In expounding the definition, however, Sapir added qualifications that distinguish his conception of language from preceding ones. First, the meaning of language is discussed and assigned to "a visual image, a class of images, or a feeling of relation." But this is not to suggest that meaning can be so simply discussed, since, like language itself, it cannot be localized in any particular part of the brain, consisting as it does in a

peculiar symbolic relation—physiologically an arbitrary one between all possible elements of consciousness on the one hand and certain selected elements localized in the auditory, motor, and other cerebral and nervous tracts on the other.

[p. 10]

Second, the association of speech and meaning is a relation that may but need not always be present, "since the flow of language itself only is constant; its inner meaning, its psychic value or intensity varies freely with attention" (p. 14).

Thought and speech, therefore, while intimately related, are not to be considered coterminous, and in Sapir's view, the best way of viewing the relation is that

From the point of view of language, thought may be defined as the highest latent or potential content of speech, the content that is obtained by interpreting each of the elements in the flow of language as possessed of its very fullest conceptual value.

[pp. 14–15.]

Since there are very many representations or substitutes for language as ordinarily conceived (that is, "primarily an auditory system of symbols" [p. 17]), it is possible to discuss "thought without language," if that means a process in which there is no awareness of auditory symbolism. The motor and other processes that are directly associated with speech pro-

[2] Edward Sapir, *Language: An Introduction to the Study of Speech*, p. 8. Copyright 1921 by Harcourt, Brace & World, Inc.; copyright 1949 by Jean V. Sapir. All quotations from *Language* appearing in this chapter are reprinted with the permission of Harcourt, Brace & World, Inc., and Rupert Hart-Davis, Ltd. Page references are to the Harvest Books edition (New York: Harcourt, Brace & World, Inc., 1949), HB 7.

duction may be put into play in such activities as thinking without our being aware of any auditory imagery.

From these two aspects of language—its indispensability for thought and the fact that the outward form of language alone remains constant, Sapir drew the conclusions that (1) language form can and should be studied for its own sake and (2) meaning must be considered, at least as the highest latent potential, at each step in the formal analysis, since the whole purpose of language is to communicate meanings.

The formal analysis, therefore, requires identification of the elements that are the vehicles of communication and the kinds of meanings that language must convey. In Chapters 2–5 of *Language* the basic units of form and meaning types are discussed.

THE ELEMENTS OF SPEECH   Chapter 2 of *Language* discusses the most fundamental units of language, radicals, grammatical elements, words, and sentences. Sapir did not use the term "morpheme," but his illustrations of radicals and grammatical elements indicate that they have the same function. By the "elements of speech," he did not mean the traditional "parts of speech," which he considers later in the book and rejects. Neither was he discussing the phonemes of the language, since an "element of speech," as Sapir used the term, must, like the morpheme, have a referential function and not merely the differential function of the sounds of language, a subject discussed in Chapter 3 of his book.

Sapir used the term "form" in several senses: in Chapter 2, a "form" is a sound or sequence of sounds that has a meaning. He also used the expression in the more traditional meaning of a determining element; in discussing the addition of affixes to radicals, he would say that the -*er* in *singer* is the "indicator of a subsidiary, and as a rule, a more abstract concept; in the widest sense of the word 'form' " (p. 26). In Chapter 4 "form" refers to grammatical processes, and in Chapter 5, to grammatical concepts. Adding the three purely linguistic uses of the term together, we can define Sapir's notion of linguistic form: it consists of the relations between linguistic forms, which can be considered as morphemes, words and sentences, grammatical processes such as affication or internal modification, and grammatical concepts. What these forms have in common is the distinction discussed in Chapter 5 of this book, that between things materially and formally considered. Materially the object of linguistic study is sound and those sound sequences that have both referential and differential function or merely differential function. It is because of their relation to meaning and meaning discrimination that the sound sequences are considered linguistic.

Sapir illustrated this point simply and effectively in his discussion of the *wh* sound we hear when blowing out a candle or starting a word like *when*. Materially these sounds could be considered the same, but formally, in view of their functions and relations, they are entirely different. The first sound is not an element of linguistic form, but the second is.[3]

In order to show that the study of linguistics can profitably consider the basic formal relations among the elements of language, Sapir developed an "algebraic formulation" to show the relations among the members of common expressions. This formulation employs four kinds of symbols: (1) capital letters, for example, *A;* (2) lower case letters, for example, *a;* (3) parenthesis; and (4) plus signs. Actually there is a fifth symbol, since the *o* he used represents zero and not the letter between *n* and *p*.

The symbols are used as follows: A capital letter stands for a radical, which may or may not be a free form. If the form is free, as in his example *hamot* ("bone"), then it can be represented as *A*. If the radical is a bound form, as it would be in the Latin word *hortus* ("garden"), it can be represented as *(A)*, since the parentheses used here and in the representation of the -*us* affix of *hortus* represent the fact that both are bound forms. The form *hortus,* therefore, is symbolized as *(A) + (b)*. The differences in the letters suggest that each stands for an overt linguistic expression which is correlated with a meaning and that the form is to be analyzed in the same order as the alphabetic representation.

In comparing the Nootka form *hamot* with English "sing" Sapir used the zero symbol to suggest that even the absence of an overt linguistic expression can be meaningful; that is, that the contrast between forms can itself be a signal, either of meaning or of a meaning difference. The point is that, like English "now" or "but," the Nootka form *hamot* is invariable and does not enter into construction with bound forms, while the English form "sing" can be constructed with -*s*, -*ing*, and so on, and, therefore, implicitly contains two or more meanings—"sing" and "non-third-singular," "non-past," "non-present participle," and so on. It is, therefore, best represented as *sing + o* or *A + (o)*, and the list of formal types is now four: *A (hamot)*, *A + (o)* ("bone," "sing"), *(A) + (b)* (*hortus*), and *A + (b)* ("singing"). Another type is possible, *A + B,* as in compound words like "fire engine," but Sapir thought that the majority of such forms are generally analyzed as having a single radical and another form that looks like a radical but considered subordinate, so that he recommended the analysis *A + b* (*Language,* pp. 25–30).

Since the *o* represents the meaning or meaning differences that have

---

[3] See Edward Sapir, "Sound Patterns in Language," *Language,* 1 (1925); also in D. G. Mandelbaum, ed., *Selected Writings of Edward Sapir* (Berkeley, Calif., 1949), pp. 33–35.

no overt phonetic representation in a word, a Latin form like *cor* ("heart") should actually be represented as $A + (o) + (o) + (o)$ to indicate the factors of number, gender, and case in this system. An objection to this procedure might seem to arise from considering an English form like *man*, since it can be found in combinations like *un + gentle + man + li + ness*, which might be symbolized as $(o) + (o) + A + (o) + (o)$. But these zero forms can be considered derivational, and, therefore, optional, while the zeros Sapir used represent inflectional categories, or required contrasts in the nature of the linguistic system. In later practice linguists have preferred to employ zeros (symbolized as $\emptyset$) to stand for allomorphs (for example, *sheep* $+ \emptyset =$ plural, vs. *sheep,* singular) rather than for morphemes.[4]

The order of the letters in such representations is not simply left to right, but the presumed order of analysis or synthesis of immediate constituents. For example, the Paiute word *wii-to-kuchum-punku-rügani-yugwi-va-ntü-m(ü)*, which is rendered "knife-black-buffalo-pet-cut-up-sit (plur.)-future-participle-animate-plural," or, "they who are going to sit and cut up with a knife a black cow [or 'bull'] is symbolized as: $(F) + (E) + C + d + A + B + (g) + (h) + (i) + (o)$ (*Language,* pp. 30–31). A similar representation of a very complex English word shows some of the alternative decisions that can be made and some of the divisions that must be made; for example, *antidisestablishmentarianism.* If this is broken up as *anti + dis + establish + ment + ari + an + ism,* and symbolized as $(d) + (b) + A + (c) + (e) + (f) + (g)$, some of the alternatives appear; we could allow *establishment* as $A + (b)$, or *disestablish* as $(b) + A$, but not *antidisestablish* as $(c) + (b) + A$. The status of *-ari-* in this word is unclear, though it is not in a word like *elementary,* despite the difference in spelling.

The notion of a word has been discussed and disputed by almost every scholar who has dealt with language. For Sapir it did not seem sensible to try to define the notion in isolation from the language under consideration nor to try to identify it with a single concept. The counterparts of single concepts are better found in radicals and grammatical elements, which do not vary from one language to another as widely as the formal units in which they must occur. This being the case, a word can often appear as a sentence, which Sapir defined as "the linguistic expression of a proposition" (*Language,* p. 35), since he was convinced that those who doubt the "prevailing cognitive character" of language have failed to prove their case. "On the whole," he said, "it must be admitted that ideation reigns supreme in language, that volition and emotion come in as distinctly secondary factors" (*Language,* p. 38). The

4 But see Noam Chomsky, *Syntactic Structures* (The Hague, 1957), p. 64.

three basic elements of linguistic form at this level, then, Sapir defined as follows:

Radical - grammatical element, the linguistic counterpart of isolated concepts.
Word, one of the smallest, completely satisfying bits of isolated "meaning" into which the sentence resolves itself.
Sentence, the linguistic expression of a proposition.

[Language, pp. 32, 34, 35]

THE SOUNDS OF LANGUAGE   Sapir had an unusually broad acquaintance with languages of many types and showed himself an acute observer of the phonetic niceties by which the sounds within a language, or sounds of several languages, could be compared and differentiated. But the predominant interest he had in linguistic phenomena of all sorts was their structural relations. It was not the bare facts of phonetic similarity or difference that were most important to him, but the patterns into which these sounds and sound differences fit. An elementary example of his interest in the patterning of language sounds is given in "Sound Patterns in Language," referred to earlier. He took the example of two speakers, A and B, and their pronunciation of *s, th,* and *sh,* and in a diagram indicated that B's *s* is not identical with his *th,* but is closer to it phonetically than to A's *s.* B's *sh* is phonetically closer to A's *s* than to his *sh:*

A :   *th*   *s*   *sh*
B: *th*$_1$*s*$_1$ *sh*$_1$

As a consequence, a classification on purely phonetic grounds might result in a pattern like:

A :   *th*   *s*   *sh*
B: *th*$_1$*s*$_1$ *sh*$_1$

whereas, in terms of significant contrasts, the pattern should obviously be:

A :   *th*   *s*   *sh*
B: *th*$_1$ *s*$_1$ *sh*$_1$

The reason is that despite the phonetic differences, the same number of contrasts, with the same number of differential functions, are involved. The phonetic differences are similar to those found in music when the same song is played in different keys.

Other differences in the sounds of a language can be automatic, and, therefore, not functional, while the same differences might be found to be functional in another language. Thus, the differences in the length of the vowels in English *bat* and *bad* seem to parallel the same differences in German *Schlaf* ("sleep" /šlāf/) and *schlaff* ("slack" /šlaf/), or in the

Latin forms *āra* ("altar," nominative) and *ārā* (ablative). The resemblance is phonetic and not one of functional pattern.[5]

Phonetic units are, therefore, to be described in terms of the usual articulatory criteria, such as the activity of the vocal cords, the passage of the air stream through the nose or mouth, the constriction of the air stream in various manners, and the various points of articulation. The phoneme, on the other hand, is incapable of definition in purely phonetic terms, since it is a "functionally significant unit in the rigidly defined pattern of configuration of sounds peculiar to a language" (*Selected Writings,* p. 46).

Although he did not use the term "allophone," Sapir illustrated some of the techniques that would be applicable to classifying phonetically different sounds as instances of the same phonemes, since the phonetic differences are predictable in terms of the linguistic system and are in complementary distribution. He gave the following data on the voiceless bilabial stop in Southern Paiute (as well as similar information about the other stops, which show marked pattern congruity):

				Postvocalic	
	Initial	1. Spirantized	2. Nasalized	3. Geminated	
				a. After voiced Vowel	b. Before unvoiced Vowel
Labial	p	β	mp	p·	p

Syllables containing /p/ will, therefore, be represented differently in phonetic and phonologic orthography: there is an additional modification to be noted, since the postvocalic forms of the stops of types 1, 2, and 3a show unvoiced spirants before an unvoiced vowel:

Phonetic Orthography		Phonologic Orthography	
1.	pa-	1.	pa-
2.	paβa-	2.	papa-
3.	paθA-	3.	papa-
4.	pap·a-	4.	pap·a-
5.	pApa-	5.	pap·a-
6.	pap·A-	6.	pap·a-

Here the *A* stands for a voiceless vowel (*Selected Writings,* pp. 49–50).

Sapir often spoke of the phonemes of a language as belonging to an "ideal system," which is known "intuitively" by the speakers of the language. This may sound as though he had no rigorous experimental

[5] D. G. Mandelbaum, ed., *Selected Writings of Edward Sapir* (Berkeley, Calif., University of California Press, 1949), pp. 35–37. All quotations from this source appearing in this chapter are reprinted with the permission of the University of California Press.

evidence for establishing such entities and their relations, but nothing could be further from the truth. Note, for example, his reply to his own rhetorical question, "How can a sound be assigned a 'place' in a pattern over and above its natural classification on organic and acoustic grounds?":

> The answer is simple. "A place" is intuitively found for a sound (which is here thought of as a true "point in the pattern," not a mere conditional variant) in such a system because of a general feeling of its phonetic relationship resulting from all the specific phonetic relationships (such as parallelism, contrast, combination, imperviousness to combination, and so on) to all other sounds.
>
> [Selected Writings, p. 42]

LINGUISTIC FORM   Sapir's preoccupation with language was first and foremost revealed in his study of linguistic form, a search for patterns among the sounds and sound sequences of a language. In one essay, "The Grammarian and his Language" (*Selected Writings*, pp. 150–159), he felt called upon to explain and defend that interest, since it appeared to be a lifeless study to many, while others thought that it ignored the meaning aspects of language. He pointed out that while it is the linguist's prime interest to study languages as formal structures, this is not to suggest that form can be studied apart from function, but that one of the most striking features of any language (even the most "primitive") is its formal completeness:

> To put this matter of the formal completeness of speech in somewhat different words, we may say that a language is so constructed that no matter what any speaker of it may desire to communicate, no matter how original or bizarre his idea or his fancy, the language is prepared to do his work. . . . The world of linguistic forms, held within the framework of a given language, is a complete system of reference, very much as a number system is a complete system of quantitative reference or as a set of geometrical axes of coordinates is a complete system of reference to all points of a given space. The mathematical analogy is by no means as fanciful as it appears to be. To pass from one language to another is psychologically parallel to passing from one geometrical system of reference to another. . . . Entirely distinct, or at least measurably distinct, formal adjustments have to be made and these differences have their psychological correlates.
>
> [*Selected Writings*, p. 153]

According to Sapir, then, there are two ideas to be considered in studying linguistic form—the basic concepts communicated by a language and the formal methods by which these basic concepts are related and modified. Grammatical processes are "formal methods for indicating the relation of a secondary concept to the main concept of the radical element" (*Language*, p. 59), and, often enough, these same formal processes are found in the language without reference to any particular grammatical function. Their study can thus be doubly profitable—as an indication of the number of grammatical differences in meaning and as a guide to the formal structure of the language without reference to its grammatical functions.

Sapir discussed six main types of grammatical processes in *Language,* some widespread, others less frequently encountered: (1) word order, (2) composition, (3) affixation, (4) internal modification of the radical or grammatical element, (5) reduplication, and (6) accentual differences. Part of the importance in studying these "processes" is the realization that there is no natural connection between the process and the meaning the process may have in any particular language. Sapir illustrated this point by putting down two English words at random, *sing praise,* and then showing that the native speaker will try to make some sensible relation between them, but will arrive at varying meanings, all of which are exploited in one language or another using a given process. In contrast to languages in which word order is important, Sapir mentioned the case of Latin, in which a sequence like (1) *hominem* (2) *femina* (3) *videt* could be equally well expressed in any order, 231, 312, 213, and so on.

Composition is considered different from word order, since it is the process of uniting two radical elements in a single word, as in *blackbird, redcoat,* or *killjoy* in English. The process shows varied limitations and combinations from one language to another, and some languages cannot employ it at all.

Of all the processes, affixation, which includes the employment of prefixes, infixes, and suffixes, is most common, and suffixing is the more general manifestation of it, although many languages use both prefixes and suffixes. Internal modification of vowels and consonants is illustrated in English forms *sing, sang, sung* in the verbs, or *wife, wives* in the nouns. It is particularly used in Semitic languages and is found in many Amerindian languages as well. Consonantal change is rarer, but English *knife, knives* is a familiar example, as is also *cloth, clothes.*

Reduplication (repeating all or part of a stem) is found frequently in English, in the kind of forms that are found almost universally in languages, such as *pooh, pooh* and *ding dong.* Other languages use the same process for a more distinctly grammatical purpose, for example, classical Greek, in which reduplication was a common phenomenon in the perfect tense: *luo* ("I loose") and *leluka* ("I have loosed"). Perhaps the most difficult to study are accentual differences, since changes of pitch and stress often affect the vocalic qualities involved as well. In many languages accentual features can be considered as inherent parts of the radical or word, and, therefore, they are not grammatically functional, while in other languages such contrasts play an important part in distinguishing grammatical as well as lexical meanings.

These "processes" are not functional parts of the language unless their presence or contrast involves a difference in meaning. The meanings they distinguish, however, vary bewilderingly from one language to another. One of Sapir's most important insights was that such grammatical meanings are often factors of which native speakers are wholly unaware. In order to show this, he submitted a seemingly simple sentence to a "destructive analysis" to show that there are many more concepts involved than the ordinary speaker would suspect. He used as an example the sentence *The farmer kills the duckling* (*Language*, p. 82).

Most people, perhaps, would analyze the sentence into three main concepts, dealing with the farmer, his killing, and the duckling. These correspond to the three concrete concepts that Sapir first distinguished as the first and second subjects of discourse (*farmer, duckling*) and the activity that links them (*kill*). These three forms can then be analyzed into three radical concepts, two verbs (*farm, kill*) and a noun (*duck*), and two derivational concepts, agentive (the *-er* of *farmer*) and diminutive (the *-ling* of *duckling*). There can then be distinguished five sets of relational concepts—two instances of definite reference (*the* with *farmer* and *duckling*); three modalities, (1) "declarative," which is expressed by the word order and implied by the *-s* suffix of the verb, (2) the "subjectivity" of *farmer*, indicated by its position before the verb with the suffix *-s*, and (3) the "objectivity" of *duckling*, expressed by its position after *kills;* two number concepts, "singularity," in both *farmer* (expressed by the *-s* of the verb and the lack of a plural suffix) and *duckling* (expressed by the lack of the plural suffix); and a time concept, expressed by the lack of the preterite suffix in the verb, as well as by the suffixed *-s*.

In all there are thirteen concepts expressed—three radical and concrete, two derivational, and eight relational. This analysis offers no surprises only because we are so familiar with our own language. When we compare sentences in other languages that deal with similar situations, we find, through this method, that there are some unusual omissions and startling inclusions. What, then, are the concepts that a language *must* express, since what a language *may* express is as various as the languages we deal with?

Sapir took it as axiomatic that the fundamental fact of language is the sentence and that the sentence is the linguistic expression of a proposition. This means, then, that

No proposition, however abstract its intent, is humanly possible without a tying on at one or more points to the concrete world of sense. . . . And secondly, such relational concepts must be expressed as moor the concrete concepts to each other and construct a definite, fundamental form of proposition.

[*Language*, p. 93]

There will, therefore, be at least two kinds of concepts that all languages must express and two other types that are commonly expressed. These can be described as concrete concepts and pure relational concepts, the two extremes in terms of which concepts can be distinguished. The linguistic expression of Type I (concrete concepts) is normally an independent word or radical element standing for things, actions, or qualities; Type IV (pure relational concepts) and the intermediate types II (derivational) and III (concrete relational) are usually expressed by one of the grammatical processes already discussed. Type IV, however, can often be expressed by an independent word, for example, preposition. The intermediate types differ from the pure relational in their relative degrees of abstractness and in the nature of their relations to the radical elements with which they are associated as well as to the rest of the proposition.

Since these are conceptual classifications, which are not of the either-or type, Sapir warned that this set of four cannot be taken as mutually exclusive nor as the complete set of distinctions that may be needed in a particular language. The forms of language can be described in an either-or fashion, but our conceptualization of things, he said, is more like a sliding scale. It was principally for this reason that he rejected the traditional definitions and divisions of the "parts of speech" as linguistic universals; they represent "wavering classifications of experience" and not natural functional units. As for formal distinctions, each language has its own set, so that he thought the search for universal "parts of speech" to be a waste of time. At the same time, Sapir recognized that languages, since they are all basically sets of propositions, must distinguish something like a noun and something like a verb (or, perhaps, something that is subject and something that is predicate), since "there must be something to talk about and something must be said about this subject" (*Language*, p. 119). The distinction between noun and verb, however, can be elusive in many languages.

There are some clear resemblances between Sapir's discussion of these topics and those we have already considered: his "destructive analysis" of *The farmer kills the duckling* can be readily understood in terms of de Saussure's signification, content, and value. Comparing *The farmer kills the duckling* and *The man takes the chick*, Sapir pointed out what has been discussed as analogy: "they are really the same fundamental sentence . . . they express identical relational concepts in an identical manner" (*Language*, p. 85). The requirement that concrete and relational concepts be expressed is a reflection of the similar analysis into the logical constants and variables called *onoma, rhēma,* and *syndesmoi* in the Aristotelian division or categorematic and syncategorematic by the medievals. The first subdivision of concrete into derivational concepts, and the intermediate division of the pure relational into concrete relational, deal with the distinctions discussed in terms of consignification by the medievals. Sapir's approach to these problems, however, was markedly superior to the medieval work, since he was in a better position to show that the formal distinctions correspond more directly to the unconscious, rather than to the conscious, organization of experience.

LANGUAGES COMPARED   The comparison of languages, dialects of the same language or different historical stages of the same language will involve the same kinds of methods and criteria. It is the data that are accidentally different. Any language description is implicitly a comparison of that language with other languages that would respond in the same or in a different fashion to the descriptive categories employed. We can, therefore, decide on the criteria by which we can classify languages and contrast their types in terms of the basic elements of linguistic form already discussed.

In erecting a linguistic typology the first problem that Sapir raised was that of the point of view. Too often, he thought, others have tried to use too simple a principle of classification or have based their work on too few examples. As a result, he found some terms that were currently being used to describe language types to be too simplistic. He was convinced that a more basic point of view could be found, and that more than a single point of view is necessary. We can classify languages according to their formal types or according to the kinds of concepts they typically communicate or in terms of both of these factors. When Sapir examined some of the purely external classifications he found them superficial.

For example, a typical opposition would distinguish Latin or Greek as **inflectional,** and Turkish as **agglutinative.** The norms for inflectional appear to be synthesis in the word forms and the use of affixation. Both of these are clearly a matter of degree relative to other languages. More reasonable, but still superficial, would be the distinctions among isolating, prefixing, suffixing, and symbolic language types; but languages of a quite different spirit share one or more of these features. The terms would be more useful if they were used to describe the method of signaling relational concepts alone. According to whether languages combine concepts into single words, they have been called **analytic, synthetic, or polysynthetic,** but these terms again are purely relative, and one language may be analytic compared to a second and synthetic compared to another. It is spurious, Sapir believed, to distinguish between languages that have and those that do not have form.

The most solid way to proceed would be first to classify languages according to what they must have in common and then to subdistinguish them according to more arbitrary properties. The concept types already distinguished provide a handy list of items languages must share, and then the formal methods they use to signal the concept types can be used for more refined classification. Languages can thus be distinguished into four types: (1) those that express concepts of types I and IV, which can be called simple pure relational languages; (2) those that express concepts of types I, II, and IV, which can be called complex pure relational languages; (3) those that express concepts of types I and III, called simple mixed relational languages; and (4) those that express concepts of types I, II, and III, called complex mixed relational languages. These groups can then be subdivided according to the formal types; for example, (1), (2), (3), and (4) can be divided into agglutinative, fusional, and symbolic subtypes, according to the prevailing method of modifying the radical element.

Using these basic classifications and the additional qualifications, three main criteria emerge: (1) the conceptual type, (2) the technique of formal expressions, particularly how the radicals are modified, and (3) the degree of fusion between radical and affix or modification. These degrees of fusion can vary from agglutination (for example, *good + ness*) to regular fusion (for example, *book + s*) to irregular fusion (for example, *deep, depth*) to symbolic fusion (for example, *goose, geese*). When languages are classified in this way it is found that in language change, it is the degree of fusion that is most susceptible to alteration; less likely to change is the normal type or technique; and the least likely to change is the conceptual type.

These classifications are based on the more obvious differences among languages. It is often very difficult indeed to assign a sensible basis for distinguishing one dialect from another. Every speaker of any language can be understood to have a different system from any other speaker, if we define "system" as "the number of units and their combinations," since all one needs in order to have a different system is a construction not used by other speakers. If we have a line of speakers who vary in this way, they would be said to speak the same dialect "because their peculiarities, as a unified whole, are not referable to another norm other than the norm of the series" (*Language,* p. 48). Like the term "dialect," then, expressions such as "language," "branch," or "stock" can be considered terms that reflect our own knowledge about the nature and degrees of language differences and language change.

Language obviously changes. De Saussure, in defining *la langue,* was not denying this, but it is interesting to see that he so defined *la langue* that it theoretically could not be changed by *la parole,* that is, what individuals say, although it obviously had to be. Sapir took up the same problem and pointed out that while language change must result from the differences in what people say (since language really exists only in use), it is still not possible to understand language change as the sum of what different people say. These differences are random (*la parole*), but the "drift" in a language has a direction, and only those variants that conform to this drift will actually contribute to language change.

One of the justifications for de Saussure's definition of *la langue* was the fact that languages change so slowly that we are unaware of the alterations. Sapir pointed out that the direction of change inherent in a language can be called its "slope," and that one of the ways of detecting the slope that contributes to drift, or patterned change, is to examine the hesitations native speakers have about the proper use of forms. This drift is not haphazard, nor the consequence of a lack of system, but is, rather, the stable dynamism of a developing, living use of language, a factor discussed as analogy in the nineteenth century.

English speakers hesitate between the use of *who* or *whom*, especially in sentence-initial position: *Who did you see?* There are several reasons for this hesitation, which reveal aspects of the linguistic system of English. For example, the preverbal position for pronouns and interrogatives is typically the subject position, where we would find *he, she,* and *they,* but not *him, her, them.* The *who* form, therefore, appears to be analogically related to subject forms. Other interrogative forms in *wh-,* such as *what, where, why,* also occur initially, and these are invariable forms; *who* seems to fit into their pattern. Too, these forms are also stressed and phonetically less "heavy" than the *whom* form, which is heavy because of its final nasal and the length of the vowel; thus again *who* seems to have more pattern relation to the short, invariable form. Finally, English shows a tendency both to fixed word order and to invariable forms, and both of these drifts would contribute to our unconscious preference for *who* in sentence-initial position.

This examination of drift, or analogy, has illustrated changes between entire forms of the language, but another illustration of drift is found in the sounds of language studied in isolation from the forms. These "sound laws," as discussed by the *Junggrammatiker,* were often conceived of as a purely mechanical process, but Sapir was of the opinion that the separation of phonetics and grammar is an unfortunate tendency. While it may be true that the laws are impersonal, to the extent that they elude the power of any individual or group to affect them, they are not ultimately mechanical so much as psychological, resulting from our appreciation of pattern in language. They can be called laws only because they allow us to set up a formula "for a consummated drift that sets in at a psychologically exposed point in the language" (*Language,* p. 178).

For example, instead of considering the changes in sounds all by themselves, it would be better to consider three strands, the first of which is very poorly understood, but seems to consist of a drift in one direction, which involves preponderantly dynamic features such as degrees of stress, voicing, and length. There is, next, an innovating analogy, which tries to restore patterns that sound changes have threatened to imbalance. Finally, there is a conservative analogy when sound changes appear to threaten morphological patterns.

An illustration of this can be shown by the old Anglo-Saxon paradigm:

	Singular	Plural
N. Ac.	*fot*	*fet* (older *foti*)
G.	*fotes*	*fota*
D.	*fet* (older *foti*)	*fotum*

This pattern was confusing, since the *o–e* alternation would be useful if it distinguished singular and plural; thus dative *fet* came to be thought out of place and was succeded by *fote*. But this then made the genitive and dative plurals contrary to the pattern, and since they were of less frequent occurrence than the nominative or accusative, they soon became *fete, feten,* resulting in the "more regular" Middle English paradigm:

	Singular	Plural
N. Ac.	*fot*	*fet*
G.	*fotes*	*fete*
D.	*fote*	*feten*

From these considerations Sapir believed that sound change cannot be studied apart from the functions of sounds in the language, and that the pattern of a language, which is affected by sound change, is best considered when we see that "every word, grammatical element, locution, sound and accent is a slowly changing configuration" (*Language,* p. 171). We must consider, therefore, phonetic, phonological, morphological, lexical, and syntactic patterning, as well as etymology and frequency of occurrence.

The possibilities of one language causing change in another through the usual cultural contacts of their users can also be explained on the phonetic, morphological, and conceptual levels. We can also establish how languages in contact are likely to modify each other.

The most usual manner in which language *A* influences language *B* is through the borrowing of vocabulary. In this way the borrowing language is open to phonetic, morphological, or semantic influence. In Sapir's view the likelihood—and historically attested influences support this—of changes in the borrowing language will depend on the drifts, phonetic and morphological, that have already set in. One language will be open to influence from another if the items to be borrowed fit that drift. Otherwise it is unlikely that the borrowed item will cause any disturbance in the patterns of the borrowing language. Sounds will be assimilated if there is some similarity in the borrowing sound system that makes them acceptable, although this may introduce a new phonemic distinction. Constructions that differ from the native pattern are unlikely to find successful adoption in the borrowing language, and the conceptual type of the borrowing language is ultimately the factor that will make the adoption of foreign forms likely or unlikely.

LANGUAGE, RACE, AND CULTURE   The relations among language, race, and culture have always been a concern of anthropologists, and Sapir was one of the scholars, in the tradition of Boas, who helped explode—at least for the scientific community—the myths about predictable connections between the racial characteristics of speakers and their linguistic habits, or between the kind of language people speak and the kind of culture the language reveals.

In *Language,* and in many articles, Sapir presented some of the evidence he had gathered in field work and study to show that while there is no necessary connection between language or race, there are often parallels between culture and language. This fact is hardly surprising, since, as he pointed out, language does not exist apart from culture, that is, apart from "the socially inherited assemblage of practices and beliefs that determine the texture of our lives" (*Language,* p. 207). But if we take language to mean the formal aspects, the "form which we call linguistic morphology," then it has already been shown that a predictable connection between the form of language and culture is by no means necessary, since there is no necessary connection between the formal aspects of language and its conceptual type. Language will not, therefore, mirror the attitude a culture takes toward its environment any more than we can determine, on the basis of whether its language is inflecting or agglutinating, whether a culture is warlike.

The most obvious connections between a culture and its language, Sapir found, will be seen on the level of vocabulary. Eskimos, for example, obviously need a more useful set of expressions to discuss snow than Polynesians, just as a literate society has more need for a word like *cause* than the Eskimo. It is also conceivable that aspectual requirements in a language could reflect both geographical and economically important places or activities, in much the same way as more familiar languages require a distinction between animate and inanimate subjects of discourse.

In one aspect of culture, however, Sapir, and one of his most brilliant pupils, Benjamin Lee Whorf, thought that language plays a central role. If we define "culture" as "what a society does and thinks"(*Language*, p. 219), then the thought aspects of different cultures are strongly conditioned by their particular languages—not, of course, by the formal side of language, nor even directly by the conceptual type, but rather language determines culture through the particular contents of the concepts that make up the world of things in which the culture is interested. In many places Sapir suggested that language is like a "prepared road or groove," which can be analyzed as "a symbolic system of reference," much like one of alternative mathematical or geometrical systems for describing situations. Although language is never, in actual use, merely a referential system, this is one of its basic properties, so that "to pass from one language to another is psychologically parallel to passing from one geometrical system of reference to another" (*Selected Writings*, p. 152).

The geometrical image appealed to Whorf as an illustration of the differences we can find between two languages. He posed the problem a European would have in attempting to discuss geometry with a Hopi Indian. Newtonian geometry requires space and time as coordinates, categories also found in most European languages. The Hopi Indian does not have a grammatically necessary distinction of time as we know it. Instead, the Hopi is required to distinguish degrees of intensity. Whorf soon found that he and a Hopi could not discuss the "same" world.[6]

In the view of both Whorf and Sapir, it is illusory to think that "experience" can occur without the formative guidance of the linguistic habits of the person experiencing, and that the world we live in is first and foremost one "to a large extent unconsciously built up on the language habits of the group" (*Selected Writings*, p. 162). At the same time, Sapir was convinced that "the latent content of all languages is the same— the intuitive *science* of experience" (*Language*, p. 218), but this is formed and patterned differently according to the language of the speaker.

According to the so-called Sapir-Whorf hypothesis, language differences introduce a new principle of relativity, according to which men are not led by their experience to the same picture of the universe unless their language backgrounds are the same or similar. This view led Sapir to question whether philosophers have not been projecting grammatical categories into their conceptions of the world, so that "innocent lin-

---

[6] Benjamin Whorf, "Science and Linguistics," in J. B. Carroll, ed., *Language, Thought, and Reality: Selected Writings of Benjamin Lee Whorf* (Cambridge, Mass.: M.I.T. Press, 1956), p. 216 ff. All quotations from the writings of Whorf appearing in this chapter are taken from this source.

guistic categories may take on the formidable appearance of cosmic absolutes" (*Selected Writings,* p. 157). In a similar vein Whorf, in comparing Hopi and Standard Average European (SAE) verbal categories, found that the basic categories of Hopi verbs could be called "manifested" vs. "manifesting" or "unmanifest," while the SAE distinctions were among present, past, and future. He considered both of these sets "cosmic forms" projected upon the universe by the observers, and he could find no common denominator between them (*Language, Thought, and Reality,* p. 59). Perhaps the traditional explanation of time as "a measure of change, according to before and after" might shed some light on the problem. SAE verbal categories could be seen as indications of previous, contemporaneous, and succeeding changes, while the aspects by which change is measured in Hopi is one of actuality "manifested," indifferent to present or past, and potentiality, "unmanifested," "what we call future, but . . . equally . . . all that we call mental" (*Language, Thought, and Reality,* p. 60). In this way it might be seen that "the latent content of all languages is the same," while still pointing out the startling differences in the way the content can be formed and related. This observation might be deduced from a remark with which Sapir concluded his discussion of language, race, and culture: "To learn what is the essential nature of speech there is perhaps no better way than to realize what it is not and what it does not do" (*Language,* p. 219).

Review Questions

1. How did Boas find language study important for anthropology?
2. What novelty was involved in Boas' methods of language analysis?
3. How did he equate form in language with relation of ideas?
4. What did he consider the three main steps for making an objective description of a language and which did he consider most important?
5. Compare Sapir's definition of language with others you know.
6. What did Sapir mean by "linguistic form"?
7. How did Sapir define "radical," "grammatical element," "word," "sentence"?
8. Be prepared to analyze words in English and other languages you know in terms of Sapir's "algebraic notation."
9. What did Sapir conclude from the differences he found between form and function?
10. What did he consider to be the basic grammatical processes, and how must they be established?
11. List the concepts he found underlying *The farmer kills the duckling.* Be prepared to analyze similar sentences in English and other languages you know.

12. How would de Saussure explain Sapir's "exaggeration of the concreteness of subsidiary concepts" in this kind of analysis?
13. Compare Sapir's list of concept types with the traditional distinctions.
14. What are the basic criteria for comparing language types? What are subsidiary criteria?
15. Why did Sapir reject the traditional parts of speech?
16. Explain the notion of drift and give Sapir's example of it in English.
17. Compare the notion of drift with analogy as understood by Thrax and the nineteenth-century linguists and *la langue* as defined by de Saussure.
18. How did Sapir explain phonetic change?
19. What relation did Sapir see among language, race, and culture?
20. Explain the Sapir-Whorf hypothesis and reconcile it with Sapir's notion that the basic meaning of all languages is the same.

Suggested Readings

Boas, F., Introduction to the *Handbook of American Indian Languages* (Washington, D.C.: Smithsonian Institution, 1911), Bulletin 40. Reprinted with a Foreword by C. I. J. M. Stuart (Washington, D.C.: Georgetown University Press, 1964).

Carroll, J. B., ed., *Language, Thought and Reality: Selected Writings of Benjamin Lee Whorf* (Cambridge, Mass.: M.I.T. Press, 1956).

von Humboldt, K. W., *Über die Kawisprache auf der Insel Jawa* (Berlin, 1836–1840). The Introduction to this work was reprinted as *Über die Verschiedenheit des menschlichen Sprachbaues und ihren Einfluss auf die geistige Entwickelung des Menschengeschlechtes*, 2d and 3d eds. (Berlin, 1876–1883).

Mandelbaum, D. G., ed., *Selected Writings of Edward Sapir* (Berkeley, Calif., 1949).

Sapir, E., *Language: An Introduction to the Study of Speech* (New York, 1921).

9

Leonard Bloomfield

Since the work of the nineteenth-century historical linguists we have seen a growing desire to make the study of language both scientific and autonomous. The desire for a scientific approach, if the term "scientific" is to be equated with "exact," is understandable. The accomplishments of the historical linguists in establishing the laws of sound change founded the hope that language could be studied scientifically, although such study was considered to be possible only on the diachronic plane. De Saussure, however, introduced the possibility that through investigation of the linguistic sign and its relations the synchronic study of language could proceed in an exact manner. This area of study, he believed, should be maximally free of dependence on other disciplines. Thus the actual sounds of speech and their meanings were not investigated in detail by de Saussure. It was Sapir who bridged the gap between the older and the newer conceptions of how to make the study of language a science.

One difficulty to be solved was the central one of language—its meaning and the relation of linguistic form to meaning. In *Language* Sapir's treatment of meaning relied on traditional psychology, but used modern structural methods to describe linguistic form. Since form alone remains constant in actual utterances, while meaning varies with attention, the object of an autonomous linguistics for Sapir was to be linguistic form.

BEHAVIORISM

Of all the authors whose works we have examined so far in this volume Leonard Bloomfield was the most concerned with making linguistics both autonomous and scientific. As the term was understood in the 1930s, "scientific" implied restricting evidence to empirical data. It should be clear that the psychological, dualistic approach of de Saussure and Sapir entailed using data that were not amenable to empirical study, understood in this simplistic sense. One reason for this approach was the lack of a persuasively presented and empirically based psychology. During the period when Bloomfield was writing his second version of *Language*, an empirical approach to psychology, called "behaviorism," was being developed by J. B. Watson. Bloomfield became acquainted with its promise and accomplishments through the work of A. P. Weiss. For readers with a humanistic, traditional psychological approach, the most characteristic—and unsatisfactory—feature of Bloomfield's book was his acceptance of behaviorist psychology as one of the ways of stating meanings. This aspect of his classic work, however, is peripheral and brought in only to illustrate how meanings could be empirically stated by another discipline. Bloomfield had no intention of making linguistics subordinate to another, nonlinguistic discipline; rather, it was his goal to make it an autonomous science by pointing out that aspect of language which he thought to be the proper object of scientific linguistics.

Behaviorism in the strict Watsonian formulation of it is all but dead.[1] But the linguistic work of Bloomfield underlies and inspires the work of many linguists still, especially in the United States. Many of his findings have been revised, some have been abandoned, but *Language* was such a thorough, significant, and suggestive survey of the field of linguistics that it has been termed the "bible of American linguistics." Much of it has been superseded by later analyses, but no single book has replaced it.

Although Bloomfield was intrigued by the promise of the behavioristic approach, a summary of Watson's views will show that his trust was most likely misplaced, whereas an account of his linguistic doctrines will show that Bloomfield's work is valid apart from that background.[2]

In a short summary of his position, developed in a debate with Oxford professor William MacDougall, Watson explained that his aim as a psychologist was to find out, "given a certain object or situation, what will the individual do, when confronted with it; or, seeing someone

[1] See O. H. Mowrer, *Learning Theory and Behavior* and *Learning Theory and the Symbolic Process* (New York, 1960), and Noam Chomsky's review of B. F. Skinner's *Verbal Behavior* (New York, 1957), in *Language*, 35 (1959), 1.

[2] See Rulon Wells, "Meaning and Use," *Word*, 10 (1954), 2.

doing something, to be able to predict what situation is calling forth that response."[3]

According to Watson, the sort of empirical study he proposed was badly needed. He considered the traditional psychology that MacDougall represented to be a poor substitute for science, because it deals with a scientifically indefensible notion of "soul." Watson found this notion to be religious in origin, a consequence of the idea of the supernatural. The latter notion, he said, can be traced to a primitive stage in human society when a group of men, too lazy to work but skilled in observing others' behavior, saw that they could put others into a state of fear through the threat of the supernatural, then require the others to support them in return for deliverance from the unknown danger. For Watson, this was the origin of religion, which he thought always builds on fear and not love (*Battle,* p. 10). The chief source of authority is, therefore, fear, as embodied in a father figure, of which God is the prime example. As a consequence of religion, we have religious authority, from which stems dogma, including the myths of soul, and human, as well as universal, purpose. Watson found these ideas to be hardly scientific: "no one ever touched the soul or has seen it in a test-tube or come into a relationship with it, as he has with other objects of experience" (*Battle,* p. 12).

Wilhelm Wundt had been the first to set up a psychological laboratory in 1869, but there he had attempted to investigate "consciousness," which Watson found to be merely a pseudoscientific term for "soul." Since such work involves introspection, Watson believed it to be scientifically useless, since there is no element of empirical control. Instead of working on the basis of an unprovable assumption, Watson intended to deal with observables—what the organism does or says, since speech is just one of many forms of behavior. He would ask when the organism started to behave, why it does what it does, whether the behavior was genetically transmitted (and, therefore, an example of an unconditioned response) or whether society teaches this form of behavior (and, therefore, an example of a conditioned response).

Watson was convinced that by investigating stimuli leading to responses behaviorism would provide a basis for predicting human behavior, a result that would be impossible in a study based on introspection. He defined "stimulus" as "any object in the general environment or any change in the physiological condition of the animal, such as the change we get when we keep it from sexual activity, feeding, or building a nest," which leads to some form of behavior.

[3] J. B. Watson and W. MacDougall, *The Battle of Behaviorism* (New York: W. W. Norton & Company, Inc., 1929). All quotations from *The Battle of Behaviorism* appearing in this chapter are reprinted with the permission of W. W. Norton & Company, Inc.

242 / LEONARD BLOOMFIELD

He defined a "response" as "that system of organic activity that we see emphasized in any kind of activity, such as building a skyscraper, drawing plans, having babies, writing books and the like" which is the consequence of some stimulus (*Battle*, p. 19). In all unconditioned responses Watson assumed that "some definite stimulus must call forth each of these responses," so that if 1 is a consequence of *A*, and *B* is always associated with *A*, then *B* can also be called forth by 1, and so on. This is the typical Pavlovian conditioning situation—the food makes the dog salivate (where food = *A*), and a bell is always rung when food is presented (bell = *B*), so that eventually *B* can call forth 1. This set of reactions has previously been called "learning," but Watson thought the stimulus-response explanation is better, since it does away with "the old hypothesis that there is any inherent or sacred connection with or association of one object with another. . . . *Order in the universe is merely a matter of conditioning*" (*Battle*, p. 22, italics his). Watson would obviously have favored the anomaly position in the anomaly-analogy dispute, but with modern trimmings.

The perception of order in the universe is explainable behavioristically as a feature of integration, by which more and more objects or situations become related in our experience as stimuli and responses, since if we apply stimulus *X* each time we apply stimuli *A*, *B*, *C*, and so on, then *X* will call forth the integrated social responses 1, 2, 3. For Watson, these integrated social responses are completely and without exception due to external, conditioning stimuli and in no way the consequence of "consciousness" or "mind" or "soul," since "*The Behaviorist* finds no scientific evidence for the existence of any vitalistic principle" (*Battle*, p. 25, italics his) such as that which Professor MacDougall claimed to investigate. "Purpose," in Watson's view, is merely a cover term for such stimuli-response combinations, which increase in complexity as we pass from infancy to adulthood. Instead of such assumptions as "soul" and "purpose," "we need nothing to explain behavior except the ordinary laws of physics and chemistry, but there one sets up a theory or hypothesis in terms of what *is* known and not on the assumption of an unknowable" (*Battle*, p. 26). It should be the same in psychology.

For Watson, fear is the most powerful of all responses, and it is found as an unconditioned response in the infant as a result of two, and only two, stimuli—a loud noise or loss of support. No other stimulus will call it forth, but *any* other stimulus co-applied with the other two can become a conditioned stimulus for the fear response. Watson pointed out that this is the reason psychoanalysts cannot eradicate fear with words alone: they must recondition the intestinal tract as well.

What has been traditionally called "thinking" is just a form of behavior: "thinking is merely talking, but talking with concealed musculature" (*Battle*, p. 33). Can we think without words? Thought is really a work of the whole bodily organization, consisting of implicit manual organization, implicit verbal organization, and overt visceral organization. If the first or third type prevails, then we can be said to be thinking without words. By "visceral," Watson meant what traditionalists call "emotional." Therefore, we could think in some fashion, even if we had no words, since thinking is largely subvocal talking:

Words are thus the conditioned stimulus for our world of objects and acts. Thinking is a device for the manipulation of the world of objects when those objects are not present to the senses. This more than doubles our efficiency. It enables us to take our day world to bed with us and manipulate it at night or when it is thousands of miles away. Psychoanalysts, when talking an individual out of a bad situation, often forget that the person carries the bad verbal set to a new location. Most of the happy results of analysis are due to the fact that the analyst builds up a new world, correlated with a new manual and a new visceral world. There is no virtue in analysis *per se*.

[*Battle*, pp. 38–39]

In the 1930s the behaviorist approach was a breath of fresh air in the field of psychology, and many valuable insights were won by applying its method of observation. But traditionalists like MacDougall were not prepared to abandon their position on so little evidence. It should be fairly clear that both Watson's and MacDougall's positions rest on an experimentally unprovable assumption: where MacDougall assumed a mind or vital force as the most economic way of accounting for the variability of human behavior, Watson assumed such variability to be the result of external stimuli alone, on the same principle of economy. But we are justified in positing an observable response as the result of a stimulus only when the stimulus is also observable; otherwise, we are merely assuming that there is a relation. "Stimulus" and "response" are mutually defining terms and are mutually required to establish each other. If we take Watson's ideas on beliefs to mean that MacDougall held the position he did as a consequence of conditioning over which he had no control, one could ask why Watson preferred his own view, which was equally the result of uncontrolled conditioning. All he could allege in its favor was that he held such a position. On such a basis one cannot sensibly choose either view, and the point of the debate comes into question: choice is the result of the integration of stimuli and responses. Inconveniences such as these led traditionalists to reject Watson's view of human behavior and resulted as well in a mistrust of Bloomfield's work.

"LANGUAGE"[4]

The 1933 version of *Language* was a revision of an earlier work, *Introduction to the Study of Language*, published in 1914. This version relied on the psychology of Wundt for the statement of meanings, while the later work illustrated meanings in behavioristic terms. In both cases the appeal to a psychology was not to be taken as a sign that the linguistic facts were derived from or dependent upon the verification of either approach. Language, as Bloomfield conceived it, is a set of signals, and the structure of the set can be studied by the linguist without commitment to any theory about what there is to signal or how it is possible for human beings to signal. The rest of this chapter is devoted to summarizing some of Bloomfield's main ideas. Since the book itself contains more than 500 tautly written pages, only some of the high points can be dealt with here.

"The Study of Language" (Chapter 1)

"The Study of Language" surveys the various views of language that we have examined earlier in this volume and the shifting points of view that inspired them. Although this account contains references to the main landmarks in linguistic study, all are assessed from a behavioristic point of view. A more balanced view of what was accomplished will be obtained by referring to the sources cited. Bloomfield concluded that all linguistic work prior to that of the historical linguists was misguided in one or more ways, principally because of the deductive or normative approach. His conclusion is a good summary of his own point of view:

The only useful generalizations about language are inductive generalizations. Features which we think ought to be universal may be absent from the very next language that becomes accessible. Some features, such as, for instance, the distinction of noun-like and verb-like words as separate parts of speech, are common to many languages, but lacking in others.

[p. 20]

"The Use of Language" (Chapter 2)

The "Use of Language" should be studied together with Chapter 9, "Meaning," since these two chapters present Bloomfield's basic convictions about the subject. Chapter 2 introduces a behaviorist explanation

---

4 Leonard Bloomfield, *Language*, copyright 1933 by Henry Holt and Company, © 1961 by Leonard Bloomfield. All quotations from *Language* appearing in this chapter are reprinted by permission of Holt, Rinehart and Winston, Inc.

of meaning and lists some of the objections, from this point of view, to the traditional "mentalist" approach. Since these chapters still occasion some misunderstanding, it will be worthwhile to discuss them in detail.

Bloomfield began by pointing out that the most difficult step in language study is the first—to view language as one form of bodily behavior. Others have approached the study of language without actually entering upon it. Instead, they have devoted their attention to manifestations of language, such as writing (which is linguistic, but derived from the central facts of language), or they have studied literature, philology, or "correct" speech, all of which are uses of language, but not language itself. All such detours can be avoided if we consider an act of speech to be behavior in simple circumstances.

Bloomfield illustrated the notion of simple circumstances with a story about Jack and Jill, walking down the lane. Jill sees an apple, makes a noise with her larynx, tongue, and lips, and Jack climbs a tree to get the apple, which Jill then devours. These simple circumstances can be broken down into

A. Practical events preceding the act of speech.
B. Speech.
C. Practical events following the act of speech.

[p. 23]

Bloomfield expressed the events listed under (A) in behavioristic terms as follows: "She was hungry; that is, some of her muscles were contracting, and some fluids were being secreted, especially in her stomach" (p. 23). Part of the speaker's stimulus can be described through the fact that the light waves reflected from the apple were striking Jill's eye: the practical events that follow upon the act of speech are called the **hearer's response**. Had Jill been alone, speech would not have entered into the circumstances and she would have had to get the apple herself. The factors that led to her desiring the apple are the stimuli, S, and her work in getting it for herself would be the normal response, R. The connection between the two can be symbolized with an arrow:

$$S \longrightarrow R$$

Since Jack happened to be available, Jill could use speech as a substitute for her own physical labor, R, so that speech in these circumstances becomes a **substitute response** for Jill, which can be symbolized by r in the same representation, whereas speech becomes a **substitute stimulus** for Jack, on the assumption that he was not hungry:

$$S \longrightarrow r -------s \longrightarrow R$$

The importance and utility of such an arrangement is manifest, since *"The gap between the bodies of the speaker and the hearer—the discon-*

tinuity of the two nervous systems—is bridged by the sound-waves" (p. 26; italics Bloomfield's).

This arrangement enables men to cooperate in a manner manifestly superior to that found among other animals.

In Bloomfield's opinion the mechanics of speech production, represented by the broken lines in the diagram, are fairly well understood, whereas the symbolic process, represented by the arrows, is not. There are two main contending theories to account for the symbolic process, which Bloomfield called **mentalism** and **mechanism.** He summarized the first as follows:

the variability of human conduct is due to the interference of some non-physical factor, a *spirit* or *will* or *mind* . . . that is present in every human being. This spirit, according to the mentalistic view, is entirely different from material things and accordingly follows some other kind of causation or perhaps none at all . . . as this mind or will does not follow the patterns of succession (cause-and-effect sequences) of the material world, we cannot foretell her [Jill's] actions.

[pp. 32–33]

Bloomfield found the second theory more satisfactory:

The *materialistic* (or, better, *mechanistic*) theory supposes that the variability of human conduct, including speech, is due only to the fact that the human body is a very complex system. Human actions, according to the materialistic view, are part of cause-and-effect sequences exactly like those we observe, say, in the study of physics or chemistry. However, the human body is so complex a structure that even a relatively simple change, such as, say, the impingement on the retina of light-waves from a red apple, may set off some very complicated chain of consequences, and a very slight difference in the state of the body may result in a great difference in its response to the light-waves. We could foretell a person's actions (for instance, whether a certain stimulus will lead him to speak, and, if so, the exact words he will utter), only if we knew the exact structure of his body at the moment, or, what would be the same thing, if we knew the exact make-up of his organism at some early stage—say at birth or before—and then we had a record of every change in that organism, including every stimulus that had ever affected the organism.

[p. 33]

Accordingly, we say that the speech-utterance, trivial and unimportant in itself, is important because it has *meaning:* the meaning consists of the important things with which the speech-utterance is connected, namely the practical events.

[p. 27]

The study of speech-sounds without regard to meanings is an abstraction: in actual use, speech-sounds are uttered as signals. We have defined the *meaning* of a linguistic form as the situation in which the speaker utters it and the response which it calls forth in the hearer. . . . We can define the meaning of a speech-form accurately when this meaning has to do with some matter of which we possess scientific knowledge. We can define the names of plants or animals by means of the technical terms of botany or zoology, but we have no precise way of defining . . . *love* or *hate* . . . and these latter are in the great majority.

[p. 139]

As long as we pay no attention to meanings, we cannot decide whether two uttered forms are "the same" or "different." . . . Since we can recognize the distinctive features of an utterance only when we know the meaning, we cannot identify them on the plane of pure phonetics. . . . [In order] to recognize the distinctive features of a language, we must leave the ground of pure phonetics and act as though science had progressed far enough to identify all the situations and responses that make up the meaning of speech-forms.

[p. 77]

From these passages it is clear that Bloomfield was far from holding the position, sometimes attributed to linguists, that language can be described without any appeal to meaning at all. At the same time his conclusion is also understandable, considering how he defined "meaning":

The statement of meanings is therefore the weak point in language-study and will remain so until human knowledge advances very far beyond its present state. In practice, we define the meaning of a linguistic form . . . in terms of some other science.

[p. 140]

This passage suggests, then, that linguistics, as Bloomfield conceived it, will never be fully autonomous, if this conception demands that forms, meanings, and their associations be the prescribed field of linguistic work. On the other hand, science as Bloomfield understood it is a unifying and unified form of knowledge, so that the scientific treatment of language form and meaning would not betray the autonomy of linguistics, although we use another name for the area of the discipline that studies meanings. Still, one is impelled to reflect that the language of science is precise, because it is artificial, to the extent that one of the reasons for our need of it is to avoid the analogous and ambiguous expressions of ordinary language. The meanings of linguistic forms can be successfully assigned when they are scientific meanings, devoid of connotation. Such meanings are not, strictly speaking, "human meanings," yet this is the sort of meaning that is behind the ordinary man's use of the word *salt*. To be told that the ordinary meaning of the English word *salt* is "sodium chloride (NaCl)" is to miss the point entirely, and is an indication of a great man's occasional naïveté.

Continuing his comparison of the mentalist-mechanist positions, Bloomfield wrote:

Adherents of the mentalist psychology believe that they can avoid the difficulty of defining meanings, because they believe that, prior to the utterance of a linguistic form, there occurs within the speaker a non-physical process, a *thought, concept, image, feeling, act of will,* or the like, and that the hearer, likewise, upon receiving the sound-waves goes through an equivalent or cor-related process. The mentalist, therefore, can define the meaning of a lin-guistic form as the characteristic mental event which occurs in every speaker and hearer in connection with the utterance or hearing of the linguistic form. The speaker who utters the word *apple* has had a mental image of an apple, and this word evokes a similar image in a hearer's mind. For the mentalist, language is *the expression of ideas, feelings,* or *volitions.*

The mechanist does not accept this solution. He believes that the *mental images, feelings,* and the like are merely popular terms for various bodily movements, which, so far as they concern language, can roughly be divided into three types:

(1) large-scale processes which are much the same in different people, and, having some social importance, are represented by conventional speech-forms, such as *I'm hungry (angry, frightened, sorry, glad; my head aches,* and so on);

(2) obscure and highly variable small-scale processes, muscular contrac-tions and glandular secretions, which differ from person to person, and, having no immediate social importance, are not represented by conventional speech-forms.

(3) soundless movements of the vocal organs, taking the place of speech-movements, but not perceptible to other people ("thinking in words").

The mechanist views the processes in (1) simply as events which the speaker can observe better than anyone else; the various problems of meaning, such as that of displaced speech (the naughty child saying *I'm hungry*), exist here no less than elsewhere. The mechanist believes that the processes in (2) are private habits left over, as traces, from the vicissitudes of education and other experience; the speaker reports them as *images, feelings,* and so on, and they differ not only for every speaker, but for every occasion of speech. The speaker who says, "I had a mental image of an apple," is really saying, "I was respond-ing to some obscure internal stimuli of a type which was associated at some time with the stimuli of an apple in my past."

The sub-vocal speech in (3) seems to the mechanist merely a derivative habit of actual speech-utterance; when we are assured that a speaker has inaudibly performed the speech-movements of a certain utterance ("thought it in words") we face exactly the same problem as when he has audibly uttered the same speech-form. In sum, then, the "mental processes" seem to the mechanist to be merely traditional names for bodily processes which either (1) come within the definition of meaning as the speaker's situation, or (2) are so distantly correlated with speech-utterance as to be negligible factors in the speaker's situation, or (3) are mere reproductions of the speech-utterances.

[pp. 142–143]

Despite the radical differences he saw between these opposed theories of meaning, Bloomfield concluded that in practice there is little or no difference between them: "the mentalist in practice defines meanings exactly as does the mechanist, in terms of speech-situations" (p. 143).

Since these passages embody views that have alienated many traditionally trained students of language, it will be worthwhile to point out some of the main points that might be misunderstood:

1. In two short paragraphs of about 120 words each Bloomfield summarized and dismissed approximately twenty-five centuries of thought on language study, leaving the impression that mentalists are all of one persuasion, faithfully reported in his account of the position. Aside from the fact that it was impossible for Bloomfield to do justice to a single position in so little space, one should be aware that there is the widest divergence among mentalists, and that the single view Bloomfield seemed to have been describing—that of Descartes—would have been rejected by many of them.

2. Much of what is ascribed to a mentalist view of language study is derived from speculative philosophy or psychology. Since these disciplines employ different methods for aims that are not the same as those in empirical linguistic investigation, their findings will not be directly comparable. There has never been a general agreement about the nature and methods of physical science, but perhaps most people would agree that philosophies attempt to tell us what things *are,* while the first goal of the scientist is to tell us how things *behave,* whatever they are. Statements drawn from fields with such divergent goals and methods are not readily comparable. Views about the basic nature of language have changed little for centuries, while linguistic science advances each time a new or more precise method of describing the facts of language becomes available. Linguistics, therefore, is a field in which there is constant growth in insight and revision of fundamental models and theories about language. Mentalism as a method of describing languages and as a philosophic position are hardly the same thing.

3. While Bloomfield also seems to have been convinced of mechanism as a valid philosophy, the core of his linguistic work was not dependent on such a basis. This seems fortunate, since from the empirical point of view of the 1930s, Bloomfield's three divisions of linguistic and prelinguistic processes do not seem hopeful: (a) the large-scale processes are those that are, to some extent, *known;* (b) the obscure, highly variable processes are *postulated;* and (c) the obscure, soundless movements that are not perceptible to others (and not to oneself) are empirically *unknowable.*

4. Bloomfield identified the prelinguistic processes with those the mentalists called "thought" and held that the traditional qualitative

distinctions between thought and material processes is not one of kind but of complexity, since the kind of measurement he used can find no differences. He believed the mentalist position to be dogmatic, since it rests on an empirically unprovable assumption. It would seem that his faith that science would one day clear up the complexities he referred to is equally unprovable, so that both positions appear no less dogmatic.

5. It is a mark of Bloomfield's integrity that he pointed out clearly the insoluble difficulty for a behaviorist approach in his notion of **displaced speech**; that is, "People often utter a word like *apple* when no apple at all is present" (p. 141). This is accounted for by the fact that the state of the speaker's body is an important part of every situation, which is to account for displaced speech, lying, irony, poetry, and narrative fiction. One's satisfaction with such a solution, as compared with the traditional mentalist account, will depend on the considerations already mentioned.

"Speech-Communities" (Chapter 3)

Bloomfield defined a "speech-community" as "a group of people who interact by means of speech" (p. 42). Like Boas and Sapir, Bloomfield did not believe that the biological consititution of speakers has any influence on their common language. The notion of a speech community suggests a way of illustrating the difficult distinction between languages and dialects within a language. Within speech communities there are differences in the **density of communication.** That is, we talk with some people more than we talk with others. If each speaker within a community were represented by a dot on a map, and then lines were drawn between those who habitually talk to each other, a network of lines showing the density of communication would result. Some dots would be connected by heavy lines and others by very light lines. Between some groups of dots there would be no connecting lines at all, or only in a few individual cases. It seems that groups of speakers, isolated from each other geographically or socially, tend to develop modes of speech that are not readily understood by those who communicate with them infrequently. When communication is not merely absent, but impossible, we have to do with two languages; when it is infrequent, but more or less easy, we have to do with two dialects within a language.

Tracing these lines of communication among dialects results in a continuous gradation and not a sharply defined line. Bloomfield classified the main types of speech roughly as follows (p. 52):

1. The **literary standard** for formal speech and writing. This dialect is generally accessible to all in a literate community regardless of their locality, through general education.

2. The **colloquial standard,** which is the informal style of the privileged class.

3. The **provincial standard,** which will resemble (2) to a greater or lesser degree, depending on the country in which it is found. There are more marked differences among English provincial standards than among American, for example.

4. **Sub-standard** clearly differs from the first three. In some countries, this will be a consequence of social position, in others, a consequence of geography.

5. The **local dialect** would be that variety of language which is not comprehensible to other speakers of the community without considerable acquaintance. It is the style often used by the least privileged classes, or it may be the language of the home, which differs from the other standards.

"The Languages of the World" (Chapter 4)

Bloomfield listed the languages of the world by their geographic distribution, the number of speakers they have, and the language family to which they belong. The summary is interesting, but will not be dealt with at length here, since it is not indicative of Bloomfield's original contributions to linguistics.

"The Phoneme" (Chapter 5)

We should remember that, as Bloomfield defined language study, the linguist as such cannot have real knowledge of what language means; that is, Bloomfield has so defined the requirements that they cannot be met. It is also the case that the study of language can be conducted without special assumptions only as long as we pay no attention to the meaning of what is spoken" (p. 75). Such a study shows that speech is a continuum, that is, something that "can be viewed as consisting of any desired number of successive parts" (p. 76). Despite the infinite variety of speech, we obviously understand each other, so that "Evidently the working of language is due to a resemblance between successive utterances" (p. 76). Thus, "as long as we pay no attention to the meanings, we cannot decide if two uttered forms are the 'same' or 'different' " (p. 77). One reason we cannot decide is that the identical phonetic forms could belong to two different languages: *man* uttered on a high or a low pitch in English is the "same" form, but the same sequence of sounds uttered on different pitches are "different" in Chinese. This points to the fact that the working of language depends upon our habitually and conventionally discriminating some features of sound and ignoring all others. The features of sound in any utterance, as they might be recorded in the laboratory, are the *gross acoustic features* of this utterance. Part of the gross acoustic features are indifferent (*non-distinctive*) and only a part are connected with meanings and essential to communication (*distinctive*).

[p. 77]

Since this varies from langauge to language, we must

act as though science had progressed far enough to identify all the situations and responses that make up the meaning of speech-forms. . . . The study of *significant* speech-sounds is *phonology* or *practical phonetics*. . . . Phonology involves the consideration of meanings.

[p. 78]

These meanings have not, so far, been scientifically established, but Bloomfield believed that in time they would be. In the meantime, phonology rests on: "the fundamental assumption of linguistics: we must assume that *in every speech-community some utterances are alike in form and meaning*" (p. 78).

A moderate amount of experimenting shows that the significant features of a speech form are limited in number, and a method results that can establish this fact—the minimal pair test—which Bloomfield illustrated with the word *pin:*

(1) *pin* ends with the same sound as *fin, sin, tin,* but begins differently; this kind of resemblance is familiar to us because of our tradition of using end-rime in verse;
(2) *pin* contains the sound of *in,* but adds something at the beginning;
(3) *pin* ends with the same sound as *man, sun, hen,* but the resemblance is smaller in (1) and (2);
(4) *pin* begins with the same sound as *pig, pill, pit,* but ends differently;
(5) *pin* begins with the same sound as *pat, push, peg,* but the resemblance is smaller than in (4);
(6) *pin* begins and ends like *pen, pan, pun,* but the middle part is different;
(7) *pin* begins and ends differently from *dig, fish, mill,* but the middle part is the same.

In this way, we can find forms which partially resemble *pin* by altering any one of *three* parts of the word . . . if we alter the first part and then the third, we get a series like *pin-tin-tick;* if we alter the second part and then the third, we get a series like *pin-pan-pack;* and if we alter all three parts, no resemblance is left, as in *pin-tin-tan-tack.*

Further experiment fails to reveal any more replaceable parts in the word *pin;* we conclude that the distinctive features of this word are three indivisible units. each of these units occurs also in other combinations, but cannot be further analyzed by partial resemblances: each of the three is *a minimum unit of distinctive sound-feature, a phoneme.* Thus we say that the word *pin* consists of three phonemes: the first of these occurs also in *pet, pack, push,* and many other words; the second also in *fig, hit, miss,* and many other words, and the third also in *tan, run, hen,* and many other words. . . . A little practice will enable the observer to recognize a phoneme even when it appears in different parts of words, as *pin, apple, mop.* Sometimes our stock of words does not readily bring out the resemblances and differences. For instance, the word *then* evidently consists of three phonemes, but (especially under the influence of our way of writing) we might question whether the initial phoneme was or was not the same as in *thick;* once we hit upon the pair *thigh* and *thy,* or upon *mouth* and *mouthe,* we see that they are different.

[pp. 78–79]

Bloomfield then expanded these basic remarks and called attention to several features of distinctive and nondistinctive differences:

1. Distinctive features occur in bundles or lumps, each of which we call a phoneme.

2. It is not possible to produce the distinctive features without the nondistinctive.

3. The phonemes of a language are not sounds but features of sounds, which the speakers have been trained to produce and recognize.

4. The range of the nondistinctive features is wide, but that of the distinctive is narrow and relatively constant.

5. Foreign speakers who produce the distinctive features of a language make themselves understood, but often speak with an accent as a result of faulty distribution of the nondistinctive features.

6. Nondistinctive features occur in all manners of distribution, but there is usually a limit on their variability.

7. Since each language has its own phonemes, established through different distinctive features, foreign speakers tend to use their own phonemes, which may seem to be the same, but often fall outside the acceptable range of the foreign phoneme they are trying to produce.

8. What saves communication is the native speaker's complementary accuracy, which makes up for the faulty pronunciation.

9. The difficulties mount when two or three of the foreign phonemes resemble some *one* native phoneme.

10. Difficulties become most acute when the foreign language makes significant use of features that play no such role in our own language.

The need of recording all these observations indicates the necessity for a symbol system that would provide a single sign for a single phoneme. The usual alphabetic writing approaches this ideal, but is not completely successful, and several systems have been invented to replace it: (1) Bell's "visible speech," which uses signs for the typical positions of the vocal organs; (2) Jespersen's "analphabetic writing," which uses Greek letters for the articulatory organs, numerals for the degree of aperture, and Latin letters for features such as voicing and nasality; and (3) the International Phonetic Association's symbols (IPA), which Bloomfield adopted, not because this is the best system but because it is the best known. It employs symbols that are used in many European languages with approximately the same values, but when several languages are being compared, each should have its own symbols.

Bloomfield distinguished several kinds of phonemes. Those that were discovered in the experiment with *pin* are called **simple primary phonemes** (often called **segmental phonemes**) and there are between fifteen and fifty in various languages. He found thirty-two simple primary phonemes in his own Chicago English. **Compound phonemes** are those made up of primary ones, but which function as units, for example, diphthongs, of which Bloomfield found eight in his dialect. **Secondary phonemes** occur when two or more forms are combined, or when simple forms are used in special ways. Bloomfield found nine in his Chicago English. Secondary phonemes include the **suprasegmental phonemes,** discussed earlier. Stress and pitch are discussed in Chapter 5 and others are treated in Chapter 7 of *Language.*

Since we have already considered one analysis of the phonemes of English, it will be interesting to list Bloomfield's earlier analysis and compare the two. Note that Bloomfield did not observe the later convention of including phonemes within slanted lines:

PRIMARY PHONEMES

[a]	alms	[amz]	[i]	pin	[pin]	[r]	rod	[rɑd]
[ɑ]	odd	[ɑd]	[j]	yes	[jes]	[s]	sod	[sɑd]
[b]	big	[big]	[ǰ]	gem	[ǰem]	[š]	shove	[šov]
[č]	chin	[čin]	[k]	cat	[kɛt]	[t]	tin	[tin]
[d]	dig	[dig]	[l]	lamb	[lɛm]	[θ]	thin	[θin]
[ð]	then	[ðen]	[m]	miss	[mis]	[u]	put	[put]
[e]	egg	[eg]	[n]	knot	[nɑt]	[v]	van	[vɛn]
[ɛ]	add	[ɛd]	[ŋ]	sing	[siŋ]	[w]	wag	[wɛg]
[f]	fan	[fɛn]	[o]	up	[op]	[z]	zip	[zip]
[g]	give	[giv]	[ɔ]	ought	[ɔt]	[ž]	rouge	[ruwž]
[h]	hand	[hɛnd]	[p]	pin	[pin]			

COMPOUND PRIMARY PHONEMES

[aj]	buy	[baj]	[ij]	bee	[bij]	[ɔj]	boy	[bɔj]
[aw]	bough	[baw]	[juw]	few	[fjuw]	[uw]	do	[duw]
[ej]	bay	[bej]	[ow]	go	[gow]			

SECONDARY PHONEMES

["], placed before primary symbols, loudest stress: *That's mine!* [ðɛt s "majn!].

['], placed before primary symbols, ordinary stress: *forgiving* [for'givin]; *I've seen it* [aj v 'sijn it].

[ˌ], placed before primary symbols, less loud stress: *dining room* ['dajnin ˌruwm]; *Keep it up* [ˌkijp it 'op].

[ˌ], placed under one of the primary symbols [l, m, n, r], a slight stress which makes this primary phoneme louder than what precedes and what follows: *coral* ['karl], *alum* ['ɛlm], *apron* [ejprn], pattern ['pɛtrn].

[.], placed after primary symbols, the falling pitch at the end of a statement: *I've seen it.* [aj v 'sijn it.].

[¿], placed after primary symbols, the rising-falling pitch at the end of a question to be answered by speech-forms other than *yes* or *no: Who's seen it?* ['huw z 'sijn it¿].

[?], placed after primary symbols, the rising pitch at the end of a yes-or-no question: *Have you seen it?* [hɛv juw 'siyn it?].

[!], placed after primary symbols, the distortion of the pitch-scheme in exclamations: *It's on fire!* [it s an 'fajr!], *Seven o'clock?!* ['sevn o "klɑk?!].

[ˌ], placed between primary symbols, the pause, often preceded by rising pitch, that promises continuation of the sentence: *John, the older boy, is away at school* ['jan, ðij 'owldr 'bɔj, iz e'wej et 'skuwl].

[pp. 91–92]

"Types of Phonemes" (Chapter 6)

After a discussion of the production of familiar sound types in articulatory phonetic terms, Bloomfield pointed out, as did Sapir (and Aristotle), that there are no particular organs that serve only for the production of speech. Bloomfield then cited some sound types that are frequently found as phonemes in familiar languages. "Noise-sounds" include stops, trills, and spirants; "musical sounds" include nasals, laterals, and vowels. Consonantal articulations are described by listing the organs involved, the place and manner of articulation, and specifying the degree of closure and friction. Vowels are defined as "modifications of the voice-sound that involves no closure, friction, or contact of the tongue or lips" (p. 102). The other sounds are consonants (for example, stops, trills, spirants, nasals, and laterals). Although they are usually voiced, some languages distinguish various kinds of vowels, such as **muffled, murmured,** or **whispered** vowels.

Each language distinguishes at least several different vowels in articulatory terms, primarily on the basis of the difference in tongue position, but also according to acoustic terms and the distribution of overtones. Bloomfield found nine vowels in his variety of English and said that the same number is found in British English, except that the distribution of the back vowels differs: the degree of closure in words like *up* and *odd* are the reverse of his pattern. In Italian he found a seven-vowel system:

	Front	Indifferent	Back
high	i		u
higher mid	e		o
lower mid	ε		ɔ
low		a	

Bloomfield listed as Italian examples:

si [si] 'yes,' *pesca* ['peska] 'fishing,' *pesca* ['pɛska] 'peach,' *tu* [tu] 'thou,' *pollo* ['pollo] 'chicken,' *olla* ['ɔlla] 'pot,' *ama* ['ama] 'loves.'

Spanish, he said, has a five-vowel system:

	Front	Indifferent	Back
high	i		u
mid	e		o
low		a	

Spanish examples Bloomfield listed as:

si [si] 'yes,' *pesca* ['peska] 'fishing,' *tu* [tu] 'thou,' *pomo* ['pomo] 'apple,' *ama* ['ama] 'loves.'

Tagalog (Philippines) has a three-vowel system:

	Front	Indifferent	Back
high	i		u
low		a	

In closing this section Bloomfield noted that the fewer the phonemes there are in the system, the more room there is for nondistinctive variation of each, so that in the Tagalog pronunciation, one would hear *o* and *e* along with other familiar qualities of European languages, but these sounds are not phonemically distinct from the three basic sounds listed.

So far, there has been no mention of phonemes that differ because of lip-rounding rather than tongue position alone. Phonemic distinctions based on this difference are found in French, which Bloomfield sketched as follows:

	Front		Back
	Unrounded	Rounded	(Rounded)
high	i	y	u
higher mid	e	ø	o
lower mid	ε	œ	ɔ
low	a		ɑ

Bloomfield gave as French examples:

fini [fini] 'done,' *été* [ete] 'summer,'
lait [lɛ] 'milk,' *bat* [ba] 'beats,'
rue [ry] 'street,' *feu* [fø] 'fire,' *peuple* [pœpl] 'people,'
roue [ru] 'wheel,' *eau* [o] 'water,' *homme* [ɔm] 'man,' *bas* [ba]
'low.'

Added to those listed are the nasalized vowels of *pain* [pɛn] 'bread,' *bon*
[bon] 'good,' *un* [œn] 'one,' banc [ban] 'bench," and a shorter variety of
[œ], which is transcribed [ə], as in *cheval* [šəval] 'horse.'

Another possibility is the use of unrounded back vowels in contrast
with the rounded, as in the three-dimensional vowel systems of Turkish:

	Front		Back	
	Unrounded	Rounded	Unrounded	Rounded
high	i	y	ï	u
low	e	ø	a	o

Tenseness and laxness may also be distinctive features, and on this
basis Bloomfield analyzed the German vowel system, with the "tenser"
on the left and the "laxer" on the right:

	Front		Indifferent	Back
	Unrounded	Rounded		(Rounded)
high	i:i	y:y		u:u
mid	e:e	ø:ø		o:o
low			a:a	

German examples Bloomfield listed as:

ihn [i:n] 'him,' *in* [in] 'in,'
Beet [be:t] 'flower-bed,' *Bett* [bet] 'bed,'
Tür [ty:r] 'door,' *hübsch* [hypš] 'pretty,' *König* ['kø:nik] 'king,'
zwölf [tsvølf] 'twelve,'
Fusz [fu:s] 'foot,' *Flusz* [flus] 'river,' *hoch* [ho:x] 'high,' *Loch*
[lox] 'hole,' *kam* [ka:m] 'came,' *Kamm* [kam] 'comb.'

"Modifications" (Chapter 7)

Because of his concept of the phoneme, with which many would disagree today, Bloomfield discussed "modifications":

The typical actions of the vocal organs described in the last chapter may be viewed as a kind of basis, which may be modified in various ways. . . .[through] the length of time through which a sound is continued; . . . loudness . . . musical pitch . . . position of organs not immediately concerned in the characteristic action; the manner of moving the vocal organs from one characteristic position to another.

[p. 109]

Some of these modifying features are employed in languages as secondary phonemes. In the section on J. R. Firth, we will see some objections to discussion of phonological entities that involve a "basis" which can add or lose features. But Bloomfield said:

Among stress-using languages, there are some differences in the manner of applying stress. In English there is a non-distinctive variation by which the vowels of unstressed words and syllables appear in a "weakened form." . . .
   In other cases the weakened syllables actually show a loss of phonemes, or substitution of one vowel phoneme for another.

[p. 112]

Once we have obtained some notion of how a phoneme is formed, we may observe various *modifications* in the way it is produced. . . .
   The most important of these is *palatalization:* during the production of a consonant the tongue and lips take up, so far as is compatible with the main features of the phoneme, the position of a front vowel, such as [i] or [e]. Thus, we may say that in English [k] and [g] are subject to non-distinctive palatalization before a front vowel.

[p. 117]

One of the modifications Bloomfield discussed is **transition,** defined as

The manner in which the vocal organs pass from inactivity to the formation of a phoneme, or from the formation of one phoneme to that of the next, or from the formation of a phoneme to inactivity. . . .

[p. 118]

Between successive consonants, the transition is said to be **close** or **open.** This difference is sometimes distinctive and sometimes not. Bloomfield stated that close transition is characteristic of English, contrasted with French, as seen in the cognates "actor," *acteur.* English stop-spirant clusters show close transition, where French explodes the stop before the spirant begins: "Betsy," "cupful," "it shall" vs. *cette scène, étape facile,* and *cette chaise.* If both types of transition occur in the same language, Bloomfield said, the distinction can be phonemic. He did not state or deny that transition contrasts in English are phonemic.

When discussing succession of phonemes, the problem of successions that seem to function as units is raised. When two vowels are found in succession, differences in their sonority are important. In general, one finds in such combinations that a low vowel is more sonorous than a high one; stress and other factors being equal, one finds any vowel more sonorous than a consonant, and a nasal, trill, or lateral more sonorous than a spirant. In any succession, then, whether of vowels or of consonants and vowels, there will be an up and down of sonority, and those sound features that, in a given environment, are more sonorous than those that precede or follow, will be a **crest of sonority** or a **syllabic.** An utterance can therefore be said to have as many syllables as there are syllabics. As a consequence, to the division of vowels and consonants, a third category must be added, that of **sonants,** since it will be found that in any language most phonemes are used as nonsyllabics, while others may either be vocalic or consonantal. Every language must be investigated individually, but in general it can be said that when the syllabic or nonsyllabic function is determined by the surrounding phonemes (or silence) the distribution is not distinctive (for example, in German, the phonemes *i* and *u* are not syllabic when they precede or follow another vowel; in other positions they are syllabic). Where the syllabic or nonsyllabic function of sonants is not determined by surrounding phonemes, the difference is phonemic, (for example in Central-western English, syllabic stress is a secondary phoneme, as in *stirring* vs. *string.*

Articulatory differences also set off the syllable from the nonsyllable function of sonants. English sonants *i* and *u* occur as nonsyllabics before and after vowels (for example, *yes, say, buy, boy,* which can be transcribed as [jes], [sej], [baj], and [bɔj], with [j] for the nonsyllabic occurrence of [i] and [w] for the nonsyllabic occurrence of [u] as in *well, go,* and *now,* [well], [gow], and [naw]. In these examples Bloomfield considered that the nonsyllabic function of *i* and *u* is determined by the "natural sonority" of the preceding or following vowels.

Therefore the actual variations in the manner of forming the sounds are here non-distinctive. . . . A non-syllabic sonant which, thanks to some modification, is phonemically distinct from the corresponding syllabic sonant is called a *semivowel.*

[p. 123]

Vowels and sonants also combine into compound phonemes, which are called **diphthongs** or **triphthongs,** depending on the number of sounds involved. Since syllabicity is a matter of the relative loudness of the phonemes, it is subject to the support or modification of stress adjustments. These stress adjustments can create stress crests of sonority, which are independent of the "natural" sonority of the phonemes.

"Phonetic Structure" (Chapter 8)

For the useful description of languages more than articulatory and acoustic phonetics is required. When either of these two approaches is used, their reputed accuracy depends on the attunement of the describer and the reader, who may or may not possess the same interests, training, and skills. This leaves a good deal open to chance and affords little hope of objectivity. For such reasons, Bloomfield said:

it is beyond our power to analyze the general acoustic effect of a language. . . .

    The important thing about language, however, is not the way it sounds. . . . For the working of language, all that is necessary is that each phoneme be unmistakably different from the others. . . . Any language can be replaced, for all its essential values, by any system of sharply distinct signals, provided that one signal is made to replace each phoneme of the language. . . . The importance of a phoneme, then, lies not in the actual configuration of its sound-waves, but merely in the difference between this configuration and the configurations of all the other phonemes of the same language.

    For this reason even a perfect knowledge of acoustics will not, by itself, give us the phonetic structure of a language. . . . For instance, [two] languages might show seven similar vowel "sounds," but in Language B these might be seven different phonemes, while in Language A . . . [the sounds] might be non-distinctive variants . . .

[pp. 128–129]

    These ideas are clearly Saussurean, and, as we have seen, were also explicitly developed by Sapir. As a consequence of these observations, however, Bloomfield concluded that the grouping of phonemes merely according to their phonetic characteristics is insufficient. Rather, he said, to show the phonological structure phonemes should be set out according to the consonant-vowel-sonant distinctions. In this way it would become clear which of the segments is always, never, or under what conditions syllabic or nonsyllabic in the typical positions—initial, medial, and final.

    After comparing some phonetic structures of various languages, Bloomfield summed up the chapter by saying,

Once we have defined the phonemes as the smallest units which make a difference in meaning, we can usually define each individual phoneme according to the part it plays in the structural pattern of the speech-forms. . . .

The phonemes so defined are the units of signaling; the meaningful forms of the language can be described as arrangements of primary and secondary phonemes. . . .

We have seen three ways of studying the sounds of speech. Phonetics in the strict sense—that is, laboratory phonetics. . . . Practical phonetics is an art or skill, not a science. . . . phonology defines each phoneme by its rôle in the structure of speech-forms. It is important to remember that practical phonetics and phonology presuppose a knowledge of meanings; without this knowledge we could not ascertain the phonemic features. . . .

Any combination of phonemes that occurs in a language, is *pronounceable* in this language, and is a *phonetic form*. . . .

When the phonology of a language is established, there remains the task of telling what meanings are attached to the several phonetic forms. This phase of the description is *semantics*. It is ordinarily divided into two parts, *grammar* and *lexicon*. . . . A phonetic form which has a meaning, is a *linguistic form*. . . . any . . . sentence, phrase, or word is a linguistic form. . . .

[pp. 136–138]

"Meaning" (Chapter 9)

Much of what the chapter on meaning deals with has already been covered. But there are some additional remarks in this chapter that deserve mention here. Bloomfield assumed that linguistic meanings are more specific than nonlinguistic acts and that each linguistic form has a constant and specific meaning. As a consequence he did not believe that there are true synonyms. An interesting conclusion he drew from these facts is that the most accurate use of language is that peculiar type called mathematics, although he noted that in this connection the basic terms of mathematics cannot be defined by the mathematician.

In drawing this conclusion he reasoned as follows: a universal feature of every language is the presence of **substitutes**—forms that have the same grammatical function as other forms, so that they can be grouped into **form classes.** Each member of a form class may be said to bear a common element of meaning, besides its own peculiar lexical meaning, which can be called a **class meaning.** Substitutes often have no other meaning than class meaning, for example, English pronouns. Pure form-class meaning gives rise to "the specially accurate form of speech which we call mathematics" (p. 147).

Despite Bloomfield's conviction that we are unable to give scientific statements of many meanings, he found that there are two main features of dictionary meanings that we cannot ignore: (1) many linguistic forms are used for more than one typical situation and (2) the addition of supplementary values in linguistic forms, which we call **connotations.**

In spite of the variety introduced by these two facts. Bloomfield found it remarkable that speakers have "assurance and agreement in viewing one of the meanings as the *normal* (or *central*) and the others as *marginal (metaphoric* or *transferred)*" (p. 149).

These facts are the sort of data that originally gave rise to the discussion of analogies—factors partially the same and partially different in successive situations but labeled with the same linguistic form. Required for any analogy is the **prime analogate,** the instance or example which, in itself or in our experience of it, represents the clearest example of the relations that are said to unite the disparate forms contained under the analogy.

Among transferred forms Bloomfield found that sometimes the transferred meaning is determined by an accompanying form, and this situation is illustrated through the uses of typical suffixes. Sometimes we hesitate in deciding whether a given form is one that has several meanings or whether we have to do with mere homonyms. One danger for the monolingual speaker in all of this is that he finds that processes of transference which are natural and necessary in his own language are not found at all in other languages. Compare this idea with the medieval linguistic study of extension and restriction of supposition, not signification, that is, the number of *things* (the environment, in Bloomfield's terms) to which a term applies when in construction with other terms.) Bloomfield found widened meanings more common than narrowed meanings.

The presence of **connotations,** supplementary values, is the other important factor in the variability of meanings and is the result of the fact that "the meaning of a form for any one speaker is nothing more than the sum of the situations in which he heard it."

These supplementary values arise from several sources, and Bloomfield listed some of the more common ones: (1) the social standing of the speaker; (2) his local provenience; (3) the perception of archaisms; (4) technical terms; (5) learned forms; (6) foreign forms or foreign-learned forms; and (7) slang. Actually, the varieties of connotation are countless and indefinable. For example, in all speech communities there are improper forms, but the reasons for their impropriety differ greatly from one language to another. Some can be used only in serious speech and other uses are considered irreverent; some are considered obscene and others, dangerous or ominous. Degrees of **intensity** are also variable, since some forms are considered animated (exclamations) and others symbolic (English stop-lateral clusters), and still others imitative (for example, *cuckoo*). There are also nursery forms, pet names, and nonsense forms.

"Grammatical Forms" (Chapter 10)

In the discussion of how the grammar of a language is to be described Bloomfield introduced several original terms, many of which have remained in use, with the same meanings he gave them. He agreed with de Saussure that the linguist should study language as it is actually spoken at the time of the study and assumed that the forms of the language have constant and definable meanings. However, the "basic assumption of linguistics" must now be modified to read: "In a speech community some utterances are alike *or partly alike* in sound and meaning" (p. 159). This restriction led him to distinguish **bound** and **free** forms, and when these are found in combination, we have to do with a **complex form**: "A linguistic form which bears a partial phonetic-semantic resemblance to some other linguistic form, is a *complex form*" (p. 160). Pursuing this line of development, Bloomfield distinguished the **ultimate** and **immediate constituents** of complex forms and opposed simple forms to them: "A linguistic form which bears no partial phonetic-semantic resemblance to any other form, is a *simple* form or *morpheme*" (p. 161).

In analyzing the sentence *Poor John ran away*, Bloomfield found that it contains five morphemes: *poor, John, ran, a-,* and *way*. They are also the ultimate constituents of the sentence, but the immediate constituents are *Poor John* and *ran away*.

Although the study of the meanings of the morphemes is not possible in the science of linguistics itself, the meaning of a morpheme can be called a **sememe**; some other science may be able to supply the meanings, Bloomfield assumed, but the linguist studies them as **signals,** since, as far as the linguist is concerned, "The signals can be analyzed, but not the things signaled about" (p. 162).

A complete list of the morphemes of a language would account for all its phonetic forms, and this sum would be called the **lexicon.** The lexicon, however, cannot account for all the meanings of a language, since there are other features of significance that do not enter into the dictionary lists. These are basically features of arrangement: "The meaningful arrangements of forms in a language constitute its *grammar*" (p. 163).

Bloomfield discussed four basic ways in which linguistic forms are arranged: (1) order, (2) modulation or use of secondary phonemes, (3) phonetic modification or change of the primary phonemes, and (4) selection or differing arrangements of the same constituents resulting in different meanings. These features of selection are complex and arbitrary, occuring with various combinations of the other methods of arrangement, but they can usually be sorted out and identified. In general, "A simple feature of grammatical arrangement is a *grammatical feature* or *taxeme*" (p. 166).

The taxeme is to the grammar what the phoneme is to the lexicon, the smallest unit of form, which distinguishes meanings, but which has no meaning itself. The smallest units of grammatical form may therefore be called **tagmemes** and their meanings **episememes**. A tagmeme may consist of more than one taxeme; the complete description of an utterance would be made in terms of its lexical and grammatical forms, since only the meanings cannot be described in linguistic science. Thus, the utterance *Duchess!* is completely described in linguistic terms as consisting of the lexical form *duchess* and the two taxemes of exclamatory pitch and the selection of a substantive expression. (Bloomfield noted that contained in the feature of selection is the **order**, *duke* + *-ess;* the **phonetic modification** of *duke* to *duch-;* and **modulation** in the stressed *duch-* vs. the unstressed *-ess*).

For Bloomfield the need for distinguishing the four taxemes exemplifies the principle (more strictly, the assumption) that

a language can convey only such meanings as are attached to some formal feature: the speakers can signal only by means of signals. . . .
a linguistic form, as actually uttered, always contains a grammatical form.
[p. 168]

In this sense isolated forms are abstractions. The grammatical forms of a language can be classed into three main types: (1) when a form is spoken alone, it appears as a **sentence type;** (2) two forms spoken as constituents of a complex form unite into a construction by virtue of the grammatical features that combine them; (3) substitutions are forms spoken as substitutes for a whole class of other forms.

"Sentence Types" (Chapter 11)

Two positions can be distinguished in the discussion of sentence types: **absolute position,** when forms are used alone, and **included position,** when forms occur as parts of other forms. These positions will help distinguish sentences from nonsentences. All languages distinguish between **full** sentences (favorite sentence types) and **minor** sentences (all the others). The two favorite sentence types in English Bloomfield called **actor-action** and **commands.** While these are also the types in many European languages, other languages have quite a variety of favorite sentence types. When there is more than a single sentence type two parts in grammatical agreement are often found, usually called the **subject** and **predicate.** This construction forms the sentence type called a **predication.** Bloomfield pointed to the impersonal expression in

German as an exception, for example, *Mir ist kalt,* "I am cold." There are many subdivisions of sentence types, such as questions that can be subdivided into yes-no-questions, supplement questions, and so on.

The problem of word vs. sentence varies from one language to another. In general, however, bound forms never appear as sentences, so that the possibility of occurring alone is one of the criteria for defining a word, which is a form in absolute, and not included, position; a word is therefore a **minimum free form**. A free form that consists of two or more lesser free forms is a phrase. While these distinctions are easily made and understood, many complexities and doubts arise in actual practice, so that supplementary criteria are required, not all of which are useful in every case. To establish the fact that a form is free, we should ideally hear it used alone. But many forms rarely occur alone. We can establish them as free forms, however, on the basis of their structural parellelism to known free forms. For example, we can establish *the,* in English, as a free form, since it is in parallel distribution with forms that occur alone, *this* and *that:*

| this thing | that thing | = | the thing |
| this | that | = | (the) |

[p. 179]

On a similar basis the **conjunct forms** of French (*je, tu, il,* and so on) can be called words, because of their parallelism to the absolute forms (*moi, lui*).

Another useful criterion, especially for distinguishing compound words from phrases, is stress, since compound words generally have a single stress, for example, *black bird* vs. *blackbird.* There are other expressions, for example, *devil may care,* which function like compound words rather than phrases, however, which show that this criterion alone is not decisive, since an expression like *devil may care,* in Bloomfield's notation, would have more than a single main stress. A better criterion is, therefore, the uninterruptibility of words. Subsidiary criteria are then the peculiar restrictions each language may put on word structure (for example, Turkish requires vowel harmony within words), or on syllable structure (for example, Hawaiian, syllables must be either V or CV), by permitting a single high stress within the word (as in English), or by restricting stress to a given position in the word (initial stress in Hungarian). Unfortunately, all of these phonetic criteria can be difficult to apply when the word is in included position.

"Syntax" (Chapter 12)

For Bloomfield syntax is the study of grammatical constructions that are different from those treated in morphology; it is, traditionally, a separate division of grammar. The constructions that syntax deals with have immediate constituents which must all be free forms; the constructions studied in morphology may have bound forms as their immediate constituents.

A **syntactic construction** is defined as a recurrent set of taxemes of modulation, phonetic modification, selection, and order. In the sentences *John ran, John fell,* and *Bill ran* there are taxemes of **selection** (the nouns and verbs, for instance, cannot fill each others functions) and **order** (for example, the noun precedes the verb). These constructions can be said to have two **positions,** and each position can be called a **function** (or functions) of the forms that can appear in that position. All the forms that can fill a given position thereby constitute a **form class.**

Since the constituents of these constructions are free forms, there are various ways in which they can be linked together. Simple juxtaposition, or **parataxis,** is a much-used device, and there are several kinds of parataxis—those with and without pause, usually nondistinctive variants in English (*It's ten o'clock. I have to go home.*); close parataxis (*Yes sir; please come*); semi-absolute forms (*John, he ran away.*); and parenthesis (*I saw the boy, I mean Smith's boy, running down the street.*). Apposition is a form of parataxis in which the forms not equivalent in meaning are grammatically linked in one construction (*John, the poor boy . . .*). A device much employed in English is a variety of this form, that is, close apposition without pause pitch (*King John, John the Baptist*).

Features of modulation and phonetic modification play a great role in syntactic constructions, and they are known as **sandhi,** an expression from the Hindu grammarians meaning "putting together." We are thus enabled to distinguish between the **absolute** and **included** form of a word, that is, the formal differences found when a word is uttered alone or with others. There are various forms of sandhi, obligatory and optional (for example, *a* and *an* are obligatory forms of sandhi, but *did you* and "*didja*" are optional). Sandhi modifications are found more often in final phonemes than in initials.

Taxemes of selection are of great importance in all languages, and syntax consists largely of a discussion of them. There is a relation between the number of selective taxemes and the form classes with which they operate: the more taxemes there are, the more subdivisions of form classes one finds. Although these subdivisions have meaning, defining them on that basis is generally of little help, since they are basically mechanical and in great variety:

	(1)	(2)	(3)	(4)
A:	I can	I run	I was	I am
B:	The boy can	The boy runs	The boy was	The boy is
C:	The boys can	The boys run	The boys were	The boys are
	A = B = C	A = C	A = B	[p. 191]

Agreement is a narrower form of selection, operating on principles similar to the larger sort, and conveniently divisible into three general types: **concord** or **congruence**, for example, the agreement in number or gender; **government**, which has to do with the selected forms that are permitted or required to occur with a concomitant form (for example, *watch me*, but *I watch*); and **cross-reference**, subclasses that contain mention of the forms with which they are joined (for example, "John, his mark," *Jean, où est-il?*).

Syntactic constructions involve free forms that may belong to different form classes, so that it is possible to identify the constructions in terms of the form classes concerned. The **resultant phrase** when free forms are in construction can be said to belong to the same form class as one (or more) of its constituents when we have an **endocentric** construction. If the resultant phrase does not belong to the same form class as either of its constituents, the construction is called **exocentric.** Of the two, endocentric constructions are more frequent. Endocentrics are **coordinative** or **serial** when the resultant phrase belongs to the same form class as two or more of its constituents (for example *"boys and girls, sheets, pillow cases, blankets* all lying around"). They are **subordinative** or **attributive** when the resultant phrase belongs to the same form class as only one of its constituents (*poor John, fresh milk*). One constituent on which this classification is based is called the **head** and the other, the **attribute.**

Phrases can be made up of more than one syntactic construction. If all of the constructions are endocentric, one of the constituents will belong to the same form class as the resultant phrase, and this constituent is called the **center** of the phrase. Since most phrases in languages are endocentric, most phrases have centers. Although it is not true of the exocentric constructions, it is usually the case that one of the constituents can serve to characterize the construction, and then it can be identified in terms of that form class. The form classes in syntax are most easily described in terms of word classes, but it is not possible to set up a consistent scheme of word classes (parts of speech), since they overlap and cross each other.

Taxemes of order are the arrangements in which form classes may occur, and great variety is found from one language to another. The English actor-action type *John ran* vs. the action-goal type *catch John* are distinguished through taxemes of order, though these taxemes in English generally occur with taxemes of selection. French, for example, has a rigid system of order taxemes for the verb conjuncts: (1) actor (2) *ne* (3) farther goals of first and second person, *me, vous, se,* (4) nearer goals, (5) farther goals of third person *lui, leur,* (6) *y,* (7) *en.* For example, *il ne me le donne pas* = 1, 2, 3, 4; *il n'y en a pas* = 1, 2, 6, 7; *il m'y en donne* = 1, 3, 6, 7; and *on le lui donne* = 1, 4, 5.

Bloomfield noted that the IE languages are exceptional in having a large number of distinguishable parts of speech. More commonly, languages have three parts of speech, one of which corresponds more or less to our noun and another to our verb. A consequence for syntax would be that in languages with fewer distinct word classes, the phrase, rather than the word, is the logical basic element of grammatical arrangements.

"Morphology" (Chapter 13)

Bloomfield described morphology as the study that deals with "the constructions in which bound forms appear among the constituents. . . . [It] includes the constructions of words and parts of words, while syntax includes the constructions of phrases" (p. 207).

Bloomfield thought morphology to be a more complex subject than syntax, an opinion that few linguists hold today. His reason for this view is that the morphologist deals with a greater number of elements and processes, and in some respects these processes are less regular and more strictly limited than syntactic constructions. Consequently, languages differ more in their morphology than in their syntax, so that the morphological classification of languages will not be conclusive.

There are some special problems in morphology. One is the elusive nature of the meanings dealt with. The selection of a basic form in morphology also provides some difficulties. Where there is an absolute form, it is taken to be basic, but a different situation is met in the study of bound forms that have the same meaning, but different shapes. For example, what should be the basic form for English plurals, since these plurals have, among other forms, the alternants found in *cats, dogs,* and *roses?* Another problem is met when a single morpheme expresses more than one meaning (for example, the noun inflections in Latin) or when no overt expression exists (for example, the plural of *sheep*). For this last problem, the Hindus invented a device called a **zero** element. Since the problems are so numerous and so various, Bloomfield thought that consistency should prevail at all costs and that the way to insure it is to insist on the method of stating the **immediate constituents** of constructions. For English this process would lead to the following classification of words:

A. *Secondary words,* containing free forms:
  1. *Compound words,* containing more than one free form: *door-knob, wild-animal-tamer.* The included free forms are the *members* of the compound word: in our examples, the members are the words *door, knob, tamer,* and the phrase *wild animal.*
  2. *Derived secondary words,* containing one free form: *boyish, old-maidish.*

the included free form is called the *underlying form;* in our examples the underlying forms are the word *boy* and the phrase *old maid.*

B. *Primary words,* not containing a free form:
  1. *Derived primary words,* containing more than one bound form: *re-ceive, de-ceive, con-ceive, re-tain, de-tain, con-tain.*
  2. *Morpheme-words,* consisting of a single (free) morpheme: *man, boy, cut, run, red, big.*

[p. 209]

After these word types are distinguished the taxemes of selection, order, modulation, and phonetic modification can be discussed in an orderly fashion. It is soon found that one of the most complex problems is that of **phonetic modification,** and a simpler one, the description of **phonetic alternants,** some of which are automatically determined by their environments (*cats, dogs, roses*), while others are grammatically determined (for example, the particular form of German plurals depends on the individual singular forms: *der Hut, die Hüte; das Jahr, die Jahre; die Frau, die Frauen*).

Such alternants appear in a variety of ways. Some have unusual shapes (*die, dice*), some do not resemble other alternants at all (*cats, dogs, roses, oxen, geese*), or they may be zero forms (*sheep, sheep*), with or without phonetic modification (*goose, geese*). These variations illustrate the need for a clear way of determining the basic alternant, and generally the criteria for such a choice will be simplicity and pattern congruity with similar forms. For example, if the masculine forms of adjectives in French are selected as basic, the feminine forms are accounted for by a very complex set of additions and mutations; if the feminine form is taken as the basic alternant, the method by which they are related to the masculines is much simpler. In some cases one would set up an artificial basic form as the clearest way of showing relations among the alternants, and this would seem to be the simplest way to explain German noun forms that do not permit a final voiced-voiceless contrast, although such a contrast is found in initial and medial positions.

Since such morphological constructions in various languages often fall into different ranks, a complex form can best be described as though the various compositions, modifications, and affixations take place in a **determined order.** Of course, the order is a consequence of the analysis and not a reality in the language. In such ranks one often finds an outer layer of **inflectional** constructions and an inner one of **word formation.** Inflectional constructions generally result in **closure** of the construction (for example, nothing more can be suffixed to *hat-s*) and in a rigid parallelism of the underlying and resultant forms; forms that are inflected differently all have different syntactic functions. Oddly enough, in his chapter on morphology Bloomfield nowhere defined "inflection."

"Morphological Types" (Chapter 14)

Bloomfield listed three main morphologic types—composition, secondary derivation, and primary derivation. Among these, the construction of primary words is much like the constructions dealt with in syntax. Compound words have two or more free forms among their constituents. Recognition of free forms may vary from one language to another, since the norms of freedom will vary, and when such forms are compounds it is sometimes difficult to distinguish them from phrases. Compounds are generally semantically more specific than phrases (*blackbird* vs. *black bird*). The favorite devices of a language are used for compounding. For example, languages that permit only a single high stress on words will also have a single high stress in compounds. Compounds will follow the phonetic restrictions of clusters in a particular language, except that they will allow combinations across compound borders, a factor which will help to identify them as compounds. This is illustrated in the English word *gooseberry,* since a voiced sibilant and a voiced stop are not found in clusters in other environments. The qualities of vowels or stops are not found in clusters in other environments. The qualities of vowels or consonants may be altered in compounds, as is seen in comparing English *holy day* vs. *holiday, moon day* vs *Monday.* The order in compounds is generally fixed, in contrast with similar phrases, for example, *to keep house* vs. *to housekeep, to slide back* vs. *to backslide.* The constituents of compounds may be stems that do not appear alone, or those that do not appear in the same form as when they stand alone. The *-ology* forms of English and their first-member combining forms, for example, *theology,* illustrate this fact. Since the constituents of this latter type are not found alone, the resultant compound is called a **synthetic** compound. The form classes from which they can be synthesized are limited; for example, we can say *meat-eater,* but not *to meat eat.* While **indivisibility** usually characterizes such compounds, just as it does simple words, compound constituents often cannot function in syntactic constructions in the same way as the compounds; for example, we can say *very black birds* but not **very blackbirds.*

While the description and classification of compound words will depend on the particular structure of the language in which they are found, there are two main lines of classification: (1) the relation among members and (2) the relation of the whole to its members. The first approach distinguishes the **syntactic** and **asyntactic** compounds along the lines used in syntactic constructions. The compounds differ from the syntactic constructions only in the essential features that distinguish compound words from phrases (for example) omission of the article, indivisibility, irreversibility, and so on) in the case of syntactic compounds. Asyntactic compounds have members that do not combine in phrases or syntactic constructions of the language.

The second approach classifies compounds in the same terms used to describe syntactic contructions, **endocentric** and **exocentric** compounds. For example, *blackbird* and *bird* have similar distribution, as do *knob* and *doorknob,* so that the compounds are endocentric. The adjective *bittersweet* is endocentric, but the plant name *bittersweet* is exocentric, since the latter compound differs from the function of its constituent adjectivals. In English *longlegs, bright-eyes, and butterfingers* are exocentric because they occur as both singulars and plurals.

Secondary derivatives have one free form, a phrase or a word as an immediate constituent. To describe them, we set up an underlying form, which is not taken to have any historical priority. The underlying form can be a compound word (*gentleman-ly*), a derived word (*actress-es*), or a theoretical underlying form (*cran-berry*). A frequent division of these is into inflectional and word-formational forms. The inflectional are the easiest to describe, since they form parallel paradigmatic sets (for example, the declensions of Latin), while the word formational are more complex and can often be dealt with only by listing, and a definite linguistic meaning is often difficult to point out. The suffix *-ess* in *duchess* and *actress* may be defined as "the female of such and such a male," but the same function is fulfilled by **composition** (*she-elephant*) and **suppletion** (*ram, ewe; boar, sow*), or by **inverse derivation** (*goose, gander; duck, drake*). The same problem occurs in determining the underlying forms in the comparison of adjectives (*to smoothe* from *smooth*). Even more difficult are decisions about the underlying forms resulting from phonetic modification (*man, men*), modulation (*cónvict, convíct*), suppletion (*go, went*) or zero elements (*cut, cut*). It is simple in English to take the irregular paradigms as **underlying** and the regular as **derived.**

Primary words have no free forms among their immediate constituents; they can be complex (*re-ceive*) or simple (*boy, run, get*). From the similarity of primary words such as *hammer, leader, rider,* we can distinguish the primary affix *-er* from the roots *hamm-, spid-, rid-,* since these affixes are limited in number and vague in meaning, whereas the roots are numerous and definite. We conclude, therefore, that primary words lacking affix-like constituents can be classed as **primary root words** (*boy, run, red*), which are free roots contrasted with *spid-* and *hamm-*.

Roots constitute the most numerous class in a language and so have the most varied and specific meanings. The vagueness of the primary affixes semantically is partially explainable in that they rarely indicate the form class they establish when added to the roots. Once the roots are set up, the complicated description of their modifications must be undertaken. Despite the complexity, however, a certain uniformity appears. For the most part, roots are morphemes, although there are series in which there is a clearly marked phonetic-semantic resemblance between elements we would consider distinct morphemes. For example, the voiced *th-* initials of English demonstratives, the *wh-* of the interrogatives, the *n-* of negatives, and the symbolic connotations of the initial clusters involving *l* and *r*. (For example, "moving light" = *fl* in *flash, flare, flame, flicker, flimmer;* "noisy impact" = *kr* in *crash, crack, creak, crunch*.) This peculiarity is also paralleled by the restriction of the otherwise unlimited occurrence of *r* and *l* as suffixes, since symbolic roots containing *r* are never followed by the determinative suffix *-er* but, rather, take *-el,* and, conversely, the *l*-roots of this type take only the *-er* suffixes.

"Substitution" (Chapter 15)

Substitutions are a type of grammatically meaningful arrangement distinct from sentence types and constructions. Bloomfield defined "substitute" as "a linguistic form or grammatical feature which, under certain conventional circumstances, replaces any one of a class of linguistic forms" (p. 247). The grammatical peculiarity of substitutes is that they replace only forms of certain classes, which are called the **domain** of the substitute. Where other linguistic forms can be said to refer to real things, substitutes refer to grammatical classes; where the use of those other forms may be correct or incorrect according to the nonlinguistic circumstances, the correct use of substitutes is more often determined on grammatical criteria alone. Other peculiarities of substitutes include the fact that they are generally short words, atonic, irregular in inflection, derivation, and in their syntactic construction, and often appear as bound forms.

Besides the meaning of the form class that is their domain, the substitutes often add a more specific meaning, such as "masculine," "feminine," "personal," or "impersonal." There is an additional element of meaning, that of the **substitution type,** which consists in "the conventional circumstances under which the substitution is made." Although Bloomfield recognized that this last item cannot be discussed competently by a linguist, as Bloomfield defined him, he did point out some of the more obvious factors involved, explaining them in quasi-behavioristic terms as "elementary circumstances of the act of speech-utterance." For example, *I* and *you* have to do with the speaker-hearer relation; *this, now,* and so on represent relations of distance from the speaker or the speaker and hearer; negatives like *nobody, nothing* exclude the possibility of a speech form. Bloomfield noted:

These types are remarkably widespread and uniform (except for details) in the languages of the world; among them we find the practical relations to which human beings respond more uniformly than to any others—numerative and identificational relations, such as positive-negative, *all, some, any, same, other,* and, above all, the numbers, *one, two, three,* and so on. These are the relations upon which the language of science is based; the speech-forms which express them make up the vocabulary of mathematics.

[p. 249]

Bloomfield considered that almost all languages have a pronominal form, although the pronominals are found in the most varied substitution types. Pronominals and nominals together form the class *substantives,* differing principally because the pronominals are not accompanied by adjective modifiers.

A pronoun that implies the substantive which it replaces is called an **anaphoric** or **dependent** substitute (for example, "Ask the policeman, and *he* will tell you"), and the replaced form is the **antecedent.** The requirement that there be an antecedent is not universal, as can be seen in the **independent substitutes** in expressions like *It's raining.*

From these considerations, Bloomfield concluded that (1) the entire meaning of substitutes = class-meaning + substitution type; (2) this meaning is more abstract and inclusive, but more constant than that of ordinary linguistic forms, since they designate classes of grammatical forms, and not things, so that (3) they can be considered linguistic forms of the second degree. Still, (4) they are more primitive than most forms and (5) occur more frequently than any of the forms of their domain that they replace.

Bloomfield then indicated, as an example, how the linguistic meaning of a substitute in English would be explained. The example is *he:*

A. Class-meanings:
   1. *Definable in terms of form-classes:*
      (a) the same as that of the form-class of singular substantive expressions, say 'one object';
      (b) the same as that of the form-class defined by the substitutes *who, someone,* say 'personal';
   2. *Creating an otherwise unestablished form-class: he* is used only of certain singular personal objects (the rest are replaced, instead, by *she*), which, accordingly, constitute a sub-class with a class-meaning, say 'male';
B. *Substitution-types:*
   1. *Anaphora: he* implies, in nearly all its uses, that a substantive designating a species of male personal objects has recently been uttered and that *he* means one individual of this species; say 'recently mentioned';
   2. *Limitation: he* implies that the individual is identifiable from among all the individuals of the species mentioned; this element of meaning

is the same as that of the syntactic category of definite nouns, and can be stated, say, as 'identified.'

[p. 251]

Examples of anaphora in English include *do, does,* and *did* for finite verbs ("Bill will misbehave and John *did*"), although verbs like *be, have, will, shall, can,* and *must* lie outside the domain of this substitute; *one* for nouns ("I prefer a hard pencil to a soft *one,* hard pencils to soft *ones*"); *does,* in subordinate clauses introduced by *than* or *as* ("Mary dances better *than* Jane" [does]). This last example shows **anaphoric zero,** as does "I haven't seen it, but I want to."

Anaphora seem to occur in all languages, though in the most varied ways; perhaps all have pronominal substitution combined with definite identification ("Ask the policeman and he will tell you"). In languages with noun gender the third-person substitutes usually differ according to the gender of the antecedent. Most languages have substitute forms for groups of people that include the speaker or the hearer or both; many differentiate the second-person substitutes according to the social relations of speaker and hearer. Demonstrative substitutes show great variety according to the number of distinctions about the relative nearness or remoteness from the speaker, hearer, subject of discourse, or combinations of all of these. Interrogatives usually require the hearer to supply the species or identification of the individual and are often found in peculiar syntactic positions. Of all the substitution types, negatives seem the most universal, whereas our relative substitutes belong to a widespread, but not universal, type.

"Form-classes and Lexicon" (Chapter 16)

One of the problems involved in meaning is the decision concerning what kind of information should be included in the grammatical description and in the lexicon. To lay the groundwork for making this decision, Bloomfield suggested and explained some terms we can use to split up the simplistic term "meaning":

(1) Smallest and meaningless unit of linguistic signaling: *phememe;*
    (a) lexical : *phoneme;*
    (b) grammatical : *taxeme;*
(2) Smallest meaningful unit of linguistic signaling: *glosseme;* the meaning of a glosseme is a *noeme;*
    (a) lexical : *morpheme;* the meaning of a morpheme is a *sememe;*
    (b) grammatical : *tagmeme;* the meaning of a tagmeme is an *episememe;*
(3) Meaningful unit of linguistic signaling, smallest or complex: *linguistic form;* the meaning of a linguistic form is a *linguistic meaning;*

(a) lexical : *lexical form;* the meaning of a lexical form is a *lexical meaning;*

(b) grammatical : *grammatical form;* the meaning of a grammatical form is a *grammatical meaning.*

[p. 264]

The term "lexical" is here extended to cover not only the basic meaning of a **lexical form** but all forms that can be stated in phonemes, even though such forms would contain certain grammatical features. Lexical forms are connected in two directions with grammatical forms: (1) through their morphological or syntactic construction and (2) through their privileges of occurrence or distribution, the sum of which make up the grammatical function of the lexical form. All forms that have a function in common belong to the same form class.

These functions also compose a complex system, in which forms may overlap (that is, belong to more than one form class, because they have more than a single function), while other functions may be limited to a very few lexical forms. Thus the grammar of a language, Bloomfield wrote:

includes, then, a very complex set of habits (taxemes of selection) by which every lexical form is used only in certain conventional functions; every lexical form is assigned always to the customary form-classes. To describe the grammar of a language, we have to state the form-classes of each lexical form, and to determine what characteristics make the speakers assign it to these form-classes.

[p. 266]

Bloomfield then explained that the traditional criterion for describing and classifying lexical forms and their combinations is through **class meaning,** such as the familiar definition of a "noun" as "the name of a person, place, or thing," and he concluded that

This definition presupposes more philosophical and scientific knowledge than the human race can command, and implies, further, that the form-classes of a language agree with the classifications that would be made by a philosopher or scientist. Is *fire,* for instance, a thing? For over a century physicists have believed it to be an action or process rather than a thing: under this view, the verb *burn* is more appropriate than the noun *fire.*

[p. 266]

These remarks seem to be based on a simplistic notion of "thing," which makes it equivalent to "body." It also seems to be assumed that scientific definitions tell us what things are, rather than provide suitable ways for observing their behavior. In such a system it is difficult to attach any real meaning to terms such as "action" or "process." On the other hand, the traditional definition of a "noun" as the "name of a person, place, or thing" is equally indefensible. As ancient thought and modern methods show, a noun is an element in a structure, and the name for it is analogical, not univocal. Nominals are therefore elements in a language that have certain relations to other structural entities, such as verbs and modifiers. Those nouns that actually do name persons, places, and things may be the clearest instances (the prime analogates), but it would be only in this way that they could serve to define the entire class. Bloomfield's own statement about this would not be difficult to express in analogical terms:

Class-meanings are merely composites, or, one might say, greatest common factors, of the grammatical meanings which accompany the forms. To state a class-meaning is to find some formula that includes the grammatical meanings in which the forms occur.

[pp. 266–267]

There are difficulties in making a useful statement of class meaning, of course, especially when a form class has more than one function, but even here, Bloomfield pointed out:

[It] is still merely a derivative of the grammatical meanings in which the forms occur. . . .

class-meanings are not clearly definable units which could serve as a basis for our work, but only vague situational features, undefinable in terms of our science. The people who speak English and keep their substantive expressions within the accepted functions, do not guide themselves by deciding whether each lexical form denotes an object.

[pp. 267–268]

The form class of a lexical item is determined by (1) the structure and constituents of a form, (2) the inclusion of a special constituent (a marker), or (3) the identity of the form itself. That is, (1) one of the forms involved determines the classification, as in endocentric and exocentric constructions when dealing with complex forms; that is why speakers do not have to consider each phrase, since the form class of a phrase is decided by one of its constituents or by the way its constituents are put together. (2) Sometimes markers, such as the *to* of infinitive phrases, determining adjectives of noun phrases, and so on, determine the class—when there is a limited number of forms whose function it is to act as markers for particular functions, our task is easier. (3) Finally, there are many irregularities, such that a given form can be known only to belong to a given class through knowledge of the language: *case* can be a noun or a verb in English, but in *in case he comes,* it serves as a subordinating conjunction. Such forms are said to belong arbitrarily to a class (that is, lacking evidence from constituents, structure, or marker). According to Bloomfield:

A complete description of a language will list every form whose function is not determined either by structure or by a marker; it will include, accordingly, a *lexicon,* or list of morphemes, which indicates the form-class of each morpheme, as well as lists of all complex forms whose function is in any way irregular.
[p. 269]

The form classes of a language are not completely exclusive; they overlap, cross over, and are included in one another. Since it is impossible to decide on an exhaustive list of "important" functions, satisfactory part-of-speech analysis presents difficulties. The task is less difficult when the basis is a set of inflectional categories, but not all categories are inflectional. Some are syntactic, such as definite and indefinite nouns, aspects of verbs, and voice in verbs. It is rash to assume that the categories of one's own language, or those of familiar languages, are universal, although, as Bloomfield noted,

a form-class comparable to our substantive expressions, with a class-meaning something like "object," seems to exist everywhere, though in many languages it is not an arbitrary class, like our substantive part of speech, but depends on the presence of markers, as in Malayan or Chinese. . . .
[pp. 270–271]

Elsewhere, Bloomfield defined a "category" as "A grammatical classification . . . which always accompanies some grammatical feature" (p. 204).

Bloomfield did not find that these categories agree with "classes of real things"; if the typical categories of objects, actions, qualities, manners, and relations do describe things as they really are, many languages lack such categories. This is shown in the existence of abstract forms and in the lack of parallel between grammatical and real gender (*the bull—he* or *it; the ship—she* or *it*), number (*Epsom salts* vs. *table salt*), cases (they range from two in some languages to twenty in Finnish), and tenses, where our "historical present" shows the lack of parallel and so too with aspects and moods.

Any function that is not determined for a form by its constituents or by the construction of its constituents is called **irregular.** The **regular** functions are therefore those that are so determined. Speakers can use or understand forms in a regular function even when they have never heard the resultant form before, but they can use or understand irregular forms only after having heard them, and this fact provides an additional criterion for distinguishing regular and irregular forms. These innovating possibilities, both for the production and understanding of previously unused or unheard constructions, are habits of substitution built on the regular analogies of the language.

Bloomfield concluded that the power and wealth of a language is found not in the number of words it has, as popular opinion asserts, but in the nature of its morphemes and tagmemes (sentence types, constructions, and substitutions). The number of words in a language is indefinite, readily expanded, and difficult to establish, since words are formed analogically: "For instance, having counted *play*, *player*, and *dance*, shall we count *dancer* as a fourth word, even though it contains no additional glosseme?" (p. 277). As for the problem of what can and what cannot be said in a language, we usually have to distinguish word meanings and categories. One language will use a phrase where another uses a word, or one will use a lexical form where another employs a grammatical category. Every language represents an arbitrary, and different, selection of situational factors for communication. Even biological relations, which would appear to be "given in nature," are dealt with in the most varied ways by the kinship terms of different languages.

"Written Records" (Chapter 17)

Within the lifetime of a single speaker there is generally no awareness of changes in his speech. Through the study of written records, however, we can see how English, for example, has changed considerably. One reason for this is that our present speech habits are a consequence of past speech habits inherited from our elders, and differences in linguistic habits can be explained through past habits plus change.

It is often not easy to interpret written records. Writing seems to have had a comparatively recent origin, beginning, perhaps, as drawings representing things or ideas. Gradually the drawings became conventionalized representations of the words that expressed the things or ideas. But all words could not be easily represented by pictures. For example, English *inn* could be more easily pictured than English *in*. There was likely a period when words that were phonetically similar were represented by the same picture. A single sign could then suggest the word *inn* or *in*. A further step was when the order of drawings followed that of speech. But even when writing reached a stage where there was a symbol for every word, such a system put tremendous burdens on the memory. It is likely that it was as the result of the exploitation of the "phonetically similar" principle that the true writing system, where characters stand for meaningless sounds, evolved.

True writing seems to have been attained first with the invention of **syllabaries.** According to this system, the characters stood for phonetic forms rather than meaningful stretches. From characters that stood for combinations of consonants and vowels it was a short step to phonemic or alphabetic writing, an advance Bloomfield believed was made only *once* in human history:

It seems that only once in the history of writing there has been any advance beyond the syllabic principle. Some of the Egyptian hieroglyphic and hieratic symbols were used for syllables containing only one consonant; in the use of these, differences of the accompanying vowel were disregarded, and the resultant ambiguities were removed by the use of classifiers and logograms. In all there were twenty-four of these symbols for one-consonant syllables. At an early date—certainly before 1500 B.C.—Semitic-speaking people became acquainted with Egyptian writing, and hit upon the idea of setting down words of their language by means of the twenty-four simplest Egyptian symbols. This was feasible because the structure of Semitic identifies each root by its consonant-scheme. . . .

The ancient Greeks took over the Phoenician system and made a decisive change. Some of the Phoenician symbols represented syllables containing consonants that were foreign to Greek; . . . The Greeks used these superfluous symbols to indicate vowel values, combining two symbols, such as TA or TO or TI, to represent a single syllable. In this way they arrived at the principle of *phonemic* or *alphabetic* writing—the principle of using a symbol for each phoneme. They fell short of complete accuracy only because they failed to invent enough symbols for vowels: they never distinguished between the long and short quantities, distinctive in their language, of the vowels [a, i, u].

[pp. 288–290]

Bloomfield assumed that the phoneme principle is applicable to any language and that the present inadequacy of writing stems from the conservatism of writers, which first freezes the written form into an authoritative norm and then proceeds to invent reasons for pseudoarchaic spellings. It is obvious that the written form of languages no longer spoken must be studied very carefully. Sometimes we are really incapable of interpreting the writing, either because we are ignorant of the language or of the phonetics of the language or of both. Bilingual transcriptions are helpful, and additional clues to the phonetics of the writing system are to be found in verse forms employing end-rhyme, alliteration, or some other phonetic pattern. The most helpful, of course, would be grammatical or phonetic information, such as is found in the Sanskrit grammar and lexicon.

"The Comparative Method" (Chapter 18)

The first thing that strikes the scholar who compares languages is that some resemble each other and others are seemingly incomparable. The resemblances could be due to several factors, such as universal, natural features of language as such (for example, phonemes, morphemes, words, and sentences are found in all languages, and some parts of speech in most). It may be due to complete accident (for example, Greek *mati* and Malay *mata* both mean "eye," but this correspondence is wholly accidental). Languages might also resemble each other as a result of borrowing or **genetic relation.** The comparative method assumes that extended similarities between languages can be studied as a consequence of genetic relation and that pervasive resemblances between contemporaneous languages are best explained by assuming that they are both developed forms of a single parent language.

In some cases it can be verified by history that languages which resemble each other are genetically related, but in other cases the task is more difficult. When there are adequate written records, as there are for the Romance languages, relations can be established fairly easily. There are resemblances among the Germanic languages that are just as evident as those found among the Romance group, but since we do not have comparable literary sources, their historical development cannot be traced as completely. When we lack such written records, the comparative method explains relations among languages by making inferences similar to those obtained by tracing the attested historical development.

Resemblances among the Germanic languages can easily be established by showing pervasive similarities in their basic vocabulary and grammatical patterns, a similarity so extensive that borrowing or accidental resemblance does not seem the likely explanation. Even the differences among the Germanic languages are systematic, appearing in whole series of dissimilar forms, from which we can conclude the characteristic changes each has undergone. We can thus reconstruct the presumed form from which the related items in two or more languages are derived.

Such a **reconstructed form,** Bloomfield said, is not taken to be an actual form once spoken so much as "a formula that tells us which identities or systematic correspondences of phonemes appear in a set of related languages; . . . a kind of phonemic diagram of the ancestral form" (pp. 302–303).

The comparative method assumes that both the resemblances and the differences among related languages are an indication of the structure of the parent language. Bloomfield warned that there are certain drawbacks to this theory, however, since

This is the same thing as assuming, firstly, that the parent community was completely uniform as to language, and, secondly, that this parent community split suddenly and sharply into two or more daughter communities, which lost all contact with each other.

[p. 310]

Such uniformity has never been found in actual speech communities, so that the strict **family-tree** image of language relations used in the comparative method is misleading, particularly when the supposedly dissociated branches of a language family show similar divergencies.

An explanation different from the family-tree image concerning how changes occur in related languages was proposed by Johannes Schmidt (1843–1901), which came to be called the "wave theory." The theory assumes that tribes spread from a geographical center in all directions and that we can picture the relations in a single direction by representing contiguous dialects by a string of letters, for example, *A, B, C, D, E, F . . . X*. Assuming then that *C* became the cultural or political center, its dialect would become the prestige form of the language during the period of its ascendancy and would most likely affect *B* and *D* first, and then, through them, *A* and *F*, and so on. Since the earlier proximity could account for dialects resembling each other more than those from which they were remote, the continued prominence of dialect *C* and its impact on its immediate neighbors would tend to make the difference between, say, *C* and *X* so great as to eventually result in two different languages and not just two different dialects.

The splitting process implied in the family-tree image and in the wave theory are the two principal types of differentiation discussed in the study of language change. But the comparative method cannot claim to give a picture of the complete historical process, since it works on the assumption of uniform speech communities, from which the varieties develop, and such communities are not found. Within these limitations, however, the information the method provides is valid and interesting. Reconstructed forms can also suggest nonlinguistic aspects of earlier times, since they help us locate the expressions dealing with basic agricultural, cultural, and economic concerns.

"Dialect Geography" (Chapter 19)

Dialect geography supplements the comparative method by giving information about the actual complexity in the forms of living languages that are obscured by the methodological assumption of uniform parent languages. According to the comparative method, indeterminacies in the parent form should not be found; dialect geography, however, shows that it is unrealistic to take a standard form of a language as the oldest type and indicates that the standard form is the result of developed local dialects. The local dialects are found to be as irregular as the standard form. Dialect geography confirms the conclusion of the comparative method that "different linguistic changes cover different portions of an area" (p. 323), but now these differences can be more accurately stated by mapping the area and showing where these differences are to be found by drawing **isoglosses** on the map. "Isoglosses" are defined as "lines

[drawn] between places which differ as to any feature of language"
(p. 51). Such a method is superior to the usual dialect dictionaries and
dialect grammars, and confirms Bloomfield's conviction that local differentiation is best pictured in terms of density of communication.
Speakers change their speech habits principally to communicate more
successfully with those they most often deal with.

Through dialect geography, surprising innovations as well as relic
forms of an older state of a language are found. The latter are easier
to trace than the former, since they are likely to be recorded in literature
or other documents. Dialect geography also shows that relic forms have
a better chance of surviving in remote areas. Innovations are not always
accepted universally, and certain forms are resistant to innovation, as is
indicated by place names. When a feature is found in a restricted area,
the isogloss that maps out the area will probably represent a weakness
in the density of communication of one solitary area.

With the development of the wave theory and methods of obtaining
geographic information about dialects it was hoped that "dialect" could
be defined more precisely in geographic terms. But as the work progressed, this possibility seemed to become less likely, since it was found
that dialect areas such as Yorkshire or Bavaria are no more uniform
speech areas than the standard language communities, but are, rather,
networks of isoglosses. Bloomfield thought that the general disappoint-
ment with these results might have been due to the mistaken idea that
all isoglosses are equally significant. More important than a few lexical
isoglosses would be the line that separates the Low and High German
areas, for example. Such divisions are often found to be linked with
geographical, political, religious, and cultural differences. Social factors
are the most important: "the spread of linguistic features depends upon
social conditions. The factors in this respect are doubtless the density
of communication and the relative prestige of different social groups"
(p. 345).

"Phonetic Change" (Chapter 20)

One of the clearest examples of linguistic change is phonetic change.
This is readily appreciated when we compare the written versions of the
same word at different periods. After the basic relations of the IE languages had been appreciated, further phonetic differences were encountered that seemed to follow no pattern. To bring order into the
picture, **phonetic correspondences** were sought that could be presumed
to be the result of **phonetic change.** Some were easy to find because (1)
voiceless stops of the earlier languages parallel Germanic voiceless
spirants—Latin *pes,* English *foot;* Latin *piscis,* English *fish;* Latin *tres,*

English *three;* Latin *tenuis,* English *thin;* (2) voiced stops in the earlier languages are paralleled by Germanic voiceless stops—Greek *kannabis,* English *hemp;* Latin *duo,* English *two;* Latin *dens,* English *tooth;* Latin *genus,* English *kin;* (3) certain aspirates and spirants in the earlier languages are paralleled in Germanic by voiced stops and spirants—where Sanskrit has *bh,* Greek has *ph,* Latin has *f,* and Germanic has *b* and *v.* These correlations were already discussed in Grimm's law, although Bloomfield thought the term "law" to be misleading. Grimm's law was supplemented by other regularities discovered by Grassmann and Verner.

Another way of stating these facts, Bloomfield said, is to say that "phonemes change." When we find facts for which we have no explanation, it may be because we have stated the correlations too narrowly or too broadly or that the apparent divergence is due to a later borrowing or that earlier pronunciations had more than one form. How are the proven resemblances to be accounted for?

The neogrammarians held that sound change is independent of semantic features and is merely a matter of articulatory habits; others felt that semantically weak forms tend to phonetic weakening and loss through irregular and regular sound change. Probably each view contains part of the explanation. We cannot really tell, however, what "semantically weak" means, but if we consider a language as consisting of a semantic and a phonemic layer, we can see how the two layers could be interdependent as well as independent. It is possible to master the phonetic layer of a language with little or no mastery of the semantic structure in a practical sense (singers do that) or to master its semantic structure with poor control of its phonetic system (as seen in foreign accent, or only reading knowledge of a language). Bloomfield saw phonetic change through history as the gradual favoring of some non-distinctive features over others. This is not, strictly speaking, "phonetic" change, which concerns the loss or addition of nondistinctive features; the problem here is that the phonemes change through original preference for allophones. There are phonetic differences that characterize different stages of a language which do not alter the structure of the phonology. For example, the change in the eighteenth-century pronunciation of *geese, eight,* and *goose, goat* from a pure, long vowel to the current diphthongized form has not introduced a new phonemic contrast into the structure of English.

"Types of Phonetic Change" (Chapter 21)

Since phonetic change was described in the previous section in terms of shifting habits of articulation, the types of phonetic change can be discussed in the same terms. One general characteristic of sound change is a simplification of the movements that make up the pronunciation of a given form. For example, consonant clusters are often simplified, especially in final position, and even single consonants in final position can be weakened and disappear. Since this is the tendency, it would indicate that the language involved would have some word-marking feature.

A common type of change is **assimilation,** in which the position of the vocal organs for the production of one phoneme is altered to a position more like that employed in producing another; more common is regressive assimilation, where the preceding phoneme is affected. In **progressive assimilation** the following consonant is altered. Very common is the weakening of consonants between vowels or other sounds or the assimilation of the consonant to the tongue position of the preceding or following vowels, the most familiar example of this being the assimilation of dentals and velars to the position of the following front vowels, called **palatalization.** Such palatalization of consonants can also undergo further modifications—velars and dentals often develop into affricates or sibilants. **Compensatory lengthening** often follows the weakening or loss of consonants in the preceding vowel, and if the lost consonant was a nasal, the vowel may be nasalized with or without compensatory lengthening or other changes. Or, with the loss of a consonant in intervocalic position, the two vowels may **contract** into a single vowel or diphthong. Assimilation of vowels into those that precede or follow is not uncommon; languages with strong word stress often weaken or lose the unstressed vowels.

Since **simplification** is the general trend in such cases, many changes can be explained in such terms, even when no additional movement is involved and they result in easier combinations. In languages that employ stress the quantity of the stressed vowels is regulated by the character of the succeeding phonemes. In general, longs and shorts in "open" syllables (that is, those before a single consonant which is followed by another vowel) result in long vowels, the short ones being lengthened, and the longs remaining long. Such loss of quantity differentiation makes articulation more uniform.

What are the causes of these changes? No one knows, but every conceivable factor has been suggested at one time or another to account for them, including race, climate, topographic conditions, diet, occupation, mode of life, or the fact that some speakers are too lazy to pronounce words clearly. When some sort of correlation emerges between such factors, the loss of "undesirable features" is generally refuted by later sound-change discoveries, resulting in the renewal of the "undesirable" feature. Bloomfield rejected the suggestion that some forms have more "semantic weight" than others, as well as the concomitant idea that the less important forms are those that are subject to change. He did not believe that a vague feature such as "semantic weight" can be objectively measured. Besides, he pointed out, phonetic changes demonstrably alter features that are semantically important. However, there is some justification for distinguishing more or less important parts of fixed formulas, which may tend to become slurred from constant repetition.

"Fluctuation in the Frequency of Forms" (Chapter 22)

If we were to assume that all linguistic changes are the result of phonetic changes, we could not account for those forms that do not show either a direct resemblance to, or a derivation from, older attested forms. We must, therefore, find some uniformity or correlation among such forms. We usually discover that forms which are not etymologically related to ancient forms are produced by analogical changes or that they enter the language through borrowing.

An important factor in all nonphonetic changes is the fluctuation in the frequency of forms. While we can often name the persons who coined terms that have come into common usage (for example, *Kodak, blurb, chortle*), and while it is possible to specify the exact time when some terms enter the language, it is clearly impossible to say when a form was dropped. Often there are competing forms—for example, *It's I* vs. *It's me, rather* vs. *"rahther"*—and if it were possible to keep score on their frequency, we might be able to tell how the battle is going, but this is not always possible.

Forms drop out of use for a number of reasons—aesthetic (in the avoidance of alliteration, assonance, or rhyme in some styles or the use of it in others); the preference for long or short words at various periods of time: and the avoidance of taboo forms or of words homonymous with such forms.

More important than phonetic considerations are factors of meaning that contribute to the avoidance of expressions or the inventions of new terms. When new situations arise, words suitable to them will be found; when certain practices are no longer in vogue, the vocabulary used to describe them will fall into disuse and may leave us with terms that are unintelligible. As an example of this situation Bloomfield cited the use of the falconry terminology in *Othello*.

Taboo forms sometimes die out (especially ritualistic or ill-omened expressions), but other types, such as obscenities, show remarkable vitality. In general, words that arouse a favorable response tend to endure, while those unfavorably received lose currency. This fact helps to account for the life of words used in advertising or the use of honorifics (for example, French *ma mère* vs. *madame, votre mère;*

German *mein Mann* vs. *Ihr Herr Gamahl;* or Italian *mia moglie* vs. *la sua signora*). The same holds for slang expressions; when they are too often repeated they tend to disappear, or they become the normal forms without any hint of wittiness. By far the most important factor in all of these situations is the prestige of the speaker whose usage another adopts. A density-of-communication diagram, using weighted arrows to bring out this factor, would be an ideal way of picturing these phenomena.

"Analogic Change" (Chapter 23)

A source of form change different from the ones discussed so far is **analogic change,** a process of linguistic coinage that is similar to that of regular analogic change on the grammatical level. One reason Bloom- field gave for this kind of change is that the formational habits of morphological constructions are comparatively more rigid than those involving syntactic constructions, so that a new phrase, which does not entail any syntactic novelty, can serve to introduce a new lexical habit. It does not appear to be possible to assign the reasons for such formation to the situational factors, but investigation of similar forms is helpful. On the principle that the meaning of a form for the individual speaker is the sum of situations in which he has heard it, we can assume that there is generally a model on which the new formation is based. When such a new form is introduced it is doubtless both a semantic as well as a grammatical displacement, but the semantic aspects are dealt with in the next chapter of Bloomfield's book.

Conflicting forms play a significant role in the success of new, analogic formations. A form like *radio,* when first introduced, had no competitors; it was unlike the innovation *cows,* which came into use at the same time as the traditional *kine.* It appears that in all stages of language development there are some elements that are stable and others that are not; in addition, when the "irregular" *cows* was first formed there were a number of other, similar "irregular" plural formations, so that this single one did not stand out alone. During the subsequent period of conflict between *cows* and *kine* we had merely to do with a difference in the frequency of the competing forms, and this factor, along with the number of new forms, is the principal one responsible for the success of any particular innovating form. Other favorable factors are similarity of meaning and frequency of occurrence in a particular context. In such situations regular forms have an advantage over ir- regular ones, although some irregular formations that occur very fre- quently are highly resistant to change; these include many of the most common words and phrases of the language. The regularizing trend is seen clearly in the inflectional paradigms of languages with numerous complex forms.

Analogic formation is not limited to complex forms, and the creation of a shorter, underlying form is called **back formation**. For example, the singular form *redels* co-existed with the singular *stone,* plural *stones,* although the usual plural form of the word was also *redels.* However, the back formation of *redel* regularized the relation between the forms, from which we get the present word *riddle.* Similarity of meaning is a powerful factor in word formation, as can be seen in our endless *-er* formations; such a type is said to be a **living analogy**. Some formations become widespread without any determined or constant community of meaning, for example, *-y, -ish, -ly,* although in our time these have acquired fairly standard meanings. Occasionally a relatively independent compounding form is reduced to an affix status, as in the case of *-ly* from *like.*

Analogic formations in phrases are common when a particular word is affected, by reason of its position in the phrase. Some English dialects drop *-r* in final position, but preserve it before vowels, hence the sandhi alternants of a word like *water.* More frequently phrasal modification results in syntactic, not lexical, innovation.

Adaptive new formations are those that have no apparent model, and these are often what Bloomfield called a facetious type, whose appeal lies in the unusual shape of the word, for example, *chorine,* on the parallel (but not on the model) of *Pauline; chlorine, colleen,* and especially, *actorine.* Mock-learned words like *scrumptious, rambunctious, absquatulate,* and so on, are also adaptive new formations. Other formations are apparently made through the influence of other forms—thus Latin had both *grevis* and *gravis* (the former probably on the analogy of *levis,* "light," vs. *grevis,* "heavy"). So-called **popular etymologies** (regularizations of new formations that disagree with the earlier structures of the forms) are largely adaptive and contaminative, for example, *shame-faced,* from the original *sham-fest,* "modest"; French *crevise* from the English *crayfish; gooseberry* probably from *groze berry.*

"Semantic Change" (Chapter 24)

When innovations lead to an alteration of lexical meaning, rather than to new grammatical functions of a form, **semantic change** is discussed. These changes can be established on the basis of (1) written records, (2) comparison with related languages, or (3) structural analysis of the forms. In linguistic terms, Bloomfield said, semantic change is "merely the result of a change in the use of it and other, semantically related speech-forms" (p. 426). An older tradition assumes that there is a root meaning, which remains unaltered despite the effect of certain processes on it—for example, **narrowing** (*mete*, "edible flesh" to *meat*); **widening** (ME *bridde*, "young birdling," to *bird*); **metaphor** (Prim. Germ. **bitraz*, "biting," participle of **bi:to*, "*I* bite," to *bitter*); **metonymy**—meanings related in space or time (OE *cēace*, "jaw," to *cheek*); **synechdoche**— meaning related as part to whole (Prim. Germ. **tu:naz*, "fence," to *town*); **hyperbole**—from stronger to weaker meanings (pre-French **extonnare*, "to strike with thunder," to French *étonner*, "surprise"); **litotes**—from weaker to stronger meaning (pre-English **kwalljan*, "to torment," to OE *cwellan*, "to kill"); **degeneration**—OE *cnafa*, "boy," "servant," to *knave*); **elevation**—(OE *cniht*, "boy," "servant," to *knight*).

Such changes indicate an alteration in the practical life of former times. English *fee* is the modern form of OE *feoh*, "livestock," "cattle," "property," or "money," and the semantic change of the forms indicates the alterations to be expected when the medium of exchange or values alter. This and the other examples can also serve to illustrate the rise of abstract from concrete meanings.

One of the first scholars to devote serious attention to problems of meaning change was Hermann Paul. He held that semantic change consists principally in expansion and obsolescence. The meaning of an expression for a speaker, he said, is the sum of situations in which the speaker has heard it. Marginal meanings are, therefore, all occasional, and we respond to them only when the situation is such that the central meaning is excluded. On the other hand, since each speaker's experience is something peculiar to him, what an individual considers marginal may be central for others.

One weakness Bloomfield found in Paul's discussion of this problem was the lack of a simultaneous consideration of the competing forms, an approach that the structuralists stress. Paul's study did represent real progress, however, especially concerning the notion of **isolation,** the process by which forms become obsolescent, thus breaking up the semantic domain, which was formerly a unity. Marginal meanings of an earlier stage may thus become central meanings later, although isolated; obsolescence of a particular construction may have an isolating effect on a particular form, and phonetic change can also contribute to this, as illustrated in our contemporary separation of the formerly related words *ready, ride, road,* Another factor contributing to meaning change can be the intrusion of analogic new formations, for example, *sloth* was formerly the quality noun of *slow,* as *truth* still is of *true,* but the increasing frequency of *-ness* formations isolated the *-th* set. Finally, changes in the practical world have decided effects on meaning.

Bloomfield considered that Paul's approach described obsolescence well but that it did not explain it. For Paul obsolescence is basically a change in frequency, but Bloomfield did not believe that meaning shift is intelligible unless it is also correlated with changes in the environment, as exemplified, for example, in the decreasing economic importance of cattle. Among the processes that account for marginal meanings in language, those involving phonetic change, analogic change, and borrowing seem to be well understood, but these account for only a small number of the wealth of marginal meanings. In Bloomfield's opinion it has been reliance on meaning rather than form that has delayed progress. It should be clear that linguistically an extension of meaning is the same process as the extension of grammatical function. The best source for investigating such processes is the contemporary language, where we are familiar with all the practical factors and connotative values involved.

"Cultural Borrowing" (Chapter 25)

Cultural borrowing projects on a grand scale what is characteristic of the learning experience for individuals. Children learn their language from one or more adults, and all constantly adapt their speech habits to those of their fellows. Speech communities, too, learn from each other in similar ways.

If a person who introduces a foreign word into his language has a good command of the phonetics of the foreign language, he may pronounce it in a manner not required by his native phonological system. This is generally not true of all the others who may adopt the expression, but in the event that they would follow the foreign patterns, it is possible for the phonology of the borrowing language to change, through change in the number or distribution of phonemes. It will be possible to sort out the borrowed words in a language, depending on their degree of integration into the borrowing language. If the entire community is familiar with the language from which a form is borrowed, or if the two phonologies are sufficiently similar, no trace of borrowing will be left, even though one may be certain of the historical importations.

Once accepted into a language, foreign sounds are subject to all the allophonic modifications of the borrowing language. This fact often helps us date the time of the borrowing. Besides exerting influence at the phonological level, borrowed forms are subject to grammatical patterns of the borrowing language as well, such as, pluralization, tense formation, and compositional rules. Occasionally, however, the borrowing language will adopt an entire construction that is foreign to the native formations. Most commonly this situation occurs in the borrowing of foreign suffixes.

One form of borrowing is the literal analysis and transliteration of foreign expressions: Greek *sympathein* was translated directly into the Latin *compatior,* and we have borrowed both forms in English—*sympathy* and *compassion.* Sometimes there is a mere word-for-word translation, as in *marriage of convenience, it goes without saying,* and *I've told him I don't know how many times,* from French.

The nature of foreign borrowings tells us a good deal about the relations of cultures to each other. No list is complete, but consider the French expressions we have for women's clothes, cosmetics, and luxuries, the Germanisms of *frankfurter, wiener, sauerkraut,* and *pretzel,* along with *zeitgeist, wanderlust, umlaut,* and so on.

"Intimate Borrowing" (Chapter 26)

Intimate borrowing, unlike cultural borrowing, can take place only when two cultures share the same geographic area and are in a dominant-to-inferior position. The dominance may be either of a military, political, or cultural nature, the result, usually, of conquest or immigration.

In such circumstances it is more generally the lower culture that borrows from the superior, but influences in the opposite direction are quite common. Usually the "lower" language dies out if the "invaders" are sufficiently numerous and strong. It if survives, it invariably shows signs of the struggle. Gypsy dialects always figure as dominated languages and show the most varied borrowings, particularly from Greek, among the European gypsies. English and American gypsies speak a substandard English dialect, with from one to several hundred lexical and grammatical forms of the old Gypsy language, but with English phonology, syntax, and vocabulary.

An example of the lower language affecting the upper is found in Chilean Spanish, which differs from that of the rest of South America and Spain as well; an unusual number of Spanish soldiers were sent there, due to the indomitability of the natives, and through intermarriage among the first comers, it is thought that the phonology of their Spanish was affected.

Some subject groups make little progress in learning the dominant language, so that their masters speak to them in a kind of "baby talk" that imitates their incorrect speech. The subjects, thus deprived of a correct model, acquire this simplified version, and the resultant speech form becomes a conventionalized **jargon.** Such a form may pass into international usage, especially among tradesman, and it is then called a *lingua franca,* a term apparently applied first to an Italian jargon in the eastern Mediterranean in the early modern period. **Pidgin English** is an example, the jargon, or *lingua franca,* used by Europeans and Chinese in their trade dealings.

When a subject group abandons its own language in favor of such a jargon (which happens in communities that have no common language), the result is called a **Creolized language.** In the case of escaped slave communities such Creolized languages avoided assimilation and developed independently, as for example, the language of the island of St. Thomas off West Africa, and the Dutch of the Virgin Islands. Afrikaans, the Dutch spoken in South Africa, shows some features that are reminiscent of Creolized languages.

"Dialect Borrowing" (Chapter 27)

The individual learns, molds, and remakes his own mode of speech in imitation of those he admires, in order to avoid ridicule, and from the simple need to communicate with speakers who have habits of speech different from his own. Every speaker acts as both an imitator and a model for others. There is no need for a single model; whether in the speech of a single person or a single locale, a great deal of leveling takes place through the neutral meeting grounds of people of varied dialectal backgrounds, for example, the market and business centers. While "prestige" is a relative factor, it is operative even in those groups where we would hardly expect it, as in school cliques and gangland groups.

Our present standard languages developed from provincial dialects prevailing among the upper middle class of the urban centers that became capitals—London and Paris for English and French. Modern standard German is not based on a particular provincial dialect, but seems to have crystallized out of an official and commercial type of speech that developed in the eastern frontier region. It was spread, but not originated, by Luther's translation of the Bible. The precise details of how many standard languages developed is not known. Estimates of co-existent provincial dialects vary in different countries. In England dialects are counted as inferior, while in Germany the standard is less rigid. While the written form gives us little information about how dialects developed, when they are in conflict the chances are in favor of the form that is the written convention. Writing also introduces new pronunciations, abbreviations, and new formations (for example, *"prof," "lab," "home ec"*). While the written form of Latin remained substantially the same for centuries, each succeeding Roman generation pronounced the written form according to the current Italian phonology, and scholars of England, Germany, and France pronounced it according to the phonology of their own languages. One result of a Latin-centered educational tradition was the introduction of many scholarly words into the vernacular, especially in the Romance languages. After the Norman Conquest many of these words were introduced into English through Norman French.

"Applications and Outlook" (Chapter 28)

Most speakers, if they reflect upon their use of language, are concerned about its correctness. This is a legacy of eighteenth-century grammatical work, which legislated, but did not discover, rules for correctness. The grammarians of that period had no need to usurp the role of issuing authoritarian pronouncements—the task was almost thrust upon them. Most speakers are convinced that some other speaker's type of language is more prestigious than their own. In the eighteenth century, with the rise to wealth and power of substandard speakers, the problem became more acute for an influential portion of the population. They were diffident about their speech; indeed, this seems to be an almost universal trait. The tendency to revise one's own speech is universal, but methods and individual motivation vary considerably, Bloomfield noted:

For the native speaker of sub-standard or dialectal English, the acquisition of standard English is a real problem, akin to that of speaking a foreign language. To be told that one's habits are due to "ignorance" or "carelessness" or are "not English" is by no means helpful. Our schools sin greatly in this regard.

[p. 499]

Considering the overwhelming preponderence of time and energy spent in schooling pupils in verbal behavior, as opposed to teaching successful behavior in their concrete environments, Bloomfield was astonished to find that our schools are utterly benighted in linguistic matters. How to teach is the pedagogue's problem, but no amount of "how" can salvage ignorance of the matter to be taught.

One of the goals of our schools is to impart literacy, yet, Bloomfield noted, nothing is more discouraging than the perusal of so-called educationalists' ideas of how to teach children to read:

At one extreme, there is the metaphysical doctrine which sets out to connect the graphic symbols directly with "thoughts" or "ideas"—as though these symbols were correlated with objects and situations and not with speech-sounds. At the other extreme are the so-called "phonic" methods, which confuse learning to read and write with learning to speak, and set out to train the child in the production of sounds—an undertaking complicated by the crassest ignorance of elementary phonetics.

[p. 500]

Granted, Bloomfield continued, that it is the teachers' specialty to decide how to teach, they must first be informed about what they are to teach; particularly, they must understand the nature of writing:

The person who learns to read, acquires the habit of responding to the sight of letters by the utterance of phonemes. This does not mean that he is learning to utter phonemes; he can be taught to read only after his phonemic habits are thoroughly established.

[pp. 500–501]

Coordination between letters and phonemes must, therefore, be established. No matter what set is taken as basic, there will be irregularities to plague us, but the teaching problem can be regularized. Two methods seem to meet elementary requirements One aims to teach the child to read a phonetic transcription first, and then, after the reading habit has been set, to teach him to read traditional writing. The other method is to give the student graphs that correspond to only one phonemic value first, and then to give him in a systematic way those letter patterns that depart from the "norm." Disparities between spelling and pronunciation will always be a problem of writing, Bloomfield pointed out:

It is wrong to suppose that writing would be unintelligible if homonyms (e.g. *pear, pair, pare* or *piece, peace*) were spelled alike; writing which reproduces the phonemes of speech is as intelligible as speech. Moreover, our present irregular writing sins exactly in this respect by using identical graphs for phonemically different forms, such as *read,* [rijd, red], *lead* [lijd, led], or *tear* [tijr, tejr].

[p. 502]

Spelling reforms run into more political and economic opposition than theoretical difficulties.

At later stages of schooling the problems of learning foreign languages is encountered. This is a valid facet of education and has many things to recommend it, but one of these reasons, often given, is invalid —that is, to learn the arbitrary glossemes of a foreign language for its "transfer value." This value can safely be estimated as zero. As things stand now, Bloomfield said (that is, 1933), it is not a question of method so much as of teacher competence. The basic fault lies in the eight-year elementary school organization of American institutions, which is by now the vested interest of the professionals. Bloomfield believed that such a program wastes four years of the pupil's time, so that he enters high school at a time when he is too mature to find satisfaction in general or elementary studies. Accordingly, after high school, "he turns to the snobberies and imbecilities which make a by-word of the American college" (p. 504). The earlier start of European students in language study accounts for their demonstrably superior performance. They begin at an age when they do not find the fantasy and make believe required in such study tedious and when the simple level of elementary reading material does not disturb them. On the other hand, Bloomfield noted, the pupil

who takes up his first foreign language at high-school age or later, is likely to substitute analysis for mere repetition, and thus to meet halfway the incompetent teacher, who talks about the foreign language instead of using it.
[p. 505]

The goal of studying ancient languages, and for many, even foreign languages, should be the ability to read. To do this successfully requires a knowledge, however "incorrect" in an historical sense, of the sounds of the language. As for method, it should be adapted to need, but one method that is obviously a waste of time is rote memorization of paradigms such as those of Latin and Greek inflections. The inflections must be learned, but they should not be taught in collocations of words such as the usual paradigm, since such groupings are not their normal use in any language.

Bloomfield made some favorable remarks about the efforts to set up an international language, but he was mainly critical of the idea in general. Any language, he thought, can deal with any problem that is sufficiently pressing. But there is too much mysticism about natural languages in general, and mathematics (merely a kind of language) in particular, much of which can be dispelled by an adequate linguistic analysis—not that Bloomfield saw linguistics as a panacea: "Lexical and grammatical analysis cannot reveal the truth or falsity of a doctrine; linguistics can merely make us critical of verbal response habits" (p. 507).

He concluded *Language* with these words:

The methods and results of linguistics, in spite of their modest scope, resemble those of natural science, the domain in which science has been most successful. It is only a prospect, but not hopelessly remote, that the study of language may help us toward the understanding and control of human events.
[p. 509]

No summary as short as this could substitute for a thorough study of Bloomfield's classic work; what has been given here is an outline of the ideas contained in it, in order to give a start on a work that might otherwise seem discouraging to beginners because of the wealth of detail it contains. But the student should remember that its attention to detail is what prevents the book from being merely unsupported dogma. No one interested in linguistics can afford not to own this book, and no one interested in language should be unacquainted with it.

BLOOMFIELD'S INFLUENCE

Bloomfield's influence on American and European linguistics has been considerable. For quite a few years after the publication of *Language,* Bloomfield's was the predominant approach to language study in this country, and European views and criticisms of American linguistics referred to Bloomfield.

Perhaps more than any other individual, he was successful in inculcating a scientific attitude toward linguistic work. The results of this attitude, which often embodied a naïve mechanism, were not universally beneficial, but doubtless they had more good effects than bad. "Mentalism" was an opprobrious label, one that linguists avoided for a considerable period, largely as a result of Bloomfield's prestige. His preoccupation with facts make him appear to have been almost a Baconian scientist, convinced that once the facts are in the significance of the collection will be self-evident. This attitude led to an emphasis on classification and description as the sole, or at least as the principal, work of scientific linguists. It has been only in comparatively recent years that linguistics has again taken up the goal of explaining, as well as describing, language. Also a recent development in linguistics is the view that meaning, defined differently from Bloomfield's conception of it, is a necessary part of a linguistic theory.

From the perspective of the development of linguistics this concentration on descriptive techniques had solid justification. The linguist took language to be a code or pattern that merited independent examination, no matter what mental or behavioral concomitants it had, and the formal study of language throve on this basis. Bloomfield's work provided the basis for considerable advances that were made later in the techniques of language description.

Bloomfield's phonetics was restricted largely to the study of single words, and later workers advanced beyond this level to the examination of more extensive data. What he called "secondary phonemes" were dealt with later as "suprasegmental phonemes" and his brief discussion of transition has been worked out more carefully in the study of junctures. The speech of people from different parts of the country has been recorded and analyzed for common patterns. One result of such work was Trager and Smith's *An Outline of English Structure,*[5] in which a framework for discussing many dialects was proposed. This work has been subsequently refined under the attack of acoustic phoneticians.

[5] George L. Trager and Henry L. Smith, Jr., *An Outline of English Structure* (Washington, D.C., 1957).

Much of the advance in more refined descriptive procedures, however, was not paralleled by a comparable advance in general linguistic theory, which could give added significance to descriptive work. Only in the past decade or so have more imaginative models of linguistic production and reception been developed, which have made a more extended and inclusive study of syntax possible. This work has shown the limitations of immediate constituent analyses, a subject to be considered in later chapters.

Review Questions

1. Explain the basic notions of behaviorism and its relevance to Bloomfield's linguistics.
2. Explain how language can be considered a substitute stimulus or substitute response.
3. What did Bloomfield mean by the statement, "The only useful generalizations about language are inductive"?
4. How did Bloomfield explain meaning in behavioristic terms?
5. Give his summary of the mentalist and mechanist explanations of meaning and their relative worth.
6. How did he compare ordinary and scientific language?
7. Explain "speech community" and "density of communication." How are these factors relevant to the distinction between languages and dialects?
8. Give and illustrate the five levels of language that Bloomfield discussed.
9. Explain Bloomfield's notion of phonemes and how they are to be discovered.
10. What is the difference between gross acoustic features and distinctive features?
11. Discuss Bloomfield's phonemic analysis of English in terms of later analyses.
12. What relations did Bloomfield see between the number of phonemes in a language and the range of nondistinctive features?
13. Explain: "palatalization"; "transition."
14. Give Bloomfield's definition of "syllable" and "semivowel."
15. What relation did he see between phonetics and phonology?
16. Explain "substitutes" and the relevance of this notion to form classes and mathematics as a form of language.
17. Give Bloomfield's views on the sameness or difference in meaning of forms in successive utterances.
18. Give some of the sources of supplementary meanings.
19. Give Bloomfield's definitions, with examples, of "complex form"; "immediate constituent"; "ultimate constituents"; "morpheme"; "free form"; "bound form."
20. Explain and illustrate Bloomfield's four ways of arranging linguistic forms.
21. Give his criteria for distinguishing taxemes and tagmemes.
22. Give his criteria for distinguishing sentence types.

23. How did he define "word"?
24. According to Bloomfield, on what basis can *the* be called a word?
25. How did he distinguish between morphology and syntax?
26. Explain agreement, concord, and government as forms of selection.
27. Distinguish, with examples in English and other languages you know, endocentric and exocentric constructions.
28. Illustrate, in English and other languages you know, Bloomfield's classification of words.
29. Give Bloomfield's criteria for distinguishing inflection and derivation (word formation).
30. On what norms can we distinguish compound words from phrases?
31. Illustrate, in English and other languages you know, the difference between endocentric and exocentric compounds and between syntactic and asyntactic compounds.
32. What are some of the differences between substitutes and other linguistic forms?
33. Give some of the substitutes in languages that you know other than English. Explain their class meanings and substitute-type meanings.
34. Define "anaphora" and "anaphoric zero."
35. What did Bloomfield understand as the grammar of a language? How are lexicon and grammar related?
36. Discuss Bloomfield's rejection of the traditional definition of "noun."
37. How are the form classes of lexical forms to be determined?
38. How did Bloomfield distinguish between regular and irregular forms? Illustrate in English and other languages you know.
39. Give his explanation of the origin of writing.
40. What is the assumption of the comparative method concerning the relations of similar languages?
41. Can this assumption be justified when we have no written records of the languages?
42. What is a reconstructed form?
43. What weakness of the family-tree image of language relations did the wave theory correct?
44. In what way does dialect geography supplement the comparative method?
45. What are the causes of phonetic change?
46. Illustrate some main types of phonetic change.
47. What are the main factors governing fluctuation in the frequency of forms?
48. Explain and illustrate analogic change.
49. What is a back formation?
50. What are the main causes and types of semantic change?
51. Define "cultural borrowing" and "intimate borrowing"; what is the difference between these terms?
52. Give Bloomfield's criteria for distinguishing jargon, *lingua franca*, pidgin English, Creolized language.
53. How did he explain the origin of standard languages?

54. What were Bloomfield's objections to the current methods of teaching children to read?
55. What were his suggestions for improving the teaching of reading?
56. What was his estimate of the transfer value of language learning?
57. Discuss Bloomfield's influence on linguistics.

Suggested Readings

Besides the basic references noted in Chapter 1, it will be useful to consult Robert A. Hall, *Introductory Linguistics* (Philadelphia, 1964). This work provides additional supplementary examples of the topics Bloomfield dealt with, and the order employed parallels that of Bloomfield's *Language* in many places.

Bloomfield's obituary and a complete bibliography of his writings are found in *Language*, 25 (1949).

Bloomfield, L., *Introduction to the Study of Language* (New York, 1911).
———, "The Linguistic Aspects of Science," in the *International Encyclopedia of Unified Science*, Vol. 1, No. 4; reprinted by the University of Chicago Press, 1960.
———, "Postulates," in *Readings in Linguistics*, ed. Martin Joos (Washington, D.C., 1957).

10

J. R. Firth
Contextual Theory and Prosodic Phonology

BRONISLAW MALINOWSKI

Bronislaw Malinowski spent most of his life in England and found prominence there in the field of anthropology. Much of his work was in the South Seas, and it was there, working with the Trobriand islanders, that his interest in linguistic problems was aroused. He found that it was impossible for him to give a word-for-word translation of many expressions these people used, especially in connection with their religion. He found this lack of word-for-word correspondence true, in varying degrees, of all of their important cultural expressions. In trying to work out this problem he found himself almost unwittingly forming a theory of meaning and language.

"Context of situation" is the expression that sums up Malinowski's basic insight into how the meanings of language should be stated. It was this idea that Firth took up and developed. This view is not unlike the behavioristic formula, since it claims that the meaning of any utterance is what it *does* in some context of situation. This is readily translated into the "practical events which follow," a linguistic utterance, in Bloomfield's system. Behaviorism, a scientific fad in the United States during the 1930s, never caused much more than a ripple of amusement in Europe, so that Malinowski's work is not simply to be equated with the behavioristic approach. It does bear out Bloomfield's contention, though, that mechanists and mentalists use the same *practical methods* for the statement of meanings.

There are some other basic ideas about the nature of language and how it should be described that are directly connected with Malinowski's view of how meanings should be stated. He assumed that (1) the *sentence* is the basic linguistic datum, and (2) the *word* is, therefore, a secondary abstraction. He defined a "sentence" as "an utterance bounded by silence or audible pauses."

Malinowski believed that Europeans, because of their familiarity with institutionalized words in printed texts, and especially because of their study of dead languages, have mistaken the relation between word and sentence. In *Coral Gardens and Their Magic* he said:

It might seem that the simplest task in any linguistic enquiry would be the translation of individual terms. In reality, the problem of defining the meaning of a single word . . . is as difficult a task as any which will face us. It is, moreover, in methodological order, not the first to be tackled. It will be obvious to anyone who has followed my argument so far that isolated words are in fact only a linguistic figment, the product of advanced linguistic analysis. The sentence is at times a self-contained linguistic unit, but not even a sentence can be regarded as a full linguistic datum. To us, the real linguistic fact is the full utterance within its content of situation.[1]

For Malinowski the sentence is most important as a social tool, and he thought, therefore, that we must consider language as "a mode of action rather than a counter-sign of thought." In a Supplement to Ogden and Richards' *The Meaning of Meaning*, he stated that this mode of examination was proper mainly for the language of primitives.[2] In *Coral Gardens* he revised his ideas, stating that such investigation is applicable to any use of language in any kind of culture. He deduced this partially from the child's initial experience with language, and in a passage reminiscent of Bloomfield he said:

In all the child's experience, words when seriously uttered *mean* in so far as they act. The intellectual function of words probably develops later, and develops as a by-product of the pragmatic function. . . . Thus the source of the magical attitude towards words is, if the theory developed here is correct, to be found in the use of words by infants and children. Thus start also those profoundly pragmatic ways of learning how to use the word by learning how to use its counterpart in the reality of behavior.

[*Coral Gardens*, II, p. 62 ff.]

According to Malinowski, then, language is a means of social activity and cooperation, and the meaning of an utterance in a particular set of

---

[1] Bronislaw Malinowski, *Coral Gardens and Their Magic* (London, George Allen & Unwin, Ltd., 1935), Vol. II, p. 11. All quotations from *Coral Gardens* appearing in this chapter are taken from this edition.

[2] See Bronislaw Malinowski, "The Problem of Meaning in Primitive Languages," Supplement to C. K. Ogden and I. A. Richards, *The Meaning of Meaning* (London: Routledge & Kegan Paul, Ltd., 1923). All quotations from "The Problem of Meaning" appearing in this chapter are taken from this source.

circumstances is to be seen in its effect on the environment, which speech seeks to preserve or alter. We have stated the meaning of an utterance when we have put it into its context of situation and we see what it does. Therefore,

$$MEANING = USE$$

One advantage that J. R. Firth saw in this approach is that it appears to escape the "entanglements of referential meaning" theories. In this system any utterance could stand for anything whatever without causing problems for the analyst, since his statement of meaning will be in terms of environmental effect. More than that, an expression thus described need not stand for anything. In fact, a great range of language use cannot be sensibly explained in terms of referential meaning, according to Malinowski.

Phatic Communion

"Phatic communion" is a term that Malinowski invented to label non-referential uses of language. But one might object that any such "escape" from referential problems is only apparent, since utterances in a society can effect something only through the mediation of the speaker's understanding, hopes, desires, and so on. Malinowski "escapes" because he presupposes referential knowledge on the part of speakers. More cogently, one might object that many forms of speech do not appear to effect anything, a difficulty similar to Bloomfield's "displaced speech."

Malinowski had answers to these anticipated objections:

1. Speakers' desires, intentions, knowledge, and so on do indeed contribute to the context of situation, but this admission does not require him to return to the traditional methods of explaining what they are; he need merely recognize that they are pertinent factors.

2. There is a great difference between literary and familiar use of language. Literary language is deliberately composed for a wide context, a specific task, and then it is meant to be forgotten. It is bound up with, and only fully understandable in, each context of situation. As for a third objection, Malinowski had an ingenious answer and an appealing expression:

there can be no doubt that we have here a new type of linguistic use—*phatic communion,* I am tempted to call it . . . a type of speech in which the ties of union are created by the mere exchange of words. . . . Are words in phatic communion used primarily to convey meaning, the meaning that is symbolically theirs? Certainly not! They fulfill a social function and that is their principal aim, but they are neither the result of intellectual reflection nor do they necessarily arouse intellectual reflection in their hearer. Once again, we may say that language does not function here as a means of transmission of thought.

["The Problem of Meaning," p. 315]

The same thought is well put by S. I. Hayakawa, a more recent author:

From these social practices it is possible to state, as a general principle, that the prevention of silence is itself an important function of speech, and that it is completely impossible for us in society to talk only when we have something to say.[3]

Translation

Since societies are unique, and their languages and the situations in which they use language are equally unique, it would appear that translation would be impossible. This was partially Malinowski's view, especially in the situations most peculiar to each community. The difficulty, he felt, is not so great among Europeans, who more or less share the same culture, but the gap between them and the Trobrianders makes the problem acute:

Now we have whittled down our paradox to the platitude that the words from one language are never translatable into another. . . . If by full translation we mean the supplying of the full range of equivalent devices, metaphoric expressions and idiomatic sayings—such a process is of course possible. But even then it must be remembered that something more than the mere juggling with words and expressions is needed.

[*Coral Gardens*, II, p. 14]

The reasons for this are expressed in terms much like the Sapir-Whorf hypothesis, that for two different cultures "an entirely different world of things to be expressed" exists. Language is essentially pragmatic in Malinowski's view, so that it can be described as a set of symbols for things (lexical items) arranged in a set of relations as men see them (grammar), and men "see" them according to their power to act upon them. Meaning, therefore, is "the effect of words on human minds and bodies, and through these, on the environmental reality as created or conceived in a given culture" (*Coral Gardens*, II, p. 53).

J. R. FIRTH

The work of J. R. Firth, and of the group called the London School that has succeeded him, is worth considering at this point, since it is in opposition to the tradition of linguistic study in America as inaugurated

---

[3] S. I. Hayakawa, *Language in Thought and Action* (London: George Allen & Unwin, Ltd., 1952), p. 72.

by Leonard Bloomfield. At the same time, it shares the basic insights into the structure of language that originated with de Saussure. Bloomfield exploited one of the possible interpretations of what is involved in the systematic nature of language as a consequence of its "linearity," but Firth considered this approach to result in a conception of linguistic structure that derives from the methods used to establish units in only one of the systems of language, phonemics. He did not think that the phonemic approach is the only way, nor indeed the best way, to reveal the phonological structure of a language. Indeed, he felt that the techniques of phonemics are principally useful for devising a writing system for a language. Nor did Firth think that the same techniques which have been used to isolate the phonemes of a language could be employed without significant adaptation to the description of the grammar.

From Malinowski Firth borrowed the idea of studying language in a context of situation, but refined the method by distinguishing various levels on which there are strictly linguistic elements. He then distinguished the specifically linguistic levels into sets of relations on the two axes discussed by de Saussure, paradigmatic and syntagmatic, and he insisted that priority could not be given to either. The over-all purpose of this contextual analysis was the statement concerning meaning. In each of these aspects Firth's work offers instructive contrasts to the Bloomfieldian and post-Bloomfieldian linguistics with which most Americans are familiar.

Firth's Conception of Linguistics

In a summary of the views he had developed over a period of twenty-five years, Firth began a discussion of the theoretical standing of linguistics with a quotation from Goethe: *Das höchste wäre zu begreifen, dass alles Faktische schon Theorie ist,* which more or less asserts that there are no such things as brute facts, but that all "facts" are seen to be relevant only in view of some theory.[4]

Older views of linguistics have been based on a discredited dualism of some psychophysical kind. American linguistics has followed the behavioristic doctrines of Watson, which amounts to another kind of realistic presupposition that Firth thought unnecessary. Malinowski too seemed to be preoccupied with what was "real" in language as opposed to what "has no existence" except in the mind of the linguist.[5]

[4] J. F. Firth, "Synopsis of Linguistic Theory, 1930–1955," in *Studies in Linguistic Analysis,* a special publication of the Philological Society (Oxford: Basil Blackwell, 1957). All quotations from "Synopsis of Linguistic Theory" appearing in this chapter are taken from this source.

[5] See J. R. Firth, "An Ethnographic Theory of Language," in R. W. Firth, ed., *Man and Culture* (London, 1957), for Firth's estimate of Malinowski's work.

In Firth's view such questions are best side-stepped, since the success of any scientific theory in *renewal of connection* with the experiential facts to which it must constantly refer is the best norm for preferring one theory over another. Firth thought that questions of "reality" can paralyze inquiry; he asked, "Where would mechanics be if it were to use as its point of departure an explanation of 'what motion really is'?" ("Synopsis of Linguistic Theory," I.)

As a consequence of these considerations, Firth pointed out that all of the structures, terms, units, and categories that he discussed are to be considered as

ordered schematic constructs, frames of reference, a sort of scaffolding to handle events. . . . Such constructs have no ontological status, and we do not project them as having being or existence. They are neither immanent nor transcendent, but just language turned back on itself.[6]

The *object* to be studied in linguistics, according to Firth, is language in actual use, since "using language is one of the forms of human life, and speech is immersed in the immediacy of social intercourse" ("Synopsis of Linguistic Theory," XII). The *purpose* of the study is to break up the meaningful aspects of language in such a way that the linguistic and nonlinguistic can be correlated, since "modes of meaning presuppose modes of experience," although "in dealing with such texts abstracted from the matrix of experience most of the environmental accompaniment of the mush of general goings-on must of necessity be suppressed" ("Synopsis of Linguistic Theory," XII). The *method* of the study is, therefore, to determine the components of linguistic activity and to state their relations in a series of congruent levels, to show the interrelationships involved, and, above all, to guarantee "renewal of connection" with the states of affairs from which they were originally abstracted.

Terminology

Firth recognized that his terminology is idiosyncratic, but he did not find this to be a drawback. He was not interested in "systematizing" or substituting a new dogmatic rigidity in linguistic description as a substitute for the other systems he criticized, but he wanted to point out and name some units and relations in linguistics that had been overlooked or insufficiently dealt with by other linguists. The terms he used are to be interpreted only within the system of all the other terms

[6] J. R. Firth, *Papers in Linguistics, 1934–1951* (London: Oxford University Press, 1957). All quotations from *Papers in Linguistics* appearing in this chapter are taken from this source.

employed. In the work of subsequent writers of the London Group, of course, we find that there is much care to use the terminology in the same fashion as proposed by Firth, and this is quite understandable, since otherwise there could be no accuracy in communication.

Although Firth would have denied vehemently that he was a structuralist if the term is taken to mean that he was aligned with the principles of the phonemicists, he was certainly a structuralist in the de Saussurean sense. The basis of much of his terminology can be understood in view of the basic distinction de Saussure drew between associative and syntagmatic axes of language. For the term "associative," linguists have accepted the amendment of the Danish linguist L. Hjelmslev and refer to "paradigmatic" relations as a corrective for de Saussure's psychological notion.[7]

For Firth, the term "structure" and all its derivatives applied solely to syntagmatic relations, and "*system*," with its derivatives, to the paradigmatic:

$$\begin{array}{c} s \\ y \\ s \\ s \ t \ r \ u \ c \ t \ u \ r \ e \\ e \\ m \end{array}$$

He noted in "Synopsis of Linguistic Theory" that structure is, therefore, concerned with syntagmatic relations between elements, and system concerns paradigmatic relations between commutable units or terms that provide values for elements.

Systems and structures are studied on various levels of analysis in **contexts of situation** for statements of meaning. A context of situation is a schematic construct that is applied especially to repetitive events in the social process, consisting of various levels of analysis. These levels, (for example, phonetic, phonological, grammatical, lexical, situational) are equally theoretical constructs and they consist of a consistent framework of categories, which are named in a restricted language in order to deal with the distinguishable aspects of meaning. Since "meaning is use," situations are set up especially to recognize use. Two such distinguishable aspects of meaning are found in **collocation** and **colligation.** On the lexical level one finds certain words in habitual company with other words and this accompaniment contributes to their meaning. This is not merely context in the usual sense, nor meaning through the examples lexicographers give, having established a meaning outside

---

[7] *Actes du Quatrième Congrès International de Linguistes, 1936,* (Copenhagen, 1938), p. 140.

those contexts. It is an order of mutual expectancy between actual lexical items. This aspect of meaning is to be distinguished from colligation, which is a relation not between actual lexical items but between the grammatical categories of which the lexical items are the exponents. In this sense, meaning, therefore, derives from the interrelations between grammatical categories in syntactic structure.

Contextual Analysis

In his review of Malinowski's linguistic work Firth mentioned that the situational approach to language began with Philipp Wegener and was then taken up by Sir Alan Gardiner and by himself.[8]

The situational approach requires that we analyze the typical speech situation as follows:

1. Interior relations of the text itself
    a. Syntagmatic relations between elements of structure considered at the various levels of analysis.
    b. Paradigmatic relations of terms or units that commute within systems to give values to the elements of structure.
2. Interior relations within the context of situation
    a. The text in relation to the nonverbal constituents, with its total effective or creative result.
    b. Analytic relations between "bits" and "pieces" of the text (for example, words, parts of words, phrases) and special constituents within the situation (for example, items, objects, persons, personalities, events).

The principal components of the whole meaning are the phonetic function (which is minor) and the major functions of lexical, morphological, and syntactic items, and of the whole context of situation. The method by which the meaning is to be explicated requires that we split up the organic whole into several levels, just as light is dispersed through a spectrum.[9]

The first level is that of phonetics, as discussed here, although the "levels" are not hierarchical in any ontological sense, and the direction of the analysis is not necessarily from phonetics to situations. This level includes what American linguists would distinguish as the levels of phonetics and phonemics or phonology. But we can retain the term,

[8] See Philipp Wegener, *Untersuchungen über die Grundfagen des Sprachlebens* (Halle, 1855); Sir Alan Gardiner, *Theory of Speech and Language* (Oxford, 1932, 1951); and J. R. Firth, *Speech* (London, 1930).

[9] See J. R. Firth, "The Techniques of Semantics," in *Papers in Linguistics, 1934–1951*.

since both phonetic and phonological levels are "levels of meaning" for Firth, a fact often asserted by him in statements like, "It is part of the meaning of a Frenchman to sound like a Frenchman." At this level, sounds have function by virtue of (1) the places in which they occur and (2) the contrast they show with other sounds that could occur in the same place.

PLACE   Using English *b* as an illustration, the sound is found to occur:

1. Initially (*bed, bid*).
2. Before any vowel.
3. Before a limited number of consonants (*bleed, bread*).
4. Never after a consonant.

CONTRAST   In studying the words in which *b* is initial we find that *p* or *m* could replace it in most of them and that:

1. Given *p* or *m*, an *s* could precede these sounds.
2. While *p* and *m* are articulated at the same place as *b*, there are contrasts between them: both *b* and *p* are bilabial, but *b* and *p* are usually non-nasal and *m* is nonplosive, and so on.
3. *d* is alveolar and contrasts differently with *b* than with the other sounds, and so on.

Such comparisons are carried on until the segmental units of the language have been established, by listing how the sounds function, how they are mutually substitutable, how they contrast, and so on:

> The phonetic or minor function of a sound is shown by studying it in relation to the phonetic contexts in which it occurs and in relation to the other sounds which may replace it in these contexts, or in whole words, in relation to the "context" of the whole phonological system. A phonetic substitution-counter has been termed a phoneme.

> [*Papers in Linguistics*, No. 3]

In this particular version Firth made no mention of the distinction he later drew between phonematic units and prosodies, which will be discussed presently. But he did note that it is one of the functions of the phonologist to state the phonematic units and prosodic processes within the text, regarding them as a mode of meaning, while it is the task of the phonetician to link these to the processes and features of utterance.

The second level is the lexical, the level on which the meanings of words can be considered. From one point of view one need not know the meanings of words, since words can be recognized as possible sequences in a language on the basis of the study made at the phonetic level. At the lexical level words can be considered "lexical substitution counters."

The meanings of the words can be stated, not only in the usual referential sense, where this is applicable, but also in terms of collocation, or the "company a word keeps." Examples of collocation are the meaning features attached to the English names for the days of the week, as opposed to the names in Chinese or Hebrew, or to the names of the English months in *March hare, August bank holiday, May week, April showers, April fool,* and the like. Such collocations are first stated for single forms of the words, and then they can be contrasted with their other forms, as *light, lightest, lights, lighted,* and so on.

The third level that Firth cited is the grammatical, which can be divided into morphology and syntax, although he later remarked that the traditional distinction between morphology and syntax, as a result of the units discoverable through collocational studies and prosodic groupings, may have been over-rated as a result of the importance the distinction had in historical linguistics. (See "Synopsis of Linguistic Theory," XII). On the morphological level, we can examine the paradigms into which words enter (here called "formal scatters"), since these also condition the meanings of the members of the paradigm.

On the syntactic level of meaning we deal with **colligations,** or syntagmatic relations between grammatical categories. Of course, these relations must always be realized in some exponents, such as in the words *I watched him,* but the grammatical relations are not, strictly speaking, between the words as such but rather between pronominal and verbal categories. Another illustration of colligations is found in the operator-negative relation. Twenty-two or twenty-four syntactical operators are required to deal with negation in English, and all of them can be regarded as terms in the ordered series of operators: *am, is, are, was, were, have, has, had, do, does, did, shall, should, will, would, may, might, can, could, must, ought, need, dare,* and *used (to).* All of these operators are colligated with the negative particle, and all negative finite verb forms are colligated with one of them. Word-form exponents of the operator-negative colligation are *can't, won't,* and so on. The need for generalizing the relation of colligation beyond the word level lies in the fact that the exponents of grammatical categories need not be words at all (see "Synopsis of Linguistic Theory," V). Firth illustrated grammatical meaning through nonsense verse, a device that can also be used to show examples of prosodic meaning (for example, groupings through intonation rather than sense, syntagmatic implication of construction and consonant-vowel types, and so on):

Finster war's, der Mond schien helle, schneebedeckt die grüne Flur, als ein Wagen blitzchnelle langsam um die Ecke fuhr.

In English the German nonsense verse is approximately:

'Twas dark, the moon shone bright, the meadow green
with snow lay thick,
When 'round the corner, slowly, slow, turned a car,
lightning-quick.

A fourth level is the situational, a level that corresponds more closely (together with the considerations on the lexical level) to what others have called a level of meaning. There is no generally accepted technical language to describe contexts of situation, but it is here that the linguist chooses the relevant items that he sets up in interrelations of "elements of structure and . . . systems of 'terms' and 'units' as end-points of mutually determined interior relations." For example, in "Synopsis of Linguistic Theory," III, Firth listed:

A. Participants (persons, personalities, and relevant features of these)
  (i) their verbal actions.
  (ii) their nonverbal actions.
B. Relevant objects, the nonverbal and nonpersonal events.
C. The effect of the verbal action.

Notional descriptions of these types of situations and their constituents seem unavoidable at this stage. Such descriptions would include distinguishing situations that are deictic, onomastic, or concerned with personal address or reference; those referring to economic, religious, and social structures of societies; situations of monologue, chorus, narrative, recitation, and so on; and language as used for drills, orders, flattery, cursing, and phatic communion; also to be included would be data concerning the age, sex, and relation of the speakers and listeners.

The order in which these types of situations and their constituents are to be stated and interrelated is not fixed, nor is any level a formal prerequisite for another. While the approach is termed *"monistic"* and avoids such dichotomies as words and ideas, it is not to be understood as excluding "the concept of mind, or to imply an embracing of materialism to avoid a foolish bogey of mentalism" ("Synopsis of Linguistic Theory," II). It is used for two principal reasons: (1) it enables us to state the *use* of an utterance in a situation, and we can equate "meaning" with "use"; (2) it is a guarantee that we are examining attested bits of language, instead of the far-fetched examples found in many grammars (see "Synopsis of Linguistic Theory," II, IV, XII).

For Firth, the study of language was the study of meaning; it is interesting, that, in view of the fact that both he and Bloomfield advocated a situational approach to meaning, one of the weaknesses Firth found in Bloomfield's otherwise laudable work was a "rejection of meaning." Of his own approach he wrote in the "Techniques of Semantics":

The techniques I have sketched here are an empirical rather than a theoretical analysis of meaning. It can be described as a serial contextualization of our facts, context within context, each one being a function, an organ of the bigger context, and all the contexts finding a place in what may be called the context of culture. It avoids many of the difficulties which arise if meaning is regarded chiefly as a mental relation or an historical process.

[*Papers in Linguistics,* No. 3]

Another way of putting this is to say that Firth tried to describe meaning, whatever it is, but had no preconceptions about what it is, whereas Bloomfield had a very clear idea about what meaning is—a physical process of associative conditioning—which only the scientist could adequately describe, so that his situational approach was makeshift.[10] Because of this definition statements concerning meaning in linguistics are the weakest point in Bloomfield's work. Firth, however, relying on his own and others' common sense, made it possible to discuss meaning because of the way he defined it. The problems that anteceded either of their definitions, of course, remained unsolved.

Prosodic Analysis

One of Firth's most characteristic contributions to the field of linguistics was alluded to above in the account of contextual analysis, where it was pointed out that Firth considered the level of phonetics to be a level of meaning. This type of phonological analysis is called "prosodic," because it contains, as one of its fundamental elements, features that are not recognized as autonomous in the phonemic approach.

All linguists seem to be in agreement that the study of language should be "formal" in the sense that linguistic units and categories should be verifiable through compositional or distributional contrast or both. They are less agreed about (1) the fundamental units to be included in such descriptions; (2) the direction in which such descriptions should proceed—from sound to sentence or sentence to sound; (3) the relevance and nature of meaning to be used in establishing the units; (4) the number of levels of analysis required; and (5) the extent to which information from one level is relevant to setting up units on another (for example, should grammatical information be considered relevant in establishing phonemic differences?).

Firth's second thoughts about the phonological level of language and its relevance to the other levels were proposed in a paper read before the Philological Society in London in 1948. He suggested a prosodic approach to phonological analysis, because he had become convinced

---

[10] See Leonard Bloomfield, *Language* (New York: Holt, Rinehart and Winston, Inc., 1931), pp. 139–140 ff.

that phonemics overemphasizes the paradigmatic relations in language and that generalization of such emphasis results in an inadequate account of the phonology as well as the grammar of languages. Firth is not easy to understand, and his paper, "Sounds and Prosodies," makes one think that he never had an editor.[11]

While the prosodic approach is highly original with Firth, others had worked along similar lines. Firth claimed to have found inspiration in the work of Panini, the Indian grammarian whose description of Sanskrit revolutionized Western linguistics in the nineteenth century.[12] One reason such work interested Firth was that Indian writing systems developed from a form in which each symbol first stood for a consonant plus the vowel a, to which diacritics could be added to indicate the presence of another vowel. Then symbols were developed for consonants with no vowels, and finally symbols for vowels without consonants. In the process the Indians arrived at a method for indicating sounds very accurately, including features that Firth would call prosodies.

To a greater extent than Firth did himself, members of the School of Oriental and African Studies at the University of London developed the prosodic method of language analysis while Firth was chairman of the Department of Phonetics and Linguistics at the school. Their publications are to be found in the *Bulletin of the School of Oriental and African Studies (BSOAS)* and in other journals not commonly circulated in the United States, which helps to account for their comparative lack of influence on American linguistics.[13]

In analyzing the phonic material of an utterance, prosodic analysis distinguishes, as at all levels, between paradigmatic and syntagmatic relations. The items in paradigmatic relations are **systemic,** while those in syntagmatic relations are **structural.** As indicated by de Saussure, there must be a succession of items on the linear plane of language in order to discuss syntagmatic relations. Typical items that can be discussed principally in terms of paradigmatic relations are the phonic segments, called phonematic units, which can be viewed as units or terms in a system. At the same time, it is possible to consider the relations between successive phonematic units, which can be studied as elements in structure. A typical structural element is a syllable, and the syllable structure of any word or piece is considered prosodic. While Firth did not seem to give a clear definition of a prosody, the illustrations he gave include features of stress, length, nasality, palatalization, iotization, labiovelarization, and

11 J. R. Firth, "Sounds and Prosodies," *Transactions of the Philological Society* (London, 1948), pp. 127–152. The paper also appears in Firth, *Papers in Linguistics,* No. 9.

12 See W. S. Allen, *Phonetics in Ancient India* (London, 1953).

13 A selection of their writings, together with Firth's "Synopsis of Linguistic Theory," is found in *Studies in Linguistic Analysis* (Oxford, 1957).

aspiration, suggesting that basic to the notion of a prosody is a sound feature associated with more than a single phonematic unit or segment. Phonematic units are segmental abstractions at the phonological level and, as such, have exponents in the phonic substance, just as grammatical units, which are abstractions at the morphological or syntactic level, also have their exponents (sometimes the same exponents) in the phonic substance. Prosodies such as stress or intonation can be considered either paradigmatically (contrasting stress, intonation) or syntagmatically (since they can succeed each other and also are realized over more than a single segmental item).

A phonematic unit, as the name suggests, both resembles and differs from a phoneme in the usual definition. While phonematic units are generally represented in general phonetic terms (for example, by International Phonetic Alphabet symbols), they should not be equated with such symbols. The phoneme is a unit defined through its ability to distinguish one lexical item from another, and part of its definition is the specification of features of a phonetic event (for example, English /p/ is typically a voiceless, bilabial stop, though not in all of its realizations). The symbols of the IPA (or any phonetic chart) stand for important kinds of articulations, without reference to their differential function on the lexical level and without implication of allophonic variations. Both the IPA and the phonemic symbols may include more or less articulatory information than the phonematic unit represents. As an initial step to understanding this kind of phonology, it might be suggested that the difference between a phoneme and a phonematic unit is a prosody; stated for a lexical item: phoneme − prosody = phonematic unit. This way of putting it is more suggestive than accurate, since prosodies, of course, are stated for more than lexical items, but many of the features called allophonic in the phonemes, which represent lexical items in phonemic analysis, would be assigned to prosodies in the prosodic approach, thus leaving the segment without such sound features. An example may help to explain.

A phonetic description of the initial consonant of an English word like *key* would include the information that *k* is a voiceless, prevelar, tense, aspirated stop. A phonemic statement about *key* would include the information that the word consists of the phonemes /kiy/ and that the initial phoneme /k/ shows the allophonic variations in this word of (1) fronting in the environment of front vowel; (2) aspiration in word-initial position; and (3) relative tenseness of articulation, since /k/ is not in intervocalic position.

The prosodic statement would include two kinds of statements: one a representation of the monosyllable type, of which *key* is an exponent, for example, $C_{13}V_7$. This statement indicates that English monosyllables, consisting of a consonant and vowel in that order, have a thirteen-term system in initial position and a seven-term system of vowels (though not all the consonants and vowels in English could combine with each other here). This very generalized phonological statement would be supplemented by others, including such formulations as:

$$\frac{h}{ki:}$$

where k is a symbol for a phonematic unit whose phonetic definition is to be given, if it is part of some larger environment (and not assumed from phonemic information, nor from IPA sources, although these would be more suggestive); h stands for a "breathy" prosody, the presence of aspiration; and the line extending over the whole word indicates that the prosody is realized over the vowel as well as over the consonant. If the word had been $kilo$, the domain of the prosody would have been only the first syllable and not the entire word.

One reason that we cannot assume the phonetic definition of the k phonematic unit from sources other than this kind of analysis is that it will depend on the environment in which it occurs. Often the information given in phonemic and prosodic analysis is quite similar. For instance, if this k sound appeared in the word ski, the formula for monosyllables beginning with a sibilant would be, perhaps, $C_1 C_6 V_6$, when the monosyllable consists of two consonants and a vowel in that order. This formula would indicate that the second consonant belongs to a six-term system (p, t, k, l, w, y) and that the vowel also belongs to a six-term system (i:, e:, a:, $ɔ$:, o:, u:). The structural representation would be as follows:

$$\frac{\bar{h}}{ski}$$

where $\bar{h}$ indicates "nonbreathy," or nonaspiration, and the phonematic unit k differs phonetically from the initial of key because it is lax in articulation. This particular example illustrates that similar phonetic information can be conveyed in prosodic and phonemic analysis (since it would be stated as one of the allophonic variants of /k/ that it is lax and nonaspirate in this same environment), but it does not show all of the differences between the two approaches. The prosodic marks of h and $\bar{h}$ indicate more clearly the domain of aspiration or its lack than the phonemic notation. Therefore, this trivial example can suggest that prosodic analysis is more deliberately focused on syntagmatic information, but in the phonetic gathering of data for the phonemic analysis, the same information would have been recorded.

It will be useful to review some of the reasons Firth offered for preferring prosodic analysis, and then to examine a few examples of how
his recommendations can be carried out. For Firth, the basic question
seemed to be, What is a unit of language? All linguists admit that the
sentence is, in an important sense, the basic datum of language, but in
practice Firth believed that unnecessary and unjustified priority is given
words and morphemes. In his "Synopsis of Linguistic Theory" he said
that the unit is the text in a context of situation, and that this unit is
then "dispersed" into modes for the purposes of study. Firth noted that
it must be remembered that all these modes or levels are abstractions
from the text, so that there is no inherent order in terms of which one
level must be considered before another. He found prosodic treatment
of a text to be necessary no matter which direction we start from—from
phonetics to grammar and context of situation or from context of situation back to phonetics. Starting at the sentence level, Firth found prosodic groups that obviousy characterize the sentence or its parts. For
example, in the West Yorkshire dialect, an expression like

a st ə 'dun t if a 'kud [I should have done it if I could]

is prosodically and grammatically holophrastic; the interrelations of the
grammatical categories stated as colligations form the unifying framework, and the phonological categories are limited by the grammatical
status of the structures. On the grammatical level, Firth found that an
example like

He couldn't have kept on running up and down the stairs all morning

is not well analyzed in terms of morphemes + distribution, but that the
verb should be considered as a polynomial periphrastic verb, not as a
set of individual words; that the analysis of grammatical or "morphe-
matic" categories should be studied syntagmatically, since they appear
paradigmatically only as units which give values to elements of structure;
and that the same sort of analysis should be applied to "pieces" and
"clauses." In such an analysis the prosodic interdependence of articles,
auxiliaries, and deictic particles according to style becomes clear. On
the lexical level, collocations show the importance of the piece, phrase,
clause, sentence, and closely knit sentence groups, so that

If the phonological analysis of longer pieces than the word is to be one of a
congruent series at a number of levels of description, there would appear to be
no alternative to some form of prosodic approach based on a theory of structures and systems.

["Synopsis of Linguistic Theory," VI]

One consequence of these considerations is the recommendation that in
analyzing a language "it will be useful to take as first isolates, prosodic

groups" ("Synopsis of Linguistic Theory," VIII) and then work down to the other phonological constituents. Using this approach, E. J. A. Henderson set up the following prosodies and phonematic units for Siamese:

Sentence prosody: intonation
Prosodies of sentence pieces: length, tone, stress, and tone relations between syllables.
Syllable prosodies: length, tone, stress, palatalization, and labio-velarization.
Prosodies of syllable parts: aspiration, retroflection, plosion, and unexploded closure.
Phonematic consonant and vowel units: velars, dentals, bilabials, front, back, rounded and unrounded vowels.[14]

One consequence of taking this direction is that some phonetic features which would be dealt with in phonemics as allophonic differences of phonemes (and some phonemic features) are assigned as prosodic markers of grammatical and larger phonological structures.

An example of the application of prosodic analysis to simplify phonological description and to bring statements at that level into more clear congruence with the grammatical description was given by John T. Bendor-Samuel.[15]

The article is principally concerned with the treatment of nasal and palatalization features in Tereno, a native language of Brazil. A phonemic analysis of the language results in the following phonemes:

stops	p t k	glottal	ʔ
laterals	l r	semivowels	y w
nasals	m n	vowels	i e a o u
fricatives	s š h hy		

The stops and fricatives are voiceless and have no allophones except an aspirated t before i. h and hy are listed with the fricatives for functional and phonetic reasons. There are two syllable types, CV and V. Apart from the features discussed here, there are no consonant clusters. Vowel clusters are found within and between morphemes when a CV syllable is followed by a V syllable. Long consonants and vowels are found only in association with stress.

The nasal phonemes are clearly established, for example (in phonetic symbols): 'ima ("her husband"), 'ipara ("his gift"), 'ina ("then"), 'iha ("his name"), l'sane ("his field"), and so on. Bendor-Samuel points out, however, that

---

[14] E. J. A. Henderson, "Prosodies in Siamese," *Asia Minor*, New Series, 1 (1949).
[15] John T. Bendor-Samuel, "Some Problems of Segmentation in the Phonological Analysis of Tereno" *Word*, 16 (1960), 348–355. All quotations from Bendor-Samuel appearing in this chapter are taken from this source.

other nasal features are not so easily interpreted by phonemic procedures. The features in question are nasalized vowels and semivowels and the consonantal sequence of nasal followed by stop or fricative, namely: *mb, nd, nz, nž,* and *ŋg*. Phonetically, the non-nasal elements of the nasal consonantal sequences under discussion, i.e., *b, d, g, z,* and *ž* are identical with the stops and fricatives *p, t, k, s,* and *š* found elsewhere in Tereno, except for the voicing. Similarly, the nasalized vowels and semivowels have the same qualities as their oral counterparts.

[p. 350]

The nasal features are linked grammatically, since they mark the category of first person, and occur elsewhere only in Portuguese loans. Phonetically, in marking the first person, it is found that:

1. All vowels and semivowels in the word are nasalized up to the first stop or fricative, and if there are no stops or fricatives in the word, the whole word is nasalized, or

2. a nasalized consonantal sequence replaces the first stop or fricative of a word: *mb* for *p, nd* for *t, ŋg* for *k, nz* for *s,* and *h* and *nž* for *š* and *hy.* For example,

e'mo?u	("his word")	'piho	("he went")
e'mõ?ũ	("my word")	'mbiho	("I went")
'owoku	("his house")	ã'nža?ašo	("I desire")
'õw̃õŋgu	("my house")	a'hya?ašo	("he desires")
'ayo	("his brother")		
'ãỹõ	("my brother")		

One phonemic solution suggested for this data would be the establishment of another nasal phoneme, /N/ (different from /m/ and /n/). The nasalized vowels and semivowels could then be considered as allophones of the vowels before /N/, and, in the case of the semivowels, after /N/. Thus ãỹõ ("my brother") would be, phonemically, /aNyoN/.

The consonantal sequences could then be analyzed as a nasal consonant followed by voiced allophones of the otherwise voiceless stops and fricatives, and /N/ would have the allophone *m* before *p, n* before *t, s,* and *š, ŋ* before *k,* and *N* before semivowels and laterals. Alternatively, the *m* and *n* could be assigned to the /m/ and /n/ phonemes, and *ŋ* could be considered an allophone of /n/ before /k/.

There is a clear advantage in the economy of the number of phonemes needed to handle the data in this solution, which adds only the phoneme /N/, and the allophones of /n/ as well as of all the vowels, semivowels, stops, and fricatives. But there are two inconveniences from the point of view of the over-all pattern of the language: this solution introduces closed syllables and consonant clusters, which are foreign to the rest of the syllable structure of the language, and thus complicates the morphophonemic statement. That is, allomorphs would have to be set up to account for words in which *h* or *hy* is the first member of the stop-or-fricative series to occur in first-person forms, since the stop or fricative would be replaced by *nz* and *nž*, respectively. For example, a form like *'ahya* ("desire") would have the alternate form *aža* occurring with the infix *-N-* (first person) as in *'aNža* ("my desire").

There are other phonemic alternatives that could be selected. For example, we could analyze the nasal features as single segments, thus setting up phonemes in addition to the present stock that would be nasalized vowels, semivowels, and consonants. But this would add twelve phonemes, and on the grammatical level, require the description of the first-person construction as a series of phoneme replacements.

As another alternative, Bendor-Samuel suggests a prosodic treatment of this Tereno material, involving the use of phonematic units and prosodies:

Phonetic features which either extend over or have implications over more than one place in the syllable are allotted to specific prosodies, while other phonetic data are assigned to the phonematic units. Prosodies may be stated for the syllable or the word.

[p. 352]

This approach would set up the phonematic units *p, t, k, s, š, h, hy, w, y, i, e, a, o, u,* and a prosody of nasalization that can be called an "n-prosody." This would most likely be regarded as a prosody of the word, since it can extend beyond a single syllable. The phonetic exponent of this prosody would include nasalization and voicing throughout the word and narrowing of the opening between the alveolar ridge and tongue, with grooving of the tongue, producing increased friction when *h* or *hy* is the first fricative. A word that can be said to be marked by this n-prosody, such as *ẽ'mõʔu* ("my word") could be symbolized as ⁿVCVCV (or $\overline{VCVCV}^{n}$). The advantages of this approach are that the syllabic pattern of the language is preserved, consonant clusters need not be postulated, and sequences which share nasality can be treated as related exponents of a single phonological category.

If we distinguish the phonemic approach as "vertical" (that is, paradigmatic) from the prosodic as "vertical and horizontal" (that is, paradigmatic and syntagmatic), we can see that there are marked differences in the economy with which nasalization in a word like *ãỹõ* ("my brother") is dealt with. If we take one phonemic representation of the word as /aNyoN/, we can see that the feature of nasalization is assigned to five phonemes: vNcvN, two instances of the nasal phoneme /N/, two allophones of the vowel, and one of the semivowel; in other words, the feature of nasality is assigned to one nasal and two non-nasal phonemes. The prosodic approach would consider the nasalized vowel ã, for example, as an exponent of the phonematic unit a as well as a (partial) exponent of the n-prosody. While the phonemic approach has the advantage of a certain over-all simplicity in that it assigns all phonetic phenomena to the segmental phoneme, the prosodic analysis might be considered to have the advantage of not subdividing what can be treated as a single phonetic feature, the exponent of one particular grammatical category, the first person.

In the phonetic exponents of the second-person category, it might be suggested that a similar treatment could be used, since, phonemically, (a) such forms beginning with any vowel except /i/ are prefixed by /y-/, and (2) other words are characterized by vowel replacements involving some type of fronting and raising, which often extends beyond a single segment. These features could be considered the phonetic exponents of a y-prosody (palatalization), and the interesting correlation would arise that the first person is phonologically marked by an n-prosody, the second person by a y-prosody, and the third person by a zero-prosody.

Despite the attractiveness of this correlation between grammatical and phonological categories, Bendor-Samuel points out one rather serious problem that would arise: the e of 'yeno ("you walked," vs. 'yono, "he walked") would be regarded as the phonetic exponent *both* of the phonematic unit o and of the y-prosody, but the e of 'yeno ("his wife," vs. 'yino, "your wife") would be regarded as the phonetic exponent of the phonematic unit e and the zero-prosody.

Monosystemic vs. Polysystemic Analysis

Firth and the London School had two principal objections to American (principally, Bloomfieldian or post-Bloomfieldian) structuralism. The objections concern American phonological procedures, but they have evident implications for the rest of language study as well. According to the Bloomfieldian view, phonemics is based on a single system of language, an assumption that goes counter to Firth's conception of linguistic structure, and this issue introduces anomalies such as the concept of redundancy. Firth did not believe that the analysis of discourse could be developed from phonemic procedures, nor even by analogy from them:

The main criticism to be offered of American structuralist linguistics based on phonemic procedures is that, having attempted just that, it has not furnished any valid grammatical analysis by means of which renewal of connection in experience can be made with systematic certainty.

["Synopsis of Linguistic Theory," VII]

Recalling that the distinction between system and structure is fundamental to Firth's whole approach to language, it can be seen that the objection to the establishment of phonemes as "basic units" of language merely on the criterion of minimal lexical contrasts can be expressed by calling the American structuralist approach "monosystemic," whereas Firth's approach is designed to be "polysystemic." Firth did not believe that any level of linguistic analysis is prior or subsequent to any other except in temporal consideration, so that units established through their function on one level, (for example, the lexical) are not truly basic. The American practice of excluding grammatical criteria (except for such fundamentals as word and sentence boundaries) from consideration in establishing phonemic contrasts seemed to Firth to be ignoring the fact that any point in a language can and should be considered the locus of many systemic and structural relations.

The objection to inability to "make renewal of connection" with phonetic reality was not a complaint about inadequate transcription, and Firth's own approach to phonology was quite evidently not intended to supply a new or better method of transcription. In fact, he believed that phonemics suffered precisely from its preoccupation with transcription, that phonemics could, therefore, be termed "prelinguistic" in much the same sense as phonetics, and that the phoneme would be better called a "transcribeme."

By "renewal of contact with experience," which was to be accomplished, apparently, through his polysystemic approach, Firth obviously meant an analysis that accounted for all the systematic and structural relations of linguistic units. This is the tenor of W. Sidney Allen's remarks about prosodic analysis in "Aspiration in Hāṛautī Nominals":

From the percepts of experience, certain phonic data are selected (and phonetically described) as characterizing the various phonological units, of which they are called the "exponents," and to which they have been "alloted." The phonological units otherwise have values given only by their mutual relations as terms of systems and elements of structure. Certain syntagmatic relations of data are found to be constantly recurrent; in such cases, the relevant data are alloted to *prosodic* units, which are to be considered the property of the whole structure within which the relations obtain. There then remain for allottment to *phonematic* units only such data as are not involved in any such constant relations: thus the phonematic units have exponents which are appropriate to their several places in structure and are devoid of syntagmatic implication.[16]

In other words, there are phonetic features regularly associated with more than a single system, (for example, lexical), some with phonological

16 W. Sidney Allen, "Aspiration in Hāṛautī Nominals," in *Studies in Linguistic Analysis,* a special publication of the Philological Society (Oxford: Basil Blackwell, 1957), p. 69. All quotations from W. Sidney Allen appearing in this chapter are taken from this source.

functions such as syllable- or word-initial features and boundaries, and some associated with grammatical categories. When such features are common to more that a single segment or have implications within structure, Allen notes, they are assigned to prosodies; otherwise they are allotted to phonematic units: "The prosodic abstractions are made only when the relation has a probability of 1 or 0, i.e., when it is one of logical implication (or exclusion)" (p. 69).

The titles of available prosodic analyses, such as Allen's "Aspiration in the Hāṛautī Nominals" and Robins' "Nasalization in Sundanese," also in *Studies in Linguistic Analysis,* might seem to suggest that prosodies are only stated for a limited number of structures. Actually, a complete prosodic analysis of a language would assign pertinent prosodies for nominal, verbal, and syllabic structures, for syllables, words, phrases, clauses, sentences, and larger pieces. It is sometimes possible that a single prosody, such as a nasalization or aspiration, could be associated with more than one structure. For example, a prosody of nasalization might be syllabic, nominal, and lexical at the same time.

Redundancy

The second objection that prosodists raise against phonemic procedures is the notion of redundancy. The term "redundancy" suggests that the phonemically relevant features in a language are what define the basic segments and that there are other, automatically predictable features which are "extra" and, therefore, not functional in the same sense. Equally involved in the procedures, the prosodists believe, is the need to "adjust" the phonemes according to their distribution, once the basic definitions have been reached by commutation in minimal pairs. Firth rather caustically summed up the situation as follows: "Some linguists seem to think that phonemics is like pure mathematics, and that morphophonemics is applied mathematics to prove it" ("Synopsis of Linguistic Theory," VIII).

The prosodists contend that these sound differences such as allophonic variations are "redundant" only on the hypothesis that phonology need investigate one system, the lexical distinctions made by phonemes. According to Allen, the fact that phonemicists then give distributional statements, listing the allophonic variants of phonemes predictable according to their environment, is proof that the initial assumption was wrong:

The distribution statement is necessitated by the phonemic assumption of a single overall system; it is in the nature of an emendatory appendix which illustrates the inappropriateness of the assumption. The present phonological approach, on the other hand, seeks to ensure that the systems should be appropriate to the position for which they were established, and if this is not achieved, the question of distribution does not arise, since one has manufactured nothing that requires it.

[p. 83]

As for the contention that information theory supports the notion of redundancy, Allen thinks this is beside the point; de Saussure held correctly that the object of linguistic science was *la langue, envisagée en elle même et pour elle même.* Linguistics, Allen says, should be linguistics, not information theory:

if a linguistic statement gives rise to the observation of redundancy, that very fact may be interpreted as an indication of inappropriateness. The prosodic abstraction of syntagmatic relations as here presented seeks to ensure that no (absolutely) implicatory data remain to be allotted to phonematic units.

[p. 84]

The phonetic features that are usually assigned to prosodies in this system are generally dealt with in phonemic practice in terms of the allophonic variants of phonemes, suprasegmental phonemes, morphophonemics, and, at the suggestion of Zellig Harris, in terms of **phonemic long components,** which discusses the occurrence of phonemically distinctive features throughout successive single segmental phonemes.[17] Such phonemic components could be called "short" which have an extent of a single segment and "long" if their extent coincides with two or more phonemes. This technique gives a more regular picture of the distribution of phonemic components, cluster limits, and some morphophonemic changes, thus tending to replace a segmental phonemic system with a componential one.

The prosodists deny that this is the same kind of information which their system provides. Robins distinguished prosodies from suprasegmental phonemes, since the latter represent quantitative features such as pitch, stress, and length, while the prosodies are concerned with qualitative features such as nasality, palatalization, and so on.[18] Prosodies differ from Harris' phonemic long components because, according to Robins, "abstraction of a component from a phoneme in one environment implies its abstraction from that phoneme in all other environments." Prosodies are associated with specific phonological and grammatical structures, while long components are not and, Robins noted, "no one phonetic feature can be stated as the mark or exponent of the long component over its domain in the way that prosodies, statable of

17 See Zellig Harris. "Phonemic Long Components," *Language* 20 (1944), 181–205.
18 See R. H. Robins, "Aspects of Prosodic Analysis," *Proceedings of the University of Durham Philosophical Society,* I.B., No. 1 (1957), pp. 1–12.

a whole structure, are associated with phonetic features exhibited by that structure as a whole." Allen denied that long components can substitute for reducing redundancy statements:

by permitting the allotment to a particular position in structure of only those features of phonemes which are not predictable from units established at other positions in structure . . . such analyses prove not to be structurally appropriate, since units at one position are made responsible for differentiation at another position . . . classable with process-statements such as assimilation.

[p. 84]

Conclusions

The main objection of Firth and the prosodists to phonemically based linguistics seems to have stemmed more from their interest in making an over-all statement of the nature of linguistic relations than from their particular preference for one kind of phonology over another. In putting the issue squarely in the realm of meaning, Firth appears to have pointed out one of the weaknesses of the Bloomfieldian approach, which worked basically with the differential function of linguistic signals, both phonological and grammatical. If it is true that more than a dichotomy must be made (for example, referential vs. differential function), then it would seem to follow that we would have to be clear about the kinds of meanings there are in order to sort out the signals for them.

The challenge Firth posed to the validity of basing phonology on the distinction of lexicon vs. grammar gives us an opportunity to reflect on the purposes of our linguistic work, since it is ultimately in terms of the many possible purposes that one or another approach will be selected. Basing these objections on an apparent neglect of the fundamental division of system and structure, a framework of reference for language that, it would seem, any linguist since de Saussure would support wholeheartedly, makes us reconsider the bases of some of the dichotomies with which we have been working. For example, we might want to reconsider the phoneme-allophone contrast, phonology-morphophonemics, morphology-syntax, and then perhaps beyond that, the usefulness of distinguishing among morpheme, word, and phrase in certain constructions, and, ultimately, the usefulness or defensibility of distinguishing lexical and grammatical meaning in linguistics.

There is probably no basic difficulty about the amount of phonetic information that is discovered in the phonemic and prosodic phonological approaches; the phonemic transcription, of course, does not show as clearly as the prosodic notation many of the phonological and grammatical correlations. But it would be most surprising if the same factors had not been considered and evaluated in the phonetic gathering of information for either of those phonologies. For the classification and correlation of such information, it would seem the prosodic approach is superior, simply because it is an explicit part of its method. If we admit that progress is made in linguistics when we are able to identify more units at a particular level and are able to correlate them with units on other levels, then prosodic phonology represents a clear advance over what is explicitly represented in phonemic transcription. Again, an operative reason for choosing one or the other approach will be our purpose, immediate or ultimate.

Firth's objection that phonemically based studies have produced no valid grammar of a language seems to be one that need not be very troublesome, since the same complaint could be made of the prosodic-contextual approach. It would appear to represent a valid division of labor, since the theoretical linguist is primarily concerned with developing linguistic theories. While this task is impossible without actual descriptive work, the complete description of a language—or even the reasonably full description of a language—is a lifelong undertaking, one that did not recommend itself even to Firth:

It is unnecessary, indeed perhaps inadvisable, to attempt a structural and systematic account of a language as a whole. Any given or selected restricted language, i.e., the language under description, is, from the present point of view multi-structural and polysystemic.

["Synopsis of Linguistic Theory," XII]

It is also clear that the term "valid" presupposes agreement about the methods used in making the grammar.

The determined inclusion of meaning considerations in Firth's approach to language also distinguishes it notably from the Bloomfieldian approach. Both employed a situational frame of reference for describing language, but neither would claim to have come any closer to solving the age-old problems concerning meaning. But Firth proposed a linguistically oriented situational approach, based on common sense, and, therefore, subjective to a great extent, which seemed intuitively to give promise of interesting and revealing developments. Compared to later semantic work by linguists, this approach seems rather uncontrolled, since it is situationally based, and situations are literally infinite in both objective and subjective characterization, whereas linguistic categories give promise of being more restricted.

In 1957 Firth was of the opinion that we have had enough of phonemics and segmental phonology for a while and believed that the next decade would likely turn to synthesis. In 1957 Noam Chomsky's *Syntactic Structures* was published, inaugurating a vigorous movement in American linguistics, based on objections to the Bloomfieldian tradition. Chomsky, like Firth, challenged the validity of phonemics, of immediate constituent structure as the totality of linguistic relations, and the usefulness of distinguishing morphology and syntax or lexical and grammatical meaning. Unlike Firth's work, however, Chomsky's is predominantly intralinguistic (involving *la langue*) and not situational (involving *la parole*).

A marked difference between the way that Firth thought synthesis could be achieved and the goals of Chomsky and his followers lies in the point of view with which Firth began his work; he refused to attach any ontological status to the linguistic entities used to describe languages and concluded the "Synopsis of Linguistic Theory" (XII) by stating:

The synopsis presents in outline a general linguistic theory applicable to particular linguistic descriptions, *not* a theory of universals for general linguistic description. . . . The business of linguistics is to describe languages, and the main features of the theory . . . should produce the main structural framework for the bridges between different languages and cultures.

Chomsky, on the other hand, with an increasing number of American linguists, claims that there are intuitively given linguistic universals that can be more carefully defined through formal linguistic investigation, and that these will provide the bridges between languages and cultures. The nature of the bridges in these two approaches is evidently quite different.

Review Questions

1. Explain Malinowski's treatment of meaning and the reason for it.
2. Explain Malinowski's term "phatic communion"; give some examples in English and other languages you know.
3. Explain Malinowski's position on translation.
4. Explain Firth's rejection of traditional dualistic realism and Bloomfield's monistic realism.
5. Compare the object of study in linguistics as recommended by Firth and de Saussure.
6. Explain Firth's distinction between system and structure.
7. What did Firth mean by "context of situation"? "level of analysis"?
8. List and explain the principal components of meaning in the contextual approach.
9. How would you explain the statement, "It is part of the meaning of a Frenchman (American, Englishman) to sound like a Frenchman"?
10. Give some examples of frequent collocations in American vs. British English.

11. In what sense can nonsense verse (for example, *Jabberwocky*) illustrate meaning?
12. Show how a context-of-situation analysis could distinguish the meaning of the same utterances by an American and an Englishman.
13. Give some examples from your speech of phonematic units and prosodies.
14. Explain the purposes that would make you choose the phonemic or the prosodic solution to the Tereno problem.
15. Explain the prosodists' objections to monosystemic analysis and give your views about the legitimacy of redundancy in linguistics.

Suggested Readings

Bazell, C. E., and Catford, J. C., *In Memory of J. R. Firth,* eds. M. A. K. Halliday and R. H. Robins (London, 1966).

Firth, J. R., "An Ethnographic Theory of Language," in R. W. Firth, ed., *Man and Culture* (London, 1957).

———, *Papers in Linguistics, 1934–1951* (London, 1957).

———, "Synopsis of Linguistic Theory, 1930–1955," in *Studies in Linguistic Analysis,* a special publication of the Philological Society (Oxford, 1957).

Malinowski, B., "An Ethnographical Theory of Language and Some Practical Corollaries," in B. Malinowski, *Coral Gardens and Their Magic,* Vol. II (London, 1935).

———, "The Problem of Meaning in Primitive Languages," Supplement to C. K. Ogden and I. A. Richards, *The Meaning of Meaning* (London, 1923).

Robins, R. H., "Obituary of J. R. Firth," *Language,* 37 (1961), 191–200.

11

Louis Hjelmslev

Glossematics

HJELMSLEV AND DE SAUSSURE

Glossematics is often described as the study that is "de Saussure taken to his logical conclusions," since it takes seriously the dictum that language is a form, not a substance. More than many linguists, Louis Hjelmslev was concerned with establishing a set of formal definitions from which theorems can be derived for the purpose of describing the patterns of language, independent of a concomitant study of phonetics or semantics. While he acknowledged his debt to de Saussure, Hjelmslev pointed out that he arrived at his conception of linguistics independently. In the work of de Saussure and Sapir, however, he found confirmation and encouragement for his own points of view. The formalism of his linguistics, Hjelmslev noted, is similar to that employed by workers in other, quite diverse fields, for example, physics and logic. In "The Structural Analysis of Language" he discussed his debt to other workers: he considered de Saussure the founder of linguistic science from the synchronic point of view because of his emphasis on the structural analysis of language, which Hjelmslev saw as a scientific description. By "scientific description" Hjelmslev meant a description of language "in terms of relations between units, irrespective of any properties which may be displayed by these units but which are not relevant to the relations or deducible from the relations."[1]

[1] *Essais linguistiques par Louis Hjelmslev* (Copenhagen: Cercle Linguistique de Copenhague, 1959), p. 27. The essays in this collection are in French and English.

That is, linguistics studies form, pattern, relations, not substance, either phonetic or semantic. This formal approach, Hjelmslev pointed out, is a method common to many studies concerned with language, such as the logistic theory of language, which had its origins in mathematical considerations developed by Whitehead, Bertrand Russell, and by the logicians of the *Wiener Kreis*. A member of the latter group, Rudolf Carnap, expressed the point of view that Hjelmslev thought is required in glossematics:

scientific statements must be structural statements in this sense of the word . . . a scientific statement must always be a statement about relations without involving knowledge or a description of the relata themselves.[2]

Hjelmslev concluded that in language study this approach entails an investigation of linguistic relations independent of phonetics or semantics and that the latter studies presuppose the structural analysis of the language pattern as he conceived it:

linguistics studies the relational pattern of language without knowing what the relata are. . . . phonetics and semantics do tell us what the relata are, but only by means of describing the relations between their parts and parts of their parts.

[*Essais Linguistiques par Louis Hjelmslev*, p. 33]

Glossematics resembles the work of de Saussure, and that of the logistic study of language as well, but it is not to be identified with either of these studies. In particular, Hjelmslev found that the logistic study of language neglects the findings of linguistics and that, as a consequence, its concept of the sign is markedly inferior to that of de Saussure. In the Saussurean tradition, the two-sided nature of the linguistic sign is stressed, and both expression and content can be studied structurally. Besides this, Hjelmslev believed that the logistic study of language overlooks commutation, the fundamental relation for the understanding of language.

In his *Prolegomena to a Theory of Language* Hjelmslev claimed that he had "attempted a structural definition of language which should account for the basic structure of any language in the conventional linguistic sense."[3] He also gave structural analyses of marginal "languages,"

2 Rudolf Carnap, *Der Logische Aufbau der Welt* (Berlin, 1928); quoted by Hjelmslev in "The Structural Analysis of Language," *Essais linguistiques par Louis Hjelmslev*, p. 32.

3 Louis Hjelmslev, *Prolegomena to a Theory of Language*, trans. Francis J. Whitfield (Madison, Wisc.: The University of Wisconsin Press, 1961). All quotations from the *Prolegomena* appearing in this chapter are taken from this edition and are reprinted with the permission of the copyright owners, the Regents of the University of Wisconsin.

such as systems of traffic lights, telephone dialing, chiming clocks, the Morse code, and prisoners' rapping codes, all to illustrate the five fundamental features that, according to his definition, are involved in the basic concept of any language in the conventional sense:

1. A language consists of a content and an expression.
2. A language consists of a succession, or a text, and a system.
3. Content and expression are bound up with each other through commutation.
4. There are certain definite relations within the succession and within the system.
5. There is no one-to-one correspondence between content and expression, but the signs are decomposable into minor components. Such sign-components are, e.g., the phonemes, which I should prefer to call taxemes of expression, and which in themselves have no content, but which can build up units which are provided with a content, e.g., words.

[*Prolegomena*, p. 35]

Such quotations serve to show the strong affinity among the work of Hjelmslev, de Saussure, and Firth, although Hjelmslev did not go into phonological and semantic detail as did Firth. The expression "glossematics" has been found apt to suggest the abstract view of mathematics through the -*matics* component of the expression. Actually, the term was formed from the Greek *glōssa* ("tongue" or "language") and *mathē* ("study") and the English combining form -*matics*. In simple arithmetic the relations studied are without doubt first perceived in or between things, but they can be stated and manipulated as though there were no "things": 5 + 3 = 8, regardless of what the numerals may stand for, or even if they stand for nothing. In Hjelmslev's view, if we can isolate the *relevant* relations among linguistic units, we should have as powerful a theory of language as we have in mathematics.

"PROLEGOMENA TO A THEORY OF LANGUAGE"

Whitfield's revised English translation of the *Prolegomena* is a slim work of 127 pages, with 23 sections and 108 definitions to which one must constantly refer when reading through the book the first few times. The summary account of the work given here, therefore, should be supplemented by a thoughtful reading of the text.

The book is divided into the following sections, which will be summarized individually in the next sections of this chapter:

1. The study of language and the theory of language.
2. Linguistic theory and humanism.
3. Linguistic theory and empiricism.

"The Study of Language and the Theory of Language"

Language is connected with everything human and can, therefore, be studied as a clue to isolated or related human characteristics, but such studies are means to an end outside language itself. In order to have a truly autonomous linguistics we should study language not as a conglomerate of nonlinguistic phenomena but according to its own, "self-sufficient totality, a structure *sui generis.*" Hjelmslev stated that the *Prolegomena* is an attempt to formulate and discover the premises of such a linguistics, to establish its methods, and to indicate its paths. Thus it will be best to put aside all previous linguistic findings and viewpoints, except for those that have proved their positive usefulness. Particularly useful in this connection are the findings of de Saussure.

"Linguistic Theory and Humanism"

The object of linguistic study is language, and, like any science, linguistics must discover the constancy in the flux of data it examines. This is to be the constancy within language that "makes a language a language, whatever language it may be, and that makes a particular language identical with itself in all its various manifestations" (p. 8).

330 / LOUIS HJELMSLEV

Humanists may object *a priori* that human activities cannot be studied in the same generalized, predictive way as natural phenomena, but in Hjelmslev's view,

A priori, it would seem to be a generally valid thesis that for every process, there is a corresponding system, by which the process can be analyzed and described by means of a limited number of premises. It must be assumed that any process can be analyzed into a limited number of elements that constantly recur in various combinations.

[p. 9]

The procedure to be followed, then, is to classify these elements and calculate their combinatory possibilities, and then to examine the data to see which of the possible combinations they exemplify. The humanities in general, and history in particular, have failed to become sciences precisely because they did not use this procedure. Whatever doubts one may have about the applicability of the method to other disciplines, language seems to be peculiarly fitted for such a procedure: "It is the aim of linguistic theory to test, on what seems a particularly inviting object, the thesis that a process has an underlying system—a fluctuation, an underlying constancy" (p. 10).

"Linguistic Theory and Empiricism"

Hjelmslev distinguished glossematics from other linguistic theories on the basis of his "empirical principle":

The description shall be free of contradiction (self-consistent), exhaustive, and as simple as possible. The requirement of freedom from contradiction takes precedence over the requirement of exhaustive description. The requirement of exhaustive description takes precedence over the requirement of simplicity.

[p. 11]

Hjelmslev's use of the term "empirical" in describing this principle may be questioned, since it usually means that findings should agree with the actual or presumed experimental data. The name of the principle could be changed, of course, but the requirements are basic to glossematics.

"Linguistic Theory and Induction"

The source of difficulties in previous linguistic theories has been the mode of investigation: they have been *inductive*, proceeding from segment to class (for example, from phones to phonemes, from phonemes to phoneme classes, and so on). Such methods are shown to be inadequate from their results, as can be illustrated in traditional definitions of a case such as the genitive, which is "hypostatized as real," but obviously is something not definable, being an entirely different category, for example, in Latin and Greek: "induction leads from fluctuation, not to constancy, but to accident. It therefore finally comes into conflict with our empirical principle: it cannot ensure a self-consistent and simple description" (p. 12).

Hjelmslev suggested that we start with the data, which impose the opposite direction on the investigator. This is because the data that the linguist is given is a text, whole and entire. The text can be considered as a class to be divided into components, and the components then as classes to be further subdivided in the same manner until the analysis is exhausted. This procedure "may therefore be defined briefly as a progression from class to component, not from component to class. It is a synthetic, not an analytic, movement, a generalizing, not a specifying, method" (p. 12). This method may be termed **deduction,** even though the use of the term disturbs epistemologists.

"Linguistic Theory and Reality"

De Saussure had remarked in passing that "the point of view creates the object." Hjelmslev inquired whether the object determines and affects the theory or whether the theory determines and affects its object. He decided that the term "theory" can be used in more than one way: if it is taken to mean "a set of hypotheses," then the influence between theory and object is in one direction—the object determines the theory, and not vice versa:

A theory in our sense is independent in itself of any experience. In itself, it says nothing at all about the possibility of its application and relation to empirical data. It includes no existence postulate. It constitutes what has been called a purely deductive system, in the sense that it may be used alone to compute the possibilities that follow from its premises.

A theory introduces certain premises concerning which the theoretician knows from previous experience that they fulfill the conditions for application to certain empirical data. These premises are of the greatest possible generality and may therefore be able to satisfy the conditions for application to a large number of empirical data.

The first of these factors we shall call the *arbitrariness* of a theory; the second we shall call its *appropriateness* . . . it follows from what has been said that empirical data can never strengthen or weaken the theory itself, but only its applicability.

[p. 14]

The most important feature of such **deductive calculi** is that they permit us to deduce theorems that are all in the form of logical implications (for example, in the Stoic formula, "If 1, then 2; but 1, therefore 2"). All such formulas tell us is that, given the fulfillment of the conditions posited, (1), the truth of a given proposition, (2), follows.

As the theory has been described so far, Hjelmslev pointed out, there are no axioms or postulates, since those required are not peculiar to linguistics but are the sort necessary to any science. Such postulates or axioms would be, for example, "there is such a thing as language," or, "we are capable of recognizing the presence or absence of language."

On the basis of such considerations Hjelmslev concluded that:

if linguistic theory, taken in this sense, is set in relation to the concept of reality, the answer to our question, whether the object determines and affects the theory or *vice versa*, is "both . . . and": by virtue of its arbitrary nature, the theory is *arealistic;* by virtue of its appropriateness, it is *realistic. . . .*

[p. 15]

"The Aim of Linguistic Theory"

As Hjelmslev understood it, the aim of linguistic theory is to provide

a procedural method by means of which objects of a premised nature can be described self-consistently and exhaustively. Such a self-consistent and exhaustive description leads to what is usually called a knowledge or comprehension of the object in question.

[p. 15]

The theory has been framed in such a way that it is supposed to account for *all possible* texts, as well as for any data that have the same structure. But linguists, of course, could not possibly examine all texts, so the theoretician must "take the precaution to foresee all conceivable possibilities—even such as he has not experienced or seen realized" (p. 17).

Did Hjelmslev think his theory the only possible one for linguistics? It is arbitrary, and, therefore, calculative; appropriate, and, therefore, empirical. It predefines the objects to which it can be applied, and it can neither be verified nor refuted by empirical data. It can be checked only for internal consistency and exhaustiveness. Alternative solutions are possible according to the theory, since alternative procedures are allowable in it, so that, according to the empirical principle, "simplicity" would be the criterion for the preferable solution. Alternative theories are conceivable, therefore, and they are to be judged according to their degree of approximation to the requirements of the empirical principle.

Of these alternative theories, "one must necessarily be the definitive one, and any concretely developed linguistic theory hopes to be precisely that definitive one" (p. 19).

"Perspectives of Linguistic Theory"

Just as de Saussure called for a "conventional simplification of the data," Hjelmslev required that linguistic investigation begin with a "circumscription of the scope" of linguistic study. To some it may appear that this procedure, which will limit study to linguistic relations, would be to ignore other linguistically relevant facts. In Hjelmslev's view one should first attain the exactness his theory aims at and then enlarge the perspectives of linguistics after this exhaustive analysis. In this approach he relied on the method of Descartes' four rules:

> The first rule was to accept nothing as true that I did not know to be evidently so, that is, to avoid carefully precipitancy and prejudice, and to apply my judgments to nothing but what showed itself so clearly and distinctly to my mind that I should never have occasion to doubt it.
>
> The second was to divide each difficulty I should examine into as many parts as possible, and as would be required the better to solve it.
>
> The third was to conduct my thoughts in an orderly fashion, starting with what was simplest and easiest to know, and rising little by little to the knowledge of the most complex, even supposing an order where there is no natural precedence among the objects of knowledge.
>
> The last rule was to make so complete an enumeration of the links in an argument, and to pass them all so thoroughly under review, that I could be sure I had missed nothing.[4]

"The System of Definitions"

In Hjelmslev's approach to linguistics definitions play a central role, as the methods sketched above suggest. Each definition is to be clearly connected with the others that premise it. Some definitions are formulated as "*If* such and such is the case. . ." in order to stress the fact that they are not intended to be *real,* but, rather, formal or structural definitions, without the existence postulates of other linguistic systems. Operational definitions will also be admitted at various stages of the analysis, but these are to be replaced by formal definitions as soon as possible, so that axioms and postulates in linguistic theory can be held at a minimum.

---

4 Réné Descartes, *Discourse on Method* (Baltimore, Md.: Penguin Books, Inc., 1960), p. 50.

"Principle of the Analysis"

The principle of the analysis is not to vary from one text to the next, and Hjelmslev recalled de Saussure's saying that "language is a form, not a substance" in order to stress the invariable nature of the procedure. This is a movement from class to component until further analysis is no longer possible and is based on this particular conception of what linguistic "form" is. While the principle sounds simple enough when expressed in this way, it is not always easy to know where to start. "Naïve realism" would assume that we simply take up the "object" and start cutting, but there is obviously more than one way to segment a text. Therefore, much more important than the starting point is the preparation of the analysis so that it "conforms to the dependences between the parts."

This is absolutely central to Hjelmslev's position, since he held that "both the object under analysis and its parts have existence only by virtue of these dependences." For science, at least, there are no "objects" to cut, only intersections of relations. The so-called "objects" of naïve realism *are* the sum total of these relations or dependences: "the dependences which naïve realism regards as secondary, presupposing the objects, become from this point of view primary, presupposed by their intersections" (p. 23).

This method of defining through relations involves a problem of circularity, as when I define *A* in terms of *B,* and *B* in terms of *A* in a relation of **interdependence,** so that the various kinds of dependences and the planes on which they hold must be carefully studied:

mutual dependences, in which the one term presupposes the other, and *vice versa,* we call conventionally *interdependences.* The unilateral dependences, in which one term presupposes the other, but not *vice versa,* we call *determinations.* And the freer dependences, in which two terms are compatible, but neither presupposes the other, we call *constellations.*

To these we add the special designations for all three such dependences as they enter into a process or into a system. Interdependence between terms in a process we call *solidarity,* interdependence between terms in a system we call *complementarity.* Determination between terms in a process we call *selection,* and a determination between terms in a system, *specification.* Constellations within a process we call *combinations,* and constellations within a system, *autonomies.*

[pp. 24–25]

The application of these terms can be made easier [pp. 24–25] if we recall that Hjelmslev used the term "system" exactly as Firth did, to refer to the paradigmatic relations, and his term "process" corresponds to Firth's "structure," which de Saussure named "syntagmatic relations."

"Form of the Analysis"

The form of the analysis consists in:

actually registering certain dependences between certain terminals . . . the parts of the text, which have existence precisely by virtue of these dependences and only by virtue of them. . . . *Analysis* we can then formally define as description of an object by the uniform dependences of other objects on it and on each other.

[pp. 28–29]

The object that is subjected to analysis is called a **class** and the other objects that are registered by the analysis as uniformly dependent on the class and on each other are called **components.**

In this first small sample of the definition system of linguistic theory, the definition of component presupposes the definition of class, and the definition of class the definition of analysis. The definition of analysis presupposes only such terms or concepts as are not defined in the specific definition system of linguistic theory, but which we posit as indefinables: *description, object, dependence, uniformity.*

[p. 29]

Hierarchies are classes of classes, and there are two main sorts: **processes** and **systems.** The analyses of these two hierarchies, and the results of the analyses, require distinct terminologies. The analysis of a process is termed a **partition.** The analysis of a system is called an **articulation.** The classes within a process are referred to as **chains,** but the classes in a system are **paradigms.** The components of chains are called **parts,** and the components of systems are named **members.** These distinctions are the result of individual analyses, but when the analysis is continued, we must discuss the **derivates** of a class in a hierarchy. These derivates are assigned a **grade,** 0, 1, 2, 3, and so on, depending on the number of classes through which they are dependent on their lowest common class. For example, parts of syllables can be considered first-degree derivates of syllables but second-degree derivates of syllable groups. Thus, "*first degree derivate* and *component* are consequently equivalent terms" (p. 33).

"Functions"

A precise terminology will be required to distinguish and state the kinds of dependences that hold among linguistic items, and Hjelmslev proposed such a terminology in the section called "Functions." A **function,** then, is a dependence that fulfills the conditions for an analysis, so that there is a function between a class and its components, such as a chain and its parts or a paradigm and its members, and between components (parts or members) mutually. The terminals of a function are called **functives,** and a functive that is not itself a function will be called an **entity.** An example of an entity would be groups of syllables, syllables themselves, and parts of syllables.

The sense in which the term "function" is used lies "midway between the logico-mathematical and the etymological." The advantage of applying this definition is that we will then be able to say that an entity has certain functions in a text, and conceive of this both in the logico-mathematical sense, that the entity has dependences with others and that such entities premise each other. In the etymological sense we can say that the entity functions in a certain way, plays a definite role, or assumes a definition position in the chain. While the etymological definition can be considered the "real" one, this is not made explicit and is not introduced into the definition system because it would be based on more premises than the formal definition, and is reducible to it.

One of the entities in relations is a **constant,** a functive whose presence is a necessary condition for another; a **variable** is a functive whose presence is not a necessary condition for the presence of another. Presupposed by such definitions are indefinables such as **presence, necessity,** and **condition,** as well as the definitions of **function** and **functive.**

Through these definitions it is possible to define **interdependence** as a function between two constants, **determination** as a function between a constant and a variable, and **constellation** as a function between two variables. As can be seen, these terms, applied to Bloomfield's distinctions of endo- and exocentric constructions, would give a slightly different picture of the possibilities.

Since it is useful to have a common name for functions in which two or more constants may appear, interdependence and determination, both can be called **cohesions.** Similarly, a common name is useful for functions with functives of a single kind: these can be called **reciprocities,** and examples would be interdependence, which involves at least two constants, and constellation, which requires two variables. These can be called reciprocities also because, unlike the function of determination, they have no fixed "orientation." The two functives of a function of determination, on the other hand, can be named with recognition of the "orientation" involved. The constant in a determination can be called the **determined** (or, in relations of selection and specification, the **selected** or **specified**) functive, and the variable can be called the **determining** (selecting, specifying) functive.

Hjelmslev distinguished between relations that are characteristic of process (structure) and those associated with system (the paradigmatic relations). The parts of the process have a both-and relation which

Hjelmslev called **conjunction** (and de Saussure termed a relation *in praesentia*). The members of the system have a relation of either-or, which Hjelmslev called **disjunction** (and de Saussure termed a relation *in absentia*). As was seen in examining Firth's work, the entities discussed in the relations of process and system can be considered the same from one point of view, yet different from another. Since they are defined by two quite different sorts of relations, the parts of the process and the members of the system are not the same. But if we define linguistic elements as those that contract both the function of conjunction (syntagmatic relations, a place in the chain) and alternation, or disjunction (paradigmatic relations), then we can say that they are the "same."

Since his goal in linguistics requires the use of a precise terminology, Hjelmslev considered that the terms just proposed should be avoided, since they already have precise definitions elsewhere. Therefore, he proposed the term **correlation** for the paradigmatic either-or relation and **relation** for the syntagmatic both-and relation. The functives that contract such relations are then called **correlates** and **relates,** respectively. Thus, "on this basis, we can define a *system* as a correlational hierarchy, and a *process* as a relational hierarchy" (pp. 38–39).

According to this view, then, language is the intersection of a system and a process: which is logically prior to the other? At first sight it would appear that they are dependences of relation or correlation, but a closer look will show that the relation here must be one of determination. That is, the system is logically prior to the process, and, therefore, it is possible to conceive of a system that is not realized in a process, but not of a process that does not have an underlying system. For example, we could conceive of a set of rules (system) for a game that would never be played (process): "it is thus impossible to have a text without a language lying behind it. On the other hand, one can have a language without a text constructed in that language. . . . The textual process is *virtual*" (p. 40).

"Signs and *Figurae*"

While he did not deny that language is a sign system, Hjelmslev found this expression inaccurate, since his deductive analysis shows that we ultimately arrive at elements that constitute, but are not, signs. These are called *figurae* and can be illustrated as phonemes or syllables or syllable parts. In the process of analysis a succession of segmentations is made; therefore, a "rule of transference" must be introduced to prevent the division of entities too early in the analysis, otherwise we would be comparing entities that do not have the same relations. For example, *i* in Latin ("go!") is a phoneme, word, syllable, clause, or sentence, depending on the point in the analysis.

This idea suggests the need not only to analyze expression and content separately but also to distinguish lexical from contextual meanings: a single expression can be considered insofar as it manifests one sign or more (for example, Latin dative plural ending *-ibus*). All meanings that we discover are contextual meanings proper to each segmentation, so that the distinction of lexical and other meanings seems to be artificial. Thus when we consider language in and for itself, we must conclude that (1) language is first and foremost a sign system, but (2) not a pure sign system, since (3) it consists ultimately of a system of nonsigns, the *figurae* which are used to construct signs. This very fact indicates that "we have found the essential basic feature in the structure of any language," since it is manageable, consisting of a limited number of *figurae,* yet infinite in capacity, since new signs can always be constructed from the *figurae.*

"Expression and Content"

Is the linguistic sign necessarily one that "has a meaning" in the sense that a linguistic sign must be a sign *for* something? Or does it result from a connection of expression and content? The latter is Hjelmslev's formulation of what he considered already established: a **sign function** is one "posited between two entities, an *expression* and a *content*," in which the content is not to be confused with the often artificial meanings assigned to lexical items independent of texts.

We have here introduced *expression* and *content* as designations of two functives that contract the function in question, the sign function. This is purely an operative definition and a formal one, in the sense that, in this context, no other meaning shall be attached to the terms. . . . lack of content must not be confused with lack of meaning: an expression may very well have a content which from some point of view (for example that of normative logic or physicalism) may be characterized as meaningless, but it is a content.

[pp. 48–49]

De Saussure had already shown that we cannot consider expression or content alone and arrive at a worthwhile study of language, since neither precedes the other in either temporal or hierarchical order. But it seems worth experimenting with the idea that there is a common factor to be abstracted or subtracted from different languages, much in the way that a logician would distinguish between a proposition and a sentence. This common factor can be called a **purport,** and its nearest analogue in the studies we have seen could be the signification, which was distinguished from de Saussure's value and content. Hjelmslev illustrated the notion with these examples:

jeg véd det ikke	(Danish)
I do not know	(English)
je ne sais pas	(French)
en tiedä	(Finnish)
naluvara	(Eskimo)

[p. 50]

These can be said to share a common purport, "the thought itself," although differently structured or formed in each of the languages, depending on the functions it has to the sentences quoted.

These sentences, despite their differences, have a factor in common, the purport, the thought itself:

This purport, so considered, exists provisionally as an amorphous mass, an unanalyzed entity, which is defined only by its external functions, namely its functions to each of the sentences we have quoted. . . . Just as the same sand can be put into different molds and the same cloud could take on ever new shapes, so also the same purport is formed or structured differently in different languages. What determines its form is solely the functions of the language, the sign function and the functions deducible therefrom. Purport remains, each time, substance for a new form, and has no possible existence except through being substance for one form or another.

We thus recognize in the linguistic *content*, in its process, a specific *form*, the *content-form*, which is independent of, and stands in arbitrary relation to, the *purport*, and forms it into a *content-substance*.

[pp. 50–52]

While these remarks are concerned with the syntagmatic relations of language, it is evident that the same kinds of factors would apply to the paradigmatic as well. These, too, show an amorphous continuum, which is differently analyzed into a content substance by each language. Color terms are a good example of this, as well as morphological paradigms for such factors as number, person, or case.

We may conclude from this fact that in one of the two entities which are functives of the sign-function, namely the content, the sign-function institutes a form, the *content-form*, which from the point of view of the purport is arbitrary and which can be explained only by the sign function and is obviously solidary with it. In this sense, de Saussure is clearly correct in distinguishing between form and substance.

[p. 54]

It is also possible to discuss a purport, or "amorphous mass" that will be structured variously according to the language, on the expression plane of language as well. The range of articulations illustrated by a general phonetic chart can be considered such a continuum, which is formed according to the peculiarities of each language. Various points on the velar, palatal, or alveolar areas are selected for exploitation, for example. We can, therefore, discuss such an **expression purport.** Because of the cohesion of system and process, one and the same expression purport may be formed differently in different languages. Part of what is meant by "speaking with a foreign accent" is the imposition of the native expression form on the foreign expression purport.

What this investigation shows is that both the functives of the expression and content planes exist solely by virtue of their role in the sign function, and the content substance and expression substance exist solely by virtue of the expression form and content form, appearing

by the form's being projected onto the purport, just as an open net casts its shadow on an undivided surface. . . . A sign is then—paradoxical as it may seem—a sign for content-substance and a sign for expression-substance. It is in this sense that a sign can be said to stand for something.

[pp. 57–58]

In holding this opinion Hjelmslev was in basic agreement with de Saussure, although they disagreed about the possibilities of studying content and expression separately (but see Section 14 of the *Prolegomena*).

Invariants and Variants

According to the principle of **simplicity,** the analysis is to result in the smallest number of elements. This must be supplemented by a principle of **economy** and a principle of **reduction.** The smallest number of elements will be attained by focusing on some common factor and disregarding as many differences as possible. Each example of an element class discovered by such a procedure is called an **invariant,** and the members of the class are called **variants.** The phoneme, as discussed by other linguists, is an example of the attempt to establish the highest-degree invariant on the expression plane, but Hjelmslev found the criteria they employ rather confused. They generally give a "real" definition, which contrasts with Hjelmslev's formal, implicit definition of the phoneme. The chief difficulties with "real" definitions is that they generally rely on phonetics and are of little use in solving doubtful cases. Hjelmslev found this to be particularly true of Daniel Jones and the English School (not Firth), but it is true of the Prague School as well, although the Prague School recognized the distinctive function as a central criterion. Hjelmslev concluded that "we must consider the distinctive factor as the relevant one in registering invariants and for distinguishing between invariants and variants." This is how he formulated the requirements that there be a difference in form, correlated with a difference in meaning, to establish a phonemic difference:

There is a difference between invariants in the expression plane when there is a correlation (e.g., the correlation between the *e* and *a* of *pet — pat*) to which there is a corresponding correlation in the content plane (the correlation between the content entities 'pet' and 'pat') so that we can register a *relation* between the expression-correlation and the content-correlation. This relation is an immediate consequence of the sign-function, the solidarity between the form of the expression and the form of the content.

[p. 65]

We can expect to find symmetry between the expression and content planes, and we find *figurae* on the expression plane. It will be worth investigating to see if there are *figurae* on the content plane as well. In order to assure the consistency of the reduction involved, a special **principle of generalization** is formulated: "*If one object admits of a solution univocally, and another object admits of the same solution equivocally, then the solution is generalized to be valid for the equivocal object*" (p. 69).

The rule that applies to the reductions discussed here can be accordingly formulated as follows: "*Entities which, on application of the principle of generalization, may be univocally registered as complex units including only elements registered in the same operation, must not be registered as elements* (p. 70).

These rules, because of the symmetry which exists between expression and content planes, can be applied on both:

If, for example, a mechanical inventorying at a given stage of the procedure leads to a registration of the entities of content 'ram,' 'ewe,' 'man,' 'woman,' 'boy,' 'girl,' 'stallion,' 'mare,' 'sheep,' 'human being,' 'child,' 'horse,' 'he' and 'she'— then 'ram,' 'ewe,' 'man,' 'woman,' 'boy,' 'girl,' 'stallion' and 'mare' must be eliminated from the inventory of elements if they can be explained univocally as relational units that include only 'he' or 'she' on the one hand, and 'sheep,' 'human being,' 'child,' 'horse' on the other.

[p. 70]

Just as exchanges of phonemes on the expression level can entail exchanges between different contents,

so exchanges between the content-entities 'ram,' 'he,' and 'sheep' can entail exchanges between three different expressions. 'Ram' = 'he-sheep' will be different from 'ewe' = 'she-sheep.' . . . The exchange of one and only one element for another is in both cases sufficient to entail an exchange in the other plane of language.

[p. 70]

The parallel that Hjelmslev discussed between *figurae* on the expression plane and on the content plane is not easy to see. On the expression plane the *figurae* are nonsign constituents of signs, entities of expression substance. But the *figurae* on the content plane are not devoid of content, even though they can be considered as constituents of content elements. One of the parallels that Hjelmslev saw between the *figurae* on the two planes is that the *figurae* belong to restricted inventories, while the elements they constitute belong to unrestricted inventories. For example, there is a restricted inventory of phonemes in a language, but an unrestricted inventory of words that the phonemes constitute; there is a restricted inventory to which the pronouns *he* and *she* pertain, but an unrestricted inventory to which the nouns, part of whose content they constitute, belong.

The effort to reduce meaningful expressions to some kind of constituents of more restricted inventories is not new. It is similar to the aim of Aristotle in setting up the categories, it underlies the classificatory principles of Roget's *Thesaurus*, and it forms a considerable part of our lexicographic tradition. Further insights are developed by Hjelmslev in his "Pour une sémantique structurale."[5] An interesting contrast to the work of Hjelmslev is found in Holger Steen Sørensen.[6] His method is similar to that of Hjelmslev, since the procedure for discovering content *figurae* appears to be that of assigning a definition, which for Hjelmslev is "a partition of a sign-content or of a sign-expression." Sørensen points out that his method is the same but his purpose is different. He finds the notion of "content *figurae*" unintelligible, and seeks instead to establish the "semantically primitive" signs. His method is to first define words, in much the same way as Hjelmslev, through other words: these words are then to be themselves defined, but defining terms cannot be used except in a single definition. When that group of defining words has been reached which cannot be defined through words (since all the words have been previously employed to define), the "semantic primitives" are given. This aspect of his work is worth comparing as well with the semantic theory of Katz and Fodor.[7]

The need of studying the expression and content planes separately and in terms of their relations is brought out in Hjelmslev's notion of **mutation:** if we are discussing items in paradigmatic relations, mutation is called **commutation;** if the mutation holds between members in a

5 *Essais linguistiques par Louis Hjelmslev*, pp. 96–112.

6 See Holger Steen Sørensen, *Word-Classes in Modern English with Special Reference to Proper Names, with an Introductory Theory of Grammar, Meaning, and Reference* (Copenhagen, 1958).

7 Jerry A. Fodor and Jerrold J. Katz, "The Structure of a Semantic Theory," *Language*, 39 (1964).

chain, either on the expression or content planes, mutation is called **permutation**. As a result of these distinctions, he would define **words** as "the minimal signs whose expressions, and likewise whose contents, are permutable."

Both commutation and permutation differ from *substitution,* which is

the absence of mutation between the members of a paradigm; substitution in our sense is therefore the opposite of commutation. It follows from the definitions that certain entities have neither mutual commutation nor mutual substitution, namely such entities as do not enter into one and the same paradigm. . . . *Invariants,* then, are correlates with mutual commutation, and *variants* are correlates with mutual substitution.

[p. 74]

Hjelmslev considered the relation of commutation to be central to linguistic study and attributed many of our difficulties to overlooking its importance. For instance, the relation shows that content elements such as *tree* and *wood* (material) are variants in Danish, but invariants in French and German. Because they neglected commutation, older grammarians "blindly transferred the Latin categories and members of categories into modern European languages." The reason is that neither content nor expression can be studied profitably in isolation:

both the study of content and the study of expression are a study of the relation between content and expression; these two disciplines presuppose each other, are interdependent, and therefore cannot be isolated from each other without serious harm.

[p. 75]

"Linguistic Schema and Linguistic Usage"

On what basis are languages best compared to bring out their similarities and differences? It has been suggested that what all languages have in common is at least their meaning. Hjelmslev thought it an illusion to believe that the purport that is formed could belong to what is common to all languages. What languages have in common, he pointed out, is their structural principle, and the basis for their differences is the manner in which this principle is carried out—"In itself, the purport is unformed, not in itself subjected to any formation, but simply susceptible of formation, and of any formation whatsoever." For this reason Hjelmslev believed that grammars based on speculative ontological systems and on the grammar of some other language are "necessarily foredoomed to miscarry" (p. 76).

It is not superfluous, in the face of certain offshoots of medieval philosophy that have appeared even in recent times, to point out the fact that generally valid phonetic types or an eternal scheme of ideas cannot be erected empirically with any validity for language. Differences between languages do not rest on different realizations of a type of substance, but on different realizations of a principle of formation, or, in other words, on a different form in the face of an identical but amorphous purport.

[p. 77]

For such reasons as these the linguistic and nonlinguistic study of purport must be undertaken separately. The sciences that should study purport "in respect of both linguistic expression and linguistic content, may in all essentials be thought of as belonging to the sphere of *physics* and partly to that of (social) *anthropology*" (pp. 77–78), since the substances of both planes should be viewed partially as physical entities and partially as conceptions of these entities. All of the sciences are required for an exhaustive description of the linguistic content purport, since, from the linguist's point of view, they are all dealing with a linguistic content. As a result, Hjelmslev saw all science as centering around linguistics; "scientific entities" can be reduced to languages and nonlanguages, and the function between them should be studied. Here the position is provisional, and the actual work will have to be undertaken later.

The task of linguistics is, then, to construct a science of expression and a science of content, and the result will be a linguistics that is quite distinct from conventional linguistics, since its "science of expression is not a phonetics, and whose science of the content is not a semantics." Glossematics is an algebra of language, operating with entities that have no natural designation, being of such an abstract relational nature, but they would be given fitting designations when "confronted with the substance." Such an entity would include the **glosseme,** which designates "the minimal forms which the theory leads us to establish as the bases of explanation, the irreducible invariants" (p. 80).

Other sciences can employ the same deductive methods as have been described for glossematics and, thereby, discover nonlinguistic hierarchies that can be correlated with the linguistic categories of glossematics. The linguistic hierarchy is called the linguistic **schema,** and the nonlinguistic hierarchies, when they are ordered to the linguistic, are called the linguistic **usage.** The linguistic usage is said to **manifest** the linguistic schema, and the relation between them is one of **manifestation.**

"Variants in the Linguistic Schema"

Variants in the linguistic schema can be considered free or bound. Those that are bound have also been called "combinatory" variants, although

Hjelmslev did not adopt this term. Bound variants are found in the chain, and they can be called **varieties,** while the free variants are discovered paradigmatically, and they are to be called **variations.** Following the terminology proper to the system and the process, the variations are combined variants, while the varieties are solidary variants.

The same sort of analysis can be applied to the content plane as well:

All so-called contextual meanings manifest varieties, and special meanings beyond these manifest variations . . . . articulation into variations presupposes articulation into varieties, since an invariant must first be articulated into varieties and after that the varieties into variations . . . . a variety that cannot thus be further articulated into varieties we shall call a *localized* variety . . . . a variation that thus cannot be further articulated into variations we shall call an *individual.*

[pp. 82–83]

"Function and Sum"

Linguistic entities are viewed in glossematics as the intersection of relations: a class that has function to one or more classes within the same rank is called a **sum.** A syntagmatic sum is called a **unit,** and a paradigmatic sum is called a **category.**

Thus a *unit* is a chain that has relation to one or more other chains within the same rank, and a *category* is a paradigm that has correlation to one or more other paradigms within the same rank. . . . It follows from the definitions that functions are always present either between sums or between functions; in other words, every entity is a sum . . . of variants. In the theory, this means that an entity is nothing else than two or more entities with mutual function, a result that further underlines the fact that only functions have scientific existence.

[p. 85]

Hjelmslev's procedure was to look first for dependences in language. This method requires two terms, and as an illustration of how the analysis would proceed, he suggested that we first choose an appropriate basis, for example, for the dependence of selection. A chain is then divided into first-degree selection units, and the result of this is a functional category, that is, the category of the functives that are registered in a single analysis, with a given function taken as the basis of analysis. *A priori,* what we will be able to find in such a dependence will be the units that select others, those that both select and are selected by others, and those that neither select nor are selected. Regardless of the basis of analysis, if we are dealing with a dependence involving only two terms (for example, A and B), there will always be only the following possibilities: *A, B, A + B,* or neither *A* nor *B.* Each possibility is called a **functival category** and is to be divided into members by the commutation test, which will reveal which of the possibilities that were foreseen have been actually realized and which have remained virtual.

"Syncretism"

Syncretism is generally a fusion of two or more forms (for example, different cases) that were originally different. Such phenomena are not restricted to the grammatical level but occur on the phonological as well, in which case the fusion is referred to as **neutralization.** An example of morphological syncretism in Latin would be a form like *templum,* which can serve as the nominative or the accusative. On the phonological level Hjelmslev cited a feature of Danish pronunciation, which allows a word that has a *p* or a *b* in syllable-final position to be pronounced either as a *p* or a *b,* indifferently. His definition of "syncretism" is in terms of **suspension,** since "the commutation between two invariants may be suspended under given conditions" (p. 88). When it is the case that a particular functive may be present or absent under certain conditions, the functive is said to **apply** when the conditions for its presence are realized, and when they do not, he speaks of the **suspension** or **absence** of the functive: "a suspended mutation between two functives we call an *overlapping,* and the category that is established by an overlapping we call (on both planes of language) a *syncretism*" (p. 88). The same situation can be described in terms of variants and invariants. When two entities are registered as invariants through the commutation test, yet under certain conditions overlap, then the two entities under those conditions will be variants, and only their syncretism is an invariant. For example, commutation shows that Latin nominative and accusative are, in the first declension, invariants. But when nominative-accusative contract a relation with neuter (for example, in *templum*), the commutation is suspended, and the entity that is the necessary condition for the nominative-accusative overlapping is that variety of neuter which is solidary with nominative-accusative. "Such a solidarity between a variant on the one hand and an overlapping on the other, we call a *dominance.*" **Obligatory** and **optional** dominance can therefore be distinguished, since the obligatory type is found when the dominant, with respect to the syncretism, is a **variety,** and the optional when the dominant is an **invariant.**

Syncretisms are of two kinds, **coalescence** (illustrated in the examples above, where, "from the point of view of the substance-hierarchy, the manifestation of the syncretism is identical with the manifestation of all or none of the functives" involved [p. 90]) and **implications,** where the manifestation is identical with one or more of the functives involved, but not with all. For example,

> if in a language, voiced and voiceless consonants are commutable, but their commutation is suspended before another consonant, so that a voiceless consonant is pronounced voiced before a voiced consonant, there is an implication.

[p. 90]

This is an if-then function, also employed in logistics. Some syncretisms are **resoluble** while others are **irresoluble**. "To *resolve* a syncretism means to introduce the syncretism-variety which does not contract the overlapping that establishes the syncretism" (p. 91). On the basis of the morphological and syntactic differences between Latin *domus-domum,* for example, we can speak of *templum* as both a nominative (like *domus*) and as an accusative (like *domum*), whereas the syncretism between the *p* or *b* final of Danish *top* cannot be so resolved.

Zero is also involved in syncretisms as well as explicit entities. In this way we can account for **latent** and **facultative** linguistic entities, for example, the latent *d* or *t* in French expressions involving *sourd* or *grand,* and the facultative *r* in some pronunciations of English words like *idea.*

> *Latency* is an overlapping with zero in which dominance is obligatory (since the dominance in respect to the syncretism is a variety) and a functive that contracts latency is called *latent. Facultativity* is an overlapping with zero in which the dominance is optional (since the dominant in respect to the syncretism is a variation) and a functive that contracts facultativity is called *facultative.*

[p. 93]

"Catalysis"

Following Carnap, a scientific statement for Hjelmslev is a statement about relations, without (necessarily) knowing what the relata are. Relations require at least two terms, yet it is conceivable that in some circumstances one term would not be expressed. In this case, the unexpressed or missing term should be supplied, and the procedure Hjelmslev proposed for this is called **catalysis.**

As an example of the need for such a procedure, he mentioned the Latin preposition *sine,* which occurs only with the ablative case. This exemplifies a unilateral dependence, determination, and on the syntagmatic level, selection is an example of determination (See Section 9 of the *Prolegomena*). That is, an ablative is required by the presence of *sine,* but ablatives can occur without *sine.* If in a given text we were to find *sine* alone, we would interpolate the missing entity, following the generalization principle. Since the interpolated item would not need to be any particular item, what is introduced by catalysis is in most instances "an irresoluble syncretism between all the entities which might be considered possible in the given 'place' in the chain" (p. 95). Hjelmslev's definition of "catalysis" is, thus, "a registration of cohesions through the replacement of one entity by another to which it has substitution" (p. 95).

"Entities of the Analysis"

The entities that Hjelmslev dealt with are not the same as those treated by other linguists or by traditional grammar. Linguistic theory as he understood it requires us to analyze a **text,** a method that leads us to recognize the form behind the "substance" which is empirically accessible, and behind the text, a system consisting of **categories,** from whose definitions we can deduce the **units** possible in the language: "The kernel of this procedure is a catalysis, through which the form is encatalyzed to the substance, and the language encatalyzed to the text" (p. 96).

This is a purely formal procedure conducted independently of the linguistic or nonlinguistic "substances" involved, so it does not result in either a phonetics or semantics, but only in a **linguistic algebra,** which provides the formal basis for deductions. Such "algebraic" entities have no natural designation, so that names are assigned them by the linguist, arbitrarily and appropriately.

In the arbitrariness of the names lies the fact that they do not at all involve the manifestation; in their appropriateness lies the fact that they are chosen so that it becomes possible to order the information concerning the manifestation in the simplest possible way.

[p. 97]

Another principle, that of **exhaustive description,** can be deduced from those employed so far:

Any analysis (or analysis-complex) in which the functives are registered with a given function as basis of analysis, shall be so made that it leads self-consistently to the registration of the highest possible number of realized functival categories within the highest possible number of functional categories.

[p. 97]

According to this principle, glossematics will investigate much more than traditional grammar by extending its analysis to more than sentences and continue its analysis longer by going below the level of the phoneme. The text to be examined is divided first on the basis of selection and reciprocity, which obtains parts of considerable extent, defined by mutual selection, solidarity, or combination. Such larger parts would be literary types, single works of authors, their chapters, paragraphs, and so on, based on premission, that is, which part presupposes the other.

Both expression and content are to be thoroughly analyzed on both planes:

the partition based on relation will reach a stage in which selection is used for the last time as the basis of analysis. The analysis at this stage will lead to an inventorying of *taxemes,* which will be virtual elements; for the expression plane the taxemes will *grosso modo* be the linguistic forms that are manifested by phonemes.

[p. 99]

This method will produce results unlike those arrived at by standard phonemic procedures.

When a taxeme inventory has been set up into systems, the logical consequence is a further partition of the individual taxemes. The endpoints of this analysis will not be the taxemes themselves but the members of the dimensions according to which they are systematized, "and if we assume that one taxeme of expression is usually manifested by one phoneme, then a glosseme of expression will usually be manifested by a part of a phoneme" (p. 100). A glosseme is such an end-point of the analysis.

After the syntagmatic deduction of the text, a paradigmatic deduction is undertaken. Here, the language is divided into categories, into which the highest-degree taxeme categories of the textual analysis are distributed, and from which the units of the language can be deduced. It will result that both sides (planes) of language have a "completely analogous categorical structure," and this appears to be a finding of great significance for our understanding of both the structural principle of a language and a semiotic.

It also appears that such a consistently carried out description of a language on the basis of the empirical principle does not contain the possibility of a syntax or of a science of parts of speech; as we have seen, the entities of syntax are for the greatest part varieties, and the "parts of speech" of ancient grammar are entities which will be rediscovered in redefined form in far different places within the hierarchy of the units.

[p. 101]

"Language and Non-Language"

One consequence of this method of analysis is that since the analysis has been conceived without reference to the substance of either plane, content or expression, it is applicable to any data that has a structure analogous to that of a natural language. By maintaining the universal nature of "system" and "process" it is also possible to include within the theory important aspects of literary science, general philosophy of science, and formal logic.

Since the theory stands or falls with the empirical principle on which it is based, it follows that substance *"cannot in itself be a definiens for a language."* That is, phonetic substance, therefore the science of phonetics, is irrelevant, and content substance, that is, whether the linguistic units that are set up do or do not have meaning, is equally irrelevant. Therefore, linguists who require that linguistics must study language as sound take a view that is "demonstrably unempirical, i.e., inappropriate because non-exhaustive." The expression substance of language is not just sound, produced by the articulatory musculature alone, but is accompanied by mimicry and gesture, which can also be substituted for it. We should, therefore, be ready to apply this procedure to any substance of expression, writing, flags, Morse code, and so on. To say that these are "derivative" from "natural" language is irrelevant, since even a derivative manifestation of a linguistic form is a manifestation. It is impossible to decide which came first on historical grounds, and such considerations are out of place in synchronic study. Language can be manifested in many substances, and the theoretical linguist's main task, according to Hjelmslev, is to "determine by definition the structural principle of language, from which can be deduced a general calculus in the form of a typology whose categories are the individual languages, or rather the individual language-types" (p. 106).

There is no problem even when these language types remain virtual or unmanifested, since manifestation is a selection-dependence in which the language is the constant and the manifestation is the variable; the constant can be called, with a reference to de Saussure, the *form:*

if the form is a language, we call it the *linguistic schema.* The variable in a manifestation (the *manifesting*) can, in agreement with de Saussure, be called the *substance;* a substance which manifests a linguistic schema we call a *linguistic usage.* From these premises, we are led to the formal definition of a *semiotic* as a *hierarchy, any of whose components admits of a further analysis into classes defined by mutual relation, so that any of these classes admits of an analysis into derivates defined by mutual mutation.*

[p. 106]

The importance of this definition is that it is not limited to natural languages, and with respect to natural languages, it is not limited to the sociological or psychological basis in de Saussure's work. It is applicable —and has been applied, especially in logistics—to sign systems other than language, for example, folk costume, art, and literature, and, especially, games, as foreseen by de Saussure in the chessman example.

From this definition arises the possibility and necessity of linking linguistics and logistics and a great number of other sciences that share this method, so that through "a mutually fructifying collaboration, it should be possible to produce a general encyclopedia of sign-structures" (p. 109).

On such a basis it should also be possible to distinguish between language and nonlanguage. A "language" may be defined as "a paradigmatic whose paradigms are manifested by all purports," and a "text," correspondingly, as "a syntagmatic whose chains, if expanded indefinitely, are manifested by all purports. By a *purport* we understand a class of variables which manifest more than one chain under more than one syntagmatic, and/or more than one paradigm under more than one paradigmatic" (p. 109).

A language, then, is a semiotic into which all other semiotics can be translated, and this is based on their ability to form any purport whatever. It is in a language, and only in a language, that we can "work over the inexpressible until it is expressed" (p. 109).

Games probably lie on the borderline between a semiotic and a nonsemiotic, and the crucial factor in distinguishing them is to fix the nature of the sign involved. Logistics approached the problem starting with the metamathematics of Hilbert,

whose idea was to consider the system of mathematical symbols as a system of expression-figurae with complete disregard for their content, and to describe its transformation rules in the same way as one can describe the rules of a game, without considering possible interpretations.

[p. 110]

This work was taken up by the Polish logicians in their "metalogic" and completed by Carnap in a sign theory, "where in principle, any semiotic is considered as a mere expression system without regard for the content" (p. 110). Linguistics took the traditional approach of defining a sign by its meaning. Hjelmslev believed that de Saussure made this precise by

introducing the concept of value, a consequence of which is the recognition of the content-form and of the bilateral nature of the sign that builds on the interplay between expression-form and content-form in the principle of commutation.

[p. 111]

This suggests another way of distinguishing language and nonlanguage, or games and semiotics that are not games. This can be done without appeal to meaning in any of the usual senses, since Hjelmslev's method posits language as a form that may or may not have an interpretation, and in this respect, chess, algebra, and languages are on the same plane. The clue will be to see if an exhaustive description requires appeal to two planes. Added to this is the requirement that the two planes be not isomorphic or **conformal.** "Two functives are said to be conformal if any particular derivate of the one functive without exception enters the same functions as a particular derivate of the other functive and *vice versa.*" This is called the **derivate test,** and for all known languages it has produced negative results. This test, linked with the commutation test, will allow us to decide between semiotics and non-semiotics. There are obviously systems that are interpretable, that is, which have content assigned to entities in the system, but which are not biplanar. These will be called **symbolic systems,** and a **symbol** is an entity that is isomorphic with its interpretation, for example, scales for the concept of justice.

"Connotative Semiotics and Metasemiotics"

The kind of language that has been described in the preceding sections is of a simple type not actually met with. For reasons of clarity and simplicity the discussion concerned a **denotative semiotic.** Approximately, this can be described as a language whose meanings are referential, not connotational, since emotional and stylistic differences of meaning are not included. More precisely, a denotative semiotic is one

none of whose planes is a semiotic. . . . any text that is not of so small extension that it fails to yield a sufficient basis for deducing a system generalizable to other texts, usually contains derivates that rest on different systems. Various parts, or parts of parts, of a text can be composed

1. in various *stylistic forms* (characterized by various restrictions: verse, prose, various blends of the two);
2. in different *styles* (creative style and the purely imitative, so-called normal style; the creative and at the same time imitative style that is called archaizing);
3. in different *value styles* (higher value-style and the lower, so-called vulgar value-style; here also a neutral value-style that is considered neither higher nor lower);
4. in different *media* (speech, writing, gesture, flag-code, etc.);
5. in different *tones* (angry, joyful, etc.);
6. in different *idioms* under which must be distinguished
    a. various *vernaculars* (the common language of a community, jargons of various cliques or professions);
    b. different *national languages;*
    c. different *regional languages* (standard, local dialect, etc.);
    d. different *physiognomies* (as concerns the expression, different "voices" or "organs").

[p. 115]

The members of this far from exhaustive list of classes are called **connotators**. The connotators form a semiotic with this interesting property: their expression plane is a denotative semiotic, with the connotators themselves as the content.

"Final Perspective"

There are two seemingly opposed results of this method of studying language as a set of dependences, or as functions between constants and variables. It would appear that the study of language has become so abstract that two of the most obvious and widely studied aspects of language, phonetics and semantics, are not considered relevant. Yet another consequence of the study is to require the investigator to look for *all* the constants and variables involved in the activity of language use. This process leads to the discovery of the complete system, and to systems of systems, some presupposed, some presupposing. Once the denotative semiotic is established, the connotative semiotic can be related to it, and then, a metasemiotic and a metasemiology must be considered. Hjelmslev found no nonsemiotics that are not components of semiotics, and no object that is not illuminated from the key position of linguistic theory. "Semiotic structure is revealed as a stand from which all scientific objects may be viewed" (p. 127).

In the final analysis the immanent method has not cut linguistics off from other studies:

Instead of hindering transcendence, immanence has given it a new and better basis; immanence and transcendence are joined in a higher unity on the basis of immanence. Linguistic theory is led by an inner necessity to recognize not merely the linguistic system, in its schema and in its usage, in its totality and in its individuality, but also man and human society behind language, and all man's sphere of knowledge through language. At that point linguistic theory has reached its prescribed goal:

humanitas et universitas.

[p. 127]

Review Questions

1. Discuss the similarity between the views of Hjelmslev and de Saussure concerning the object of linguistic science.
2. In what sense are scientific statements structural?
3. Give a structural description of a traffic light system.
4. What are the five requisites for a language, according to Hjelmslev?
5. How does Hjelmslev answer the humanists' objection that language cannot be studied like natural phenomena?

6. Explain his empirical principle.
7. What objection did he have to inductive methods?
8. Explain what he meant by the arbitrariness and appropriateness of theories.
9. How do the objects of structural study differ from those of "naïve realism"?
10. Give examples of interdependence, determination, and constellation.
11. Express these three relations in terms of functions between constants and variables.
12. Which is prior, system or process?
13. Explain *figurae* on the plane of expression.
14. Must all signs have a meaning, according to Hjelmslev? Explain.
15. Explain the notion of purport on the expression and content planes.
16. Explain the analogy between signification and purport: in what sense could signification (as attributed to de Saussure) be an "amorphous mass"?
17. Explain *figurae* on the content plane. How are they comparable to those of expression?
18. What does Sørensen mean by semantically primitive signs?
19. What is meant by the linguistic schema and the linguistic *usage?*
20. How did Hjelmslev explain *syncretism?*
21. What is meant by catalysis?
22. In what sense are phonetics and semantics irrelevant to the glossematic definition of language?
23. How did Hjelmslev define language?
24. How did he distinguish between a denotative and a connotative semiotic?
25. How does the relation of denotative and connotative semiotics point to *humanitas et universitas* as the "prescribed goal" of linguistics?

Suggested Readings

Bazell, C. E., Review of Louis Hjelmslev's *Omkring Sprogteoriens Grundlaeggelse,* in *Archivum Linguisticum,* I (1949).

Fischer-Jørgensen, E. Review of Louis Hjelmslev's *OSG,* in *Miscellanea Phonetica,* II (1954).

Garvin, P., Review of Louis Hjelmslev's *OSG,* in *Language,* 30 (1954), 1.

Haugen, E., Review of Louis Hjelmslev's *OSG,* in *International Journal of Applied Linguistics,* 20 (1954), 3.

Hjelmslev, L. *Essais linguistiques par Louis Hjelmslev* (Copenhagen, 1959).

———, *Principes de grammaire générale* (Copenhagen, 1928).

———, *Prolegomena to a Theory of Language,* trans. Francis J. Whitfield (Madison, Wisc., 1961).

———, and H. J. Uldall, *An Outline of Glossematics* (Copenhagen, 1957).

Lamb, Sidney M., "Epilegomena to a Theory of Language," in *Romance Philology,* 19 (1966).

Siertsema, B., *A Study of Glossematics: A Critical Survey of Its Fundamental Concepts* (The Hague, 1955).

12

Noam Chomsky
Transformational Grammar and Linguistic Universals

The work of Noam Chomsky and his colleagues in linguistics represents an interesting summary and commentary on the value of the work we have examined so far. It embodies a recognition of the strengths of traditional grammar and structural work, but formalizes the descriptive mechanisms of these studies and suggests means of correcting weaknesses in their presuppositions and methods. The sources of inspiration for Chomsky and his colleagues, then, are to be found in modern as well as in older studies. Among modern linguists Chomsky acknowledges that the writings of Zellig S. Harris have been influential in forming his thought, and that in less obvious ways the logical and speculative writings of Willard Quine have been significant (see the Bibliography).

Formalism is nothing new in modern linguistics, but most readers are particularly struck by this aspect of transformational work when they first become acquainted with it. While formulaic abbreviation can be an annoying and often unmotivated stylistic feature, this was far from being the origin or intent of such formalism in Chomsky's work. He has shown convincingly that by a rigorous formalization a theory can be pushed to its logical conclusions, whereas intuitive discussion may fail to reveal its limits. Formalization can also suggest remedies for inconsistencies and inadequacies that other forms of investigation cannot.

From the literature we will find that transformational grammar has undergone several stages of development. The first generally available statement of this program of linguistic investigation is to be found in Chomsky's *Syntactic Structures*.[1] In this chapter our account of transformational grammar will be drawn from two other important works, *An Integrated Theory of Linguistic Descriptions* by Katz and Postal and *Aspects of the Theory of Syntax* by Chomsky.[2] The account which follows assumes that these three works can be cited and summarized as a fair account of the work of those interested in developing a common view of transformational grammars. The form of the account is, therefore, that of summary of these three texts, with occasional comments and comparisons with previous work in linguistics.

GOALS OF LINGUISTIC THEORY

To decide upon suitable goals in linguistics we should be clear about the object we are studying, the purpose of the study, and, therefore, the best methods to be used to obtain this goal. Chomsky suggests that considering the grammar of a language as involving a theory of that language, as well as a theory of language in general, is one way to see how the goals of linguistics can be formulated clearly and what methods are required to attain these goals. Such a linguistic theory is also to be a scientific theory, according to Chomsky, and when we reflect how scientific theories are constructed, we can gain insight into the nature of linguistic theories and the entities they concern.

Take, for example, a physical theory about the behavior of bodies. Like any scientific theory, this should be based on (1) a finite number of observations, (2) an attempt to relate the observed phenomena, (3) an attempt to predict new phenomena. The prediction will be made because of the postulation of a general law, which will involve certain hypothetical constructs, for example, mass and velocity, if we were attempting to formulate a law of gravity. In grammatical work we have similar conditions: we have observed a finite number of utterances, and we can distinguish some from others as being grammatical. In order to relate the grammatical sentences to each other and to distinguish them from the ungrammatical, we postulate a general law that concerns the predictable relations among grammatical sentences. This will involve the construction of entities such as phonemes, morphemes, grammatical categories, and so on, and in terms of the general law we can then predict what combinations of such entities will be, or will represent, grammatical

[1] Noam Chomsky, *Syntactic Structures* (The Hague: Mouton & Company, 1957).
[2] J. Katz and P. Postal, *An Integrated Theory of Linguistic Descriptions* (Cambridge, Mass.: M.I.T. Press, 1964); Noam Chomsky, *Aspects of the Theory of Syntax* (Cambridge, Mass.: M.I.T. Press, 1965).

sentences. In terms of the same general law we should be able to account for the deviations that will result in ungrammatical sentences.

Chomsky shows that there are considerable problems involved in the method by which we can go about selecting the correct theory. First, he notes that the theory should meet certain conditions of **external adequacy,** which include the prediction of sentences that the native speaker of the language in question would accept. Second, there should be a **condition of generality,** since a linguistic theory, unlike a particular grammar of a language, should be so constructed as to be helpful in deciding what makes a language a language and how a particular language differs from another. A third criterion is the notion of **simplicity,** and in discussing this Chomsky says it is worth considering in what sense particular grammars, or particular forms of grammars, can be said to follow from the general linguistic theory.

One way of conceiving the relation between our general linguistic theory and a grammar constructed as a consequence of the theory is to see that we have been provided with a **discovery procedure,** so that we have a practical and mechanical way of discovering the grammar (the general laws) of a given language. A weaker connection between a general linguistic theory and particular grammars of languages Chomsky sees in the claim that the general theory provides us with a **decision procedure,** so that we could take two proposed grammars for a language and, by means of the theory decide in a practical and mechanical way which is the better grammar. An even weaker claim would be one that Chomsky thinks more realistic in view of our present state of knowledge, that our general theory is required only to provide an **evaluation procedure.** That is, it should enable us to decide that particular grammars of a language, or particular forms of grammars, are either better or less desirable ways of formulating the general laws underlying the grammatical character of a finite set of observed sentences.

The question of simplicity is relevant in making a choice between alternative theories or descriptions, and there are various ways of making such a choice. Chomsky shows that when we try to choose between grammatical theories there is no *a priori* norm we can use to decide which account is the simpler, although some obvious examples of comparative simplicity come readily to mind. For example, two proposed phonemic systems for a language may be compared in terms of simplicity if one has fewer phonemes than the other. However, positing a smaller number of phonemes may complicate the syllabic structure and the morphophonemic statement, so that "simplicity" from one point of view may result in complexity from another. When applying this criterion to choosing between linguistic theories, Chomsky points out that there is nothing obvious or given about the notion simplicity and that it is a concept we must define for linguistic theories. It is obviously to be judged in terms of the entire language and the theory concerning the nature of language, so that we might expect to be on the right track when we find that one simplification leads to further simplification. In general, simplicity may be considered a function of the generalizing power of our analysis.

The Object of Linguistic Study

Since the time of de Saussure linguists have been agreed more or less in principle that the object of linguistic study should be *la langue,* when the term is broadly interpreted to mean the set of pervasive patterns in terms of which *la parole,* actual utterances, are to be described. Chomsky has basic objections to some of the consequences of de Saussure's conception of the linguistic system, which will be examined, but he proposes another contrastive set of terms that distinguishes possible objects of linguistic study. According to Chomsky, we can study either a speaker's **competence** (his knowledge of the language) or his **performance** (his actual use of the language in concrete situations). The knowledge that the speaker possesses is not conscious but is, rather, the ability he has to produce and understand indefinitely many sentences. In fact, Chomsky points out, a speaker's expressed opinions about the presumed mechanisms by which he produces sentences can be quite mistaken, so that linguistics, taking a speaker's competence as an object of study, is interested in what the speaker really knows rather than in what he thinks he knows.

Chomsky finds one way of appreciating what kind of knowledge the speaker may be presumed to possess by considering the conditions that must hold in order for a child to learn any language. When a child has learned a language Chomsky holds that he has developed what we can describe as an internal representation of a system of rules that determines how sentences are to be produced and understood. This is a kind of theory of the child's own language, and the data from which it was constructed can be presumed to be correctly and incorrectly formed sentences. Further, it can be assumed that unless the child already had a knowledge of language in some sense, he could not have learned a *particular* language:

A theory of linguistic structure that aims for explanatory adequacy incorporates an account of linguistic universals, and it attributes tacit knowledge of these universals to the child. It proposes, then, that the child approaches the data with the presumption that they are drawn from a language of a certain antecedently well-defined type, his problem being to determine which of the (humanly) possible languages is that of the community in which he is placed. Language learning would be impossible unless this were the case.[3]

As a consequence of these assumptions, Chomsky sees it as one of the main tasks of linguistic theory to

develop an account of linguistic universals, that, on the one hand, will not be falsified by the actual diversity of languages, and, on the other, will be sufficiently rich and explicit to account for the rapidity and uniformity of language learning, and the remarkable complexity and range of the generative grammars that are the product of language learning.

[*Aspects of the Theory of Syntax*, p. 28]

Linguistic Universals

Chomsky distinguishes two types of linguistic universals, **substantive** and **formal**. A theory of substantive universals claims that items of a particular kind in any language must be instances of a determined set. For example, Jakobson's theory of distinctive features holds that there are fifteen or twenty distinctive features of a determinable acoustic or articulatory character independent of any particular language. Similar universals appear to be the traditional notions of noun, verb, and so on.

Formal universals are more abstract, for example, the claim that the grammar of any language must meet certain specified formal conditions. This would not imply that any particular rule would have to appear in all or even in any two grammars. Chomsky points out in *Aspects of the Theory of Syntax* that among substantive universals are those that concern the vocabulary required to describe a language (for example, "noun," "verb," "vowel," "sentence"), while the formal universals are concerned with types of relations, in terms of which grammatical rules are formulated (for example, endocentric, coordinate, transformation). Aristotle's categories appear to be implicitly formal universals.

FORMS OF GRAMMARS

Formalism in Linguistics

As has been noted before, all linguists are agreed in principle that the most desirable kind of linguistic description is a **formal description**, but there are disagreements concerning the methods of identifying and defining linguistic forms. The decisions made by the linguist have several

---

[3] Noam Chomsky, *Aspects of the Theory of Syntax*, p. 27. Copyright © 1965 by The Massachusetts Institute of Technology. All quotations from *Aspects of the Theory of Syntax* appearing in this chapter are reprinted with the permission of M.I.T. Press.

consequences for our conception of language as viewed by linguistics and other disciplines. One consequence is that the linguist concentrates first (though not exclusively) on the sounds and sequences of a language as well as on the patterns into which they enter. Another is that the linguist tries to find ways of classifying large numbers of such forms together in order to reduce the number of items his description must concern directly. A third consequence is that the linguist must determine the kinds of relations among forms linguistics is competent to study (for example, grammatical vs. stylistic, denotational vs. connotational, and so on). Formalism in this sense is another expression of the power of generalization contained in an analysis.

The language of descriptive linguistics with reference to a particular natural language it describes can be called a **metalanguage** (a language about language), and the vocabulary of descriptive linguistics in a formal analysis should refer to as many accurately distinguishable forms and relations among linguistic forms as possible. When descriptive theories have been formulated with sufficient exactness, it will be possible to submit them to an analysis similar to that applied to natural languages, and a formal expression of the linguistic theory can be established. Such an expression can then be compared to the form of other grammatical theories, and all of these can be tested against the known properties of natural languages. In this way it will be readily appreciated whether one form of linguistic description is inherently capable of handling the facts of natural languages in a manner that is "simple, general, and adequate" (descriptively and explanatorily).

Formalization of an Elementary Linguistic Theory

In *Syntactic Structures* Chomsky was particularly concerned to explicate the nature of syntax and to show how this level of analysis is dealt with in various approaches to language. He therefore defined "Syntax" as "the study of the principles and processes by which sentences are constructed in particular languages . . . more generally, linguists have been concerned with the problem of determining the fundamental underlying properties of successful grammars."[4] Chomsky can then view a grammar as a device of some sort for producing all of the grammatical, and none of the ungrammatical, sentences of a language. Such a grammar usually contains several linguistic "levels," for example, phonemics, morphology, and phrase structure. These too are best considered as devices made available for the construction of grammars, that is, as methods for

---

[4] Noam Chomsky, *Syntactic Structures* (The Hague: Mouton & Company, 1957), p. 11. All quotations from *Syntactic Structures* appearing in this chapter are reprinted with the permission of Mouton & Company.

representing utterances. As a consequence, "We can determine the adequacy of a linguistic theory by developing rigorously and precisely the form of grammar corresponding to the set of levels contained within this theory" (*Syntactic Structures*, p. 11). Theories will then be seen to be adequate if simple and revealing grammars can be constructed according to them.

Defining "language" as "a set (finite or infinite) of sentences, each finite in length and constructed out of a finite set of elements" (*Syntactic Structures*, p. 13), Chomsky points out that the notion "grammatical" with respect to sentences is assumed as intuitively given in *Syntactic Structures*, and suggests in passing that one test of this is acceptability to the native speaker. This point was widely misunderstood as an operational definition of "grammatical."[5] In *Aspects of the Theory of Syntax* Chomsky gives some operational criteria for acceptability and points out that both grammaticality and acceptability are matters of degree, "but the scales of grammaticalness and acceptability do not coincide" (p. 11). In *Syntactic Structures* his discussion of how to characterize grammatical sentences is reminiscent of Durkheim's position on the role of scientific definitions (see Chapter 7 of this book).

Our investigation of the former [grammatical sentences] is a preparatory study, proceeding from the assumption that before we can characterize this relation clearly, we will have to know a great deal more about the formal properties of each of these sets.

[*Syntactic Structures*, p. 55]

Assuming, then, that we know that many sentences are grammatical, although we may be in doubt about others, and that a grammar is to produce all the grammatical and none of the ungrammatical sentences, we can ask how the grammar is to perform this task. In intermediate cases the grammar itself, when "set up in the simplest way, so that it includes the clear sentences and excludes the clear nonsentences" (*Syntactic Structures*, p. 13), can decide between grammatical and ungrammatical products.

One possibility that Chomsky immediately rejects is the assumption that the grammar is merely a description of a finite number of observed sentences. The notion "grammatical sentence" must be richer than this, since, quoting von Humboldt, Chomsky notes that "language makes infinite use of finite means,"[6] and Quine's formulation has it that a

5 See A. A. Hill's article "Grammaticality," *Word*, 17 (April 1961), pp. 1–10, and Chomsky's reply, "Some Methodological Remarks on Generative Grammar," *Word*, 17 (August 1961), pp. 219–239. Both articles are reprinted in Harold B. Allen, ed., *Readings in Applied English Linguistics*, 2d. ed. (New York, 1964).

6 W. von Humboldt, *Über die Verschiedenheit des menschlichen Sprachbaus* (Darmstadt, 1949); quoted in Chomsky, *Aspects of the Theory of Syntax*, p. v.

linguistic theory gives a general explanation for what could be in a language on the basis of "what *is* plus *simplicity* of the laws whereby we describe and extrapolate what is."[7] First, any grammar must *project* a presumably finite set of grammatical utterances on the basis of the finite set observed.

Second, "grammatical" cannot, in Chomsky's view, be identified with "meaningful" or "significant" in *any* semantic sense. This statement lacks a certain amount of force, to the extent that no definition is given of "semantic," but Chomsky seems to believe that semantic theories have not been made sufficiently exact to justify proposing a notion of meaning that could give us a practical way of deciding on the grammatical status of pairs of sentences such as the following:

(1) *Colorless green ideas sleep furiously.*
(2) *Furiously sleep ideas green colorless.*[8]

[*Syntactic Structures*, p. 15]

From such considerations Chomsky notes that "we are forced to conclude that grammar is autonomous and independent of meaning" (*Syntactic Structures,* pp. 15 and 19).

Considered as a device for producing only grammatical sentences, then, a grammar should have the following properties: (1) it should be finite; (2) it should predict an infinite number of sentences; (3) it should be describable in purely formal terms without reliance on meaning. To understand the kinds of formal properties of some proposed forms of grammars Chomsky suggests three very elementary kinds of "languages" and illustrates possible "sentences" in them.

Take languages that consist only of the symbols *a* and *b*. Sentences in such languages are formed exclusively from these symbols in various arrangements. For example,

(10) (i) ab, aabb, aaabbb . . . ;

That is, all sentences consist of a certain number of *a*'s followed by a certain number of *b*'s.

(ii) aa, bb, abba, baab, aaaa, bbbb, aabbaa, abbba . . . ;

That is, all sentences can be considered "mirror images" of each other, since they consist of reversed combinations of preceding sentences or entirely of one kind of two possible symbols.

---

[7] W. Quine, *From a Logical Point of View* (Cambridge Mass., 1953), p. 54; quoted in Chomsky, *Syntactic Structures,* footnote 1, p. 14.

[8] Example numbers in parentheses are those given in the various sources and will not be found in consecutive order in this chapter. While this system may seem confusing, it will facilitate consulting the original works.

(iii)   aa, bb, abab, baba, aaaa, bbbb, aabaab, abbabb . . . ;

That is, all sentences have sequences of *a*'s and *b*'s, and successive sentences are formed out of the preceding constituents.

Take the first requirement, a grammar should be *finite*. We can illustrate a grammar, considered as a finite device, in (7).

(7)

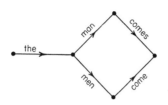

Fig. 12.1.

[*Syntactic Structures*, p. 19]

Such a diagram can be called a "state diagram."[9] It illustrates a device that can be in any one of a finite number of states, and it switches from one state to the next by producing a symbol (for example, an English word): one state is **initial**, another is **final**. The device illustrated in (7) can produce only two "sentences"—*The man comes* or *The men come*. A grammar like (7) can be called a **finite state grammar**, since it consists of a finite number of states, and the language it produces is a *finite state language*. Since this grammar cannot produce an infinite number of sentences, it obviously could not produce any of the simple languages sketched in (i), (ii), and (iii) above. The same kind of grammar *can* be made to produce an indefinite number of sentences, by adding closed loops, and it would then be able to produce sequences like *the old man comes, the old old man comes, the old men come, the old old men come,* and so on:

(8)

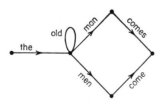

Fig. 12.2.

[*Syntactic Structures*, p. 19]

9 See Chomsky, *Syntactic Structures*, p. 19, and C. E. Shannon and W. Weaver, *The Mathematical Theory of Communication* (Urbana, Ill., 1949), pp. 15 ff.

The grammar described in (8) can now meet two of the criteria for a grammar of a natural language, since (a) it is finite and (b) it can produce an infinite number of sentences. But it is clearly incapable of producing *all* the grammatical sentences in English and incapable as well of producing the synthetic languages (i), (ii), and (iii), for the simple reason that neither these nor English are finite state languages. One of the more obvious indications of this fact is that both in the languages (ii), and (iii) and in English we have *a*'s and *b*'s that are *embedded* in other strings (for example, aa, bb, a*bb*a, b*aa*b) and that are not, therefore, *consecutive* (for example, as in (1) *the*, (2) *old*, (3) *old*, (4) *old*, (5) *men*, (6) *come*). In English for example, we find sentences whose form can be symbolized as

(11)   (i)   If S_1, then S_2.
     (ii)   Either S_3, or S_4.
     (iii)   The man who said that S_5 is arriving today.

                                            [*Syntactic Structures,* p. 22]

Here *S* stands for any declarative sentence, which could be of the form of any of the examples given in (11), and Chomsky shows that this possibility of embedding sentences within sentences demonstrates clearly that English is not a finite state language and, therefore, cannot possibly be handled by a grammar of the type indicated in (7) and (8). Such devices are known mathematically as "finite-state Markov processes," and Chomsky points out that this is the formalized explication of the kind of grammar developed by Hockett.[10]

    Chomsky finds that another weakness of the Markov-process type of grammar in dealing with such sentences lies in the familiar fact that there are links of dependence between the words *if . . . then* and *Either . . . or* in the sentences listed in (11). But the Markov process has no way of selecting, for example, *then* instead of *or* when it starts producing sentence (11i) or of preferring *or* to *then* when it is producing sentence (11ii). It will produce grammatical as well as ungrammatical sentences, and, therefore, it again is disqualified as a type of grammar intrinsically capable of describing all and only the grammatical sentences of English. From this Chomsky concludes in *Syntactic Structures* that at least one linguistic level in a grammar capable of dealing with English *cannot* have the simple structure described in the Markov type.

Formalization of Phrase-Structure Grammar

In Chapter 3 of this volume we discussed constructions and their constituents—immediate, mediate, and ultimate. It was noted that our ability to distinguish these depends upon a certain grammatical intui-

---

10 See Charles Hockett, *A Manual of Phonology* (Bloomington, Ind., 1955), p. 3.

tion concerning the relations of elements of sentences. In addition, the formal criteria given for identifying the constituents depends ultimately on our intuitive knowledge of what a grammatical sentence in English is. Chomsky formalizes the relations we are using in such phrase-structure grammars (that is, grammars concerned with the identification of the constituents of constructions and how they are related) and illustrates the process with the simple sentence *The man hit the ball.* We know that this statement is a sentence and that it consists of a subject and predicate, which happen to be represented by a nominal and a verbal phrase, each of which has more than a single constituent. By starting with the basic notion *Sentence* Chomsky represents the derivation of this sentence from its more abstract representations:

(13) (i)   *Sentence* $\longrightarrow$ NP + VP

 (ii) NP $\longrightarrow$ T + N

 (iii) VP $\longrightarrow$ *Verb* + NP

 (iv) T $\longrightarrow$ *the*

 (v) N $\longrightarrow$ *man, ball,* etc.

 (vi) *Verb* $\longrightarrow$ *hit, took,* etc.

[*Syntactic Structure,* p. 26]

Here, each rule X → Y is to be read as "rewrite X as Y," and (13) can be considered the "grammar" for sentences like *The man hit the ball.* Set (14) shows how the sentence is derived according to the rules of the grammar (13).

(14) *Sentence*

NP + VP	(i)
T + N + VP	(ii)
T + N + *Verb* + NP	(iii)
the + N + *Verb* + NP	(iv)
the + *man* + *Verb* + NP	(v)
the + *man* + *hit* + NP	(vi)
the + *man* + *hit* + T + N	(ii)
the + *man* + *hit* + *the* + N	(iv)
the + *man* + *hit* + *the* + *ball*	(v)

[*Syntactic Structures,* p. 27]

This derivation (14) can also be represented in a *diagram* (15).

(15)

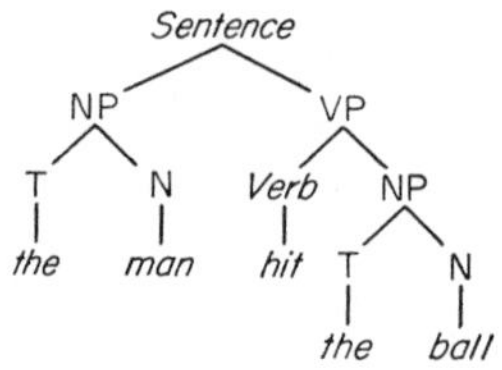

Fig. 12.3.

[*Syntactic Structures,* p. 27]

Chomsky notes that both the derivation and the diagram that represents it give us similar information, but the diagram, of itself, does not tell us the order in which the grammatical rules listed in (13) were applied. It would be possible, then, to have more than a single derivation represented by the diagram (15), and in this case, such derivations can be considered **equivalent.** The diagram, however, clearly distinguishes between the immediate constituents, since we can trace an expression like *the man* back to a single common symbol (placed over a "node") such as *NP,* but there is no single node or symbol to which a combination like *man hit* can be traced. For similar reasons Chomsky would like to be able to put some restrictions on the rewrite rules in derivations: a single symbol only should be rewritten on each line, since it is by this means that we know how to assign the nodes that will indicate the constituency relations among elements they dominate. For example, Chomsky points out that if NP + VP were to be rewritten by a single rule, it would not be clear in what sense *man hit* is not a constituent of the sentence. Second, there should be the possibility of restricting the form of a rewrite rule according to context, so that for T + N we would rewrite T as *a* in the context of a singular N, but not in the context of a plural.

We can now describe more generally the form of grammar associated with the theory of linguistic structure based upon constituent analysis. Each such grammar is defined by a finite set Σ of initial strings and a finite set F of "instruction formulas" of the form X $\longrightarrow$ Y interpreted: 'rewrite X as Y.' Though X need not be a single symbol, only a single symbol of X can be rewritten in forming Y. In the grammar (13), the only member of the set Σ of initial strings was the single symbol *Sentence,* and F consisted of the rules (i)–(vi); but we might want to extend Σ to include, for example, *Declarative Sentence, Interrogative Sentence,* as additional symbols. Given the grammar [Σ, F], we define a *derivation* as a finite sequence of strings, beginning with the initial string of Σ, and with each string in the sequence being derived from the preceding string through the application of one of the instruction formulas of F. Thus (14) is a derivation, and the five-termed sequence of strings consisting of the first five lines of (14) is also a derivation.

[*Syntactic Structures*, p. 29]

(14) is also a **terminated** derivation, although the first five lines of it are not; the last line of a terminated derivation Chomsky calls a **terminal string,** and if such strings are the terminal strings of an [Σ, F] grammar, they constitute a **terminal language.** Comparing the finite state model and the phrase-structure formalization, Chomsky points out that all finite state languages are terminal languages, but not all terminal languages are finite state languages, for example, the languages (10i) and (10ii) cited earlier. Neither of these languages can be produced by a finite state grammar of the type illustrated in (7) and (8), but they are produced by a phrase-structure grammar, which could be represented as:

(18) Σ : Z

    F : Z $\longrightarrow$ ab

          Z $\longrightarrow$ aZb

[*Syntactic Structures*, p. 30]

In such a grammar the initial string is Z, similar to the initial string *Sentence* in (13), and the two rules illustrated produce the sentences *ab* and *aabb* (since the Z in the second step is already equivalent to *ab*). Language (10ii) can also be produced by a phrase-structure grammar, but not language (10iii).

It is worth noticing in the case of a phrase-structure grammar that each terminal string, such as *the man hit the ball,* has a number of representations, which can be as abstract as Σ (*sentence*) and as immediate as the string of words just quoted. But since we have sentences embedded within sentences, NP's within NP's and VP's, and so on, Chomsky thinks it would be inefficient to try to establish a hierarchy of representations such as sentence, clause, phrase, and word. The entire set of representations can, therefore, be considered a **single level.** This distinguishes the level of phrase structure, which consists of a set of strings, from the morphemic and phonemic levels, which represent sentences by a single string.

Limitations of Phrase-Structure Grammars

Although a phrase-structure grammar is demonstrably superior to the finite state type, Chomsky shows that there are certain language problems it can handle only clumsily, and simplicity is one of the features he is looking for in a grammar. For example, it would be necessary to make cumbersome adjustments in a phrase-structure grammar in order to enable it to handle a language like (10iii), and there are familiar features of English that indicate the sources of this weakness.

The first example of a weakness inherent to phrase-structure grammars Chomsky sees in the ordinary formation of new sentences by conjunctions. This process is possible only when there is a similar relation of constituency between the elements so conjoined and their respective sentences. This constituency relation can be checked by examining a diagram like (15) and seeing if the two constituents in question can both be traced back to comparable nodes. If this requirement is met, we can form the new sentence (21) *The scene of the movie and of the play was in Chicago* from the pair of sentences

(20)   the scene - of the movie - was in Chicago
       the scene - of the play - was in Chicago

[*Syntactic Structures*, p. 35]

Ungrammatical sentences will be produced if the proper relation of constituency is not found in the sentences from which new ones are formed by conjunction, since

(22)   the - liner sailed down the - river
       the - tugboat chugged up the - river

[*Syntactic Structures*, p. 36]

would result in

(23)   the - liner sailed down the and the tugboat chugged
       up the - river

[*Syntactic Structures*, p. 36]

Nonsentences can also be produced when the elements conjoined are immediate constituents of their respective sentences [which in (22) was not the case], but are constituents of a different kind:

(24)   the scene - of the movie - was in Chicago
       the scene - that I wrote - was in Chicago

[*Syntactic Structures*, p. 36]

would result in

(25)   the scene - of the movie and that I wrote - was in Chicago

[*Syntactic Structures*, p. 36]

A rule that would specify which combinations are possible and which are not can be formulated, and this would greatly simplify a phrase-structure grammar. But Chomsky shows that a phrase-structure grammar cannot accept the kind of rule that is required, since it would be necessary for the rule to apply to elements whose constituency relations are known at the time of application, and this would mean that the **derivational history** would have to be indicated at that point in a derivation where the rewrite rule applies. But when we examine the formalization of what we do in a phrase-structure grammar, Chomsky shows that the rules in (13) specify how a given symbol is to be rewritten and that these rules are applied in a derivation like (14) because of the *shape* of the symbol there, not because of previous steps in the derivation. For example, the third string in the derivation (14) has applied rule (iii) to the symbol VP from the second string, rewriting it as *Verb* + NP, simply because that is the rule, and not in virtue of any constituency relations that Vp has to the sentence involved.

Viewed in terms of a sort of mechanical operation, Chomsky shows that a phrase-structure grammar has an initial state (for example, *Sentence*) and moves through several others (for example, NP → T + N or VP → *Verb* + NP) until there is a terminal string such as *The man hit the ball,* to which none of the rules of (13) apply. In so doing the machine applies its rules at each state, without possible reference to previous or subsequent states. The machine, Chomsky points out, cannot "look back," as it must, in order to check the constitutent status, for example, of *of the movie* or *that I wrote* in (24), much less the status of both of these in two different sentences when producing the nonsentence *the scene of the movie and that I wrote was in Chicago.*

Chomsky finds a similar weakness in phrase-structure grammar when attempting to deal with forms of the verb other than the simple forms produced by rewriting rules like *Verb* → *hit* or *take,* since we may be required to have in other contexts, forms like *takes, has + taken, will + take,* and so on. Assuming that we now have modified (13) so that it can accept contextual restrictions for rewriting rules, Chomsky suggests that we could add rules such as the following for the required forms of the verbs:

(28) (i)   *Verb* ⟶ *Aux* + V

(ii) V ⟶ *hit, take, walk, read,* etc.

(iii) *Aux* ⟶ C(M) (*have* + *en*) (*be* + *ing*) (*be* + *en*)

(iv) M ⟶ *will, can, may, shall, must*

(29) (i)   C ⟶ $\begin{cases} \text{S in the context } NP_{sing} \\ \emptyset \text{ in the context } \mathbf{NP_{pl}} \\ past \end{cases}$

(ii) let *Af* stand for any of the affixes *past,*
S, $\emptyset$, *en, ing.* Let *v* stand for any M or V,
or *have* or *be* (i.e., for any non-affix in the
phrase *Verb*). Then:
$$Af + v \longrightarrow v + Af \,\#,$$
where # is interpreted as word boundary.

(iii) Replace + by # except in the context *v–Af.*
Insert # initially and finally.

[*Syntactic Structures,* p. 39]

Rule (28iii) is to be understood as requiring us to select C, and zero or more of the parenthesized elements in the given order, and (29i) allows us to rewrite C as any of the three morphemes according to the contextual restrictions. To show how these rules apply, Chomsky gives the following derivation of

(31) the man has been reading the book

in the manner of (14), but omitting the initial steps:

(30) *the + man + Verb + the + book*   from **(13 i-v)**
    the + man + Aux + V + the + book   **(28i)**
    the + man + Aux + read + the + book   **(28ii)**
    the + man + C + have + en + be + ing
    + read + the + book   **(28iii)**—we select the
    the + man + S + have + en + be + ing   elements C, *have + en*,
    + read + the + book   and *be + ing*
    the + man + have + S # be + en # read   **(29i)**
    + ing # the + book
    # the # man # have + S # be + en # read   **(29ii)**—three times
    + ing # the # book #   **(29iii)**

[*Syntactic Structures*, pp. 39–40]

In the same way every other auxiliary verb phrase can be generated.

There are several factors here that indicate the shortcomings of phrase-structure grammars that cannot utilize some of the generalizations indicated by these rules. In order to apply (29i) to insure the proper concord between the singular noun and verb, Chomsky points out that we had to know that *the + man* was an example of NP$_{sing}$, and this requires information concerning the earlier steps in the derivation, which goes beyond the scope of the elementary Markovian type of phrase-structure grammar. Rule (29ii) also requires information about the derivational history, and, within the terms of phrase-structure grammar, there is no way of expressing the required inversion. Elements such as *have . . . en* and *be . . . ing* are really discontinuous (for example, "he seems to *be* sleep*ing*") and, as Chomsky has shown, interdependent discontinuities cannot be handled by an [Σ, F] grammar.

Of course, these rules in themselves are complex, but a glance at Table 4 of some verb phrases in English involving auxiliary forms (including an optional adverb) indicates the complexity that would be involved in formulating a rewrite rule providing for only this one set, which exemplifies only the third-person forms. The structure of such phrases *is* complex, and Chomsky considers the rules given above a "simplification" because they are sufficiently general to be applicable to any auxiliary verb phrase.

A third limitation of phrase-structure grammar Chomsky finds in

Table 4: Some Auxiliary Verb Phrases

It	(Adverb)							
It	(Adverb)	is/was						heating
It		has/had			been			heating
It		has/had						heated
It		will						heat
It		will		have				heated
It		will		have	been			heating
It		should						heat
It		ought	to			be		heating
It		ought	to	have	been			heating
It		is/was						heated
It		has/had			been			heated
It		is/was					being	
It		has/had			been		being	heated
It		will		have	been			heated
It		will				be		heated
It		will				be	being	heated
It		will		have	been		being	heated
It		ought	to	have	been		being	heated

the treatment of the active-passive relation. Passive sentences are formed when we select the element *be + en* of rule (28iii). But there are many restrictions on the possibility of selecting the element *be + en* in order to produce grammatical sentences that make this element unique among the auxiliaries. First, the *Verb* that follows *be + en* must be transitive or we produce sentences like *It was occurred;* second, *be + en* cannot precede an NP, even when the verb is transitive, or we would produce sentences like *Lunch is eaten John;* third, if the verb is transitive and is followed by the prepositional phrase *by + NP,* then we must almost always select the element *be + en,* or else sentences like *John is eating by lunch* could be produced along with *John is eating by candlelight.* Finally, in order to enable a phrase-structure grammar like (13) to handle such sentences, extensive restrictions would have to be placed in the rules to insure the proper combinations of subjects and objects with V, to allow sentences like *John admires sincerity* and *John plays golf,* but not *Sincerity admires John* or *Golf plays John.* And since there is a corresponding sentence of the form NP_2 - *is* + *Ven* - *by* + NP_1 for each NP_1 - V - NP_2, the same restrictions would have to be stated for the passives in the reverse order of that for the actives. (Note that the hyphen is used occasionally instead of the plus sign "to symbolize concatenation. We do this to call special attention to a subdivision of the utterance with which we happen to be particulary concerned at the moment" [*Syntactic Structures*, p. 109].)

Because of this complexity, Chomsky concludes that it would be better to exclude the passives from the phrase-structure grammar and reintroduce them later through such a rule as (34). This rule, of course, would have to be further specified for subclasses of V—:

(34) If S_1 is a grammatical sentence of the form

NP_1 - *Aux* - V - NP_2

then the corresponding string of the form

NP_2 - *Aux* + *be* + *en* - V - *by* + NP_1

is also a grammatical sentence.

[Syntactic Structures, p. 43]

Such a rule enables us to drop the element *be* + *en* and all of its special restrictions from (28iii), since they are now an automatic consequence of the developed rule (34). But again Chomsky reminds us that such a rule is clearly beyond the limits of an [Σ, F] grammar, which can rewrite only a single symbol at a time, cannot "look back" to check the derivational history of the symbols it is rewriting, and cannot introduce an inversion in the order of elements because of their constituency relations to preceding strings that have been rewritten.

A New Model of Grammar

The preceding section presented Chomsky's demonstration that it is possible to formulate rules which will: (1) insure the correct production of new sentences by conjunction, according to suitable IC relations of the items conjoined—rule (26); (2) assign rules to guarantee the production of sentences with the correct concord of noun and verb and the proper selection and combination of auxiliaries—rule (29); and (3) guarantee the formation of passive sentences from active ones without allowing ungrammatical sentences to result—rule (34). But none of these rules can be accepted in an [Σ, F] grammar.

When the nature of these rules is studied Chomsky finds that they lead to a new conception of linguistic structure, since the changes they effect are not merely the rewriting of a grammatical category into a more explicit representation (for example, VP → V + NP) nor of a symbol into a more familiar instance of the class it represents (for example, T → *the*). These rules, which can be called **grammatical transformations,** operate on a string or on a set of strings that have one constituent structure and convert them into strings with a different constituent structure (for example, $NP_1 + V + NP_2$ becomes $NP_2 + is + Ven + by + NP_1$). Where the rewrite rules of an [Σ, F] grammar apply only to individual symbols singly, and do not change, but, rather, make explicit the constituent structure, it can be seen that the transformational rules could be considered to apply to the entire constituent structure found in the derivations according to the grammatical rules, since the result of the transformation is a string that would have to have been produced by an entirely different set of grammatical rules in a derivation.

Chomsky concludes that a grammar which can incorporate such rules will, therefore, have at least these two components, an [Σ, F] component and a transformational component. A third component will also be required, consisting of morphophonemic rules that rewrite the terminal strings into the proper phonemic representation.

The **phrase-structure component** of such a grammar will consist of a sequence of rules, of the form X → Y. It begins with the initial symbol *Sentence* and constructs derivations through the application of the rules of F. The result is a string of morphemes, which may or may not be in the correct order.

The **transformational component** will consist of rules that will add, delete, or change the order of morphemes in the terminal strings produced by the phrase-structure component. Some of the transformations will be **obligatory**—for example, rule (29)—and others will be **optional** —for example, rule (34). Chomsky thus distinguishes two kinds of sentences. Those that are produced by the application of obligatory transformations to the terminal strings of the phrase-structure component he calls **kernel sentences,** and in this way every sentence of the language will be either a kernel sentence or one produced by a combination of obligatory and optional transformations. Transformations will be so set up that they can apply either to the underlying strings of kernel sentences or to strings already transformed by other transformation rules.

Chomsky finds that a grammar which contains a transformational component will be essentially more powerful than description in terms of phrase structure. For example, he shows that it can easily generate the language (10iii), which could not be done by a phrase-structure grammar. To illustrate, let G be a phrase-structure grammar with the initial string *Sentence,* and let this G be the phrase-structure component of a grammar G'. The output of the phrase-structure part is all the finite strings of *a*'s and *b*'s, and G' contains the transformational rule T that rewrites any string K which is a *Sentence,* as K + K.

The **morphophonemic component** will rewrite the morphemic representation into a proper string of phonemes, with rules of the form X → Y. Such rules for English would include

(19)   (i)   *walk* ⟶ /wɔk/

    (ii)   *take* + *past* ⟶ /tuk/

    (iii)   *hit* + *past* ⟶ /hit/

    (iv)   /. . . D/ + *past* ⟶ /. . . D/ + /ɨd/   (where D = /t/ or /d/),

etc.

[Syntactic Structures, p. 32]

and these rules must be ordered, but each rule need not be restricted to rewriting a single symbol.

This form of grammar meets several of Chomsky's requirements for a scientific theory: it takes a set of observed phenomena (for example, "grammatical sentences"), tries to formulate the laws by which these are related (for example, through phrase-structure and transformational rules), and invents a mechanism by which we can predict new phenomena of the same type (for example, through the phrase-structure, transformational, and morphophonemic components, which produce actual grammatical utterances).

Obviously Chomsky does not propose this process as a discovery procedure, but he finds that it does provide us with a way of comparing and evaluating proposed grammars. Both the finite-state type and phrase-structure grammar, compared to this model, have been found to be either incapable of producing parts of a natural language (English) or able to do so only with extreme complexity. Therefore, we would be led, Chomsky thinks, to prefer this model on the grounds of simplicity. He does not mean that it is simpler because it is necessarily more practical or shorter than other procedures, but basically because its generalizations result in giving a more uniform representation of relations among linguistic elements at different levels.

It has been pointed out that there is danger of circularity in our methods if we define morphemes in terms of phonemes and then use morphological considerations in phonemic analysis. In this approach Chomsky suggests that we can define "tentative phoneme set" and "tentative morpheme set" and develop a relation of compatibility between them. This does not, however, tell us how to *discover* phonemes and morphemes, he notes, but no other theory meets this requirement either. On the morphemic level Chomsky thinks we also have some simpler statements, as in the morphophonemic rules (19) that allow us to state the relation between *take* and *took* as *take* + *past,* just as *walked* is represented as *walk* + *past*. The idea that higher levels (for example, the morphemic) are literally constructed out of lower ones (for example, the phonemic) he finds untenable, and this makes it more natural to consider such abstract systems of representation as transformational structure as constituting a linguistic level.

The use of a transformational level of analysis in a grammar has the effect of simplifying several aspects of the structure of English. For example, take the terminal strings

(37) (i)   NP - C - V . . .

    (ii)   NP - C + M . . .

    (iii)   NP - C + *have* . . .

    (iv)   NP - C + *be* - . . .

[Syntactic Structures, p. 62]

Given a string analyzed into three parts such as these, a negative transformation, T_{not}, adds *not* (or *n't*) after the second segment of the string. Applied to (37iv), it gives, with application first of (29i) but before (29ii,) *they + be + n't − ing + come,* which is finally converted by the morphophonemic rules to *They aren't coming.*

A terminal string like (37i) can be

(38) *John - S - come*

[Syntactic Structures, p. 62]

which provides the kernel sentence *John comes* by rule (29ii). Applying T_{not} to this gives us

(39) *John - S + n't - come*

[Syntactic Structures, p. 62]

Rule (29ii) rewrites an *Affix + Verb* as *Verb + Affix#*, but this particular string does not contain an affix + verb sequence, giving us the familiar problem of how to introduce *do* into such expressions. Chomsky meets this difficulty by introducing a new obligatory transformation, to apply after (39):

(40) $\#Af \longrightarrow \#do + Af$

[Syntactic Structures, p. 62]

The new transformation has the effect of saying that *do* is the bearer of an unaffixed affix; applying the morphophonemic rules to (39) along with this transformation (40), we get *John doesn't come.* With rule (37), transformation (40) allows us to derive all the grammatical forms of sentence negation.

Chomsky shows that this same pair of formulas is also required for the class of yes-no questions. A question transformation, T_q, will have the effect of interchanging the first and second elements of the strings in

(37) and is required to apply *after* (29i) but *before* (29ii). When we apply T_q to (41i), *they - ∅ - arrive,* which is an example of (37i), we get (42i) *∅ - they - arrive.* When the obligatory rules (29ii, iii) and (40) are applied to this we derive (43i), *do they arrive.* In similar fashion we can derive (43ii) *can they arrive,* (43iii) *have they arrived,* and (43iv) *are they arriving.* Without the use of T_q we would have derived the statement forms of the same strings. These transformational possibilities indicate that negative and interrogative sentences in English have substantially the same structure. Chomsky shows that it is also possible to show a simple correlational correspondence between such sentences and the insistent affirmations such as "John *does* arrive" and the use of zero anaphora in sentences like *John has arrived and so have I.*

Another advantage of the transformational component, as Chomsky shows, is the fact that it indicates that the behavior of some elements in English which appear to be very irregular on the level of immediate constituents turn out to be quite regular from the transformational point of view. The forms *be* and *have,* for example, do not behave like the forms of verbs in many instances. For example, we can have *John isn't my friend,* but not *John readsn't books,* or "John *is* here," but not "John *does* be here." In the case of *have* it is found that we could have either *John doesn't have a chance to live* or *John hasn't a chance to live,* a double possibility that does not hold for other transitive verbs. Part of the significance of (28iii), Chomsky notes, is that there are instances of *have* which are not instances of V, or that there are diagrams in which we cannot trace *have* back to a node for *Verb,* whereas in other cases (for example, *I have money*) *have* is a V.

Chomsky also shows that the same simplification is found in the ability of transformations to distinguish between utterances like *The book seems interesting, The book is interesting,* and *The child is sleeping* vs. *The child seems sleeping.* Where phrase-structure grammars are incapable of handling discontinuous items easily, because of transformations the analysis of utterances like *The police brought the criminal in* or *The police brought in the criminal* or *The police brought him in* can be handled readily. Chomsky demonstrates that utterances like *Everyone in the lab considered John incompetent* or *John was considered incompetent by everyone in the lab* can be analyzed by employing two further rewrite rules for verbs:

(84) $V \longrightarrow V_1 + Prt$ (e. g., *bring in*)
(91) $V \longrightarrow V_a + Comp$ (e. g., *consider incompetent*)

[*Syntactic Structures,* pp. 75–76]

and adding the required transformations that provide the variable positions of the nonverbal element.

Some of the formulations discussed may appear artificial, and some of the decisions reached may also seem to be capable of other interpretations, but Chomsky is at pains to point out that the illustrations used, as a matter of fact, produce results that are intuitively supported. What is even more convincing is that alternatives are shown to lead to undesirable complexity or to ungrammatical formulations. As for artificiality, Chomsky points out that this device is really nothing new in linguistics, as he indicates by quoting Bloomfield, who saw the need for setting up artificial basic forms to give a simpler and clearer explanation of morphology.[11]

Another defense for a transformational component is that it is capable of resolving, in a formal way, ambiguities that cannot be explained on the level of phrase structure. It would seem that expressions which are represented in a similar fashion on some level of analysis would also be "understood" in an analogous fashion, suggesting that there can be a close relation between the notion of "understanding a sentence" and "linguistic level." For example, we understand all simple, active sentences in roughly the same fashion. They differ radically from their corresponding passive sentences, yet we understand pairs of active and passive sentences in the same way, for example, *John killed Bill* and *Bill was killed by John*. Other pairs of sentences can have identical constituent structures, yet be understood in more than one way, for example, *Stone the architect of the new library* as a newspaper headline. Part of the problem of "understanding" is rooted in the nature of kernel sentences, since these simple, active declarative sentences, with no complex noun or verb phrases, can be considered the basic "content elements" from which our more usual sentences are formed by transformational development. Seeing the difference in transformational development enables us to distinguish between the two meanings that we can assign to *What did you think of the paintings of the madmen?* in which *the paintings of the madmen* has the phrase structure *the* - V + *ing* - *of* + NP. The NP can be taken as a transformation of either the kernel sentence *The madmen paint* or *They paint madmen*.

Finally, the addition of a transformational representation of sentences, Chomsky shows, corresponds generally to the simplest classification and to our intuitive classification as well. This can be seen in the kernel declarative sentence and the transformations in:

(115)   (i)   John ate an apple.   - declarative

(ii)   Did John eat an apple?   - yes or no question ⎫
                                                     ⎬ interrogative
(iii) What did John eat?   ⎫   ⎭
                            ⎬ - *wh-* question
(iv)   Who ate an apple?   ⎭

[*Syntactic Structures*, pp. 77–91]

11 See Leonard Bloomfield, *Language* (New York, 1933), p. 218.

Phrase-Structure and Transformational Grammar

From such considerations as summarized in the previous section Chomsky concludes that we must abandon one of the presuppositions of those who have proposed phrase-structure grammars, that is, that we can now develop a mechanical discovery procedure that will reveal the grammar of a language through the application of the theory. Instead he believes that it would be more realistic to aim at an evaluation procedure for proposed grammars. This has several advantages when transformational components are included—one of which is the validity of mixing levels of analysis.

Chomsky's formalization of proposed phrase-structure grammars has shown that the finite state Markov process and the usual context-free rewrite rules of phrase-structure grammars are inadequate for handling the familiar facts of natural languages in a simple and revealing way. Chomsky does not think that the study of grammar is actually dependent on meaning, although certain obvious connections between syntax and semantics cannot be ignored. It will be more useful at the outset, however, to develop a syntactic analysis that can support a semantic interpretation rather than beginning by basing our syntax on meaning.

The description is simplified because kernel sentences can be recognized, and sentences produced by further transformations can be examined according to the various kernels from which they can be produced. The grammar should, therefore, be tripartite, involving a phrase-structure component, a transformational component, and a morphophonemic component. Neither the phrase-structure nor the morphophonemic rules require information concerning the history of derivation, whereas the elementary transformation rules do consider both the "shape" of the symbols and their derivational history.

As a consequence, many constituents whose behavior seems unpredictable and irregular in phrase-structure description are seen to be regular and simply explainable through transformational representation. The fact that many constructions can be considered ambiguous at one or more levels of representation indicates the need of an additional level of transformational representation.

This notion of "understanding a sentence" indicates the need of a refined grammatical analysis, since we most likely understand sentences through reconstructing them at various levels of representation, and the sentences of the kernel can be considered elementary contents of transformed sentences. The result of such analysis should be a syntax free from meaning, but one that can support semantic analysis. From this

DEVELOPMENTS IN TRANSFORMATIONAL GRAMMAR / 379

point of view, then, Chomsky finds the distinction between lexical and grammatical meaning suspect. The typical argument for making such a distinction, he points out, is usually to quote sentences in which so-called grammatically functioning morphemes such as -ing, -ly, prepositions, and so on can be distributed in nonsense frames that seem to have at least grammatical meaning, as, for example, *Pirots karulize elatically*. For Chomsky the distinction is not a sharp one and seems to indicate only the productivity or "open-endedness" of the categories of noun, verb, and so on, as opposed to other, closed classes:

Whatever differences there are among morphemes with respect to this property are apparently better explained in terms of such grammatical notions as productivity, freedom of combination, and size of substitution class than in terms of any presumed feature of meaning.

[*Syntactic Structures,* p. 105]

DEVELOPMENTS IN TRANSFORMATIONAL GRAMMAR

Since it was proposed generally in *Syntactic Structures* there has been considerable research into the bases and development of a transformational approach to syntax, and although the basic insights remain unchanged, the appearance of this work now seems quite different. One of the reasons for this is the explicit inclusion of a semantic theory that gives an interpretation of the sentences produced by the syntactic component of the grammar. The need for such a theory was alluded to earlier in our considerations of the problems of linking syntax and semantics. The discussion of sentences such as *Colorless green ideas sleep furiously* pointed out a sense in which grammar is independent of meaning. The subsequent distinctions concerning degrees of grammaticalness point out the need for a formal specification of how these degrees are to be judged. There are sentences that we would call ungrammatical yet acceptable, and there are other sentences that are grammatical but unacceptable. It is where semantic and grammatical criteria overlap that this problem is raised.

Another feature that seems to distinguish present work from earlier efforts is the more explicit recognition that traditional grammatical concepts are, in the main, quite correct, as is the traditional concept of universal grammar. There were obvious gaps in the traditional account of syntax, as well as some inconsistencies in the distinction of substantial vs. formal universals. Chomsky believes that the distinction between deep structure and surface structure enables us to appreciate the lasting contribution of traditional grammar, and to see why the structural linguist rejects universal grammar.

Deep Structure versus Surface Structure

The original form of the transformational grammar was tripartite; it involved (1) a phrase-structure grammar that produced terminal strings; (2) a transformational component that, through obligatory and optional additions, deletions, and rearrangements, produced the final grammatical representation of all sentences in the language; and (3) a morpho-phonemic component that rewrote these sentences into the proper sequence of phonemes. The distinction between the phrase-structure component (the base) and the transformational component suggests the difference between **deep structure** (what the base produces) and **surface structure** (the grammatical representation effected by transformations, and the phonological representation produced by the morphophonemic component). Chomsky finds that this distinction, though variously formulated, is as old as syntactic theory itself:

In place of the terms "deep structure" and "surface structure" one might use the corresponding Humboldtian notions "inner form" of a sentence and "outer form" of a sentence. . . . I have adopted the more neutral terminology to avoid the question, here, of textual interpretation. The terms "depth grammar" and "surface grammar" are familiar in modern philosophy in something like the sense here intended (cf. Wittgenstein's distinction of *"Tiefengrammatik"* and *"Oberflächengrammatik."*[12] Hockett uses similar terminology in his discussion of the inadequacy of taxonomic linguistics.[13] Postal has used the terms "underlying structure" and "superficial structure"[14] for the same notions.

The distinction between deep and surface structure, in the sense in which these terms are used here, is drawn quite clearly in the Port-Royal *Grammar.*[15]

[*Aspects of the Theory of Syntax,* p. 199]

This kind of distinction recalls the opinion of Roger Bacon (see Chapter 5 of this volume) that all languages are substantially the same and only accidentally different. But it is part of the program of transformational grammar to specify just what the "substantial" resemblances and the "accidental" differences are. The use of "substantial" here, of course, is not the same as Chomsky's use of the term in distinguishing between substantial and formal universals.

The elements that comprise deep structure and the relations among them, as opposed to the elements and relations of the surface structure, will be examined in detail in a later section. It is sufficient to point out

12 Ludvig Wittgenstein, *Philosophical Investigations* (New York, 1953).
13 Charles Hockett, *A Course in Modern Linguistics* (New York, 1958), Chap. 20.
14 P. Postal, "Underlying and Superficial Linguistic Structure," *Harvard Educational Review,* 34 (1964), pp. 246–266.
15 C. Lancelot, A. Arnauld, *et al.,* Grammaire générale et raisonné (Paris, 1660).

here that the elements of deep structure include grammatical relations, functions, and categories, while surface structure includes the actual formatives, phonetic signals, and combinations of perceived utterances. Basic to this distinction is Chomsky's conviction that we do not understand utterances merely in terms of the surface signals but rather in terms of the structures underlying them and from which they can be considered to be transformationally produced. For such reasons Chomsky concludes that modern linguistics of the IC type as well as anthropological investigations have by no means refuted the doctrines of classical universal grammar; what they have done instead, is to show the great diversity of surface structures in languages, but they have not dealt with deep structures. The evidence so far has produced nothing to suggest to him that the underlying structures are as diverse as the surface structures:

Since the origin of this work in the *Grammaire générale et raisonnée,* it has been emphasized that the deep structures for which universality is claimed may be quite distinct from the surface structures of sentences as they actually appear. . . . and the findings of modern linguistics are thus not inconsistent with the hypotheses of universal grammarians. Insofar as attention is restricted to surface structures, the most that can be expected is the discovery of statistical tendencies, such as those presented by Greenberg.[16]

[*Aspects of the Theory of Syntax,* p. 118]

In *Syntactic Structures* the kernel sentences were proposed as the "elementary content elements" out of which a given sentence is constructed. The term "kernel sentence," however, was often pointed out as an abbreviation for the underlying terminal strings of a phrase-structure grammar. Therefore, Chomsky's statement in *Aspects of the Theory of Syntax* (p. 117) that "The base Phrase-markers may be regarded as the elementary content elements" out of which actual sentences are constructed and interpreted serves to point up the clearer notion of deep structure that he later developed. In *Syntactic Structures* Chomsky defines a "phrase-marker" as "a set of phrase-grammar strings that represents a sentence." In later work it is suggested that it is uneconomical to exclude transformational rules from the base.

A New Model of a Transformational Grammar

It has already been noted that a grammar is to be a description of a speaker's competence. Insofar as the grammar is perfectly explicit, leaving nothing to the reader's intuition, but providing symbols and rules for all the operations on the items described by the grammar, Chomsky

---

[16] Joseph H. Greenberg, ed., *Universals in Language* (Cambridge, Mass., 1963).

states that it can be called a **generative grammar**. Such a grammar must be finite, yet generate an infinite number of sentences and assign to each a structural description, allowing them to be phonetically and semantically interpreted. There will be three major components of such a grammar:

1. A **syntactic component** that contains all the information needed for the phonological and semantic interpretation of a particular sentence.

2. A **phonological component** that determines the phonetic form of a sentence generated by the syntactic rules.

3. A **semantic component** that determines the semantic interpretation of a sentence.

As a consequence, the syntactic component specifies the deep structure of a sentence, for which the semantic interpretation is specified, and via transformations, the surface structure, for which a phonetic interpretation is determined by the phonetic component. Since it is the syntactic component that generates, while the other two interpret, the syntactic component can be called the **base.**

The two interpretive components are related differently and independently to the base. The phonological component assigns a phonetic interpretation to surface structure, but the semantic component assigns an interpretation to the deep structure underlying a sentence. The base itself can be variously conceived, and a chief source of such variety lies in its relations to the semantic component. Depending on how various problems concerning the relation of syntax and semantics are to be dealt with, the base can contain a context-free or a context-sensitive phrase-structure component.

In either case the functioning of the phonological component would seem to be unaffected, since it is to determine surface structures, while the problems involved in relating the base and the semantic component are concerned with deep structures. It is assumed that sentences are understood in terms of (1) their lexical items and (2) the grammatical relations among the lexical items, not merely in the surface presentation of an utterance but especially through the processes by which the surface sentence has been formed; this formational process, operating on lexical items and the syntactic relations into which they enter, is referred to as the "deep structure." To illustrate, Chomsky notes the distinction that the Port-Royal logicians made between "what we think" and "what we say." Citing their example, we can say "The invisible God created the visible world," but we understand this sentence because we have made the following judgments: (1) God created the world, (2) God is invisible, and (3) the world is visible.

At this stage of the investigation, Chomsky feels, "it should not be taken for granted, necessarily, that syntactic and semantic considerations can be sharply distinguished" (*Aspects of the Theory of Syntax*, p. 77).

Deep Structure and the Base

One way to sort out the kind of information that we would want to assign to the base and to the semantic component is to examine what information traditional grammatical analysis gives with respect to a single sentence. Chomsky proceeds as follows:

(1)   sincerity may frighten the boy

Concerning this sentence, a traditional grammar might provide information of the following sort:

(2)   (i)   the string (1) is a Sentence (S); *frighten the boy* is a Verb Phrase (VP) consisting of the Verb (V) *frighten* and the Noun Phrase (NP) *the boy; sincerity* is also an NP; the NP *the boy* consists of the Determiner (Det) *the,* followed by a Noun (N); the NP *sincerity* consists of just an N; *the* is, furthermore, an Article (Art); *may* is a Verbal Auxiliary (Aux) and, furthermore, a Modal (M).

   (ii)   the NP *sincerity* functions as the Subject of the sentence (1), whereas the VP *frighten the boy* functions as the Predicate of the sentence; the NP *the boy* functions as the Object of the VP, and the V *frighten* as its Main Verb; the grammatical relation Subject-Verb holds of the pair (*sincerity, frighten*), and the grammatical relation Verb-Object holds of the pair (*frighten, the boy*).

   (iii)   the N *boy* is a Count Noun (as distinct from the Mass Noun *butter* and the Abstract Noun *sincerity*) and a Common Noun (as distinct from the Proper Noun *John* and the Pronoun *it*); it is, furthermore, an Animate Noun (as distinct from *book*) and a Human Noun (as distinct from *bee*); *frighten* is a Transitive Verb (as distinct from *occur*), and one that does not freely permit Object deletion (as distinct from *read, eat*); it takes Progressive Aspect freely (as distinct from *know, own*); it allows Abstract Subjects (as distinct from *eat, admire*) and Human Objects (as distinct from *read, wear*).
   [*Aspects of the Theory of Syntax*, pp. 63–64]

The kind of information contained in (2i) is represented in the usual phrase-structure grammar's rewrite rules, as seen above. The verbal description can be formalized by showing that a vocabulary of **category symbols** (for example, S, NP, VP) and **formatives** (for example, *the, boy*) is required, and that the formatives can be subdivided into **lexical** items (*sincerity,* boy) and **grammatical** items (*perfect, possessive,* and so on, perhaps *the*.)

Chomsky assumes that these can be given some "language-independent characterization" (*Aspects of the Theory of Syntax*, p. 5) and that, therefore, they pertain to the study of universal grammar, at least in the case of the grammatical formatives and category symbols.

The establishment of these grammatical categories in the formalized version of a phrase-structure grammar was portrayed as the construction of a derivation through the application of rewrite rules, which begin with the initial symbol *Sentence*. These rules successively show each grammatical category that the symbols represent as being realized in a string of categories such as NP, VP, until the **terminal string** of a **terminated derivation** consists of a string of formatives, at which point no further rewriting rules are applicable.

These formatives are distinguished from morphemes: "The set of *morphemes* for a language is not necessarily identical with the set of *formatives* (because transformations may add or delete terminal symbols), and in fact it almost certainly never is."[17]

Formatives are elements of surface structure, and, therefore, Chomsky defines them as "minimal syntactically functioning units," to which the phonological rules of the phonological components apply, "first to the minimal elements (formatives), then to the constituents of which these are parts" (*Aspects of the Theory of Syntax*, p. 143). The morphemes appear to pertain primarily to deep structure: Katz and Postal note that the terminal symbols of underlying P-markers are referred to as "morphemes."

The rewriting rules of the phrase-structure grammar can be represented by the formula:

(4) $A \longrightarrow Z \mid X - Y$

[*Aspects of the Theory of Syntax*, p. 66]

indicating that A, a single-category symbol, is to be rewritten as a string, Z, of non-null symbols in the environment $X - Y$. If neither X nor Y are null, the rule is, in effect, context-sensitive. If X and Y are null, the rule is context-free. A phrase-structure grammar that contains unordered, context-free rewrite rules is also called a **constituent structure grammar**. Chomsky has already rejected this kind of grammar on the grounds that it is inadequate for describing natural languages. In the base, therefore, Chomsky assumes the phrase-structure part will consist of **ordered rules** that produce a **sequential derivation**.

To provide a phrase-marker such as (3) the base component could contain such a sequence of rewriting rules:

17 J. J. Katz and P. Postal, *An Integrated Theory of Linguistic Descriptions* (Cambridge, Mass.: M.I.T. Press, 1964). All quotations from *An Integrated Theory of Linguistic Descriptions* appearing in this chapter are reprinted with the permission of M.I.T. Press.

(5) (I) S ⟶ NP Aux VP

         VP ⟶ V NP

         NP ⟶ Det N
         NP ⟶ N
         Det ⟶ *the*
         Aux ⟶ M
    (II) M ⟶ *may*
         N ⟶ *sincerity*
         N ⟶ *boy*
         V ⟶ *frighten*

                          [*Aspects of the Theory of Syntax*, p. 65]

(3)

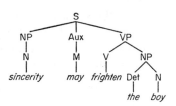

Fig. 12.4.

                          [*Aspects of the Theory of Syntax*, p. 65]

Chomsky points out that the information given by traditional grammar in (2ii) indicates an important difference between grammatical categories and grammatical functions. The latter are purely **relational** notions, whereas the former are capable of positive definition. Defining such grammatical functions as "subject of" and "object of" formally helps to point out that in simpler sentences grammatical categories may have only a single function, whereas in sentences like

(7) (a) John was persuaded by Bill to leave
     (b) John was persuaded by Bill to be examined
     (c) what disturbed John was being regarded as incompetent

                          [*Aspects of the Theory of Syntax*, p. 70]

we can have several grammatical functions realized by the same phrase. For example, in (7c) *John* is simultaneously object of *disturb*, object of *regard (as incompetent)*, and subject of the predication *as incompetent*.

Relations such as *subject of* for English can be considered as the relation holding between, for example, the NP of a sentence of the form NP Aux VP and the whole sentence. Such relations are defined by the rewriting rules, although not all such relations have traditional names.

Chomsky believes, then, that the information contained in (2i) and

(2ii) is handled adequately by the rewriting rules, even though there are various ways in which the functional notions discussed could be modified or extended. For example, in the grammar the rules that introduce lexical formatives (5II) have been distinguished from those that introduce the grammatical formatives (5I). Chomsky calls a category that appears on the left of the lexical rules a **lexical category.** He notes that any category which dominates a string, . . . X . . . , where X is a lexical category, we could call a **major category,** and it would be in accord with traditional grammar to restrict discussion of functional relations to major categories.

If we assume that the semantic component is to be purely interpretive, then the syntactic component must supply all the information needed for interpretation. We must decide whether to include the information contained in (2iii) in the syntactic component or leave it to the semantic component. It is possible to formulate some of the subcategorizations in (2iii) in syntactic terms. Chomsky gives a few examples of deviant and nondeviant sentences to illustrate the problem at hand:

(13)   (i)   the boy may frighten sincerity

       (ii)   sincerity may admire the boy

       (iii)   John amazed the injustice of the decision

(14)   (i)   sincerity may frighten the boy

       (ii)   the boy may admire sincerity

       (iii)   the injustice of that decision amazed John

(15)   (i)   sincerity frighten may boy the

       (ii)   boy the frighten may sincerity

(16)   (i)   oculists are generally better trained than eye-doctors

       (ii)   both of John's parents are married to aunts of mine

       (iii)   I'm memorizing the score of the sonata I hope to compose some day
       [*Aspects of the Theory of Syntax,* pp. 75–77]

If the semantic component is to interpret such sentences, Chomsky thinks it fairly clear that the sentences will not be handled by the same kind of rules that are used to deal with the sentences of (14), and it would appear that the best way to start is to formulate rules for the unequivocal cases and then figure out how to handle the various kinds of deviance illustrated in the others:

it should not be taken for granted, necessarily, that syntactic and semantic considerations can be sharply distinguished. . . . A priori there is no way to decide whether the burden of presentation should fall on the syntactic or semantic component of the generative grammar.

[*Aspects of the Theory of Syntax*, pp. 77–78]

The problem, however, is clearly delineated; we can permit the syntactic component to generate sentences like (14) by introducing selectional restrictions such as animateness and abstractness, and sentences like (13) by relaxing these restrictions, or allow the syntactic component to generate both (13) and (14), leaving the specification of deviance to the semantic component. In either case we must try to formulate the kind of information given in (2iii) in explicit rules, either for the syntactic component or for the semantic component.

Chomsky finds that rewriting rules seem apt for this purpose until it is appreciated that the subcategorization involved is not strictly hierarchic. For example, English nouns are either proper or common, human or nonhuman. But some syntactic rules concern complexes of different groupings of these subcategorizations, and it would be uneconomic to have rewrite rules that concern unrelated features.

This kind of problem, which involves cross-reference, Chomsky shows to be formally identical with one in phonology: there are rules, for example, that apply to voiced consonants, [b], [z], but not to unvoiced consonants, [p], [s], and some that apply to continuants, [s], [z], but not to stops, [p,] [b]. Therefore, it is useful to consider each phonological unit as a set of features and to formulate the rules so that they can be applied to any segment with a certain complex of features. Chomsky thinks the same solution seems indicated in the syntactic problem raised here. It will be useful, then, to sketch the operation of the phonological component.

The Operation of the Phonological Component

The details of how the phonological component is conceived are to be found in works by M. Halle.[18]

The lexical formatives are represented by segments that consist of sets of features in a **distinctive feature matrix,** where the columns represent successive segments and the rows the particular features. A mark such as + or − in a particular box formed by the intersection of rows and columns indicates whether a particular segment is specified or unspecified for the feature in question. Segments are distinct, therefore, when they do not share a positive specification.

[18] See M. Halle, "Questions of Linguistics," *Nuovo Cimento,* 13 (1959); *The Sound Pattern of Russian* (The Hague, 1959); and "Phonology in Generative Grammar," *Word,* 18 (1962), reprinted in J. J. Katz and J. Fodor, *The Structure of Language* (Englewood Cliffs, N.J., 1964).

A typical phonological rule is of the rewrite type:

(18) $A \longrightarrow Z \mid X - Y$

[Aspects of the Theory of Syntax, p. 81]

where A, Z and X, Y represent matrices, but A and Z are segments (that is, matrices with a single column).
A rule such as

(19) [+continuant] $\longrightarrow$ [+voiced] / — [+voiced]

[Aspects of the Theory of Syntax, p. 82]

will rewrite a **continuant** as a **voiced continuant** in the environment of a voiced sound, and so converts [sm] into [zm] and [fd] into [vd], but would not affect [st] or [pd], for example, since the *s* is not in a voiced environment and the *p* is not a continuant.

Lexical Subcomponent of the Base

These rules, Chomsky suggests, can be adapted without essential change to the formation of a lexicon, which will be an unordered set of the lexical formatives of the language, and each entry can be represented as (D, C). D will stand for a distinctive feature matrix, the "spelling" of the entry, and C will stand for a **complex symbol** standing for syntactic features.

For example, a lexical entry such as *bee* could be represented as consisting of the syntactic features + Noun + Common + Animate + Count − Human − Abstract, and so on, and of the phonological features represented by the distinctive feature matrix. This matrix representation could be symbolized by putting a number over the columns for segments and then indicating which features are specified or not specified for them, as in *bee* + Consonantal$_1$, − Vocalic$_1$, − Continuant$_1$, and so on, and − Consonantal$_2$, + Vocalic$_2$, − Grave$_2$, and so on.

The effect of introducing such context-sensitive rewrite rules, Chomsky explains, is to do away with such lexical rules as (5II) (for example, N → *boy*) in the grammar and transfer them to a **lexical subcomponent**. The rewrite rules of the base now produce derivations that terminate in strings of grammatical formatives and complex symbols, which Chomsky calls **preterminal strings,** from which terminal strings are formed by the introduction of lexical formatives.

Separating the lexicon from the grammar enables Chomsky to specify the grammatical and phonological peculiarities of each lexical entry in the lexicon, rather than having to do so in the rewrite rules. It also enables him to classify in the lexicon those verbs that do or do not allow object deletion, so that the transformational rule which deletes objects will be applicable only to those entries so specified for it. The grammar will be greatly simplified when the lexicon specifies phonetic peculiarities not predictable by the rule, transformationa¹ possibilities, features relevant to semantic interpretation, or restrictions on the positions where the lexical formatives can be inserted.

Since the base now contains ordered rules, and especially since it employs complex symbols, it is no longer a simple phrase-structure grammar, because the conventions for the use of complex symbols, for one thing, make it a kind of transformational grammar. Chomsky points out, therefore, that it cannot be adequately represented by a tree diagram.

The syntactic features discussed so far have been features of nouns. In trying to specify the syntactic features of verbs Chomsky shows that it soon appears that their subcategorization is better expressed in terms of contextual features rather than in terms of syntactic features of the verb itself. Instead of considering as part of its lexical entry the specification for ± Abstract Subject, ± Concrete Object, ± Transitive, and so on, Chomsky finds it better to recognize, for example, that a verb is transitive precisely when it is in the environment of —NP as an object following it, and similarly for the other subcategorizations. A different kind of rule can then be introduced, one that analyzes a category (for example, V) into a complex symbol in terms of the frame in which the category appears. Instead of stating its subcategorization in terms of syntactic features (for example, ± Abstract Subject, ± Concrete Subject), Chomsky has these rules analyze a symbol in terms of its **categorial context** (for example, "in the environment NP," "in the environment Adjective"). Rules that subcategorize a symbol in terms of categorial context Chomsky calls **strict subcategorization rules,** and those that analyze symbols (generally complex) in terms of syntactic features of the frames in which they appear he calls **selectional rules.**

Both of these types of rules will have to be further specified, he says, since it is clear not only that the immediate categorial environment is pertinent to the subcategorization of V, for example, but that every frame in which V appears in the VP is relevant to its strict subcategorization. For example, VP will dominate such strings as the following:

(43) (i)   V   (*elapse*)

   (ii) V NP   (*bring the book*)

   (iii) V NP *that-S*   (*persuade John that there was no hope*)

   (iv) V Prep-Phrase   (*argue with John about the plan*)
                  [*Aspects of the Theory of Syntax*, p. 96]

In the case of the selectional rules it is clear that *every* syntactic feature imposes a corresponding classification on the Verb, for example, which is found in its subject or object, so that all of the lexical features already discussed for nouns would be relevant.

The Transformational Subcomponent

The phrase-structure component of the base, Chomsky explains, produces phrase markers, which, in the case of a simple phrase-structure grammar, consist of the derivations according to rules that can be associated with tree diagrams. Such P-markers can be considered the deep structure or underlying structure of actual sentences. The transformational subcomponent of the base operates on the finite set of P-markers produced by the phrase-structure subcomponent to produce new P-markers, which he calls **derived P-markers.** A **final derived P-marker** is the last one, which is the result of all the transformations that have been applied, and the elements of its last line are the formatives of which the sentence consists, in the correct order. This Chomsky calls the surface structure of the particular sentence.

Chomsky notes that while the output of the phrase-structure part of the syntactic component is a finite set of P-markers, the output of the transformational subcomponent is an infinite set of final derived P-markers, plus a set of transformation markers (T-markers), which indicates the configurations of transformations applied to derive the final string of formatives. Such transformations he calls either **singular** (they operate on only a single P-marker) or **generalized** (they operate on a set—usually two—of P-markers, by **embedding** part of one or all of one P-marker into another or by **conjoining** the two in some way). In this way the grammar meets the basic requirements of being finite, while producing infinitely many sentences and assigning their structural description.[19]

The Semantic Component

The semantic component consists of two parts, a **dictionary,** which will provide a meaning for the lexical items of the language, and a finite set of **projection rules** to

assign a semantic interpretation to each string of formatives generated by the syntactic component. The semantic interpretation that a string of formatives has assigned to it provides a full analysis of its cognitive meaning.

[Katz and Postal, p. 12]

The semantic interpretation is obtained by first assigning each of the lexical formatives in the string the meanings found in the dictionary,

19 See Katz and Postal, pp. 6–12.

and these are then combined by the projection rules according to the syntactic description. Information from the syntactic description is basic to the semantic interpretation, so that the output of the syntactic component must be the input to the semantic component.

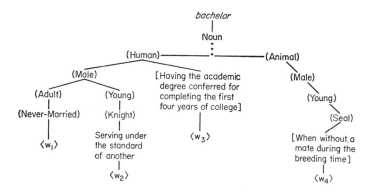

Fig. 5. (From J. Katz and P. Postal, **An Integrated Theory of Linguistic Descriptions** [Cambridge, Mass.: M.I.T. Press, 1964], p. 14.)

The dictionary entries in the semantic component are to be in a **normal form;** that is, a full analysis of the meaning of each lexical item is broken down into its most elementary concepts, with a statement indicating the semantic relations among the items. In the illustration of the dictionary entry *bachelor* in Figure 5 the following are noted: **semantic markers** are enclosed in parentheses, **distinguishers** within brackets, and **selection restrictions** within angles. The **syntactic markers** are not enclosed, and the dots below the syntactic marker *noun* indicate the possibility of other syntactic categorizations (for example, common, animate, count).

All the features noted here for *bachelor* may be found in other dictionary entries except the distinguishers: these will appear only once in the dictionary. Following the lines from any entry to an end-point, or from the selection restriction to an entry, gives a **reading** for a lexical item, and such an item will be semantically ambiguous in as many ways as it has such readings. For example, in a sentence like

(2) he enjoys wearing a light suit in the summer

[Katz and Postal, p. 15]

the dictionary would include readings for *light,* one of which would have the semantic marker *color,* but exclude *weight,* and at least one more where *weight* is included but *color* is excluded. (2) is therefore *ambiguous* because it contains an ambiguous lexical item. This is necessary, but not a sufficient, condition for ambiguity, since in a sentence like

(3) the stuff is light enough to carry

[Katz and Postal, p. 15]

the selection rules would determine what reading of *light* would be ad-missible as a combination when a projection rule is applied (for example, it would allow the reading with weight as compatible with the readings of *carry*).[20]

The projection rules operate in the following way: the syntactic component provides the semantic component with a sentence like *the man hits the ball*. With this sentence is associated the appropriate struc-tural description. First, the semantic component assigns the semantic interpretations to each lexical item. These interpretations are compatible with the syntactic markers of each lexical item (for example, *hit* as a verb, not as a noun) both in the dictionary entry and in the structural description. The semantic readings can be called **expanded** in the sense that to the dictionary meanings are added, for each lexical item, the meanings each item acquires through its syntactic relations. The ex-panded readings are then combined to form derived readings, and these in turn are combined until derived readings are obtained that express the meaning of the whole sentence. In this process meanings will be assigned to *the, man,* "past," *hit, the, ball;* they will be expanded in terms of the immediate constituent relations, for example, of *the man* and *hit the ball,* but not for substrings like *the man hit* or *hit the.* The derived meanings of *the man* and *hit the ball* can then be combined to produce the derived meaning of *the man hit the ball.*

This exemplifies the process of **amalgamation:**

Amalgamation is the operation of forming a composite reading made up of a reading from each of the sets of readings dominated by a given node in a P-marker. A pair of readings is joined if one of them satisfies the selection restriction in the other.

[Katz and Postal, p. 21]

The projection rules by which this process is accomplished can be dis-tinguished as Type 1 projection rules (P1) and Type 2 projection rules (P2). Katz and Postal note that originally P1 rules were designed to interpret the final derived P-markers of kernel sentences (those that have only obligatory, singulary transformations in their T-markers), P2 rules were intended to interpret other sentences, which could involve optional singulary transformations, just in case these changed the meaning of the final derived sentence with respect to the underlying structures.

It will be recalled that a singulary transformation operates on a single phrase marker, while a generalized transformation usually oper-ates on two phrase markers, either by embedding all or part of the first

---

[20] See Katz and Postal, pp. 13–17.

into the second or by producing a new, derived phrase marker by conjoining the two (or parts of them). The phrase marker that has a subpart embedded in it can be called the **matrix** phrase marker, and the one that provides the embedded part is called the **constituent** phrase marker.

The following relations can now be stipulated:

We claim that all Matrix P-markers will be characterized by the presence of one or more specified *dummy elements* in their last lines. A dummy element is a morpheme which necessarily never occurs in any sentence (i.e., is never a *formative*). There will be at least two types of dummy elements which are found universally in the terminal strings of the underlying P-markers of all languages. The first type is found only in Matrix P-markers and will henceforth be referred to as *Matrix dummies* (md). . . . We further specify the notion of embedding transformations by requiring that each operate by substituting the Constituent P-marker for some occurrence of md.

[Katz and Postal, p. 48]

Besides these specifications two more are added: (1) all syntactic components are to contain nonterminal symbols in their phrase-structure subpart, including at least **relative** (Rel) and **complement** (comp), each of which is developed into a terminal representation of the matrix dummy; (2) besides a universal vocabulary of grammar, therefore, a certain set of universal phrase-structure rules is assumed: *all* languages are held to have elements like relative and complement as possible expansions of lexical heads like noun and verb. As a result, besides the finite number of noun phrases in English such as *the book,* substitutions for the matrix dummy representative of relative can produce an indefinite number of other noun phrases—for example:

(35) the book which was taken by the man who Mary saw on her way to the red school

[Katz and Postal, p. 49]

ALTERNATIVE ORGANIZATION OF THE GRAMMAR

The development of transformational grammars so far can be illustrated by giving the phrase markers and the transformation marker which Chomsky provides for a sentence like:

(4) the man who persuaded John to be examined by a specialist was fired
[*Aspects of the Theory of Syntax,* p. 130]

This discussion will illustrate the most important aspects of the base and will also suggest some alternative relations between the base and the semantic component. The relations of both the base and the semantic component to the phonological component remain unaltered.

(1)

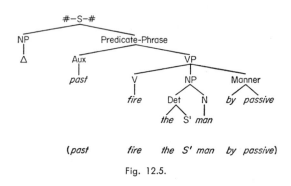

#–S–#
NP
Predicate-Phrase
Δ
Aux
VP
past
V
NP
Manner
fire
Det
N
by passive
the
S'
man
(past fire the S' man by passive)

Fig. 12.5.

(2)

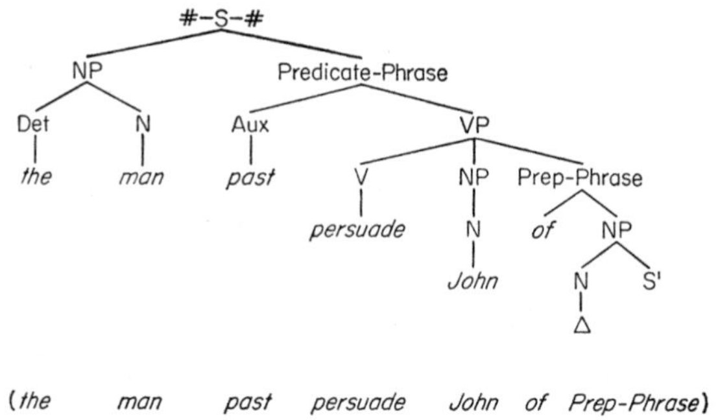

#–S–#
NP
Predicate-Phrase
Det
N
Aux
VP
the
man
past
V
NP
Prep-Phrase
persuade
N
of
NP
John
N
S'
Δ
(the man past persuade John of Prep-Phrase)

Fig. 12.6.

Diagram (5) is Chomsky's informal representation of a transformation-marker, detailing the transformations applied in (1), (2), and (3), to give the derived phrase marker of sentence (4), and ultimately its surface structure. Chomsky interprets this as follows:

First, apply the Passive transformation T_P to the base Phrase-marker (3); embed the result in the base Phrase-marker (2), in place of S′, by a generalized (double-base) substitution transformation T_E, giving a Phrase-marker for "the man persuaded John of △ John *nom* be examined by a specialist"; to this apply first T_D, which deletes the repeated NP "John," and then T_{to}, which replaces "of △ *nom*" by "to," giving a Phrase-marker for "the man persuaded John to be examined by a specialist"; next embed this in the position of S′ in (1) by T_E; to this apply the relative transformation T_R, which permutes the embedded sentence with the following N and replaces the repeated phrase "the man" by "who," giving a Phrase-marker for "△ fired the man who persuaded John to be examined by a specialist by *passive*"; to this Phrase-marker apply the passive transformation and agent deletion (T_{AD}), giving (4). [*Aspects of the Theory of Syntax,* p. 131]

(3)

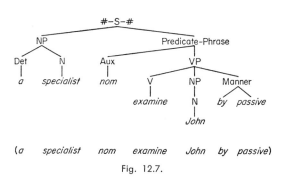

$(a \quad specialist \quad nom \quad examine \quad John \quad by \quad passive)$

Fig. 12.7.

(5)

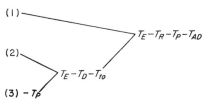

Fig. 12.8.

[*Aspects of the Theory of Syntax*, pp. 129–130]

Chomsky reports that, as a consequence of considerable research, several means have been suggested for simplifying the organization of the grammar, which will be worked out in detail as the work progresses. First, it has been recommended that many transformations which have been considered optional should be reformulated as obligatory for forms with suitable syntactic markers. It has also been appreciated that the sole function of transformations is to relate phrase markers, which have already been semantically interpreted, in a fixed way. The consequence is that transformations cannot introduce new semantic elements, and the semantic interpretation will be independent of all aspects of transformation markers, except insofar as they show how the base structures are interrelated.

Second, it has been noted that singular transformations are generally subject to ordering, while generalized transformations are not. This suggests that the notions "generalized transformation" and "transformation marker" should be eliminated, so that when there is a phrase marker where "sentence" can be introduced (for example, (1) and (2) above), the position is filled by #S#, which initiates derivations, and the ordered rules of the base apply as usual:

We have thus revised the theory of the base by allowing #S# to appear on the right in certain branching rules, where previously the dummy symbol S′ had appeared, and by allowing the rules to reapply (preserving their order) to the newly introduced occurrences of #S#.

[*Aspects of the Theory of Syntax*, p. 134]

In addition to the rules of the base with these modifications, the grammar now has a linear sequence of singulary transformations, which are applied to the constituent sentences before embedding and to the matrix sentences after the embedding.

Thus the syntactic component consists of a base that generates deep structures and a transformational part that maps them into surface structures. The deep structure of a sentence is submitted to the semantic component for semantic interpretation, and its surface structure enters the phonological component and undergoes phonetic interpretation.

[*Aspects of the Theory of Syntax*, p. 135]

As a consequence of this refinement Chomsky has no need for transformation markers, generalized transformations, or projection rules, on the assumption that (1) the semantic interpretation of a sentence depends only on its lexical items and the grammatical relations and functions of the underlying structures; (2) the base contains a categorial component that is context-free, specifying the grammatical relations and functions; and (3) the lexicon in the base characterizes the individual properties of particular lexical items that are inserted in specified positions in the base phrase markers.

Another consequence of these refinements may appear quite surprising, although it has always been inherent in the relation of the transformational component to the phrase-structure part: the transformational rules "act as a 'filter' that permits only certain generalized Phrase-markers to qualify as deep structures" (*Aspects of the Theory of Syntax*, p. 139). That is, a sequence of base phrase markers could have been selected that could not underlie any sentence, and application of certain transformations could cancel each other out or cause some other kind of block because of inconsistencies: "If none of the transformations blocks, we derive in this way a well-formed surface structure" (*Aspects of the Theory of Syntax*, p. 143).

Chomsky shows that the form of the grammar may be as follows:

A grammar contains a syntactic component, a semantic component, and a phonological component. The latter two are purely interpretive; they play no part in the recursive generation of sentence structures. The syntactic component consists of a base [a sequence of context-free rewriting rules] and a transformational component [a sequence of singulary transformations]. . . . The base, in turn, consists of a categorial subcomponent and a lexicon [an unordered set of lexical entries and certain redundancy rules]. . . .

Each lexical entry is a set of features . . . [some] . . . phonological . . . [some] . . . semantic. . . . We call a feature "semantic" if it is not mentioned in any syntactic rule. . . . Thus the lexical entries constitute the full set of irregularities in the language.

The base generates deep structures [an infinite set of generalized Phrase-markers]. A deep structure enters the semantic component and receives a semantic interpretation; it is mapped by the transformational rules into a surface structure, which is then given a phonetic interpretation by the phonological component. Thus the grammar assigns semantic interpretations to signals, this association being mediated by the recursive rules of the syntactic component.

[*Aspects of the Theory of Syntax*, pp. 141 and 142]

Conclusions

Chomsky specifies the conditions that a theory of language and of linguistic structure must meet if it is to be adequate both as a description and as an explanation:

1. It must contain a universal phonetic theory that defines the notion "possible sentence."
2. It must contain a definition of "possible structural description."
3. It should contain a definition of "generative grammar."
4. It should contain a method for determining what the structural description of a sentence is, given a grammar.
5. It should provide a way of evaluating alternative proposed grammars.

He is convinced that the first four requirements must be met by a linguistic theory in order to be considered an adequate descriptive device. In his view all phrase-structure grammars so far proposed fail to meet these criteria. In order for a linguistic theory to give an adequate explanation, it must also meet the last-named criterion.

If we assume that we are making real progress in linguistics as we become better at defining linguistic units and linguistic levels, as well as in relating the units of various levels to each other in a systematic way, then it is obvious that the work of Chomsky represents an attainment of the highest degree. It also gives promise of considerable further development.

In Chomsky's own view, "Real progress in linguistics consists in the discovery that certain features of given languages can be reduced to universal properties of language, and explained in terms of these deeper aspects of linguistic form" (*Aspects of the Theory of Syntax*, p. 35).

Review Questions

1. Explain the basic requirements for the construction of a scientific theory and relate them to grammar.
2. Explain the criteria for the selection of the "correct" theory.
3. What are some possible goals for linguistic theory?
4. Relate de Saussure's distinction between *la langue* and *la parole* to Chomsky's distinction between a speaker's competence and his performance.
5. Distinguish substantial and formal universals in language.
6. In what sense would you accept the sentence, *Colorless green ideas sleep furiously* as grammatical? What definition of grammar would require you to reject it as ungrammatical?
7. Construct a finite state grammar that will produce the equivalent of *The (old) (old) man comes* and *The (old) (old) men come* in another language you know and point out the problems involved.
8. Give an example of embedding from other languages you know.
9. Write a derivation, with the associated diagram, according to specific grammatical rules for the equivalent of *The man hit the ball* in other languages you know.
10. Why can phrase-structure representation be considered as a single level of linguistic analysis?
11. What is the problem for phrase-structure grammars in the formation of new sentences by (a) embedding (b) conjunction?
12. In what sense can the transformational rules for dealing with verbal auxiliaries in English be considered a "simplification"?
13. List some of the limitations of phrase-structure grammars in dealing with a language like English.
14. Sketch the basic outline of a transformational grammar as presented in Chomsky's *Syntactic Structures*.
15. How do the rules of the phrase-structure component differ from those of the transformational and morphophonemic components?
16. Give some of the simplifications a transformational component can introduce into the description of English.
17. How are the notions "understanding a sentence" and "level of linguistic analysis" related?
18. Explain the distinction between lexical and grammatical meaning.
19. What is the distinction between deep and surface structure?
20. Sketch the revised version of a transformational grammar and explain the difficulties involved in defining the components.
21. How does the information given by traditional grammar in examples (2i), (2ii), and (2iii) differ?
22. What is the distinction between morphemes and formatives?
23. How can notions like "subject of," "object of," and "main verb of" be formally established? What are the problems?

24. Give some advantages of separating the lexicon and grammar.
25. Give some of the problems and advantages of subcategorizing nouns and verbs in the lexicon, grammar, or semantic component.
26. Explain the basic functions of (a) the syntactic component, (b) the semantic component, and (c) the phonological component.
27. Give an original example of a dictionary entry like that for *bachelor* (Fig. 5).
28. Explain the operation of the projection rules.
29. Explain the difference between singulary and generalized transformations.
30. Explain the suggested simplifications of the transformational grammar and their advantages.

Suggested Readings

Bach, E., *An Introduction to Transformational Grammars* (New York, 1964).

Bolinger, D., "The Atomization of Meaning," *Language,* 41 (1965), 555–573.

Chomsky, N., *Aspects of the Theory of Syntax* (Cambridge, Mass., 1965).

———, *Current Issues in Linguistic Theory* (The Hague, 1965).

———, Review of B. F. Skinner's "Verbal Behavior" (1957), *Language,* 35 (1959).

———, *Syntactic Structures* (The Hague, 1957).

Katz, J. J., and J. Fodor, *The Structure of Language* (Englewood Cliffs, N.J., 1964).

Katz J. J., and P. Postal, *An Integrated Theory of Linguistic Descriptions* (Cambridge, Mass., 1964).

Lees, R. B., Review of N. Chomsky's *Syntactic Structures* (1957), *Language,* 33 (1957).

Postal, P., *Constituent Structure: A Study of Contemporary Models of Syntactic Description* (Bloomington, Ind., 1964).

———, "Underlying and Superficial Linguistic Structure," *Harvard Educational Review,* 34 (1964).

13

Summary and Conclusions

The preceding chapters of this book are organized to show that there are lines of investigation which have constantly recurred in the study of language, from the most ancient to modern times. One of the differentiating factors at different periods of language study has been a shift in purpose and interest, which has either heightened the value of preceding work and developed it or ignored the progress already made and resulted in a less satisfactory view of language.

Among the ancients the main purpose in studying language was for the development of logic. Initially this study aimed at establishing a formal, quasi-automatic method for arriving at accurate definitions (Plato) or at a method by which the accuracy of arguments and the truth of their conclusions could be checked (Aristotle and the Stoics). Plato's work resulted in a clear difficulty: his divisions were made on an intuitive either-or basis, and such divisions required more information than a person who wanted to use the method for resolving doubts would normally possess. It is instructive to examine the means by which Aristotle and the Stoics were able to advance beyond this point. Their work, as well as that of later linguists, illustrates one of the conditions for progress in language study: the introduction of more defining criteria for the units under discussion. In the case of Aristotle the subjects and predicates of syllogisms were "quantified" through the use of the *syndesmoi,* and a more flexible range of combinations was thus introduced, which could handle either necessary or contingent facts. The Stoics studied logical relations expressed in a more varied set of sentence types than the categoric syllogisms of Aristotle, and, therefore, brought more units and levels of analysis into consideration.

It is clear that the work of the logicians was not grammatical in intent, although their terminology (especially that of the Stoics) became part of the grammatical tradition. What they had in common with all studies of language was an interest in correct combinations. The criteria by which correctness was established, as well as the terms of the combinations, varied considerably from one study to the next. In rhetoric correct combinations were those that moved the audience to action. In logic correct combinations were those that yielded valid syllogisms or true conclusions. In both cases such correctness can be called, in de Saussure's terms, a "motivated" correctness, which appeals to nonlinguistic factors; in formal grammatical work the basis for correctness is, again in de Saussure's terms, only "relatively motivated," since the source of motivation is intralinguistic. That is, linguistic combinations are called correct because they usually show a formal analogy to other linguistic combinations, and this similarity is what is meant by the structural patterns of the language. To that extent a grammar is independent of meaning, although there may be many parallels between the linguistic and non-linguistic structures.

The formal approach to the study of grammar was found first in the work of Dionysius Thrax, whose pioneering approach shows the characteristics of all scientific work on language. His grammar was formal (only the conjunctions were defined on the basis of extralinguistic criteria alone), and its stated aims included the search for the analogies (the intralinguistic regularities) of Greek. We have seen that the notion of analogy is readily translatable into our current formulations of "structure" and "levels of analysis," since an analogy is a relation of similarity between terms that may differ more or less widely in some respect, but where the differences are ignored for the sake of the perceived unity the statement of the analogy gives us. Just as analogies can be considered more powerful and interesting the more differences they enable us to ignore, so too the definitions of language units are more interesting and useful when we can relate them to more units and to units on other levels of analysis.

The Roman adaptation of Greek grammar marked a basic departure from Thrax's approach. This different approach has helped characterize traditional grammar. Instead of concentrating on form, as did Thrax, the Romans took the meaning categories used by the Greeks as basic to defining parts of Latin and seemed to think that there was some prelinguistic, or extralinguistic, set of meaning types in terms of which language should be analyzed. Priscian claimed this view to be the basis for grammatical work. The fact that he did not (and really could not) apply this criterion exclusively in practice actually tended to obscure what the grammarian does in describing a language. When he relied on semantic criteria alone, his statements about Latin are often illogical or wrong. Using semantic criteria, he stated that the nominative form of the noun is basic. This is clearly incorrect for many nouns. He was guilty of his greatest failure as a grammarian when he denied the clear morphological analysis of forms like *vires* into the morphemes represented by *vir-* and *-es*. The possibility of this analysis was denied because he could not justify it on semantic grounds.

The medieval period contributed little to the study of linguistic form as such and so continued some of the ambiguity inherent in the ancient work, especially in the application of morphological terms. A persistent source of difficulty was the lack of an adequate system of phonetics, which would have enabled the medievals to analyze the typical root-plus-affix construction of Latin or Greek morphology in a consistent way. They discussed word endings, but were unable to specify where roots ended and suffixes began. Instead, they developed the psychological theory implicit in the traditional semantic-grammatical definitions and correlated it with current metaphysical doctrines. The Modistae, in particular, saw that there was no isomorphism among the formal categories (modes of signification), the psychological categories (modes of understanding), and the metaphysical categories (modes of being). It was a commonplace among the dialecticians of this period that an argument should be about things, not words, but that a careful study of language is required in order to insure against being misled by resemblances among expressions that do not correspond to resemblances among the things discussed.

Such extensive technical study of the properties of terms, and particularly the distinction made between signification and supposition, was an activity repugnant to the humanists, particularly those at Orleans, who had long fought against the logicization of all studies that developed in Paris from the eleventh to the early fourteenth century. This Aristotelian-Scholastic logic was conceived as a study of *formal* relations, but was expressed in the Latin language and was, therefore, subject to restrictions peculiar to the grammar of that language, even though it was used in a technical and restricted sense. Renaissance humanists derided the latinity of the medieval schoolmen as well as the study of language in and for itself. The medievals did not take the ancient authors as the norm of grammatical and stylistic correctness. They knowingly preferred the usage of contemporary authors to the ancient models. The study of logic began to be considered a study of the laws of thought, and not of the workings of a formal system independent of actual usage, and when the traditional material of logic was discussed, it was under the tautological expression "formal logic." This perversion of the term lasted until well into the nineteenth century, when the work of Frege and his successors restored the direction initiated by the pre-Renaissance logicians. But in the nineteenth century, under the influence of mathematics, logic became a study of formal relations among symbols that were not taken from a natural language, and which were, therefore, considered independent of the capricious restrictions imposed by natural languages. The lack of sympathy between the logicians and humanists of the medieval period is not unlike the split between the linguistic and traditional conceptions concerning the definition of a grammar and the role of the linguist.

The prescriptivists of the eighteenth century had no quarrel with the established conceptions of language. They admitted that languages are arbitrary and conventional systems and recognized that usage alone makes a particular word, or combination of words, "correct." But authors were becoming increasingly sensitive to the variety of usage they observed and thus sought to establish norms of correctness in orthography, pronunciation, and grammar. The works of Johnson and Lowth were seen as authoritative answers to this need, and the legitimate place of such works in a literate society seems unquestionable. However, it no longer seems defensible that the idiosyncratic imposition of personal preferences can be tolerated in modern lexicography and grammar. While there is always the need for some authority or group of authorities to decide what is "good taste," there is also a need for accurate information concerning how people actually use language. The descriptive linguist as such cannot supply the good taste, but he can supply the facts. Linguists have sometimes been considered too permissive by grammatical purists, since the linguist merely reports the forms he finds in use. The imposition of prescriptive norms without the facts of actual usage seems as undesirable a procedure as the alleged permissive acceptance of forms because they are used.

The nineteenth-century work on the relation between the classical and modern languages shifted the focus of controversy and provided a field in which many of the long-lived prejudices about the nature of grammar had a lesser place. The development of articulatory phonetics during this period represents one of the most significant advances in the history of linguistic science, since it enabled scholars to see that sounds which otherwise might be conceived as wholly different can be analyzed into constituents shared by more than one sound. Such work, in turn, aided in distinguishing between the root and affix. In addition, the advances in articulatory phonetics made it possible to formulate more accurately the regularities that underlie the variable forms of words in the classical languages, since it could be seen that only certain properties of sounds, and not the entire sounds themselves, are altered when forms are composed or when sounds change with time. The result was a more rational and revealing view of the morphology of the classical and modern languages.

We have come to the modern period, which began with de Saussure. From his time until recently the basic problems of linguistics and the framework in which problems are discussed remained substantially the same. While there have been many developments that might appear to be revolutionary, there is more continuity of viewpoint and development than would appear on the surface. To bring this out it will be more convenient here to review the topics and problems examined by the linguists discussed above.

PHONETICS AND PHONOLOGY

Until the nineteenth century the phonetic information and methods of description were of the most rudimentary kind. In the modern authors we have considered we find illustrations of the use of the two most reliable kinds of phonetic description developed: articulatory phonetics and acoustic, or instrumental, phonetics. According to his editors, de Saussure was familiar with the phonetic works of Sievers, Jespersen, and Roudet.[1] In discussing phonology de Saussure employed the symbols used by Jespersen, providing a specification of the various places and manners of articulation, as well as the degree of aperture (particularly in oral articulations) and the presence or absence of voicing and nasality.

Boas, Sapir, Bloomfield, and Firth all used a type of articulatory phonetics such as that found in the *Principles of the International Phonetic Association,* developed by Henry Sweet and Paul Passy (who founded the Association).[2]

The International Phonetic Alphabet is perhaps the most widely used set of symbols for phonetic transcription, particularly in Europe (Table 5). The upper half of the table contains a section of consonant symbols, distinguished across the top according to the place of articulation, and down the side by the manner of articulation. The lower section indicates the vowel symbols, distinguished as close (high), half-close, half-open, and open (low); and as front, central, and back, and rounded or unrounded. The bottom half consists of other sounds and "modifiers" such as indications of nasality, breathiness, voicing, and so on. (By convention the

---

[1] E. Sievers, *Grundzüge der Phonetik* (Leipzig, 1904); J. O. Jespersen, *Lehrbuch der Phonetik* (Leipzig, 1904); Paul Roudet, *Elements de phonologie générale* (Paris, 1910).

[2] See *Principles of the International Phonetic Association* (London, 1949).

Table 5: The International Phonetic Alphabet

CONSONANTS

	Bi-labial	Labio-dental	Dental and Alveolar	Retroflex	Palato-alveolar	Alveolo-palatal	Palatal	Velar	Uvular	Pharyngal	Glottal
Plosive	p b		t d	ʈ ɖ			c ɟ	k g	q ɢ		ʔ
Nasal	m	ɱ	n	ɳ			ɲ	ŋ	N		
Lateral Fricative			ɬ ɮ								
Lateral Non-fricative			l	ɭ			ʎ				
Rolled			r						ʀ		
Flapped			ɾ	ɽ					ʀ		
Fricative	ɸ β	f v	θ ð s z ɹ	ʂ ʐ	ʃ ʒ	ɕ ʑ	ç j	x ɣ	χ ʁ	ħ ʕ	h ɦ
Frictionless Continuants and Semi-vowels	w ɥ	ʋ	ɹ				j (ɥ)	(w)	ʁ		

VOWELS

		Front	Central	Back	
Close	(y ʉ u)	i y	ɨ ʉ	ɯ u	
Half-close	(ø o)	e ø		ɤ o	
Half-open	(œ ɔ)	ɛ œ	ɜ	ʌ ɔ	
Open	(ɒ)	æ	a	ɑ ɒ	

(Secondary articulations are shown by symbols in brackets.)

OTHER SOUNDS.—Palatalized consonants: ƫ, ɖ, etc. Velarized or pharyngalized consonants: ɫ, đ, ẕ, etc. Ejective consonants (plosives with simultaneous glottal stop): p', t', etc. Implosive voiced consonants: ɓ, ɗ, etc. ř fricative trill. σ, ʑ (labialized θ, ð, or s, z). ɋ, ʒ (labialized ʃ, ʒ). ʇ, ʗ, ʖ (clicks, Zulu c, q, x). ɺ (a sound between r and l). ʍ (voiceless w). ɪ, ʏ, ʊ (lowered varieties of i, y, u). ɹ (a variety of ə). ɵ (a vowel between ø and o).

Affricates are normally represented by groups of two consonants (ts, tʃ, dʒ, etc.), but, when necessary, ligatures are used (ʦ, ʧ, ʤ, etc.), or the marks ‿ or ͡ (t͡s or t͡ʃ, etc.). c, ɟ may occasionally be used in place of tʃ, dʒ. Aspirated plosives: ph, th, etc.

LENGTH, STRESS, PITCH.—ː (full length). · (half length). ˈ (stress, placed at beginning of the stressed syllable). ˌ (secondary stress). ˉ (high level pitch); ˍ (low level); ˊ (high rising); ˏ (low rising); ˋ (high falling); ˎ (low falling); ˆ (rise-fall); ˇ (fall-rise). See Écriture phonétique internationale, p. 9.

MODIFIERS.—˜ nasality. ˳ breath (ḷ = breathed l). ˬ voice (ş = z). ʻ slight aspiration following p, t, etc. ˌ specially close vowel (ẹ = a very close e). ˏ specially open vowel (ẹ = a rather open e). ̫ labialization (n̫ = labialized n). ̪ dental articulation (t̪ = dental t). ˓ palatalization (z̧ = ʑ). ˔ tongue slightly raised. ˕ tongue slightly lowered. ˒ lips more rounded. ˓ lips more spread. ʃ variety of ʃ resembling s, etc. Central vowels ï (= ɨ), ü (= ʉ), ë (= ə˔), ö (= ɵ), ɛ̈, ɔ̈, (e.g. n̩) syllabic consonant. ˘ consonantal vowel.

SOURCE: Louis H. Gray, *Foundations of Language* (New York: The Macmillan Company, 1939). Reprinted by permission of Crowell Collier and Macmillan, Inc.

consonant symbols written to the left are voiceless, those to the right in the same set are voiced.)

In the revised version of Chomsky's *Aspects of the Theory of Syntax* he noted that a probable way of representing sentences will be through the use of Jakobson's distinctive features arranged in matrices.[3] These distinctive features can be described in either articulatory or acoustic terms and would include the contrasts between vocalic and nonvocalic, consonantal and nonconsonantal, grave and nongrave, flat and nonflat, and so on. This method of representing sounds in terms of the features that compose them is apparently not segmental in the same sense as phonemes or the symbols of the International Phonetic Alphabet, but it is based on essentially the same kind of analysis. Such segments can be taken as the unit being analyzed into simultaneous features, rather than a syllable or some larger unit being analyzed into successive segments. Since the "features" are distinctive features, this approach can still be called phonemic in an extended sense. The role of allophones in such a system will be slightly different, however, as will that of morpho-phonemics, since the spelling of lexical items will be assigned, in the revised version of the generative grammar, in the lexicon, which will specify any alterations not called for by predictable phonological rules. The phonological rules apply cyclically first to the minimal elements (formatives) and then to the constituents of which these are parts, and so on until the maximal domain of a phonological process is reached.

In Chapter 5 of *Language* Bloomfield pointed out that we can study language without referring to meaning problems on only the phonetic level, and that phonology involves the examination of meanings. Phonology need not be identical with phonemics. It seems clear that a linguist's stand on meaning questions is directly related to his position in phonology. Phonemics, for example, as generally applied, takes the phoneme to be a fundamental unit because it distinguishes one *lexical* meaning from another. That is, morphemes and words can be distinguished because of the contrast in the phonemes by which they are represented. If the fundamental unit of phonology is not to be defined on the basis of its signaling only lexical differences, then a different kind of unit, or more than a single kind of unit, can be established. Such is the case with Firth, who divided questions of meaning on a different basis from that used in other studies. He recognized that there are phonetic, phonological, lexical, grammatical, and contextual levels of meaning and then set up phonetic correlations for all of them.

The purpose of the phonological study will also contribute to the

---

[3] See R. Jakobson, and M. Halle, *Preliminaries to Speech Analysis* (Cambridge, Mass., 1952); and M. Halle, "On the Bases of Phonology," in J. J. Katz and J. Fodor, eds., *The Structure of Language* (Englewood Cliffs, N.J., 1964).

selection of an apt unit. The subtitle of Pike's classic text *Phonemics* is *A Technique for Reducing Languages to Writing*.[4] Traditionally the best writing systems have been alphabetic or syllabic. The phonemic technique is of the alphabetic type. If the purpose of a phonology is not to provide a writing system, then a different unit can be expected to be more useful. It was not Firth's purpose to establish a usable orthography through his prosodic approach. By the same token it is not for orthographic purposes that Chomsky leans toward the use of Jakobson's distinctive features as the phonetic representation of the sentence his grammar produces. Neither Chomsky nor Firth take the anthropologist's discovery procedure, although this method has been a significant factor in the development of American linguistics. Boas, Sapir, and Bloomfield were interested in techniques for learning and describing languages unknown to the linguist at the beginning of his work in the same terms, and the phonemic technique allows us to learn the distinctive sounds of a language by comparing minimal pairs, of which words are the most manageable instances. The approach of both Chomsky and Firth is more adaptable to the analysis of a language we already know well than to the discovery of the phonological system of a language of which we are ignorant.

With these considerations in mind we can review the basic phonological positions of the various authors we have examined. De Saussure employed the term "phoneme," but not without a certain amount of ambiguity.[5] On the one hand it would appear that the phoneme is an entity in *la langue*, since it is obtained by analyzing *signifiants*. On the other hand "phoneme" is a term used for entities of *la parole*, and sometimes for vowels or consonants in general. As an entity of *la langue* the phoneme would not have to be defined in terms of positive phonetic properties, since it would be a point of difference only; but as an entity of *la parole* exact positive phonetic criteria would be required. An additional problem arises out of the fact that de Saussure did not consider the distinction between lexical and grammatical meaning to be convincing.

Sapir did not use the term "phoneme" in his *Language*, but in a footnote he proposed the view he developed elsewhere that the phoneme is an "ideal sound" at which we aim in pronunciation, but fail to produce exactly as we intend or in exactly the same fashion as we hear it.[6]

---

[4] Kenneth L. Pike, *Phonemics: A Technique for Reducing Language to Writing* (Ann Arbor, Mich., 1947).

[5] See Robert Godel, *Les Sources Manuscrites du Cours de Linguistique Générale* (Paris, 1957).

[6] Edward Sapir, *Language* (New York, 1921), p. 56, footnote 16. See also Sapir's "Sound Patterns in Language" and "The Psychological Reality of the Phoneme," in David G. Mandelbaum, ed., *Selected Writings Of Edward Sapir* (Berkeley, Calif., 1949).

He did not discuss the distinction between lexicon and grammar, nor the role of the phoneme in view of this distinction, but the examples he gave indicate that he based phonemic distinction on lexical differences.

It is interesting to note that Boas, who perhaps exerted the greatest influence on the linguistic formation of Sapir, considered that the distinction made between lexicon and grammar was a consequence of the accidental proportion of root to affixed morphemes in the IE languages. On this matter Boas is close to the opinion of de Saussure.

In Bloomfield the nature and function of the phoneme, as well as the criteria by which it is established, are clearer. He distinguished primary (segmental) and secondary (suprasegmental) phonemes, and these are discovered by comparing minimal pairs of lexical items to establish the primary phonemes, and usually pairs of lexical items or sentences to establish the secondary phonemes. In both cases the phoneme is not a "sound" (that is, an actual disturbance of the air or the articulatory movements with all their factual components, acoustic or articulatory) but a feature of the sound by which one meaning is distinguished from another. These minimal units of distinctive sound feature are always accompanied by the nondistinctive, and, therefore, the phoneme as such cannot be pronounced. In his list of English phonemes Bloomfield did not include open internal juncture (plus juncture) as a phoneme, although he discussed the phenomenon in terms of open and close transition.

A consequence of the phonemic approach is the notion of redundancy; that is, more signals are given than are minimally required for distinguishing between phonemically different utterances. Besides the phenomenon of grammatical redundancy (for example, the use of numerical expressions as well as plural concord in English), allophonic differences are considered redundant from the phonemic point of view. Firth objected to the notion of redundancy, since in his system predictable phonetic features are to be assigned to meaningful features not necessarily on the lexical level. He posited two fundamental phonological units, the phonematic unit and the prosody. The prosodies include features that would often be considered allophonic in the phonemic system, such as English nasalization, aspiration, and palatalization. The phonematic units, even in this system, are most easily discovered by commutation of minimal pairs on the lexical level, but phonematic units are definitely not to be confused with phonemes commonly used to represent them. One difference between the phonematic units (which usually stand at least for the place and manner of articulation) and the IPA segments is the convention that assigns voice or voicelessness by contrast in the position of the symbol in the chart and by the choice of symbol (for example, p or b). A prosody of voicing or voicelessness could contain in its domain, in this system, either a *p* or *b* phonematic unit. The prosodies are also comparable to the "modifiers" in the IPA chart and often share the same labels, for example, "breathiness" and "palatalization"; the IPA diacritics are designed to apply to single segments, whereas the prosodies are ordinarily stated for more than a single segment or phonematic unit. It is clear that the difference in prosodic and phonemic phonology is a consequence of a purpose different from that of the Pikean approach; no one would claim that prosodic analysis provides us with a handy way of writing a language.

Hjelmslev had no need to discuss phonology at length in the *Prolegomena,* but he pointed out that phonological units, insofar as they are elements of system or process, can be defined in terms of the relations of interdependence, constellation, and determination.

Chomsky seems to take two different positions concerning phonology. In *Syntactic Structures* he does not reject the phonemic representation of sentences as a valid level of linguistic analysis, although he does cast doubt on the validity of distinguishing between lexical and grammatical meaning. He also suggests there that the morphophonemic component can represent sentences in the proper sequence of either phonemes or morphophonemes. In subsequent work Chomsky rejects phonemics as a valid level of linguistic representation of a sentence. One reason for this rejection is his negative attitude toward an alleged argument from perception that supports use of phonemics. This argument suggests that speakers first recognize the lexical items of which sentences are composed and understand the sentence through the lexical items and their grammatical relations. Chomsky believes that speakers understand sentences through their initial perception of the grammatical relations, to which analysis of the lexical content is secondary. It is not necessarily to be concluded from this statement that Chomsky denies the usefulness of phonemics in linguistic work any more than he rejects the value of discovery procedures. He is merely calling attention to the difference between a manual of descriptive procedures and a linguistic theory. While Chomsky believes that such procedures are desirable, he points out in *Syntactic Structures* that they should ideally be based on an adequate linguistic theory.

MEANING

Whatever else is clear about the difficult problems connected with meaning—and here one finds the most astounding varieties of confusion—it is an inescapable fact that meaning entails a relation. The real difficulty is that meaning involves a very complex set of relations.

In dealing with meaning, therefore, it is necessary to identify (1) the kind of terms that are to be considered in the relations, (2) the number of such terms to be dealt with, and (3) the type of relation or relations to be discussed. For the linguist one obvious term in such relations is a linguistic unit, and the number and types of other terms in the relation(s) are then to be determined. Chomsky shows in *Syntactic Structures* that one approach to such problems has been through a consideration of differential meaning or, more generally, through an appeal to differential function. A phoneme or a morpheme can be established in this way by discovering that phonemic or morphophonemic contrasts signal differences in meaning. The difference between the phonemes and morphemes in this approach is that the phonemes, as such, are not considered to have a recurrent connection with a constant aspect of the nonlinguistic environments in which they occur, while the morpheme is a unit that does or can have such a relation.

Depending on the kind of relation discussed, we have two fundamentally different sorts of meaning statements. The first tells us what meaning *is*—for example, a concept. The second tells us *how* meaning is to be described, whatever it *is*—for example, by enumerating the other units of the same kind that contrast with a given unit in some environment. There is a further development of this notion of describing rather than defining meanings, and that is a statement about what meaningful language *does,* whatever it *is.* In the authors we have studied we have found one or the other of these approaches used, and sometimes a combination of them.

De Saussure approached meaning by discussing both what it is and how it is to be described. His understanding of meaning coincides with the traditional dualistic approach outlined in the medieval period, except that he did not go into any details concerning the psychological elements involved. His identification of the sign as an association of an acoustic image and a concept merely suggests the framework within which his use of the term "concept" makes sense. His insistence that all facts of language (with the exception of signification, the positive association of the acoustic image and the concept) are facts of value, and, therefore, differential, could align him with the purely differential approach to meaning. When suggesting how meaning is to be described he appealed to the linear nature of the sign, which can be investigated according to the associative and syntagmatic relations that every part of language must contract. This view gave rise to the fruitful distinction that can be made among signification, value, and content, concepts that make the most sense when meaning is considered to be basically referential—that is, a naming relation.

Sapir followed the traditional, referential discussion of meaning, and made this point of view cardinal to his entire concept of language. For him sentences are linguistic representations of propositions. The basic concept types by which human language is defined take the type of reference into account, and he summed up the whole traditional position on meaning by saying that "ideation reigns supreme in language." Although Sapir's conception of what meaning is departs little from the Aristotelian position, his method for describing it is distinctly modern. He noted that meaning may or may not be an actual term in relation to linguistic forms, that the form of language alone remains constant, and, therefore, can and should be studied for itself alone. Like his traditional predecessors and some of his successors, for example, Chomsky, Sapir believed that there are pervasive and important aspects of language which are universal. In particular he held that the latent content of all languages is the same: the science of experience, which is variously formed in the structure of the language in which it is communicated. This implies a departure from the original Aristotelian doctrine that things, and, therefore, concepts, are the same for all men.

Bloomfield deals with meaning in both fashions. His explanation of what meaning is amounts to a crude form of associationism. According to this view, meaning is basically referential, but the mechanism by which a linguistic unit refers is not via conceptualization or intellectual classification but through a kind of Pavlovian conditioning that underlies Watson's behaviorism. Consistent with this view, we are to describe meanings in terms of the relevant and partial aspects of the situations in which linguistic forms regularly occur. This is not a very satisfactory or informative process, however, since for Bloomfield "science" is the sole source of definitive meanings, and he saw that it has progressed little in defining the most common linguistic expressions. As a consequence, we are to "act as though" science had so progressed and confine linguistic study to the distribution of meaningful signals, since distribution is at least the surest indication of differential function. Form classes, established through distribution, have constant, positive meaning types, and substitutes share that meaning. Makeshift statements of meaning are made through pointing, paraphrase, or translation or in terms of practical events. The distinction between central and derived meanings seems universal and can be explained through the concept of density of communication. Not all members of a speech community actually interact through their language, so that meanings central for one group can be marginal for another. Meanings are said to change, depending on the usage of the successive prestige groups.

Firth avoided using a psychological approach to meaning, not necessarily because he did not believe in mind, ideas, and the like but because such concepts are disputed, and he did not think he needed them for the kind of statements of meaning he made. He considered his divisions theoretical constructs to be applied to language and believed that their usefulness would determine whether they were to be rejected or accepted. He compared meaning in language to light passing through a prism. Although from one point of view meaning can be considered one thing, using his levels of meaning enables us to discuss various components of meaning, analogous to the prism's dispersion of white light into distinctive color bands. The terms in his meaning relations vary. On the level of phonetic meaning the basic terms are the speaker and the noises he makes, and phonetic meaning informs us more about the speaker than what he is speaking about. The terms in phonological meaning are principally phonematic units, prosodies, and meaning differences. Phonematic units can be established on the lexical level through the usual method of commutation, marking differences in lexical meaning. These units can also be signals on the syntagmatic level of differences in style, because of the consonant-vowel clusters that are characteristic of different styles or because of the the co-occurrence of certain phonematic or prosodic units that are syntagmatic signals of different styles. On the lexical level the basic terms in relation are lexical items and their referents, and through this relation we can be informed about the aspects of the speaker's environment to which he reacts or upon which he is acting. Syntagmatically collocations are also relevant to stylistic meaning differences. Grammatical meanings have grammatical categories, not lexical items, as the terms of their meaning relation, and the functions are both differential and referential. The terms in the two contextual levels of meaning are the relevant aspects of speaker and environment, with both differential and referential functions involved. This treatment is very similar to Bloomfield's, but Firth's extra, social level of context appeals beyond the individual contexts Bloomfield seemed to envisage.

Hjelmslev's approach to meaning resembles and at the same time differs from de Saussure's. In de Saussure's conception of language the notion of value, a network of contrasts, is paramount. Applied to meaning this notion led him to the distinction between signification (the association of a concept and an acoustic image) and content (the statement of meaning that takes into account the positive fact of signification and the negative element of contrast which value-study stresses, especially between terms in two languages that have the same signification). It was pointed out that the distinctions among signification, value, and content as explained in the study of de Saussure are not explicit in his treatment but are consonant with his teaching. In Hjelmslev there is no discussion of concepts involved in signification, and the connection between Saussurean signification and the notion of purport in Hjelmslev can be understood in this way: in signification there is a relation between a concept and a referent, as well as between a concept and an acoustic image. Hjelmslev's purport is the referent of a concept in de Saussure's system. Now, even though it is possible for two languages to have the same signification (that is, linguistic items that refer to the same thing, as in English *sheep* or *mutton* and French *mouton*), still, divorced from the system of both languages, there really is no determinate "thing" to which either refers. We can profitably compare de Saussure's distinction among value, content, and signification with the distinction Hjelmslev made among linguistic schema, linguistic usage, and purport. The linguistic schema is a pure set of relations (values); linguistic usage is this set of relations as holding among referents (content); purport is the as yet unorganized, unstructured, amorphous realm of things that can be meant (the referent in in de Saussure's signification, but here divorced from the linguistic system). It is interesting to see a mixture of both anomaly and analogy in Hjelmslev's approach. On the level of purport we find complete anomaly; on the level of linguistic schema or usage, analogy. Another peculiarity of this approach is the search for *figurae* on both the expression and content planes. On the level of expression the *figurae* are the nonsign constituents of signs (for example, phonemes), but on the level of content they are the more generic sign components of more specific signs. Instead of assigning to the *figurae* the meanings of the classes for which they substitute, the meaning of these items is discussed in terms of the *figurae*.

Chomsky in *Syntactic Structures* foresaw the possibility of incorporating a semantic theory into the transformational approach to grammar, but he was not primarily concerned with such problems. It is not possible to state what meaning is or how it is to be described from the discussion there. In later work he incorporated the semantic theory of Katz and Fodor, resulting in what appears to be an elegant, intralinguistic method of describing meaning without making a commitment to any of the disputed theories about what meaning is. The semantic markers are reminiscent of the *figurae* alluded to by Hjelmslev, and the process of amalgamation of readings suggests as well the restriction of supposition discussed by Petrus Hispanus. The inclusion of a semantic distinguisher, which is to appear once in the formalized dictionary entries, seems to involve a factor wholly lacking in previous genus-and-species–type analyses.

GRAMMAR

As noted previously, all students of language have been concerned primarily about correct linguistic combinations. The criterion for correctness has varied with the purpose of the study, with the result that various units for combinations, as well as different criteria for determining proper constructions, have been proposed. Depending on the purpose of the study, we can make a good or bad choice of fundamental units, and our implicit or explicit psychological conception of language (or lack of such a theory) will also affect the adequacy of our linguistic explanation. Linguists have proposed the morpheme, word, phrase, and sentence as the basic unit of study, from different points of view and for differing purposes. Paralleling these choices has been a conviction concerning the necessity or justifiability of distinguishing between the levels of lexical and grammatical meaning, and in grammar between morphology and syntax.

De Saussure did not believe any useful distinction could be made among lexicon, morphology, and syntax, since, according to his view, *la langue* is a system of pure values. For him such distinctions were linguistic identities (that is, distinctions the linguistic system allows, so that they could be recognized by means of the criteria proposed—for example, the dative case of English nouns), but not linguistic realities (that is, distinctions other than those the linguistic system itself demands). De Saussure reasoned as follows: the distinction between lexical and grammatical meaning is illusory, since what is grammatical in one language is lexical in another. One would have thought, however, that he would have noted that what is grammatical and part of *la langue* in one language can be lexical and part of *la parole* in another. His denial of the reality of a distinction between morphology and syntax seems better founded. He held such a distinction to be manifestly illusory, since it is impossible to separate the members of a morphological paradigm, such as a noun declension, without appealing to their distinctness in syntax. This follows directly from his definition of the sign as the association of a concept and an acoustic image, in which the unity of each is to be established through the unity of the other, by examining their syntagmatic and associative relations. For de Saussure, "Grammar is a question of a complex and systematic object governing the interplay of coexisting values. . . . Grammar studies language as a system of means of expression."[7]

It was not Sapir's intention to develop a thorough system of grammatical description in *Language,* and his description of grammar is like that of de Saussure: "grammar . . . is simply a generalized expression of the feeling that analogous concepts and relations are most conveniently symbolized in analogous forms" (p. 39). He did not discuss the validity of distinguishing among lexicon, morphology, and syntax, but his distinction of the four concept types and his proposed method of "algebraic"

---

[7] Ferdinand de Saussure, *A Course in General Linguistics,* trans. Wade Baskin (New York: Philosophical Library, 1959), p. 134.

classification of morphological constructions would suggest that he found such a distinction useful. His system of symbolizing morphological constructions amounts to a kind of immediate-constituent analysis; it is the order of immediate constituency, not the left-to-right order, that determines which letter to use.

Bloomfield proposed the most complete and consistent technique for describing a grammar up to his time. As for what grammar is, he used a behavioristic definition: "The grammar of a language, then, includes a very complex set of habits (taxemes of selection) by which every form is assigned to a certain form-class and is used only in certain conventional functions."[8] He did not discuss the validity of distinguishing among lexicon, morphology and syntax, but he did provide the norms by which lexicon and grammar, as he used the terms, can be distinguished, and then how morphology and syntax can be subdistinguished within grammar. For Bloomfield the lexicon is the list of all the meaningful forms of the language and their meanings. But differences in meaningful arrangements introduce distinctions not dealt with in the lexicon, and the study of these is the province of grammar. Morphology and syntax are distinguished according to the ICs of the constructions each studies. Only free forms can be the ICs of syntactic constructions, while bound forms may appear among the ICs of morphological constructions. Bloomfield pointed out that lexical items do not appear alone as such in actual language use but are always found with two or more of four taxemes: phonetic modification (*sit, sat, duke, duchess*); modulation (*Harry! Harry?*); selection (*Harry!, Run!*); and order (*Man bites dog, Dog bites man*).

In line with his descriptive, classificatory purposes Bloomfield developed a rigorous technique and terminology for classifying and comparing forms. First he discussed absolute and included positions of forms (according to whether or not the form is a member of a larger construction). Next, and as a result of the first step, he distinguished between free and bound forms and between basic and sandhi forms (according to their shape in absolute or included position). The alterations forms undergo in included position Bloomfield distinguished as obligatory (for example, the use of *a* before consonants and *an* before vowels) or optional (for example, /ə/ or /ey/ forms of the English article). Constructions, morphological and syntactic, are classified as endocentric (*John Smith, poor John, very quickly*) or exocentric (*John runs, to the town*), depending on whether the resultant construction has the same distribution as one, both, or neither of its ICs. Compounds are either syntactic or

8 Leonard Bloomfield, *Language*. Copyright 1933 by Henry Holt and Company; © 1961 by Leonard Bloomfield. Reprinted by permission of Holt, Rinehart and Winston, Inc.

asyntactic (*redcap, red cap, bottle opener, open the bottle*), depending on whether the morphological ICs are related in the same way as the syntactic ones. Bloomfield classified sentences into major and minor types on the basis of frequency. He gave subdivisions of sentence types semantic labels (actor-action, action-goal). He also suggested the order of grammatical description: phonetic, phonemic, morphological, syntactic, semantic. Bloomfield considered that semantic description would always be the weakest part of linguistics. The grammatical description of a language as he proposed it would, therefore, list the phonetic characteristics, the phonemic units, the morphemes and their meanings, the constructions of morphemes and words, and phrases and clauses according to the four taxemes, the principal sentence, and substitution types.

Firth added little to the study of grammar as the discipline is usually understood, and his discussion of meaning on the grammatical level is distinguished principally by his introduction of the term "colligation," which he employed to describe the linkage between grammatical categories, as opposed to collocation, the habitual associations between lexical items. Firth shifted the purposes and techniques of linguistic investigation in a novel and interesting way by pointing out a scheme according to which the facts that had been discussed by others in isolation from each other could be integrated into a whole.

In Hjelmlev's *Prolegomena* there is no discussion of the difference between lexicon and grammar, but it is clear that for him the distinction which Bloomfield would draw between morphology and syntax is merely a difference in the degree of derivation of the units studied. Hjelmslev assumed *a priori*, but not without considerable experience, that any language can be profitably described in terms of the three relations of interdependence, determination, and constellation, on both the paradigmatic and syntagmatic axes. A grammar constructed on such principles would, therefore, resemble the kind of IC grammar proposed by Bloomfield. Such a grammar, however, would include more control over the paradigmatic axis than appears to be possible in the usual IC approach, since it would be systematically required that the degree of derivation involved in the items substituted in syntactic frames be specified. Such a technique has been used to help distinguish "degree of grammaticalness."[9]

Chomsky is the one author who has made explicit his concept of what grammar is and what it is not, and why he prefers his approach to other alternatives. While there is still considerable need for the development and refinement of the mechanisms involved in the tripartite

[9] See Noam Chomsky, "Some Methodological Remarks on Generative Grammar," *Word*, 17 (1961).

model of grammar so far proposed, this form of linguistic description appears more apt to win the interest and sympathy of the traditional grammarian and, at the same time, to satisfy the demands for rigor among other linguists. When it was first published Chomsky's *Syntactic Structures* was greeted with considerable hostility, but most of the objections and misunderstandings have now been more clearly formulated, and it would appear that all linguists, however more useful they find their own approaches for their own particular interests (for example, the description and establishment of a writing system for unknown languages), will have to take the developments in transformational grammar into account.

This form of grammar calls for a base, which has been variously formulated, the prime purpose of which is to specify the underlying grammatical structures in terms of which sentences can be said to be understood and described. This may consist of a context-free phrase-structure grammar, a sequence of singulary transformations, and a lexicon. The syntactic component of the base is to generate deep structures that are interpreted by the semantic component (with its dictionary) and map the deep structures into surface structures, which will then be assigned the proper phonetic interpretation by the phonological component.

In the process of applying this form of grammatical description to languages it is hoped that the intuitive universals presupposed in traditional grammars will be more sharply identified. Substantive universals are those that exemplify a particular, positive type of unit, such as consonants and vowels, nouns and verbs, relative clauses and complements. Formal universals are found in the kinds of relations that must exist among the substantive ones, such as the fact of transformational relations and, perhaps, some particular types of transformations and other grammatical relations.

MODELS OF LANGUAGE

In reviewing the basic points of view of the linguists studied with respect to phonology, grammar, and meaning we have already sketched their particular "models" of language, but it will be useful here to recapitulate these more explicitly. It can be said that all of the modern linguists are structuralists in the sense that all consider it basic to define linguistic units by relating them to each other intralinguistically on as many levels of analysis as they consider required. They differ principally in their conceptions of the number and nature of admissible units and levels and kinds of relations that hold among them.

Language for de Saussure in synchronic study is a static, unchangeable system of pure values, which can be established through the associative and syntagmatic relations of signs. The sign is an indissoluble association between an acoustic image and a concept, and the two most important characterisitcs of the sign are its linearity and arbitrariness. From the first property follows the need for value study on the two axes; from the second, the recognition of the supremacy of the notion of value, as well as the comparative unimportance of either phonetic or semantic substance (signification is the "sole positive fact" of *la langue*). The sign itself, in de Saussure's view, is indifferent to the distinction among lexical, morphological, or syntactic units or meanings. While the distinction may be useful, it is not necessary. From the synchronic point of view language is a succession of discrete, self-defining systems whose changes are brought about by the innovating factors that are introduced by the individual deviations of the mass of people speaking the language through time.

For Sapir language is a dynamic, shifting set of patterns holding among elements capable of signaling four or more concept types, but necessarily signaling at least two types. The sentence is the major functional unit of speech, and since it is defined as "the linguistic expression of a proposition," the conclusion that "ideation reigns supreme" in language follows. Words are psychological units whose properties vary from language to language; they can often be analyzed into radical and affixed (grammatical) elements. The mechanisms of relation in morphological constructions include order, composition, affixation, internal modification, reduplication, and accentual differences.

As seen by Bloomfield language is a set of conditioned human responses to physical or chemical stimuli. These responses are conditioned; that is, they are neither instinctive nor inherited, and they are substitutes for other forms of bodily behavior. They are important because they link otherwise separated nervous systems and facilitate social cooperation. The study of the connection among the physico-chemical stimuli, the conditioned linguistic activity, and the effect this connection has on the environment is the study of meaning. Linguistic activity for the linguist, then, is restricted to the study of a set of signals connected with environmental factors.

The typical integral response is a sentence. Various types of sentences are distinguishable on the basis of frequency (major or minor types) and environmental effect (actor-action, command, question). Complex sentences can be analyzed into syntactic constructions, and these, in turn, into morphological constructions. Such constructions are types of relations into which lexical forms can enter, and all forms that can occur in a position of a construction belong to the same form class. All linguistic forms are considered to have a constant and specific meaning (although the distinction of central and marginal meanings seems universal), but the degree of specificity varies. Grammatical forms have a more general and lexical forms a more specific association with aspects of the situations in which they always occur. The problem of displaced speech indicates that the motion environment cannot be restricted to factors external to the speaker, since the body, as a receptacle of increasingly complex stimuli and conditioning, is always part of any environment in which speech takes place.

The linguist studies language apart from its connection with the environment, although he must appeal to other sciences to inform him about that connection. He views language as a set of signals of three principal types: (1) phonemes, which signal meaning differences but which themselves cannot have meaning; (2) morphemes and morpheme constructions (lexical items), which have a constant and specific connection with environmental factors, although the connection may neither be known nor specified; and (3) grammatical forms, the taxemes of order, selection, modulation, and phonetic modification, which signal meanings not contained in the lexical forms.

Firth viewed language as an activity by which men, who are immersed in the world, seek to either preserve or alter their environment. Although this idea is readily expressible in behavioristic terms, Firth avoided both the dualism of Sapir, de Saussure, and the traditionalists and the mechanistic monism of Bloomfield. Firth saw language as essentially a meaningful activity, which can be described on different levels. The speaker identifies himself (phonetic meaning), the mode of his participation in the speech situation (phonological, collocational meaning), and the elements of the situation on which he acts or to which he responds (lexical meaning) according to the restrictions of the sound and the grammatical systems of his language (phonological and grammatical meanings). The grammatical system of a language can be described in terms of the items and relations involved in the immediate situation (interior relations of the context of situation) and can be related to the larger cultural setting of the speech activity (exterior relations of the context of situation).

Hjelmslev studied language as a network of dependence relations that can be considered as independent of phonetics or semantics, but which are instantiated in a given text. A text must consist of a system, and it may or may not also include a succession or process. A language is a hierarchy, or class of classes, and elements can be compared and defined in terms of relations of dependence at different levels of degrees of derivation. The entities of a language are found in those elements that are terms in a relation, but not in the relations themselves. In the *Prolegomena* Hjelmslev spoke of the variability of linguistic phenomena as being explainable principally through one cause or constant—denotation. He added that this is an insufficient criterion by which to account for the reality of language, which has more than a denotational constant. This group of other constants can be called "connotational," and it includes factors of style, value, media, tone, idiom, and the like.

As set forth in *Syntactic Structures,* language for Chomsky appears to consist of three components. The first is a core set of constructions whose structural description can be satisfactorily assigned by IC analysis. This analysis is represented by three diagrams that are associated with derivations. The derivations are performed according to specific rules and produce terminal strings. The latter are transformed into kernel sentences by obligatory transformation rules. The elements of this first part of language appear to be syntactic categories that underlie all sentences, either directly (as in the case of the kernel sentences via obligatory transformations) or indirectly (as in the case of others produced by combinations of obligatory and optional transformations). The second component is a set of transformation rules, obligatory and optional. There is an implicit restriction here. Chomsky noted that for interesting work the transformations should not merely permit us to relate sets of sentences through the rules but that something should remain constant or recoverable under transformation, since it should be possible to formulate the transformation of any linguistic structure into any other. The original concern was to show that there is a regular relation between sentences with differing IC structures which have the same meaning and between similar explanations of pairs of ambiguous constructions which have the same IC structures. Later work has shown that the semantic aspect can remain unaltered by transformation. The third component is a set of rules for expressing the grammatically correct sentences in the phonologically correct representation.

After the appearance of *Syntactic Structures* language was viewed as consisting of a certain set of substantive and formal factors that are shared by all languages. Just how this set is to be specified will depend on a more careful examination of the available data, but it would appear that the basic assumptions of traditional grammar with respect to linguistic universals are substantially correct. Linguistics has done nothing to disprove this assumption, and the demonstration that the surface structures of languages are markedly different has been a valuable contribution, but does nothing to weaken the case for linguistic universals, which are to be found principally in the deep structures of languages.

OBJECT STUDIED

Language, as understood in the models presented above, should be the object studied by these linguists. But it will be useful, following de Saussure's lead, to state as well what these scholars were *not* studying.

De Saussure was concerned with a system of values that holds between signs, and he focused primarily on the values, not on the concepts or acoustic images, and, hence, not on semantics or phonetics. He was not primarily concerned with linguistic change. He did not study the immediate constituents of signs or constructions nor did he study the transformational potential of either. Since he was interested in *la langue,* he did not devote attention to linguistic behavior (*la parole*) and relegated phonetics, semantics, and the study of actual speech to the linguistics of *la parole,* an area of investigation he thought desirable but which he did not pursue himself.

Unlike de Saussure, Sapir conceived of language as a slowly changing mechanism that signals meanings. The principal meanings signaled are concept types. At least two of these concept types must be signaled by any language. Because the signal system is subject to drift, the match between the forms and their meanings can shift in time. Sapir was not studying individual semantics, phonetics, or other forms of linguistic behavior, and he did not investigate the transformational relations of constructions.

Bloomfield viewed language as one form of human behavior comparable to any other form, except that the activities associated with language happen to be socially significant as a set of signals. Logically his study should have been concerned with *la parole,* because of his insistence on empirical data. Implicit in his approach is the idea that the relations among individual linguistic forms used by a single speaker can base a generalized pattern valid for all speakers of the same speech community. This is another expression of the conventionality of language. He was not studying concepts or meaning in terms of concepts, and he did not consider the transformational potential of constructions.

It was Firth's ideal to study actual sentences in contexts of situation, in order to guarantee their genuineness. Like Bloomfield, then, he should have been studying *la parole,* which is then somehow generalized to *la langue.* The apparent difficulty illustrates that, as de Saussure said, the objective entities of *la langue* are not immediately accessible to us and that in all such studies, whatever their conception of empiricism, *la parole* is the necessary source of the study, not precisely the object of it. Firth did not consider the ICs of utterances explicitly, and he did not deal with concepts or with the transformational relations of constructions, nor was he concerned with studying linguistic change.

In the *Prolegomena* Hjelmslev was primarily concerned with dependence relations. He did not deal there directly with phonetics or concepts, nor did he consider linguistic change.

Chomsky is studying *la langue,* but not in terms of ICs alone. The speaker's competence is describable as a systematic set of relations between deep structures and (probably the constructions generated by a context-free phrase-structure grammar) their semantic interpretation and phonetic representation in surface structures, which represents the speaker's performance. Neither the deep structures nor the surface structures are literally the individual's competence or performance. The generative mechanisms as such are neutral with respect to the speaker's production or analysis of sentences, and in this sense, both could be considered under the general aspect of *la langue*. Understood as individual linguistic behavior, Chomsky does not study *la parole*. Neither does he consider language change, although a transformational account of such change would undoubtedly be revealing. It would give a truer picture of linguistic reality than de Saussure's study of arrested language states.

LANGUAGE CHANGE

Since de Saussure was more interested in establishing the synchronic study of language, he did not dwell on the facts and mechanisms of linguistic change. He pointed out that one reason for linguistic change is the fact that successive generations do not analyze forms in the same way. For example, some signs previously held to be complex would be analyzed as simple (English *only, ugly*). In order to make synchronic linguistics a science he had called for a conventional simplification of the data, especially the abstraction from linguistic change. He noted that for a realistic consideration of language we would have to reintroduce the causes of linguistic change that this simplification has omitted—the speakers and the effects of time (that is, *la parole,* the innovations of individuals, *le langage,* community innovations, and *temps,* diachronic considerations).

Sapir's treatment of linguistic change is reminiscent of Firth's polysystemic approach to synchronic study. Neither thought that phonetics should be separated from grammar. In his discussion of the hesitation between the English forms *who* and *whom* Sapir illustrated this belief. Among the factors he considered involved were (1) syntax, where pre- and postverbal position must be considered, with the English tendency to fixed word order; (2) paradigmatic relations, since all the *wh-* forms of English are invariable with the exception of *who, whom*; (3) morphology, since English shows a tendency to invariable word forms; (4) accentual features, since most *wh-* forms are short and stressed, while *whom* is long. When all of these factors converge in a particular *who-whom* choice, there is no hesitation, and *who* is used. Where some factors are missing, there is hesitation, though a preference is shown for *who*.

Sapir's over-all explanation of sound change is similar to this inclusive structural study and involves the relative weight to be assigned to (1) automatic, regular sound changes; (2) the "psychologically exposed points" in patterns when these factors converge; (3) the innovating drive of language to impose pattern where it seems to be lacking; and (4) the conservative trend of languages to preserve analogies that seem to be threatened by other changes, such as phonetic shifts. In all of these factors the prestige of the speakers plays a central role. Sapir noted that one source of sound change is the preference for one kind of articulation.

Bloomfield surveyed several accounts of linguistic change and concluded that sound change is (1) mechanical and independent of meaning considerations; (2) regular; and (3) arises from the preference for one nondistinctive variant of a phoneme over another, thus giving rise ultimately to a new phonemic contrast. He explained lexical or semantic change primarily through his notion of speech communities and the density of communication within them. Thus here too the prestige of the speaker is important. For this reason Bloomfield preferred the wave theory of Schmidt to the family-tree image of linguistic relations and changes, since the former represents the variability of influences between languages at different times, while the latter portrays languages as completely isolated in time and local contact. Grammatical change, in Bloomfield's view, is partially explained through the loss of phonemic contrasts in sound change and through the prestige of one analysis of constructions over others.

Firth, Hjelmslev, and Chomsky did not discuss linguistic change.

CHARACTERISTIC TOPICS

The primary interests of these linguists are frequently reflected in the terms they introduced. With de Saussure, then, the synchronic study of language is the most characteristic approach. A consequence of this approach was the distinction he made among *la langue, la parole,* and *le langage* and the importance he placed on value in studying signs. According to de Saussure, every sign must be defined through its association of sound image and concept. These distinctions amounted to a summary of what the structural study of language must be.

The same insights, but not the same terminology, were shared by subsequent linguists, for example, Sapir, with his notions of analogy and pattern. More characteristic of Sapir's work as an innovator, perhaps, was his concern for studying the relations between language and culture. He did not believe that language, defined as a morphological system, does or can determine culture, since this formal aspect of language is shown to be changeable and independent of concept type, while the

424 / SUMMARY AND CONCLUSIONS

conceptual type of language is "massively" resistant to change. But given a language of a particular formal and conceptual type at a particular time, and, especially, given the content of the concepts, language can be considered as a "prepared groove" for our experiences and as a "garment wrapped about our thought" when we try to communicate our experiences. A language makes it easier and more natural for speakers to see things in a certain light. It does not make it impossible, or even inordinately difficult, as Whorf seemed to suggest, to see things differently.

In discussing Bloomfield, we tend to think of behaviorism, but this particular form of psychology is peripheral to his linguistics. It would be fairer to say that his most characteristic accomplishment was his effort to make linguistics an autonomous and scientific discipline. For these purposes he introduced a precise and restricted technical vocabulary for linguistic description, and he initiated immediate constituent analysis.[10] Bloomfield also introduced an ideal of empirical description on a mechanistic basis, which Chomsky characterized as "simply an expression of lack of interest in theory and explanation . . . perhaps . . . fostered by certain ideas . . . that were considered briefly in positivist philosophy of science, but rejected forthwith, in the early nineteen-thirties."[11] In addition, Bloomfield provided techniques for the survey of a wide variety of linguistic problems, both synchronic and diachronic.

Firth was characteristically associated with meaning and phonology apart from phonemics. Both of these areas of study resulted from his rejection of the American structuralist (post-Bloomfield) "monosystemic" approach, which, he believed, neglected syntagmatic relations.

Hjelmslev is perhaps best known through the esoteric name of his study: *Glossematics*. As a consequence of his empirical principle, he deliberately worked in a deductive way, as opposed to the inductive methods of the anthropologically oriented linguist. This approach represents an alternative conception of linguistic "science" which we are to entertain, since linguistics for other workers is scientific because it is inductive.

Chomsky's development of transformational analysis and his methodological studies of alternative forms of grammars have extended the notion of linguistic "structure." His work posed further challenges to our definitions "linguistic" and to our notion of "linguistic science":

[10] Later developed by others; see, for example, Rulon Wells, "Immediate Constituents," and Leonard Bloomfield, "Postulates," in Martin Joos, ed., *Readings in Linguistics* (Washington, D.C., 1957).

[11] Noam Chomsky, *Aspects of the Theory of Syntax*, pp. 193–194. Reprinted by permission of the M.I.T. Press. Copyright 1965 by The Massachusetts Institute of Technology.

One may ask whether the necessity for present-day linguistics to give such priority to introspective evidence and to the linguistic intuition of the native speaker excludes it from the domain of science. . . . The social and behavioral sciences provide ample evidence that objectivity can be pursued with little consequent gain in insight and understanding. On the other hand, a good case can be made for the view that the natural sciences have, by and large, sought objectivity primarily insofar as it is a tool for gaining insight (for providing phenomena that can suggest or test deeper explanatory hypotheses).

[*Aspects of the Theory of Syntax*, p. 20]

The goal of explaining rather than merely classifying facts of language goes beyond previous goals; the introduction of the semantic component into the grammar and the rejection of phonemics as a significant level in a generative grammar undercut two long-held positions in American linguistics. The distinction he made between deep and surface structure as well as his recognition of and search for linguistic universals, substantive and formal, align Chomsky with the traditional grammarians, although the rigor of his method adequately separates him from most traditional and many structural grammarians. All of these factors require us to rethink the goals we have set ourselves in terms of a purely empirical general linguistic theory, and, indeed, to ask whether such a theory is possible.

CONCLUSIONS

It was suggested that there is a greater amount of continuity in the development of linguistic studies than generally appears in modern linguistic works, especially when traditional studies are discussed. Chomsky has explicated this continuity more than other linguists, and the notion of a formal universal suggests the kind of continuity that was intended in the present volume. It appears that in the field of linguistics the form of investigation and the form of the conditions under which progress is made are remarkably similar. Progress in linguistics is measured by our ability to relate a given unit of linguistic description to successively more systems. Required implicitly, of course, is the ability to show that there *is* another system.

During the course of our investigation we have considered various kinds of linguistic systems. Some of these were seen to be autonomous and others, interrelated. Not all linguists agree in their conceptions of how the systems discussed are related. We have distinguished phonetic, phonological, lexical, syntactic, semantic, and stylistic systems on synchronic and historical planes. Our understanding of these successive systems has been enriched by our study of these linguists, both separately and conjointly, giving promise that we will be able to progress to a more unified and satisfying explanation of linguistic facts and their relations to other systems important to mankind. In particular, the distinctions between deep and surface structure and between formal and substantial universals in language are comparable to the influential distinction made in the fifth century B.C. between substance and accidents. The distinctions of both periods focus our attention on the formal rather than on the material aspects of an object of study and both can be considered formulations of the insights that initiated the structural, patterned study of language in modern linguistics.

One of the obvious differences between the approach to language used by the ancients and that of the moderns is that modern linguistics has provided us with a growing range of accurate studies of the material aspects of many languages, in phonetics and grammar, in addition to a formal, unifying point of view. Only concrete, detailed evidence of instances that make such insights more than bright ideas can guarantee solid progress.

Formal linguistic study has appeared to some to be alien or indifferent to more pervasive humanistic goals. It is to be hoped, on the basis of the studies considered here, that Hjelmslev's estimate of the relation of linguistics to other studies of man and his work will prove to be more accurate:

Linguistic theory is led by an inner necessity to recognize not merely the linguistic system . . . in its totality and in its individuality, but also man and human society behind language, and all man's sphere of knowledge through language. At that point linguistic theory has reached its prescribed goal:

humanitas et universitas.[12]

[12] Reprinted with the permission of the copyright owners, the Regents of the University of Wisconsin, from Louis Hjelmslev, *Prolegomena to a Theory of Language,* trans. Francis Whitfield (Madison, Wisc.: University of Wisconsin Press, 1961), p. 127.

Selected General Bibliography

General Linguistic Works

Allen, W. Sidney, *On the Linguistic Study of Language*. Cambridge, England: The University Press, 1957.

Anderson, W., and N. Stageberg, *Introductory Readings on Language*, 2d ed. New York: Holt, Rinehart and Winston, Inc., 1966.

Bach, Emmon, *An Introduction to Transformational Grammars*. New York: Holt, Rinehart and Winston, Inc., 1964.

Bastide, R., ed., *Sens et usages du terme "structure" dans les sciences humaines et sociales*. The Hague: Mouton & Company, 1962.

Bazell, Charles, *Linguistic Form*. Istanbul: Istanbul Press, 1953.

Bloch, B., and G. Trager, *Outline of Linguistic Analysis*. Baltimore, Md.: Waverly Press, 1942.

Bloomfield, Leonard, "Why a Linguistic Society," *Language*, I (1925), 1–5.

————, Obituary of Albert P. Weiss, *Language*, 7 (1931), 219–221.

————, *Language*. New York: Holt, Rinehart and Winston, Inc., 1933.

————, Review of Edward Sapir's *Language* (1921), *The Classical Weekly*, 15, 142–143.

————, Review of J. Otto Jespersen's *Language, Its Nature, Development and Origin*, (1922), *American Journal of Philology*, 43, 370–373.

————, Review of Ferdinand de Saussure's *Cours de linguistique générale*, in *Modern Language Journal*, 8, 317–319.

————, "The Linguistic Aspects of Science," in the *International Encyclopedia of Unified Science*, Vol. 1, No. 4; reprinted by the University of Chicago Press, 1960.

Boas, Franz, *Handbook of American Indian Languages*. Washington, D.C.: Smithsonian Institution, Bureau of American Ethnology, Bulletin 40, 1911;

Introduction, with a Foreword by C. I. J. M. Stuart, reprinted by Georgetown University Press, Washington, D.C., 1964.

———, *Race, Language, and Culture.* Toronto: Crowell Collier and Macmillan, Inc., 1940; reprinted as a paperback by The Free Press of Glencoe, New York, 1966.

Bolinger, Dwight L., "On Defining the Morpheme," *Word,* 4 (1948), 18–23.

———, *Generality, Gradience and the All-or-None.* The Hague: Mouton & Company, 1961.

———, "Syntactic Blends and Other Matters," *Language,* 37 (1961), 366–381.

———, "The Atomization of Meaning," *Language,* 41, 4 (1965), 555–573.

Buchanan, Cynthia D., *A Programmed Introduction to Linguistics.* Boston: D. C. Heath & Company, 1963.

Carroll, John B., *The Study of Language.* Cambridge, Mass.: Harvard University Press, 1953.

———, *Language, Thought, and Reality: Selected Writings of Benjamin Whorf.* Cambridge, Mass., M.I.T. Press, 1956.

Cassirer, Ernst, *Substanzbegriff und Funktionsbegriff.* Berlin, 1910.

Chomsky, Noam, *The Logical Structure of Linguistic Theory.* Cambridge, Mass., M.I.T. Library, 1955, mimeographed.

———, "Semantic Considerations in Grammar," Monograph No. 8, Georgetown University, Washington, D.C., 1955.

———, Review of Roman Jakobson and Morris Halle's *Fundamentals of Language,* (1956), *International Journal of American Linguistics,* 23 (1957), 234–241.

———, *Syntactic Structures.* The Hague: Mouton & Company, 1957

———, "A Transformational Approach to Syntax," *Proceedings of the Fourth University of Texas Symposium on English and Syntax.* Austin, Texas, 1958.

———, "Explanatory Models in Linguistics," *Proceedings of the International Congress on Logic, Methodology, and Philosophy of Science.* Stamford, Conn., 1960.

———, "On the Notion 'Rule of Grammar' " in R. Jakobson, ed. *The Structure of Language and Its Mathematical Aspects,* Proceedings of the Twelfth Symposium in Applied Mathematics. Providence, R. I., 1961.

———, "Some Methodological Remarks on Generative Grammar," *Word,* 17 (August, 1961), 219–239.

———, *Aspects of the Theory of Syntax.* Cambridge, Mass.: M.I.T. Press, 1965.

———, *Current Issues in Linguistic Theory.* The Hague: Mouton & Company, 1965.

———, M. Halle, and F. Lukoff, "On Accent and Juncture in English," in *For Roman Jakobson.* The Hague: Mouton & Company, 1956.

Cohen, Marcel, *Instruction d'Enquête linguistique.* Paris: Institute of Ethnology, 1950.

Cook, Walter, S.J., *On Tagmemes and Transforms.* Washington, D.C.: Georgetown University Press, 1964.

Diderichsen, P., "Morpheme Categories in Modern Danish," in *Recherches Structurales.* Copenhagen: Travaux du Cercle Linguistique de Copenhague, 1949.

——, "The Importance of Distribution vs. other Criteria in Linguistic Analysis," in *Proceedings of the Eighth International Congress of Linguists.* Oslo, 1958, pp. 156–181.

Dingwall, William Orr, *Transformational Generative Grammar: A Bibliography.* Washington, D.C.: Center for Applied Linguistics, 1965.

Elson, B., and V. Pickett, *Beginning Morphology and Syntax.* Santa Ana, Calif.: Summer Institute of Linguistics, 1960.

Firth, J. R., *Papers in Linguistics, 1934–1951.* London: Oxford University Press, 1957.

——, "Synopsis of Linguistic Theory, 1930–1955," in *Studies in Linguistic Analysis,* a special publication of the Philological Society. Oxford: Basil Blackwell, 1957.

Fodor, J., and J. Katz, eds. *The Structure of Language: Readings in the Philosophy of Language.* Englewood Cliffs, N.J.: Prentice-Hall, Inc., 1964.

Garvin, Paul, *On Linguistic Methods: Selected Papers.* The Hague: Mouton & Company, 1964.

Gleason, H. A., Jr., *An Introduction to Descriptive Linguistics,* rev. ed. New York: Holt, Rinehart and Winston, Inc., 1961.

——, *Linguistics and English Grammar.* New York: Holt, Rinehart and Winston, Inc., 1965.

Goldschmidt, W., ed., *The Anthropology of Franz Boas.* New York, Memoir 89 of the American Anthropological Association, Vol. 61, No. 5, Part 2, October 1959.

Gray, Louis H., *The Foundations of Language.* New York: Crowell Collier and Macmillan, Inc., 1939.

Greenberg, Joseph, *Essays in Linguistics.* Chicago: University of Chicago Press, 1957.

——, ed., *Universals in Language.* Cambridge, Mass.: M.I.T. Press, 1963.

Hall, Robert A., Jr., *Linguistics and Your Language.* New York: Doubleday & Company, Inc., 1960.

——, *Introductory Linguistics.* Philadelphia: Chilton Company, 1964.

Halle, Morris, *The Sound Patterns of Russian.* The Hague: Mouton & Company, 1959.

——, "On the Role of Simplicity in Linguistic Descriptions," in R. Jakobson, ed., *The Structure of Language and Its Mathematical Aspects,* Proceedings of the Twelfth Symposium in Applied Mathematics. Providence, R.I., 1961.

Hamp, Eric P., *A Glossary of American Technical Linguistic Usage, 1925–1950.* Utrecht: Spectrum, 1958.

Harris, Zellig S., *Methods in Structural Linguistics.* Chicago: University of Chicago Press, 1951.

——, Review of D. Mandelbaum, ed., *Selected Writings of Edward Sapir,* in *Language,* 27 (1951), 288–322.

————, "Discourse Analysis," *Language,* 28 (1952), 18–23 and 474–494.

————, "Distributional Structure," *Word,* 10 (1954), 146–194.

————, "Co-occurrence and Transformation in Linguistic Structure," *Language,* 33 (1957), 283–340.

————, *String Analysis of Sentence Structure.* The Hague: Mouton & Company, 1962.

Hjelmslev, L., and H. J. Uldall, *An Outline of Glossematics.* Copenhagen: Travaux du Cercle Linguistique de Copenhague, 1957.

Hockett, Charles, *A Course in Modern Linguistics.* New York: Crowell Collier and Macmillan, Inc., 1958.

Hughes, John, *The Science of Language: An Introduction to Linguistics.* New York: Random House-Alfred A. Knopf, Inc., 1962.

von Humboldt, W., *Über die Verschiedenheit des menschlichen Sprachbaus.* Darmstadt: Claasen and Roether, 1949.

Jespersen, J. Otto., *Language, Its Nature, Development, and Origin.* London: Allen & Unwin, Ltd., 1922.

————, *Essentials of English Grammar.* New York: Holt, Rinehart and Winston, Inc., 1933.

————, *Analytic Syntax.* Copenhagen: Munksgaard, 1937.

Joos, Martin, ed., *Readings in Linguistics.* Washington, D.C.: American Council of Learned Societies, 1957.

Juilland, Alphonse, *Structural Relations.* The Hague: Mouton & Company, 1961.

Katz, J., and P. Postal, *An Integrated Theory of Linguistic Descriptions.* Cambridge, Mass.: M.I.T. Press, 1964.

Lees, Robert B., Review of Noam Chomsky's *Syntactic Structures* (1957), in *Language,* 33 (1957), 375–407.

————, *The Grammar of English Nominalizations.* Bloomington, Ind.: Research Center in Anthropology, Folklore, and Linguistics, 1960.

————, "A Multiply Ambiguous Adjectival Construction in English," *Language,* 36 (1960), 207–221.

Lenneberg, Eric, *New Directions in the Study of Language.* Cambridge, Mass.: M.I.T. Press, 1964.

Leroy, Maurice, *Les grands courants de la linguistique moderne.* Brussels: Presses Universitaires, 1964.

Longacre, R., *Grammar Discovery Procedures: A Field Manual.* The Hague: Mouton & Company, 1964.

Malmberg, Bertil, *Structural Linguistics and Human Communications: An Introduction to the Mechanisms of Language and the Methodology of Linguistics.* New York: Academic Press: 1963.

Marouzeau, Jacques, *Lexique de la terminologie linguistique français, allemand, anglais, italien,* 3d ed. Paris: Geuthner, 1951.

Martinet, A., and U. Weinreich, *Linguistics Today.* New York: Linguistic Circle of New York, Publication No. 2, 1958.

Mandelbaum, D., ed., *Selected Writings of Edward Sapir.* Berkeley, Calif.: University of California Press, 1949.

Miller, George A., *Language and Communication*. New York: McGraw-Hill Book Company, Inc., 1951.

Nida, Eugene, *Morphology: A Descriptive Analysis of Words*, 2d ed. Ann Arbor, Mich.: University of Michigan Press, 1949.

Ornstein, J., and W. Gage, *The ABC's of Languages and Linguistics*. Philadelphia: Chilton Company, 1964.

Perrot, Jean, *La Linguistique*. Paris: Presses Universitaires, 1953.

Postal, Paul, *Constituent Structure: A Study of Contemporary Models of Syntactic Description*. Bloomington, Ind.: Indiana University Publications in Folklore and Linguistics, 1964.

Potter, Simeon, *Modern Linguistics*. London: André Deutsch, 1957.

Reichling, Anton, "Principles and Methods of Syntax: Cryptanalytical Formalism," *Lingua*, 10 (1961), 1–17.

Reid, T. B. W., *Historical Philology and Linguistic Science*. Oxford: Clarendon Press, 1960.

Ries, J. *Was ist Syntax?* Marburg, 1929.

Robins, R. H., "Noun and Verb in Universal Grammar," *Language*, 28 (1952), 289–298.

———, "Aspects of Prosodic Analysis," *Proceedings of the University of Durham Philosophical Society*, I.B. No. 1 (1957), 1–30.

———, "In Defence of WP," *Transactions of the Philological Society*. London, 1960, pp. 116–144.

———, *General Linguistics: An Introductory Survey*. London: Longmans Green, 1964.

Sapir, Edward, *Language: An Introduction to the Study of Speech*. New York: Harcourt, Brace & World, Inc., 1921.

———, *Selected Writings in Language, Culture, and Personality*. Berkeley, Calif.: University of California Press, 1949.

de Saussure, Ferdinand, *A Course in General Linguistics*, trans. Wade Baskin. New York: Philosophical Library, 1959.

Schlauch, Margaret, *The Gift of Language*. New York: Dover Publications, Inc., 1955.

Schuchardt, H., *Schuchardt Brevier*. Halle, 1928.

Siertsema, Berta, *A Study of Glossematics: A Critical Survey of Its Fundamental Concepts*. The Hague: Martinus Nijhoff, 1955.

Spang-Hanssen, H., *Probability and Structural Classification in Language Description*. Copenhagen: Rosenkilde and Bagger, 1959.

Sørensen, Holger Steen, *Word Classes in English with Special Reference to Proper Names, with an Introductory Theory of Grammar, Meaning, and Reference*. Copenhagen: Gad, 1958.

Togeby, Knud, *La Structure immanente de la Langue française*. Copenhagen, 1951.

Wackernagel, Jacob, *Vorlesungen über Syntax*, 1–2. Reihe: Basel, 1920–1924.

Wartburg, Walther von, *Problèmes et méthodes de la Linguistique*. Paris: Presses Universitaires, 1963.

Whatmough, Joshua, *Language: A Modern Synthesis*. New York: Mentor Books, 1957.

Whitney, W. D., *The Life and Growth of Language*. New York: Appleton-Century-Crofts, 1875.

———, *Language, and the Study of Language*. New York: Charles Scribners' Sons, 1885.

Phonetics and Phonology

Fant, G., *Acoustic Theory of Speech Production*. The Hague: Mouton & Company, 1960.

Heffner, R., *General Phonetics*. Madison, Wisc.: University of Wisconsin Press, 1949.

Hockett, Charles, *A Manual of Phonology*. Bloomington, Ind.: Indiana University Press, 1955.

Jakobson, R., and M. Halle, *Fundamentals of Language*. The Hague: Mouton & Company, 1956.

Jones, Daniel, *An Outline of English Phonetics,* 6th ed. New York: E. P. Dutton & Company, Inc., 1940.

———, *The Phoneme, Its Nature and Use*. Cambridge, England: Heffer, 1950.

———, *The Pronunciation of English*, 3d ed. Cambridge, England: Heffer, 1950.

Joos, Martin, *Acoustic Phonetics,* Language Monograph No. 23, Linguistic Society of America (Baltimore, Md., 1948).

Kenyon, John S., *American Pronunciation: A Textbook of Phonetics for Students of English,* 8th ed. Ann Arbor, Mich.: University of Michigan Press, 1940.

Ladefoged, Peter, *Elements of Acoustic Phonetics*. Chicago: University of Chicago Press, 1962.

Llorach, Emilio Alorcas, *Fonologia Española*. Madrid: Editorial Gredos, 1954.

Martinet, André, *Économies des changements phonétiques: Traité de phonologique diachronique*. Berne: Francke, 1955.

———, *La description phonologique*. Geneva: Droz, 1956.

Pike, Kenneth, *Phonetics*. Ann Arbor, Mich.: University of Michigan Press, 1943.

———, *Phonemics*. Ann Arbor, Mich.: University of Michigan Press, 1947.

———, *Tone Languages*. Ann Arbor, Mich.: University of Michigan Press, 1948.

Potter, R. K., G. Kopp, and H. Green, *Visible Speech*. Princeton, N.J.: D. Van Nostrand Company, Inc., 1947.

Robins, R. H., "The Phonology of the Nasalized Verb in Sundanese," *Bulletin of the School of Oriental and African Studies,* New York, 15 (1953), 138–145.

Stetson, R. H., *Motor Phonetics: A Study of Speech Movements in Action*. Amsterdam: North Holland Company, 1951.

Thomas, C. K., "An Introduction to the Phonetics of American English," University of Buffalo, Studies in Linguistics, No. 3, 1951.

Trager, G. L., "Phonetics: Glossary and Tables," University of Buffalo, Studies in Linguistics, Occasional Papers No. 6, 1958.
Troubetzkoy, N. S., *Grundzüge der Phonologie*. Prague: Cercle Linguistique de Prague, 1939; French edition, *Principes de Phonologie*, trans. Jean Cantineau. Paris: Klincksiek, 1949.
Westermann, D., and I. Ward, *Practical Phonetics for Students of African Languages*. New York: Oxford University Press, 1933–1964.

Historical Linguistics

Bloomfield, M. W., and L. D. Newmark, *A Linguistic Introduction to the History of English*. New York: Random House–Alfred A. Knopf, Inc., 1963.
Gabelentz, Georg von der, *Die Sprachwissenschaft*. Leipzig, 1891.
Hoenigswald, Henry, *Language Change and Linguistic Reconstruction*. Chicago: University of Chicago Press, 1960.
Meillet, Antoine, *Linguistique historique et linguistique générale*. Paris: I, 1926; II, 1938.
Noreen, Adolf, *Einführung in die wissenschaftliche Betrachtung der Sprache*. Halle, 1923.
Paul, Hermann, *Prinzipien der Sprachgeschichte*. Halle: Niemeyer, 1909.
Pedersen, Holger, *Linguistic Science in the Nineteenth Century*, trans. J. W. Spargo. Cambridge, Mass.: Harvard University Press, 1931; Bloomington, Ind.: Indiana University Press, 1959.
Sturtevant, Edgar H., *An Introduction to Linguistic Science*. New Haven, Conn.: Yale University Press, 1949.
———, *Linguistic Change*. Chicago: University of Chicago Press, 1961.

History of Linguistics

Arens, H., *Sprachwissenschaft*, Munich: Karl Alber, 1955.
François, A., *La grammaire du purisme et l'Académie française au XVIIIe siècle*. Paris, 1905.
Garvin, P., et al., *Current Trends in Linguistics*. Vol. 1. *Soviet and East European Linguistics*. The Hague: Mouton & Company, 1963.
Hall, Robert A., "American Linguistics, 1925–1950," *Archivum Linguisticum*, 3, 101–25; 4, 1–166.
Jellinek, M. H., *Geschichte der neuhochdeutschen Grammatik von den Anfängen bis auf Adelung*, 1–2. Heidelberg, 1913–1914.
Jeep, L., *Zur Geschichte der Lehre von den Redetheilen bei den lateinischen Grammatikern*. Leipzig, 1893.
Livet, Ch. L., *La grammaire française et les grammariens du XVIe siècle*. Paris, 1859.
Mohrmann, C., A. Sommerfelt, and J. Whatmough, *Trends in European and American Linguistics 1930–1960*. Utrecht: Spectrum, 1961.

Steinthal, H., *Geschichte der Sprachwissenschaft bei den Griechen und Römern.* Berlin: Dümmlers, 1963.

Trabalza, Ciro, *Storia della grammatica italiana.* Milan, 1908.

————, ed., *Il concetto della grammatica.* Città di Castello, 1912.

Vachek, Josef, *A Prague School Reader in Linguistics: Studies in the History and Theory of Linguistics.* Bloomington, Ind.: Indiana University Press, 1964.

————, *The Linguistic School of Prague.* Bloomington, Ind.: Indiana University Press, 1966.

Waterman, John T., *Perspectives in Linguistics.* Chicago: University of Chicago Press, 1963.

Ancient Works

Allen, W. Sidney, "Ancient Ideas on the Origin and Development of Languages," *Transactions of the Philological Society.* London, 1948.

Barth, P., *Die Stoa.* Stuttgart, 1946.

Barwick, K., *Remmius Palaemon und die römische ars grammatica.* Leipzig, 1922.

Bochenski, I. M., *Ancient Formal Logic.* Amsterdam: Noord-Hollansche, 1951.

Collart, Jean, *Varron, de Lingua Latina Livres V.* Strasbourg, 1954.

Egger, Emile, *Appolonius Dyscole, Essai sur l'histoire des théories grammaticales dans l'antiquité.* Paris, 1854.

————, *De l'étude de la langue latine chez les grecs dans l'antiquité.* Paris, 1885.

Pohlenz, M., *Die Begründung der abendländischen Sprachlehre durch die Stoa.* Göttingen: Vandenhoeck & Ruprecht, 1939.

Robins, R. H., "Dionysius Thrax and the Western Grammatical Tradition," *Transactions of the Philological Society.* London, 1957, pp. 67–106.

Sandys, D., *History of Classical Scholarship.* Cambridge, England, 1903.

Schoemann, G. F., *Die Lehre von den Redetheilen nach den Alten dargestellt.* Berlin, 1862.

Schneider, R., *Apollonii Dyscoli Quae supersunt.* Leipzig, 1878–1910.

Stöhr, H., "Die Abhängigkeit der kategoriellen Logik von dem IE Sprachbau," in H. Junker, *Sprachphilosophisches Lesebuch.* Heidelberg, 1948.

Thrax, D., edition by I. Bekker. Berlin: W. De. Gruyter & Co., 1814–16.

Uhlig, Gustavus, ed., *Dionysii Thracis ars grammatica.* Leipzig, 1883.

————, *Zur Widerherstellung des ältesten occidentalischen Kompendiums der Grammatik,* Annuaire de l'Association pour l'Encouragement des études grecques, XI. Heidelberg, 1887.

Medieval Works

Baebler, J. J., *Beiträge zu einer Geschichte der lateinischen Grammatik im Mittelalter.* Halle, 1885.

Bochenski, I. M., *Summulae Logicales Petri Hispani.* Rome: Marietti, 1947.

(See also, J. P. Mullaly, *The Summulae Logicales of Peter of Spain*, Medieval Studies of the University of Notre Dame, 8. Notre Dame, Ind., 1945.)

Chenu, O. P., *Grammaire et Théologie aux 12e et 13e siècles.* Paris: Vrin, 1957.

Clerval, P., *Les écoles de Chartres au moyen âge.* Chartres, 1895.

Curtius, E. R., "Das mittelalterlische Bildung und Grammatik," *Romanische Forchungen,* 40 (1947).

d'Andely, Henri, *La bataille des sept arts,* in L. Paetow, *University of California Memoirs,* Vol. 4, No. 1. Berkeley, Calif.: University of California Press, 1914.

Grabmann, M., *Auslegung der Aristotelischen Logik aus der Zeit von Boethius bis Petrus Hispanus,* Abhandlungen der Preussischen Akademie der Wissenschaft. Berlin, Jahrgang 1937, Phil.-Historisches., No. 5.

———, *Thomas von Erfurt und der mittelalterliche Aristotelismus.* Munich: Beck, 1943.

———, *Mittelalterliches Gesitesleben,* 3 vols. Munich, 1956.

Heiddegger, M., *Die Kategorienlehre und Bedeutungslehre des Duns Scotus.* Tübingen: Mohr, 1916.

Gottfried, Hermann, *De emendanda ratione graecae grammaticae.* Leipzig, 1801.

Isaac, J., *Le Peri Hermeneias en Occident de Boèce à S. Thomas.* Paris, 1933.

Manthey, Franz, *Die Sprachphilosophie des hl. Thomas von Aquin.* Paderborn: Ferdinand Schöningh, 1937.

Moody, E. A., *Truth and Consequence in Medieval Logic.* Amsterdam, 1953.

Patch, H. R., *The Tradition of Boethius.* New York: Oxford University Press, 1935.

Roos, H., S.J., "Martinus de Dacia und seine Schriften de modis significandi," *Classica et Medievalia,* 8 (1946), 87–115.

———, "Sprachdenken im Mittelalter," *Classica et Medievalia,* 9 (1949).

———, *Die Modi Significandi des Martinus von Dacia.* Münster, 1952.

Thomas of Erfurt, *De Modis Significandi seu Grammatica Speculativa,* ed. F. M. Fernández García. Quarrachi, 1902.

Thurot, Charles, *Extraits de divers manuscrits latins pour servir à l'histoire des doctrines grammaticales au moyen âge.* Paris, 1869.

Vann, G., *The Wisdom of Boethius.* London: Thomistic Society, 1952.

Wallerand, G., *Les Oeuvres de Siger de Courtrai.* Louvain, 1913.

Warnach, J., "Erkennen und Sprechen bei Thomas von Aquin," *Divus Thomas,* 15 (1937).

———, "Das äussere Sprechen und seine Funktionnen in der Lehre von Thomas von Aquin," *Divus Thomas,* 16 (1938).

Werner, K., "Die Sprachphilosophie des Johannis Duns Scoti," *Sitzungsberichte der Wiener Akademie der Wissenschaften,* 85 (1877), 545–597.

Philosophical Treatments of Language

Anmann, H., *Die menschliche Rede, Sprachphilosophische Untersuchungen.* Lahr im Breisgau, 1925.

Arnault, A., and C. Lancelot, *Grammaire raisonnée, contenant les fondemens de l'art de parler expliquez d'une manière claire et naturelle.* Paris, 1660.

————, *Logique ou l'art de penser.* Paris, 1662. Reprinted as *The Art of Thinking: Port Royal Logic.* Indianapolis, Ind.: The Bobbs-Merrill Company, 1964.

Beauzée, N., *Grammaire générale ou Exposition des éléments nécessaires du langage pour servir de fondement à l'étude de toutes les langues.* Paris, 1767.

Becker, K. F., *Organism der Sprache als Einleitung zur deutschen Grammatik.* Frankfurt am Main, 1827.

Brunot, F., *La doctrine de Malherbe, d'après son "Commentaire sur Desportes"* Paris: Thèse, 1891.

————, *La Pensée et la langue.* Paris: Masson et Cie, 1922.

Burggraff, P. *Principes de grammaire générale, ou Exposition raisonée des éléments.* Liège, 1863.

Courtourat, L., ed., *Opuscule et Fragments de Leibniz.* Paris, 1903.

————, *La Logique de Leibniz d'après des documents inédits.* Paris, 1910.

————, "Des Rapports de la logique et de la linguistique," *Revue de Métaphysique et de Morale.* Paris, 1911.

————, "Sur la structure logique du langage," *Bulletin de la Société de Philosophie.* Paris, 1912.

————, *Pour la Logique du langage.* Paris, 1913.

Dumarsais, C. C., *Logique et principes de grammaire.* Paris: Drouet, 1769.

Fiesel, Eva, *Die Sprachphilosophie der deutschen Romantik.* Tübingen, 1927.

Funke, O., *Innere Sprachform. Eine Einführung in A. Martys Sprachphilosophie.* Reichenberg, 1924.

————, *Studien zur Geschichte der Sprachphilosophie.* Berne, 1927.

Gazae, T., *Introductive grammatices libri quattuor.* Venetiis, in aedibus Aldi Romani, 1495, folio. Cologne edition, 1525, octavo, in Bibliothèque Nationale, Paris.

de Gebelin, Court, *Monde primitif: Histoire naturelle de la parole, ou Précis de l'origine du langage et de la grammaire.* Paris, 1776.

Girard, Abbé Gabriel, *Les vrais principes de la langue française, ou la Parole réduite en méthode.* Paris, 1747.

Harris, James, *Hermes, or a Philosophical inquiry concerning universal grammar; also Hermes . . . traduit . . . avec des remarques et additions par François Thurot.* Paris, 1796.

Hjelmslev, L., *Principes de grammaire générale.* Copenhagen: Munksgaard, 1927.

Jespersen, J. Otto, *Philosophy of Grammar.* London: Allen & Unwin, Ltd., 1924.

Leibniz, G. W., von, *De arte combinatoria.* Leipzig, 1666.

————, *Nouveaux essais sur l'entendement.* Paris, 1886.

————, *La Monadologie.* Paris, 1881.

Lenz, R., *La Oración y sus partes.* Madrid, 1920.

Linacre, T., *De emendata structura latini sermonis.* London, 1524.

Marty, Anton, *Untersuchungen zur Grundlegung der allgemeinen Grammatik und Sprachlogik.* Halle, 1908.

Meiner, J. W., *Versuch einer an der menschlichen Sprache abgebildeten Vernunftlehre oder philosophische und allgemeine Sprachlehre.* Leipzig, 1781.

Ollion, H., *Philosophie de la grammaire, ou Essai d'une détermination des catégories par l'analyse des procédés du langage*. Grenoble, 1900.

Rotta, P., *Filosofia del linguaggio nella patristica e nella scolastica*. Turin, 1919.

de Sacy, A. J. S., *Principes de grammaire générale, mis à la portée des enfants, et propres à servir d'introduction à l'étude de toutes les langues*, 2d. ed. Paris, 1804.

Sanctii, F., *Minerva, seu de causis linguae latinae*. Salamanca, 1587.

Scaligeri, J. C., *De causis linguae latinae libri tredecem*. Lyons, 1540.

Serrus, C., *Le parallélisme logico-grammaticale*. Paris: Alcan, 1933.

Vossi, Joannis Gerardi, *De grammatica arte*. Amsterdam, 1635.

Vossler, K., *Gesammelte Aufsätze zur Sprachphilosophie*. Munich, 1923.

Wittgenstein, L., *Tractatus Logico-philosophicus*, 1921; English edition, trans. C. K. Ogden. London, 1922.

Meaning

Anshen, Ruth N., ed., *Language: An Enquiry into Its Meaning and Function*. New York: Harcourt, Brace & World, Inc., 1940.

Bar-Hillel, Y., "Logical Syntax and Semantics," *Language*, 30 (1954), 230–237.

Bréal, M., *Essai de Sémantique*. Paris: Hachette, 1897. Reprinted as *Semantics: Studies in the Science of Meaning*. New York: Dover Publications, Inc., 1964.

"Les commencements du verbe," *Mémoires de la Société linguistique de Paris*, II (1900), 264–284.

Brøndal, V., *Les Parties du discours*, trans. Pierre Naert. Copenhagen: Munksgaard, 1948.

Brown, Roger W., *Words and Things*. New York: The Free Press of Glencoe, 1958.

Carnap, Rudolf, *Meaning and Necessity: A Study in Semantics and Model Logic*. Chicago: Phoenix Books, 1958.

———, *The Logical Syntax of Language*. Paterson, N. J.: Littlefield, Adams & Company, 1959.

Cassirer, E, *Die Begriffsform im mythischen Denken*, Studien der Bibliothek Warburg, I. Leipzig, 1922.

———, *Philosophie der Symbolischen Formen*. I, *Die Sprache*. Berlin, 1923.

———, *Language and Myth*, trans. Susanne K. Langer. New York: Dover Publications, Inc., 1946.

Cohen, L. J., *The Diversity of Meaning*. New York: Herder & Herder, Inc. 1963.

Conklin, Harold C., "Lexicographical Treatment of Folk Taxonomies," *International Journal of American Linguistics*, 28 (1962), 2.

George, F. H., *Semantics*. London: English Universities Press, 1964.

Gibson, Walker, ed., *The Limits of Language*. New York: Hill & Wang, Inc., 1962.

Goodenough, Ward H., "Componential Analysis and the Study of Meaning," *Language*, 32 (1956), 195–216.

Guiraud, Pierre, *La Sémantique*. Paris: Presses Universitaires, 1955.

Hayakawa, S. I., *Language in Thought and Action*. London: Allen & Unwin, Ltd., 1952.

———, *The Use and Misuse of Language*. New York: Fawcett World Library, 1962.

Hymes, Dell H., "On Typology of Cognitive Styles in Languages," *Anthropological Linguistics*, 3 (1961), 22–54.

Johnson, Alexander Bryan, *A Treatise on Language* (1836). Berkeley, Calif.: University of California Press, 1959.

Joos, Martin, *The English Verb: Form and Meanings*. Madison, Wisc.: University of Wisconsin Press, 1964.

Lounsbury, Floyd G., "A Semantic Analysis of the Pawnee Kinship Usage," *Language*, 32 (1956), 158–194.

Morris, Charles W., *Signs, Language, and Behavior*. Englewood Cliffs, N.J.: Prentice-Hall, Inc., 1955.

———, *Signification and Significance*. Cambridge Mass.: M.I.T. Press, 1964.

Mowrer, Hobart O., *Learning Theory and the Symbolic Process*. New York: John Wiley & Sons, Inc., 1960.

Nida, Eugene, "A System for the Description of Semantic Elements," *Word*, 7 (1951), 1–14.

———, "Analysis and Dictionary Making," *International Journal of American Linguistics*, 24 (1958), 279–292.

Ogden, C. K., and I. A. Richards, *The Meaning of Meaning*. London: Routledge and Kegan Paul, 1923.

Osgood, C., G. Suci, and P. Tannenbaum, *The Measurement of Meaning*. Urbana, Ill.: University of Illinois Press, 1957.

Phenix, Philip H., *Realms of Meaning*. New York: McGraw-Hill Book Company, Inc., 1964.

Schaff, Adam, *Introduction to Semantics*. New York: Pergamon Press, Inc., 1962.

Skinner, B. F., *Verbal Behavior*. New York: Appleton-Century-Crofts, 1957.

Stern, Gustaf, *Meaning and the Change of Meaning*. Bloomington, Ind.: Indiana University Press, 1931, 1964.

Ullmann, S., *Précis de Sémantique française*. Berne: Francke, 1952.

Vygotski, L. S., *Thought and Language*, E. Hanfmann and G. Vaker, eds. and trans. Cambridge, Mass.: M.I.T. Press, 1965.

Whitehead, Alfred North, *Symbolism, Its Meaning and Effect*. New York: Capricorn Books, 1959.

Wittgenstein, Ludwig, *Philosophical Investigations*. New York: Crowell Collier and Macmillan, Inc., 1953.

Ziff, Paul, *Semantic Analysis*. Ithaca, N.Y.: Cornell University Press, 1960.

Linguistics and Allied Fields

Bloomfield, Leonard, *An Outline Guide for the Practical Study of Foreign Languages*. Baltimore, Md.: Special Publications of the Linguistic Society of America, 1942.

Bram, Joseph, *Language and Society*. New York: Random House–Alfred A. Knopf, Inc., 1961.

Chadwick, John, *The Decipherment of Linear B*. New York: Random House–Alfred A. Knopf, Inc., Modern Library Paperback, 1958.

Frake, Charles C., "The Ethnographic Study of Cognitive Systems," in *Anthropology and Human Behavior*. Washington, D.C.: Anthropological Society of Washington, 1962.

Friedrich, Johannes, *Extinct Languages*. New York: Wisdom Library, 1957.

Gudshinsky, Sarah, *Handbook of Literacy*. Glendale, Calif.: Summer Institute of Linguistics, 1957.

Hall, Edward, *The Silent Language*. New York: Fawcett World Library, 1961.

Halliday, M. A. K., Angus McIntosh, and Peter Strevens, *The Linguistic Sciences and Language Teaching*. London: Longmans Green, 1964.

Henle, Paul, ed., *Language, Thought, and Culture*. Ann Arbor, Mich.: University of Michigan Press, 1958.

Hoijer, Harry, *Language in Culture*. Chicago: University of Chicago Press, 1954.

Hymes, Dell H., "Lexicostatistics So Far," *Current Anthropology*, I (1960), 3–44.

————, ed., *Language in Culture and Society: A Reader in Linguistics and Anthropology*. New York: Harper & Row, Publishers, Inc., 1964.

Kurath, Hans, *Linguistic Atlas of New England*, Vol. 1, *Handbook of the Linguistic Geography of New England*. Providence, R.I.: Brown University Press, 1939.

————, *A Word Geography of the Eastern United States*. Ann Arbor, Mich.: University of Michigan Press, 1949.

Lado, Robert, *Linguistics across Cultures: Applied Linguistics for Language Teachers*. Ann Arbor, Mich.: University of Michigan Press, 1957.

————, *Language Teaching: A Scientific Approach*. New York: McGraw-Hill Book Company, Inc., 1964.

————, *Language Testing*. New York: McGraw-Hill Book Company, Inc., 1965.

Nida, Eugene, *Learning a Foreign Language*. New York: Foreign Missions Conference of North America, 1950.

Politzer, Robert L., *Foreign Language Learning*, prelim. ed. Englewood Cliffs, N.J.: Prentice-Hall, Inc., 1965.

Pop, Sever, *La Dialectologie: Aperçu historique et méthodes d'enquêtes linguistiques*, Vols. I and II. Louvain, Presses Universitaires, 1950.

Quine, Willard V., *A System of Logistic*. Cambridge, Mass.: Harvard University Press, 1934.

————, *Mathematical Logic*, rev. ed. Cambridge, Mass.: Harvard University Press, 1951.

————, *From a Logical Point of View*. Cambridge, Mass.: Harvard University Press, 1953.

————, *Methods of Logic*, rev. ed. New York: Holt, Rinehart and Winston, Inc., 1959.

————, *Word and Object*. Cambridge, Mass.: M.I.T. Press, 1960.

Rice, F. A., and A. Guss, *Information Sources in Linguistics*. Washington, D.C.: Center for Applied Linguistics, 1965.

Shaughnessy, Amy E., ed., *Dissertations in Linguistics*. Washington, D.C.: Center for Applied Linguistics, 1965.

Stevick, Earl, *Helping People Learn English*. Nashville, Tenn.: Abingdon Press, 1957.

Thomas, Owen, *Transformational Grammar and the Teacher of English*. New York: Holt, Rinehart and Winston, Inc., 1965.

Walters, T. W., S.J., *The Georgetown Bibliography of Studies Contributing to the Psycholinguistics of Language Learning*. Washington, D.C.: Georgetown University Press, 1965.

Weinreich, Uriel, *Languages in Contact: Findings and Problems*. New York: Linguistic Circle of New York, 1953.

Weir, Ruth, *Language in the Crib*. The Hague: Mouton & Company, 1962.

Linguistics and English

Allen, Harold B., ed., *Readings in Applied English Linguistics*, 2d ed. New York: Appleton-Century-Crofts, 1964.

Baugh, Albert C., *A History of the English Language*, 2d ed. New York: Appleton-Century-Crofts, 1957.

Brooks, G. L., *A History of the English Language*. New York: W. W. Norton & Company, Inc., 1958.

Clark, John W., *Early English*. New York: W. W. Norton & Company, Inc., 1957.

Francis, W. Nelson, *The Structure of American English*. New York: The Ronald Press Company, 1958.

Fries, Charles C., *American English Grammar*. New York: Appleton-Century-Crofts, 1940.

———, *Teaching and Learning English as a Foreign Language*. Ann Arbor, Mich.: University of Michigan Press, 1945.

———, *The Structure of English*. New York: Harcourt, Brace & World, Inc., 1952.

Hill, Archibald A., *Introduction to Linguistic Structures: From Sound to Sentence in English*. New York: Harcourt, Brace & World, Inc., 1958.

Jespersen, J. Otto, *Essentials of English Grammar*. New York: Holt, Rinehart & Winston, Inc., 1939.

———, *Growth and Structure of the English Language*, 9th ed. Oxford: Basil Blackwell, 1960.

Markwardt, Albert H., *American English*. New York: Oxford University Press, 1958.

Nida, Eugene, *A Synopsis of English Syntax*. Norman, Okla.: Summer Institute of Linguistics, 1960.

Pyles, Thomas, *The Origins and Development of the English Language*. New York: Harcourt, Brace & World, Inc., 1964.

Roberts, Paul, *Patterns of English*. New York: Harcourt, Brace & World, Inc., 1956.

———, *English Sentences*. New York: Harcourt, Brace & World, Inc., 1962.

————, *English Syntax*, Alternate ed. New York: Harcourt, Brace & World, Inc., 1964.

Sledd, James, Review of G. L. Trager and H. L. Smith's *An Outline of English Structure* (1957), *Language*, 31 (1955), 312–335.

————, "Some Questions of English Phonology," *Language*, 34 (1958), 252–258.

————, *A Short Introduction to English Grammar*. Chicago: Scott, Foresman & Company, 1959.

Strang, Barbara, *Modern English Structure*. New York: St. Martins Press, 1962.

Trager, G. L., and H. L. Smith, Jr., *An Outline of English Structure*. Studies in Linguistics, Occasional Papers No. 3. Reprinted. Washington, D.C.: American Council of Learned Societies, 1957.

Index